ARCHBISHOP ALEMANY LIBRARY
DOMINICAN UNIVER⸗
SAN RAFAEL, CALIFORN

S0-BME-604

HUMAN
RIGHTS
WATCH

WORLD REPORT

2008

EVENTS OF 2007

Copyright © 2008 Human Rights Watch
All rights reserved.
Printed in the United States of America

ISBN-13: 978-1-58322-774-9

Front cover photo: *Monks and others protest military rule and government economic mismanagement in Rangoon, Burma, September 26, 2007.* © 2007 Reuters

Back cover photo: *Migrant workers at the construction site of the Beijing Olympic stadium.* © 2007 Kadir van Lohuizen/Noor

Cover design by Rafael Jiménez

Human Rights Watch

350 Fifth Avenue, 34th floor
New York, NY 10118-3299 USA
Tel: +1 212 290 4700
Fax: +1 212 736 1300
hrwnyc@hrw.org

1630 Connecticut Avenue, N.W.,
Suite 500
Washington, DC 20009 USA
Tel: +1 202 612 4321
Fax: +1 202 612 4333
hrwdc@hrw.org

2-12 Pentonville Road, 2nd Floor
London N1 9HF, UK
Tel: +44 20 7713 1995
Fax: +44 20 7713 1800
hrwuk@hrw.org

6 rue des Graviers
92200 Neuilly sur Seine, France
Tel: +33 (0) 1 41 92 07 34
Fax: +33 (0) 1 47 22 08 61
paris@hrw.org

Avenue des Gaulois, 7
1040 Brussels, Belgium
Tel: + 32 (2) 732 2009
Fax: + 32 (2) 732 0471
hrwbe@hrw.org

64-66 Rue de Lausanne
1201 Geneva, Switzerland
Tel: +41 22 738 0481
Fax: +41 22 738 1791
hrwgva@hrw.org

Poststraße 4-5
10178 Berlin, Germany
Tel: +49 30 2593 06-10
Fax: +49 30 2593 0629
berlin@hrw.org

www.hrw.org

Human Rights Watch is dedicated to protecting the human rights of people around the world.

We stand with victims and activists to prevent discrimination, to uphold political freedom, to protect people from inhumane conduct in wartime, and to bring offenders to justice.

We investigate and expose human rights violations and hold abusers accountable.

We challenge governments and those who hold power to end abusive practices and respect international human rights law.

We enlist the public and the international community to support the cause of human rights for all.

HUMAN RIGHTS WATCH

Human Rights Watch conducts regular, systematic investigations of human rights abuses in some seventy countries around the world. Our reputation for timely, reliable disclosures has made us an essential source of information for those concerned with human rights. We address the human rights practices of governments of all political stripes, of all geopolitical alignments, and of all ethnic and religious persuasions. Human Rights Watch defends freedom of thought and expression, due process and equal protection of the law, and a vigorous civil society; we document and denounce murders, disappearances, torture, arbitrary imprisonment, discrimination, and other abuses of internationally recognized human rights. Our goal is to hold governments accountable if they transgress the rights of their people.

Human Rights Watch began in 1978 with the founding of its Europe and Central Asia division (then known as Helsinki Watch). Today, it also includes divisions covering Africa, the Americas, Asia, and the Middle East. In addition, it includes three thematic divisions on arms, children's rights, and women's rights. It maintains offices in Berlin, Brussels, Chicago, Geneva, Johannesburg, London, Los Angeles, Moscow, New York, Paris, San Francisco, Toronto, and Washington. Human Rights Watch is an independent, nongovernmental organization, supported by contributions from private individuals and foundations worldwide. It accepts no government funds, directly or indirectly.

The staff includes Kenneth Roth, Executive Director; Carroll Bogert, Associate Director; Michele Alexander, Development and Outreach Director; Clive Baldwin, Senior Legal Advisor; Barbara Guglielmo, Finance and Administration Director; Peggy Hicks, Global Advocacy Director; Iain Levine, Program Director; Andrew Mawson, Deputy Program Director; Suzanne Nossel, Chief of Operations; Dinah PoKempner, General Counsel; Aisling Reidy, Senior Legal Advisor; James Ross, Legal and Policy Director; and Joseph Saunders, Deputy Program Director.

The division directors of Human Rights Watch are Brad Adams, Asia; Joseph Amon, HIV/AIDS and Human Rights; Peter Bouckaert, Emergencies; Bruni Burres, International Film Festival; Holly Cartner, Europe and Central Asia; Richard Dicker, International Justice; David Fathi, United States; Arvind Ganesan, Business and Human Rights; Bill Frelick, Refugee Policy; Steve Goose, Arms; Janet Walsh, Women's Rights; Scott Long, Lesbian, Gay, Bisexual and Transgender Rights; Joanne Mariner, Terrorism and Counterterrorism; Peter Takirambudde, Africa; José Miguel Vivanco, Americas; Lois Whitman, Children's Rights; and Sarah Leah Whitson, Middle East and North Africa.

The advocacy directors of Human Rights Watch are Steve Crawshaw, United Nations; Juliette De Rivero, Geneva; Jean-Marie Fardeau, Paris; Marianne Heuwagen, Berlin; Lotte Leicht, European Union; Tom Porteous, London; and Tom Malinowski, Washington DC.

The members of the board of directors are Jane Olson, Chair, Bruce J. Klatsky, Vice-Chair, Sid Sheinberg, Vice-Chair, John J. Studzinski, Vice-Chair, Lloyd Axworthy, David M. Brown, Jorge Castañeda, Tony Elliott, Hassan Elmasry, Michael G. Fisch, Michael E. Gellert, Richard J. Goldstone, Vartan Gregorian, James F. Hoge, Jr., Wendy Keys, Robert Kissane, Joanne Leedom-Ackerman, Susan Manilow, Kati Marton, Linda Mason, Barry Meyer, Pat Mitchell, Joel Motley, Samuel K. Murumba, Catherine Powell, Sigrid Rausing, Victoria Riskin, Shelley Rubin, Kevin P. Ryan, Darian W. Swig, John R. Taylor, Shibley Telhami.

Emeritus board members are Roland Algrant, Lisa Anderson, Robert L. Bernstein (Founding Chair 1979-1997), William Carmichael, Dorothy Cullman, Adrian W. DeWind, Edith Everett, Jonathan F. Fanton, Chair (1998-2003), Alice Henkin, Steve Kass, Marina Pinto Kaufman, Josh Mailman, Peter Osnos, Kathleen Peratis, Bruce Rabb, Orville Schell, Gary Sick, and Malcolm B. Smith.

ACKNOWLEDGMENTS

A compilation of this magnitude requires contribution from a large
number of people, including most of the Human Rights Watch staff.
The contributors were:

Fred Abrahams, Brad Adams, Daniel Ades, Bashair Ahmed, Niki Akhavan, Chris Albin-Lackey,
Nada Ali, Emily Allen, Joseph Amon, Assef Ashraf, Leeam Azulay-Yagev, Jo Becker,
Clarisa Bencomo, Nicholas Bequelin, Olivier Bercault, Andrea Berg, Nicki Boehland,
Carroll Bogert, Michelle Born, Peter Bouckaert, Maria Brant, Sebastian Brett, Selena Brewer,
Jane Buchanan, David Buchbinder, Maria Burnett, Elizabeth Calvin, Juliana Cano Nieto,
Holly Cartner, Haleh Chahrokh, Dominique Chambless, Grace Choi, Sara Colm, Tatyana Cooper,
Andrea Cottom, Zama Coursen-Neff, Steve Crawshaw, Sara Dareshori, Jennifer Daskal,
Juliette De Rivero, Farida Deif, Rachel Denber, Alison Des Forges, Thodleen Dessources,
Boris Dittrich, Corinne Dufka, Andrej Dynko, Mike Eisner, Helen Epstein, Liz Evenson,
Jean-Marie Fardeau, David Fathi, Jamie Fellner, Conor Fortune, Bill Frelick, Diana Galperin,
Meenakshi Ganguly, Neela Joy Ghoshal, Allison Gill, Sebastien Gillioz, Giorgi Gogia,
Anne Goldin, Eric Goldstein, Rachel Good, Ian Gorvin, Brian Griffey, Inara Gulpe-Laganovska,
Julia Hall, Ali Dayan Hasan, Harun Hassan, Angela Heimburger, Marianne Heuwagen,
Peggy Hicks, Charu Hogg, Andrew Hogue, Alisha Holland, Andrea Holley, Nadim Houry,
Lee-Sean Huang, Chris Huggins, Sarah Jackson, Rachel Jacobson, Rafael Jimenez,
Tiseke Kasambala, Elise Keppler, Kennji Kizuka, Sonya Kleshik, Kathryn Koonce, Phelim Kyne,
Katie Lane, Katherine Lay, Leslie Lefkow, Lotte Leicht, Iain Levine, Maria Lisitsyna,
Joseph Logan, Diederik Lohman, Scott Long, Lucy Mair, Joanne Mariner, David Mathieson,
Veronica Matushaj, Andrew Mawson, Maria McFarland, Megan McLemore, Anna McTaggart,
Lisa Misol, Amha Mogus, Charmain Mohamed, Ashoka Mukpo, Jim Murphy, Saloua Ouchan,
Alison Parker, Elaine Pearson, Sasha Petrov, Sunai Phasuk, Carol Pier, Dinah PoKempner,
Vitalii Ponomarev, Tom Porteus, Lutz Prager, Clara Presler, McKenzie Price, Mia Psorn,
Tarek Radwan, Ben Rawlence, Emina Redzic, Aisling Reidy, Sophie Richardson, Lisa Rimli,
Celeste Robinson, James Ross, Kenneth Roth, Abby Rubinson, Joe Saunders,
Rebecca Schleifer, Kay Seok, Dustin Sharp, Carmen Silvestre, Emma Sinclair-Webb,

Param-Preet Singh, Mickey Spiegel, Joe Stork, Rania Suidan, Judith Sunderland, Veronika Szente Goldston, Peter Takirambudde, Lara Talsma, Tamara Taraciuk, Sarah Tofte, Wanda Troszczynska-van Genderen, Bill Van Esvald, Anneke Van Woudenberg, Nisha Varia, Jose Miguel Vivanco, Igor Vorontsov, Danielle Wainer, Janet Walsh, Benjamin Ward, Lois Whitman, Sarah Leah Whitson, Christoph Wilcke, Daniel Wilkinson, Beth Wolfram, Minky Worden, Elijah Zarwan, Kreshnik Zhega, Sam Zia-Zarifi, and Iwona Zielinska.

Ian Gorvin edited the report with assistance from Andrew Mawson, Joe Saunders, and Iain Levine; Leeam Azulay-Yagev coordinated the editing process. Layout and production were coordinated by Andrea Holley and Rafael Jiménez, with assistance from Grace Choi, Anna Lopriore, Veronica Matushaj, Amha Mogus and Jim Murphy.

Emily Allen, Assef Ashraf, Leeam Azulay-Yagev, Nicki Boehland, Michelle Born, Dominique Chambless, Conor Fortune, Brian Griffey, Lee-Sean Huang, Rachel Jacobson, Kennji Kizuka, Kathryn Koonce, Katie Lane, Clara Presler, and Beth Wolfram proofread the report.

For a full list of Human Rights Watch staff, please go to our website: www.hrw.org/about/info/staff.html.

TABLE OF CONTENTS

Despots Masquerading as Democrats

By Kenneth Roth

Rarely has democracy been so acclaimed yet so breached, so promoted yet so disrespected, so important yet so disappointing. Today, democracy has become the sine qua non of legitimacy. Few governments want to be seen as undemocratic. Yet the credentials of the claimants have not kept pace with democracy's growing popularity. These days, even overt dictators aspire to the status conferred by the democracy label. Determined not to let mere facts stand in the way, these rulers have mastered the art of democratic rhetoric that bears little relationship to their practice of governing.

Why else would as ruthless a leader as Uzbekistan's President Islam Karimov choose to stage elections? Why bother? Karimov heads a government that has imprisoned some 7,000 people for political and religious reasons, routinely tortures detainees, and as recently as 2005 massacred hundreds of protesters in Andijan. He is hardly a democrat, and he faces no real opponents in December 2007 elections because no one dares mount a serious challenge to his rule. Even a constitutional prohibition against a third seven-year presidential term has not stood in his way.

Yet this brutal president finds utility in holding electoral charades to legitimize his reign. So do, among others, Robert Mugabe of Zimbabwe, Pervez Musharraf of Pakistan, Hosni Mubarak of Egypt, Meles Zenawi of Ethiopia, and Vladimir Putin of Russia.

Even China has gotten into the game. In an October 2007 speech to the Communist Party Congress, President Hu Jintao used the word "democracy" more than 60 times in calling for more of it within the party. Yet that has not stopped him from barring independent political parties, blocking legal efforts to uphold basic rights, and shutting down countless civil society organizations, media outlets, and websites. And there are no national elections. So what did he have in mind? The party allowed 221 candidates to contest 204 seats for its Central Committee.

The techniques used by such autocrats to tame the nettlesome unpredictability of democracy are nothing if not creative. The challenge they face is to appear to embrace democratic principles while avoiding any risk of succumbing to popular preferences. Electoral fraud, political violence, press censorship, repression of civil society, even military rule have all been used to curtail the prospect that the proclaimed process of democratization might actually lead to a popular say in government.

Part of the reason that dictators can hope to get away with such subterfuge is that, unlike human rights, "democracy" has no legally established definition. The concept of democracy reflects the powerful vision that the best way to select a government and guide its course is to entrust ultimate authority to those who are subject to its rule. It is far from a perfect political system, with its risk of majoritarian indifference to minorities and its susceptibility to excessive influence by powerful elements, but as famously the "least bad" form of government, in the words of Winston Churchill, it is an important part of the human rights ideal. Yet there is no International Convention on Democracy, no widely ratified treaty affirming how a government must behave to earn the democracy label. The meaning of democracy lies too much in the eye of the beholder.

By contrast, international human rights law grants all citizens the right to "take part in the conduct of public affairs, directly or through freely chosen representatives" and to "vote" in "genuine periodic elections" with "universal and equal suffrage" and "secret ballot" so as to "guarantee[] the free expression of the will of the electors." It also grants a range of related rights that should be seen as essential to democracy in any robust and meaningful form, including rights protecting a diverse and vigorous civil society and a free and vibrant press, rights defending the interests of minorities, and rights ensuring that government officials are subject to the rule of law. The specificity and legally binding nature of human rights are their great strength. But when autocrats manage to deflect criticism for violating these rights by pretending to be democrats, when they can enjoy the benefits of admission to the club of democracies without paying the admission fee of respect for basic rights, the global defense of human rights is put in jeopardy. Why bother complying with so intrusive a set of rules as international human rights law when, with a bit of maneuvering, any tyrant can pass himself off as a "democrat"?

The misuse of the democratic name is not entirely new. The one-time German Democratic Republic (the name of the now-defunct one-party Communist state in East Germany) or today's Democratic People's Republic of Korea (the improbable, official name of North Korea) are prime examples. But few gave any credence to these Orwellian claims. The sad new development is how easy it has become for today's autocrats to get away with mounting a democratic facade.

It is not that pseudo-democratic leaders gain much legitimacy at home. The local population knows all too bitterly what a farce the elections really are. At best, these leaders gain the benefit of feigned compliance with local laws requiring elections. Rather, a good part of the motivation today behind this democratic veneer stems from the international legitimacy that an electoral exercise, however empty, can win for even the most hardened dictator. Because of other interests—energy, commerce, counterterrorism—the world's more established democracies too often find it convenient to appear credulous of these sham democrats.

Foremost has been the United States under President George W. Bush. In a troubling parallel to abusive governments around the world, the US government has embraced democracy promotion as a softer and fuzzier alternative to defending human rights. Democracy is a metric by which the United States still measures up fairly well, but human rights are a standard by which the record of the Bush administration is deeply troubling. Talk of human rights leads to Guantanamo, secret CIA prisons, waterboarding, rendition, military commissions, and the suspension of habeas corpus. Despite the 2000 presidential elections, discussion of democracy takes place on a more comfortable terrain.

Such divorcing of democracy from the international standards that give it meaning helps to convince autocrats that mere elections, regardless of the circumstances, are sufficient to warrant the democrat label. Bush's response to then-General Musharraf's November 2007 declaration of "emergency rule" illustrates the problem. Even after Musharraf's effective coup and his detention of thousands of political opponents, Bush said that Musharraf had somehow not "crossed the line." Bush could hardly trumpet Musharraf's human rights record, so he declared that Musharraf is "somebody who believes in democracy" and that Pakistan was "on the road to democracy." But if, unlike human rights law, "the road to democracy" permits locking up political opponents, dismissing independent judges, and silencing the independent press, it is easy to see why tyrants the world over are tempted to believe that they, too, might be eligible. As such unworthy claimants as the leaders of Egypt, Ethiopia, Kazakhstan, and Nigeria wrap themselves in the democracy mantle with scant international objection, the concept of democracy gets cheapened, its human rights component cast aside.

To make matters worse, the Bush administration's efforts to rationalize the invasion of Iraq in terms of democracy promotion has made it easier for autocrats to equate pressure on them to democratize with an imperial, militarist agenda. Sadly, that cynical ploy often works, because much of the world today views any Washington-led campaign for democracy as a pretext for military invasion or regime change, if not also as a recipe for chaos. Dictators have learned that conjuring up visions of Iraq can be a useful way to blunt pressure to democratize. And governments that might have defended a more robust vision of democracy are reluctant to do so for fear of being seen as joining the Bush agenda.

Other governments, too, have treated empty elections as an excuse to re-start business as usual with dictatorships that merit denunciation, not partnership. A prime example is the treatment of Kazakhstan by the Organization for Security and Cooperation in Europe (OSCE), a body that comprises 56 governments from Europe and Central Asia as well as the United States and Canada. In August 2007, President Nursultan Nazarbaev staged parliamentary elections in which the OSCE found vote-counting flaws in 40 percent of the polling stations it visited. The predictable result: Nazarbaev's party won all the seats in the lower house of parliament with a declared 88 percent of the vote, and no opposition party was said to have surpassed the 7 percent threshold needed for parliamentary representation. This fraud occurred against a backdrop of continuing, widespread human rights violations: government loyalists dominate the broadcast media, independent journalists are threatened and harassed for criticizing the president or the government, libel continues to be used as a criminal offense, and opposition activists risk imprisonment, such as Alibek Zhumbaev, currently serving a five-year prison term for insulting Nazarbaev.

But the OSCE, in evidence-be-damned fashion, claimed that the elections had "moved Kazakhstan forward in its evolution towards a democratic country." This wishful thinking was apparently designed to avoid keeping Kazakhstan from its long-sought goal of becoming the first former Soviet republic to chair the OSCE. Preoccupied by energy concerns, Germany joined Russia in supporting this inappropriate candidacy. Although the US and British governments led the opposition, they, too, ultimately wavered. In November 2007, OSCE states by consensus granted Kazakhstan the chairmanship in 2010. Kazakhstan, rather than having to demonstrate respect in fact for the democracy and human rights standards that are at the heart of the OSCE, had only to pledge to undertake media and electoral reform and to stop trying to undermine the OSCE's human rights mandate. Dumbing down democracy in this form, with little protest from the governments that are best placed to serve as its guardians, has made it easier for authoritarian leaders like Nazarbaev to masquerade as democrats and deflect pressure for more meaningful human rights reform.

Of course, insisting on real democracy is not the only test of the international community's commitment to human rights. Also of fundamental importance is its response to mass atrocities in places such as eastern Chad, Colombia, eastern Congo, the Ogaden region of Ethiopia, Iraq, Somalia, Sri Lanka, and the Darfur region of Sudan, as well as to closed societies or severe repression in countries such as Burma, China, Cuba, Eritrea, Libya, North Korea, Saudi Arabia and Vietnam. These urgent situations are addressed in detail within this volume. But the human rights cause must be concerned not only with these severe cases but also with governments that may be slightly more open but still use repressive means to prevent any challenge to their rule. Their task is eased when mere gestures toward democracy are allowed to displace respect for the full panoply of human rights.

To avoid this shell game, to prevent the appeal of "democracy" from being abused as a poor surrogate for more exacting rights standards, there is an urgent need to reclaim the full meaning of the democratic ideal. That does not mean advocating a narrowly defined form of governance. Democracy legitimately comes in many varieties, including systems based on proportional representation and first-past-the-post models, those featuring a strong president and those centered around a powerful prime minister, those that entrust authority primarily to the executive branch and those that prefer a stronger legislature. But all democracies worthy of the name have certain common characteristics, including periodic com-

5

petitive elections that are freely held as well as transparently and accurately tabulated, a meaningful array of political parties, independent media outlets, civil society organizations that give citizens—including minorities—a broad range of opportunities to band together with others to make their voices heard, and a legal system that ensures that no one—and especially no government official—is above the law.

In 2007, democracy showed continuing vitality in, for example, Sierra Leone, Jamaica, Poland, and Australia—all countries where power alternated and opposition parties took office after elections that were widely considered free and fair. In Turkey, when the military launched a so-called email coup in an effort to block the democratically elected, moderate Islamic government from appointing one of its officials, Abdullah Gül, as president, the government called an early general election, received an overwhelming reaffirmation of its mandate, and proceeded to appoint Gül anyway. The Turkish people's desire for democracy proved strong.

Still, many dictators are eager to legitimize themselves on the cheap. If they can get away with a sham election, they will. Their ability to do so depends in large part on the vigilance of established democracies in insisting on democracy in all its dimensions, including respect for a broad array of human rights and the rule of law. A principled commitment to democracy is not easy. It may mean putting pressure on dictatorial friends or promoting rights that even some established democracies would prefer not to highlight. But a principled commitment is needed if the promotion of democracy is to serve as a source of real pressure to respect human rights rather than a new tool to bypass international standards in favor of a feel-good, empty alternative.

To recapture the powerful ideal of democracy, so central to the human rights cause yet so at risk of being manipulated as a false but beguiling substitute, requires heightened attention to the clever subterfuges of its detractors. What follows is a summary of recent trends as governments violate human rights to subvert democracy or trumpet democracy to avoid discussion of human rights.

Upholding democracy also requires avoiding some of the pitfalls that have undermined recent efforts to defend it. As described below, many established democracies have fallen victim to the tendencies to bank on the "democrat" rather than democratic principles, to accept the false dichotomy that the only alternative to the despot one knows is the despot one fears, to claim that democracy could flourish even if divorced from the human rights that give it meaning, or to modulate demands for genuine democracy according to the strategic value of the democracy pretender. These tendencies must be resisted if democracy promotion is to reach its potential as a positive force for human rights.

Rhetorical Games

Authoritarian leaders' evasive use of democracy often begins with word games and rhetorical sleights of hand suggesting that restrictions undermining democracy are really necessary to save it. In Pakistan, for example, Musharraf imposed "emergency rule" to prevent the then-independent Supreme Court from ruling illegal his election as president while he remained the head of the military. Despite this very personal motivation, he claimed the coup was necessary to "preserve the democratic transition." Similarly in Bangladesh, an army-appointed caretaker government banned all political and trade union activities and limited press freedoms, all in the name of preparing credible national elections.

Many repressive leaders have tried to redefine democracy by introducing a devastating qualifier or an antithetical adjective. President Vladimir Putin, as he cripples democracy by shutting down all competing centers of influence in Russia, has become a proponent of "sovereign democracy," meaning in effect that democracy is whatever the sovereign wants it to mean. As the Burmese junta rounded up protesting monks and violently suppressed dissent, it spoke of the need for "disciplined democracy." China has long promoted "socialist democracy," by which it means a top-down centralism that eliminates minority views.

Musharraf in Pakistan justified "emergency rule" as "genuine democracy," explaining: "We want democracy, we want human rights, we want civil liberties but we will do it our own way." Libya's Mu`ammar al-Qadhafi uses the term "participatory democracy" to justify abolishing independent political parties on the grounds that the population does not need them as intermediaries because it participates directly in governance through government-staged assemblies. In the Cuban version of the same concept, candidates must be pre-approved by mass organizations controlled by the government, and the constitution severely limits any political organization other than the Communist Party.

Electoral Fraud

Ordinary electoral fraud is one of the most common strategies to circumvent the uncertainties of democracy. In addition to the case of Kazakhstan, cited above, Nigeria and Chad are recent examples.

In Nigeria, facing the first transfer of power from one civilian leader to another since the country's independence in 1960, the ruling People's Democratic Party resorted to massive fraud to ensure that its candidate, Umaru Yar'Adua, succeeded Olusegun Obasanjo as president in April 2007 elections. In an effort to redeem some legitimacy, Yar'Adua, to his credit, has launched an electoral reform process, has allowed the courts to overturn several of his party's fraudulent state-level victories, and continues to face judicial review of his own tainted election. But no one has been prosecuted for the blatant ballot-stuffing, vote-buying, and political intimidation that were central to his "election," so the Nigerian people are losing confidence that he will translate his reformist rhetoric into a new democratic reality.

In Chad, President Idriss Déby, who seized power in 1990, has given his rule the imprimatur of democracy by holding three sham presidential elections. In 2005, he did away with a provision barring him from seeking a third five-year term by amending the constitution in a referendum plagued by irregularities. Anticipating fraud, opposition groups refused to field candidates for the 2006 presidential elections, leaving Déby to prevail easily over four weak challengers including two government ministers. The United States and European Union declined to send observers, while the balloting was marred by low voter participation, underage voting, and multiple voting.

Controlling the Electoral Machinery

Fair elections depend on the independence of the people running them, so it should come as no surprise that one favorite way for rulers to manipulate elections is to stack electoral machinery with their supporters. In Azerbaijan, where electoral fraud has been a persistent problem, the ruling party of President Ilham Aliev names the chairperson and maintains a majority on the election commission. In Zimbabwe, opposition parties are excluded from the Electoral Commission. In Thailand, the new military-sponsored constitution allows members of the National Election Commission to be selected by the Senate, which was once elected but is now appointed.

The case of Malaysia illustrates why governments seek control of the electoral machinery. Its government-dominated Election Commission rejected opposition efforts to remove alleged phantom voters from the electoral rolls, eliminate the widespread use of absentee ballots by government workers, and permit access to state-controlled media by all political parties. Similarly, Cambodia has made an art of holding elections staged by a National Election Commission controlled by the ruling Cambodian People's Party, which then simply ignores claims of violence, fraud, or intimidation by independent monitors or opposition parties.

Because of such failings, national electoral monitoring mechanisms are often supplemented by international institutions. But these, too, have been targeted by those seeking to manage elections. The Kremlin effectively prevented observers from the Office for Democratic Institutions and Human Rights, the main election monitoring body of the OSCE, from reviewing Russia's December 2007 parliamentary elections by delaying visas, limiting the number of international monitors to be admitted, and threatening to prevent the OSCE from offering its assessment until long after Russia's government-controlled media had shaped public perceptions of the balloting.

Blocking and Discouraging Opposition Candidates

One obvious way to fix an election is to prevent opposition candidates from running. Iran has perfected this method, with its Council of Guardians having rejected some half of the candidates for the 2004 parliamentary elections, most of whom it apparently deemed too reform-minded. In Cuba, the Communist Party-controlled National Assembly has the authority to reject any prospective candidate for public office. Tunisia refuses to legalize most genuine opposition parties. In Thailand, the military government's election commission adopted stringent new rules permitting disqualification of candidates for such trivial offenses as playing music at rallies or having posters not of an approved size—evidently with the goal of eliminating candidates of the People's Power Party, the successor to ousted Prime Minister Thaksin Shinawatra's Thai Rak Thai party.

In several cases, more punitive measures were used. In 2005, just months before Uganda's first multiparty parliamentary and presidential elections in 26 years, the government jailed the leading opposition presidential challenger, Kizza Besigye, on politically-motivated charges of treason and rape. He was later released, but the detention significantly impaired his ability to contest elections a few months later, which he lost to President Yoweri Museveni. In Zimbabwe, the government sent a similar message of discouragement to would-be challengers in March 2007 by dispatching police to severely beat opposition leader Morgan Tsvangirai and to arrest scores of other opposition members.

Turkmenistan had the chance to finally give its people a real choice after the December 2006 death of Saparmurat Niazov, the tyrant who ruled the country for 21 years and laid waste to its social welfare system. Instead, the chair of parliament, who was the constitutionally designated successor to Niazov as interim president, was imprisoned on charges of driving a relative to attempt suicide, paving the way for Gurbanguly Berdymukhamedov to take over. Five low-ranking "alternative" candidates, all representing the country's sole political party, ran unsuccessfully against Berdymukhamedov. No opposition leader was allowed to return from exile to stand as a candidate.

Sometimes, opposition candidates are permitted to run for office but then are punished for having done so, discouraging such challenges in the future. Under President Alexander Lukashenko of Belarus, the government detained both opposition candidates who challenged him in the March 2006 presidential election. One of them is serving a five-and-a-half-year prison term on "hooliganism" charges.

Similarly, in 2005, at a time when Egyptian President Mubarak was still facing pressure from the US government to democratize, he allowed other candidates to run against him. Ayman Nour, his most energetic and popular opponent, won an officially reported 7 percent of the vote. But to ensure that Nour's candidacy would not encourage more formidable future challengers, the Egyptian government convicted him after an unfair trial on politically-motivated charges of forgery and sentenced him to five years in prison.

Again following the powerful showing in the 2005 parliamentary elections of the Muslim Brotherhood, the country's largest opposition group, the Egyptian government detained more than a thousand of its members, holding some for up to eight months. The government has prohibited political activity with a religious basis, eliminating the possibility that the Muslim Brotherhood could become a legally recognized political party. The government has also discussed preventing candidates from running as independents, which is how Muslim Brotherhood members have managed so far to participate in elections.

Israel took this process to a new level by detaining candidates even after they had won an election. Dismayed that Hamas won parliamentary elections in 2006, Israel arrested Hamas legislators so that the party could not obtain a quorum in parliament.

Political Violence

Violence is a tool commonly used to tame democracy. In Lebanon, unidentified assailants have assassinated a series of figures from the parliamentary majority, which has been engaged in an ongoing political struggle with Syria and its allies in Lebanon. In Chechnya, Ramzan Kadyrov—the president installed by the Kremlin—uses security forces known as the "Kadyrovtsy" to brutally enforce his rule. Cambodia's Hun Sen, prime minister since 1985, has used violence in election after election to muffle dissent, including numerous assassinations of opposition party members, independent journalists, human rights defenders, and trade union leaders. Ethiopian authorities reacted to unexpected opposition wins in the 2005 elections by violently dispersing peaceful demonstrations and detaining most of the opposition leadership.

In Zimbabwe, which has scheduled presidential and parliamentary elections for March 2008, the government has let loose youth militia and "war veterans" to beat, torture and rape opposition figures, and the police have used excessive force, sometimes lethal, to break up opposition demonstrations. In the Democratic Republic of Congo, soldiers and police used excessive force, killing more than 100 civilians in the course of crushing sometimes-violent protests against electoral corruption in January-February 2007. In Nigeria, the ruling party recruited gang-like "cults" to curb opposition in advance of April 2007 elections. In Egypt's 2005 parliamentary elections, as return polls showed an increasing number of candidates affiliated with the Muslim Brotherhood winning seats, the Egyptian security forces physically blocked voters from reaching polling stations in Muslim Brotherhood strongholds, and in the ensuing violence killed 11 people trying to vote.

Silencing the Media

A meaningful election requires a free press—to highlight issues demanding governmental attention and to permit public scrutiny of candidates' competing political visions. The media is also essential for conveying popular concerns between elections—necessary input because a single vote cast every few years is a crude and insufficient method to make popular concerns known. It is thus no surprise that governments trying to control the democratic process seek to silence the press.

One of the first targets of Russian President Putin was the independent media. Today, all major television and radio stations and most major newspapers are in the hands of Kremlin loyalists. This controlled media landscape was one of Putin's most important tools for ensuring that the opposition had no chance to threaten his political dominance, whether in the parliamentary elections of December 2007 or the planned presidential elections of March 2008.

Venezuelan President Hugo Chávez, making arbitrary use of a regulatory process, refused to renew the license of RCTV, one of the country's four leading private television stations and the only one with national coverage that had dared to maintain an anti-Chávez editorial line. Under Zimbabwe's repressive media laws, the only independent daily newspaper, the Daily News, was shut down in 2003.

Egypt imprisoned journalists and bloggers for such offenses as criticizing Mubarak, "undermin[ing] the dignity of the country," and publishing "false news ... likely to disturb public order." Azerbaijan imprisoned at least 10 journalists on a range of trumped-up charges to prevent criticism of President Aliev and his government. It also shut down the leading independent newspaper. Kazakhstan closed a television station and weekly newspaper owned by the president's estranged son-in-law, now a political opponent. Like Azerbaijan, it also uses criminal libel laws to jail critics for such charges as "insulting the honor and dignity" of the president. At least six journalists have died in suspicious "accidents" in Kazakhstan since 2002.

Preventing Opposition Rallies

One way for candidates to speak to supporters and to demonstrate political strength is to organize public rallies. Yet because large opposition rallies can show the emptiness of a government's claim to broad popular support, these demonstrations are another favorite target of repression.

In Malaysia, for example, which bans public gatherings of more than five people without a permit, the police used chemical-laced water and tear gas to break up an orderly and peaceful march of protesters demanding electoral reforms ahead of planned elections expected in early 2008. In Russia the authorities beat, detained, and harassed participants in peaceful political protests, including, in November 2007, the former chess champion and current opposition leader Garry Kasparov.

In Zimbabwe, armed riot police violently disrupted political rallies in February 2007, firing tear gas at opposition supporters and arresting more than 70 of them in the cities of Harare and Bulawayo before imposing a three-month ban on all political rallies and demonstrations in Harare, the capital. Authorities also violently broke up rallies in Egypt and the Democratic Republic of Congo.

Shutting Down Civil Society

In addition to political parties, a vibrant democracy requires a variety of associations and organizations so that people can mobilize support for their policy preferences and make their voices heard. These civil society organizations thus are another common target of autocratic rulers.

In Russia, for example, a 2006 law regulating nongovernmental organizations (NGOs) has served as a pretext for growing harassment. The law requires groups to submit annual reports on their activities and their use of foreign funds on pain of liquidation—a sanction that already has been used. Meanwhile, organizations have been subject to intrusive inspections, and a 2007 law allowing any politically or ideologically-motivated crime to be designated "extremist" and subject to harsh punishment raises concerns that the law will be used to silence dissent.

In Turkmenistan, severe legal restrictions on NGOs include the need to register every grant with the government, inform the government of every meeting, and allow a government representative to participate. Just three independent NGOs have been registered since 2003, only one of which has anything to do with human rights or public accountability. In Uzbekistan since the 2005 Andijan massacre, at least 17 human rights defenders have been imprisoned on politically-motivated charges, dozens have had to stop their human rights work or flee the country altogether, and numerous international organizations have been forced out. The United Arab Emirates bans most civil society organizations, and in August 2007 the Palestinian Authority announced that it would shut down 103 civil society organizations on a variety of technical grounds.

In countries where domestic funders of critical NGOs risk governmental wrath, a limitation on external sources of funding is a serious impediment to organized independent voices. Yet Egypt shut down a local human rights group engaged in vigorous anti-torture advocacy by reviving a years-old complaint against it for using funds from a foreign donor without government permission. Jordan and Bahrain have proposed similar legislation requiring government permission to use funds from abroad. Iran and Syria have already enacted this requirement and exercise complete control over the day-to-day operations of civil society. The Tunisian government has blocked European Union grants to the Tunisian Human Rights League and other independent organizations.

Undermining the Rule of Law

Much of the repression and manipulation outlined above is illegal. Governments seeking to use it thus must avoid independent legal oversight. Sometimes, this can be accomplished by beating and arresting lawyers, as in Zimbabwe or China.

Other times it occurs by way of amnesties for any crimes committed. Pakistan's Musharraf and the military rulers in Thailand, for example, pushed through constitutional changes granting them impunity for actions taken during their respective coups. Musharraf also dismissed the Supreme Court judges who threatened to rule against the legitimacy of his selection as president, replacing them with pliant loyalists who promptly validated the choice.

The Weak International Response

The use of these techniques to trivialize democracy does not occur in a political vacuum. Abusive governments may want to legitimize themselves on the cheap, but it takes their peers to let them do so. To a significant degree, half-baked democrats succeed in passing themselves off as the real thing because they are beneficiaries of diminished expectations from the more established democracies.

In part the problem is one of competing interests. Would-be defenders of a more meaningful vision of democracy are too ready to allow commercial opportunities, access to resources, or the perceived requirements of fighting terrorism to override concern with a government's democratic credentials. In part, though, the problem is one of hypocrisy avoidance. Even seemingly flourishing democracies can, as noted, find it inconvenient to embrace all the rights that constitute genuine democracy lest the subject lead to their own violations.

The problem is compounded by inconsistency in promoting democracy—a longstanding problem. These days, for example, the US government's vigorous criticism of democratic shortcomings tends to be reserved mainly for long-time adversaries or pariahs, such as Syria, Burma or Cuba. Washington has largely exempted such allies as Saudi Arabia, Tunisia, or Ethiopia, while its short-lived pressure on others, such as Egypt or Jordan, has waned. Indeed, the US government is often a major funder of these allied governments despite their repressive practices. This obvious double standard makes the promotion of democracy seem like an act of political convenience rather than a commitment of principle, weakening the pressure for real democratic change.

Ethiopia has been an illustrative beneficiary of this double standard. The government of Prime Minister Meles Zenawi arrested thousands of demonstrators protesting against fraud in the 2005 elections and charged 18 journalists with treason. These arrests were part of a broader pattern of repression, including the use of torture, detention, and intimidation of people perceived as political opponents and, more recently, extraordinary brutality in suppressing an insurgency in the Ogaden region and fighting Islamic forces in neighboring Somalia. The US government has expressed dismay about the post-election crackdown, but Ethiopia, a key counterterrorism partner, remains Washington's biggest aid beneficiary in sub-Saharan Africa.

Ethiopia is also among the top African recipients of European Union aid. After the 2005 election violence, the EU, along with the World Bank and the United Kingdom, suspended portions of their direct budget support to Ethiopia, but the UK has since increased its aid.

Jordan has also benefited from diminished democratic expectations, due largely to the US government's fear that Islamists in the country might replicate Hamas's victory in the Occupied Palestinian Territories, but also to Washington's apparent gratitude for Jordan's assistance in fighting terrorism by providing secret detention centers where US-delivered suspects could be tortured. Jordan's municipal elections in July 2007 were reportedly tainted by massive fraud, including soldiers bussed to opposition strongholds to vote for the government, multiple voting, and manipulated voter rolls. Yet both the US ambassador and Congress congratulated Jordanians on the exercise of their democratic rights. Some of these faults were allegedly replicated in parliamentary elections in November, but the US State Department "commend[ed]" the Jordanian government for "ensuring another step has been taken on the country's path of political development." The State Department praised in particular the use of "independent national observers" without noting that, as mentioned, the government had reneged on its promise to allow them to enter polling places, forcing them to try to observe the proceedings from outside.

The European Union's reaction to the Jordanian elections was no more principled. It issued no known public protest, even though Jordan, as a member of the European Neighborhood Policy (ENP), has signed an Association Agreement with the EU, of which respect for democratic principles and fundamental human rights is supposed to constitute an "essential element." This failing reflects broader problems with the ENP, since unlike the successful Copenhagen criteria for accession to the EU, there are no benchmarks or timelines associated with it, and it is becoming increasingly focused on issues such as cooperation for border management and migration control.

Such unprincipled endorsements suggest that Washington and often the European Union will accept an electoral facade so long as the "victor" is a strategic or commercial ally. The fairness of the vote and the openness of campaign conditions seem to matter less than the political orientation of the democracy pretender.

A False Dichotomy: The Tyrant You Know or the Tyrant You Fear

The weak international response to the manipulation of democracy is founded in part on fear that an autocrat might be replaced by someone or something worse. Beginning with the FIS parliamentary victory in Algeria in 1991, the rise of political Islam has made that fear especially acute. Savvy dictators have learned to use a me-or-them logic to justify continued rule, but the dichotomy is often a false one.

For example, Egypt's Mubarak has profited from Western concern that Islamists will win any fair election in the country. As evidence, Mubarak can point to the parliamentary elections of 2005, when candidates backed by the Muslim Brotherhood captured a majority of the seats they contested. There is no doubt that the Muslim Brotherhood is genuinely popular, but some of that popularity is a product of limited choice. In thirty years, the Egyptian government has refused to register more than 60 political parties while accepting only two, one of which it later suspended. Many of these parties could have served as a rallying point for a secular opposition.

The Muslim Brotherhood, as noted, is also banned as a political party, but it has been able to build a following by providing social services and developing a reputation as above corruption. So, today, if an Egyptian seeks an alternative to Mubarak and his ruling National Democratic Party, the Muslim Brotherhood appears to be the only real game in town. That serves Mubarak well, because Western acquiescence in his electoral manipulations is more likely in light of this false political choice. US pressure for democratization largely ended with the strong Muslim Brotherhood showing of 2005.

Pakistan's Musharraf has played a similar game. He justified "emergency rule" as the only alternative to rule by al Qaeda and Islamic extremists. The West accepted and even embraced Musharraf's manipulation of the political landscape as a form of "moderation" and a step on the road to "democracy." Never mind that Pakistanis historically have voted for centrist political parties (corrupt and inept as they often were), that Islamist political parties never gained more than 11 percent of the vote in a competitive national election, that Musharraf's attacks on the moderate center have forced him to seek alliance with and, in turn, bolster the Islamists, and that the lack of opportunity under a military government for peaceful political change is a powerful recruiting force for the Islamists.

The Bush administration's inconsistent response to Musharraf's declaration of emergency rule was illustrative. On the one hand, Deputy Secretary of State John Negroponte flew to Islamabad to ask Musharraf to lift emergency rule and to release the thousands of political prisoners who had been detained. He even said, appropriately, that "[e]mergency rule is not compatible with free, fair and credible elections." Even Bush urged Musharraf to "take off your uniform."

But at this writing, the US government has never asked Musharraf to reinstate the independent Supreme Court judges whom he had dismissed in favor of the pliant allies who blessed his selection as president while still military chief. Nor has Washington suspended any of its massive military assistance. The message sent was that rather than risking the tenure of its counterterrorism ally, Washington would divorce democracy from the rule of law. Washington also seemed to want to stop the courts from continuing to free suspects who had disappeared into the custody of Pakistan's abusive Directorate for Inter-Services Intelligence (ISI), a detention and interrogation service that the US government has had occasion to avail itself of.

Fear of rising Islamic militancy seems also to lie behind a mixed international response to Bangladesh. At first, the international community promoted a more principled vision of democracy. The United Nations and the European Union found elections planned for January 2007 to be too compromised to warrant sending observers, thus contributing to their postponement. However, the caretaker government brought in ostensibly to ensure free and fair elections has instead declared a "state of emergency" and become a vehicle for de facto military rule, presiding over large numbers of arbitrary arrests, cases of torture, and custodial killings by security forces acting with impunity. The US, UK, and Indian governments have expressed concern about the slow pace of election preparations but not the country's poor human rights record. Nor have they called on the army to return full powers to a civilian government. However, the EU has been more outspoken and is providing financial assistance for governance and human rights.

Such complicity in dictatorial rule is sometimes rationalized with patronizing claims that the people in question—often Muslim, frequently Arab—are not "ready" for democracy, that the risks in these societies are simply too great to afford them the same rights of freedom and self-governance that people everywhere else aspire to. Put another way, Western governments sometimes complain that there is no opposition worthy of support. But that supposed lack of readiness, the lack of political alternatives, is no more than the warped political conditions that, with Western acquiescence, these countries' leadership has bequeathed them. The entire point of the pseudo-democrats' repression is to cripple the emergence of an effective opposition. Indeed, in the case of Saudi Arabia, lack of readiness is an excuse that the government itself has used to avoid elections. Pakistan's Musharraf made similar excuses, charging that the West has an "unrealistic obsession with your form of democracy, your human rights and civil liberties ... which you took centuries to (evolve), but you want us to adopt in months .... [T]his is not possible."

To reject that logic is not to suggest that immediate, unfettered elections are the answer, either. Just as extremism flourishes in a constrained political environment, so it may prevail in a snap election called in such an environment. A more sophisticated response is needed, one that would push autocrats to allow a range of political choices before rushing to elections—that is, to prioritize respect for an array of essential political rights over the balloting itself. Instead of accepting a dictator's crimped set of options as the only conceivable ones, democracy promoters should press to transform the political landscape so that voters will face a meaningful range of political options before marking their ballot. That genuine choice tends to be an enemy of extremism.

Banking on the "Democrat" Rather than Democratic Principles

One common failing is to support a particular proclaimed "democrat" rather than the human rights principles that make democracy meaningful. Established democracies seem increasingly to look for individuals—rather than institutions—to save the day, hoping that people will equate the ascendance of a leader prone to democratic rhetoric with the arrival of democracy itself, even though the first lesson of democratic theory is that unrestrained power tends toward tyranny. This failing has certainly characterized Western policy toward Pakistan's Musharraf, but it has also played a central role in the response to such disparate countries as Russia, Nigeria and Georgia.

Bush famously embraced Putin in 2001 after "look[ing] into his eyes and s[eeing] his soul." Putin proceeded systematically to undermine nearly every competing center of influence in Russia—the Duma, the regional governors, the press, the NGOs, even the oligarchs. The US government ultimately did react, but it had lost an early opportunity to build US-Russian relations around principles rather than personal chemistry.

Germany, which traditionally plays a leading role in shaping the European Union's policy toward Russia, had a mixed record in 2007. German Chancellor Angela Merkel, perhaps because she grew up in the East under Soviet domination, sees Putin with clearer eyes than her mercantilist predecessor, Gerhard Schröder. She has spoken out several times about the disturbing trends in Russia, and during her first trip to Moscow in 2006, made a point of visiting human rights NGOs. That led to hope that Germany would elevate the importance of human rights when it assumed the EU presidency during the first half of 2007. In fact, human rights continued to be consigned largely to low-level consultations. Merkel did raise human rights during the EU-Russia summit in May 2007, when demonstrations were quashed, but the next EU presidency, under the Portuguese government, undermined that effort by equating the raising of human rights issues with "lecturing."

The US and UK governments as well as the EU were candid about the blatant fraud that marred Nigeria's presidential and parliamentary elections in April 2007, but these Western governments seemed eager to work with President Yar'Adua because his rhetoric was reformist, even though the circumstances of his election set a far more powerful precedent than his conciliatory words. Nor did Yar'Adua translate his reformist message into prosecution of anyone responsible for the fraud and parallel political violence. Again, the message seems to be that, so long as the leader in question is friendly to the West, even fake elections will suffice to legitimize him.

In Georgia, the 2003 Rose Revolution brought to power a government with a strong commitment to democratic principles and a vibrant civil society. But serious human rights problems persisted in the years that followed, particularly in the criminal justice system. Yet international organizations and governments—the US most prominently among them—resisted robust criticism, wishing to believe in the good intentions of a Western-educated ally, President Mikheil Saakashvili. The danger of embracing a person rather than democratic principles became apparent when in November 2007 the Georgian government unleashed a violent crackdown on protesters and imposed a nine-day state of emergency.

As noted, US policy toward Pakistan has been dominated by this tendency to reduce democracy to favored personalities. In addition to accepting Musharraf's dismissal of the Supreme Court to preserve his presidency, the Bush administration devoted enormous energy to negotiating a deal between Musharraf and its preferred prime ministerial candidate, former Prime Minister Benazir Bhutto, paving the way for her return from exile to Pakistan. But in September, when the Musharraf government blocked the initial attempt to return of exiled former Prime Minister Nawaz Sharif, her chief civilian competitor, the US State Department spokesman said, "[T]his is wholly and entirely a Pakistani issue to resolve."

Failing Turkey

Turkey presented perhaps the most important test of the European Union's commitment to democracy and human rights. In principle, the EU is committed to admitting Turkey as a member—a step of enormous importance—if Ankara meets the Copenhagen criteria on democracy and human rights. But key European lead-

ers—especially German Chancellor Merkel and French President Nicolas Sarkozy—
have spoken out against Turkey's membership in the EU. As the possibility of
Turkey's accession to the EU is perceived as more remote, the EU has lost leverage itself and diminished the clout of those in Turkey who have cited the
prospect of EU membership as a reason for reform. Unsurprisingly, the military
has begun once more to intrude into governmental affairs, going so far as to
launch the above-mentioned email coup attempt to block the naming of Abdullah
Gül as president. The civilian government's successful deflection of that coup
attempt owed far more to the insistence of the Turkish people than to the EU's
fading promise of membership to a democratic, rights-respecting Turkey.

Conclusion

It is a sign of hope that even dictators have come to believe that the route to
legitimacy runs by way of democratic credentials. Broadly shared and deeply felt
values underwrite the principle that sovereignty lies with the people of a nation
and that the authority to govern is ultimately theirs. But that progress is fragile,
its meaning dependent in large part on the commitment of the world's established democracies. If they accept any dictator who puts on the charade of an
election, if they allow their commitment to democracy to be watered down by
their pursuit of resources, commercial opportunities, and short-sighted visions of
security, they will devalue the currency of democracy. And if dictators can get
away with calling themselves "democrats," they will have acquired a powerful
tool for deflecting pressure to uphold human rights. It is time to stop selling
democracy on the cheap and to start substituting a broader and more meaningful
vision of the concept that incorporates all human rights.

This Report

This report is Human Rights Watch's eighteenth annual review of human rights
practices around the globe. It summarizes key human rights issues in more than
75 countries worldwide, drawing on events through November 2007.

Each country entry identifies significant human rights issues, examines the freedom of local human rights defenders to conduct their work, and surveys the
response of key international actors, such as the United Nations, European

Union, Japan, the United States, and various regional and international organizations and institutions.

This report reflects extensive investigative work undertaken in 2007 by the Human Rights Watch research staff, usually in close partnership with human rights activists in the country in question. It also reflects the work of our advocacy team, which monitors policy developments and strives to persuade governments and international institutions to curb abuses and promote human rights. Human Rights Watch publications, issued throughout the year, contain more detailed accounts of many of the issues addressed in the brief summaries collected in this volume. They can be found on the Human Rights Watch website, www.hrw.org.

As in past years, this report does not include a chapter on every country where Human Rights Watch works, nor does it discuss every issue of importance. The failure to include a particular country or issue often reflects no more than staffing limitations and should not be taken as commentary on the significance of the problem. There are many serious human rights violations that Human Rights Watch simply lacks the capacity to address.

The factors we considered in determining the focus of our work in 2007 (and hence the content of this volume) include the number of people affected and the severity of abuse, access to the country and the availability of information about it, the susceptibility of abusive forces to influence, and the importance of addressing certain thematic concerns and of reinforcing the work of local rights organizations.

The World Report does not have separate chapters addressing our thematic work but instead incorporates such material directly into the country entries. Please consult the Human Rights Watch website for more detailed treatment of our work on children's rights, women's rights, arms and military issues, business and human rights, HIV/AIDS and human rights, international justice, terrorism and counterterrorism, refugees and displaced people, and lesbian, gay, bisexual, and transgender people's rights, and for information about our international film festivals.

Kenneth Roth is executive director of Human Rights Watch.

CHALLENGES FOR A "RESPONSIBLE POWER"

By Sophie Richardson

In 2007, China's harsher critics across the world pointed with alarm to its growing international presence, highlighting what they describe as its preference for doing business with abusive and autocratic governments like itself, its export of tainted toys and medicines, and its rapacious quest for energy resources across the defenseless developing world. Chinese officials paint a very different picture, describing their foreign policy as a "process of forging [China's] destiny with the international community in a closer and more genuine way," insisting it is a "responsible power," and suggesting that such relentless criticism violates the rights of China's 1.3 billion citizens.

One thing is certain: as China becomes ever more enmeshed in the international system, its foreign policy is changing in small ways and is under more scrutiny than ever. As the 2008 Beijing Olympic Games approach, which Chinese officials consider a unique opportunity to show off a modern China to the world, the leadership may be more willing to factor human rights considerations into its decisions. Successfully encouraging it to be more open to human rights promotion, however, will require understanding several key dimensions of Chinese foreign policy and what they mean for human rights globally.

Human rights activists expect all governments to uphold internationally recognized human rights obligations, regardless of borders. But China's approach is one of non-interference, respect for sovereignty, unconditional development aid, refusal to base international relations on regime type or commitments to reform, and resistance to international scrutiny of domestic affairs. This leads to some key questions: how does the Chinese government's approach harm international human rights promotion? In particular, will China's policies of non-interference and unconditional aid obstruct crucial traditional human rights instruments and institutions, such as UN Security Council-imposed pressure and sanctions? Is there a particular logic to Chinese foreign policy? Has recent international pressure prompted the Chinese government to respond more constructively in the face of human rights crises, such as in Darfur and Burma? And, ultimately, can a government that assiduously represses rights at home be expected to work for their defense elsewhere?

How Chinese Foreign Policy Undermines International Human Rights Protection

Few bother to note that it is a tenet of Chinese foreign policy to have relations with and provide aid (a considerable amount of it for a developing country) to rights-respecting governments on the same basis as it provides aid to abusive ones. This is a reflection of China's core policy of "non-interference" in the internal affairs of other states. As a growing power, China's close relations with abusive governments come in for great criticism, as they should, but there is little evidence in recent years that the Chinese government actively encourages human rights abuse by others. China's willingness to provide aid and political support regardless of a recipient's human rights record may, depending on the situation, deserve criticism, but no more so than other countries that do the same thing.

Yet there are many ways in which the model and practice of Chinese foreign policy crucially undermines international efforts to defend human rights. First, the Chinese Communist Party's (CCP) model of development—rapid economic growth without a commensurate increase in civil or political rights, alongside general resistance to international pressure—is hardly a positive example. Economic development in China has brought a greater degree of social freedoms, and of course reduced the number of people in poverty, but the fact remains that it is a government highly repressive of its critics, often on the grounds that their criticism jeopardizes state stability and growth. In addition, that rapid growth has been enabled by gross violations of labor rights, rampant expropriation of land and other public resources by officials, environmental devastation, and suppression of public discontent about these developments. In this sense, the Chinese "model" is, needless to say, not one rights activists wish to see replicated.

Second, after regaining United Nations membership in 1971 and spending about 20 years reinvigorating China's international diplomacy, Chinese diplomats have become more adept at undermining or obstructing the work of international institutions important to the promotion of human rights. For example, Chinese officials consistently block UN Security Council resolutions that entail sanctions, such as (along with other countries) a proposed resolution in January 2007 on Burma and a later resolution condemning the Burmese junta's September 2007 assault on thousands of peaceful demonstrators. By obstructing a means of swiftly disciplining an abusive government or impeding investigations into the nature and scope of human rights abuses, such actions directly contribute to the misery of those who are already suffering.

China's actions at the UN Human Rights Council (HRC) also demonstrate a concerted effort to roll back structures and procedures for protecting rights. China was one of several countries to propose that country mandates and "special procedures" be abandoned or restricted. It suggested that only governments should be able to submit statements in the universal periodic review (UPR) process. Chinese diplomats have complained that nongovernmental organizations' involvement in the HRC should be "controlled." In 2006, China objected to the HRC accepting a report on human rights conditions in Darfur on the grounds that the authors had not actually been inside the country and therefore its report could not be accurate. That entry into the country had been denied by precisely the people thought to be responsible for human rights abuses (and precisely in order to evade scrutiny) seemed immaterial to China.

Third, while Beijing may have deep philosophical differences with the rest of the international community on the efficacy of conditioning aid, it has indisputably provided a crucial financial lifeline to countries with poor human rights records. This has often undermined efforts made by other international actors to use financial pressure to improve rights. Without steady flows of Chinese aid, investment, weapons, and political support, it is possible that the governments of Burma's General Than Shwe, Sudan's President Omar Bashir, and Zimbabwe's President Robert Mugabe, among others, would either already have been consigned to history or would have had their ability to abuse their citizens dramatically limited by a lack of resources.

It is these kinds of actions that earn the Chinese government its reputation as the patron of abusive regimes. Beijing defends its decisions to maintain these relationships with three arguments: first, that to alter them would be to discriminate on the basis of "internal affairs," which it insists it will not do; second, that withdrawing such support would only worsen at least the economic situation of the countries in question, particularly for ordinary people; third, that developed countries at various points continue to support equally abusive governments when it suits them, and thus China's approach cannot be criticized. That these arguments find sympathy in some quarters around the world does nothing to relieve China of complicity in the human suffering that results from its relations with abusive governments.

The Logic Behind Chinese Foreign Policy

Many assume that Chinese diplomats simply do not care about the human rights of other people. After all, they argue, the Chinese government does not care about the rights of its own citizens. Its leaden rhetoric about international human rights and non-interference often sounds callous and seems to eschew any sympathy or responsibility for victims. But those who make assumptions about China's global agenda—that it only supports dictatorships or communists, that its aid brings no benefits to ordinary people, that it seeks to dominate its region—do so at their own peril, as they ignore much evidence to the contrary. More important, these arguments fail to apprehend the internal logic and thinking of Chinese leaders about their international role and aspirations.

China's leaders often point to their efforts to lift hundreds of millions of Chinese out of poverty as evidence of their commitment to human rights domestically. Rather than seeing all rights as equally important, the CCP continues to argue that economic and social rights, which it often equates with economic development, take precedence over civil and political rights. Poverty, they argue, causes serious instability and makes it impossible for any rights to be secured. Even assuming that poverty reduction is their overarching priority, the logic of Chinese officials is flawed. Respect for civil and political rights can also assist poverty reduction efforts, but one does not hear Chinese officials arguing that China must immediately remove barriers to free expression and the free flow of information so as to free up space for more robust public criticism of bad governance and policy failures. This failure to acknowledge the importance of such civil and political rights, it is worth noting, has created a domestic threat to the CCP more serious than it has grappled with in decades as unprecedented numbers of Chinese protestors and petitioners spill into China's streets to make their complaints known.

China's foreign policy employs a similar logic—that economic development is key to real independence and therefore also to securing individual countries' "rights" in the international community. This thinking is augmented by several other closely-held beliefs, including a half-century of hostility towards the principles and practices of American foreign policy, which China continues to see as profoundly imperialistic, hypocritical, and, directly or indirectly, the cause of conflict. Beijing also remains skeptical about the merits of international institutions and norms, many of which were developed in the two decades during which China was frozen out of the international system, and which the CCP believes were created in part to criticize, take advantage of, and marginalize developing countries. As long as the United States remains committed to defending Taiwan, the CCP also believes it remains vulnerable to actual threats to its territorial security. Finally, by forgoing its claim to examine other countries' human rights conditions, it is much easier for Beijing to reject scrutiny of its own.

These convictions and rhetoric often sound and are obstructionist, particularly when deployed in the face of gross human rights abuses. Yet they remain popular in many parts of the developing world, where China is now seen as almost as desirable a partner as the United States, the European Union, and international financial institutions.

The term "non-interference" seems to contradict other Chinese foreign policy rhetoric, which regularly states the importance of China's membership in the international community. But many Chinese officials genuinely do not believe that pressing countries to adopt rights-respecting political or economic systems, or selecting aid recipients based on their human rights records, let alone deposing a particular political leader, achieves progress. To many Chinese leaders, non-interference does not mean uninvolved or uninterested, but rather conducting international relations in a highly circumscribed way so as not to alter the domestic balance of power or induce significant change other than that which local authorities want; it also means reducing the role of international organizations to talk shops for deferential governments, not activist bodies.

Whether local leaders are human rights heroes or war criminals, and regardless of how they came to power or what sort of system they run, China believes it is best to leave crucial decisions about human rights policies to domestic politics. This is the opposite of the approach the United States, European Union, UN, and others often adopt (though with glaring exceptions and highly inconsistent emphases). Many Chinese foreign policy officials, however, view any intervention as distorting domestic politics and relieving domestic actors of responsibility for their actions, ultimately making those countries less independent and stable.

China's insistence on sovereignty also seems in tension with its own rapidly growing interconnections with the rest of the world. But one has to bear in mind Chinese leaders' obsession with maintaining control of Tibet and Hong Kong, and gaining control of Taiwan. These goals are inextricably linked to the CCP's lore about its own legitimacy: that it came to power and has stayed in power because it has popular support, and no foreigners have the right or even the information needed to make good decisions about what happens inside China. Similarly, in the international arena Chinese leaders view conditioned aid and pressure for major economic or political change as undermining sovereignty by leaving too many important decisions to foreigners. Those leaders also believe that international interventions are likely to fail because the people pushing for intervention often lack an adequate understanding of on-the-ground reality or a sufficient commitment to remain involved long enough, or are actually using human rights as a Trojan horse for hidden political agendas.

Are Things Changing?

As it has increasingly come under the international spotlight for its foreign policy positions, China has recently made modest policy adjustments that appear to promote human rights. It is too soon to tell whether they constitute a shift away from the traditional policy of non-interference, or whether they are idiosyncratic changes made in response to intense international pressure.

One sign of change is that, in response to considerable international pressure, China has taken some steps to respond to the human rights crisis in Sudan. China has been harshly criticized for not making better use of its leverage as the primary purchaser of Sudanese oil to discipline a government that is almost certainly guilty of—at a minimum—crimes against humanity. From 2004 to 2006, China helped shield Sudan from the threat of individual and other types of sanctions at the Security Council. It provided diplomatic support to Sudan's refusal of a UN deployment in Darfur, for instance, by abstaining on resolution 1706 in August 2006, which authorized such a force.

Yet just months later, in November 2006, Chinese diplomats apparently took a more assertive position at a key meeting to discuss Darfur deployment in Addis Ababa. In March 2007 China removed Sudan from a list of countries in which Chinese investors were encouraged to do business. In May, Beijing took the highly unusual step of appointing a special envoy for Africa with a focus on Darfur, tapping veteran diplomat Liu Guijin. In August China supported resolution 1769 at the Security Council, which authorized the deployment of a hybrid UN-African Union peacekeeping force. In October, it sent 300 engineers to join the peacekeeping operation.

What changed? China says that it was quietly pushing Sudan all along to resolve the Darfur crisis. But the Chinese government clearly was deeply dismayed over the international focus on its role—which was concentrated, in the words of one Chinese diplomat, "in a way we have never before experienced"—and efforts to link the abuses in Sudan to the 2008 Beijing Olympics. As a result, it decided to intervene more actively with Khartoum, and to be more visible in doing so. The Chinese government made more public statements explaining how it was trying to convince the Sudanese government to accept international demands. The tone and timing of Chinese statements and actions also suggest growing concern in Beijing that ongoing instability in southern Sudan would jeopardize China's plans for oil development across the country. There is, of course, a great deal more China should push Khartoum to do: rapidly deploy the hybrid force, ensuring that it is fully equipped with a robust protective mandate; surrender the ICC indictees; end rape and "ethnic cleansing"; and create conditions for voluntary safe return of the displaced. These actions will have far more of an impact than a special ambassador ever will.

News also began to trickle out in June 2007 of an "unprecedented" effort by Chinese diplomats to bring together leaders of Burma's exile government with members of the ruling State Peace and Development Council (SPDC). Since the Burmese military government solidified its grip on power after annulling elections in 1990, it has been increasingly isolated by Western sanctions. Yet China has provided a crucial financial and diplomatic lifeline even in the face of attacks on peaceful democratic opponents, continued brutal assaults on ethnic minorities, the systematic use of rape as a weapon of war, and ongoing recruitment of child soldiers. After the government used force to break up street protests led by monks in September 2007, China publicly called for restraint and dialogue on all sides and agreed to a Security Council statement critical of the government. It gained credit for quietly pressuring the Burmese government to allow a special UN envoy access to opposition leader Aung San Suu Kyi and for supporting the "good offices" of the UN secretary-general. However, China failed to halt arms transfers or publicly challenge the SPDC over the killing and arrest of protestors.

This relative assertiveness is far more likely a function of China's desire not to have a large border state deteriorate into chaos than a shift in loyalties—although China has long had a relationship with the SPDC, it had no trouble congratulating the pro-democracy forces for their electoral victory in 1990. If Burma implodes, not only would China's considerable investments there be compromised, but so would its ability to manage a border area already rife with drug trafficking and serious public health crises. Of course, should China want to work for a truly stable Burma, it should recognize that the source of instability in Burma is a deeply unpopular, repressive, and rapacious military government that has done almost nothing to address the economic needs of its own people. So long as it stays in power, the country is likely to remain unstable.

Another interesting development came in late August 2007, when a senior British diplomat suggested that China was taking a harder line against Zimbabwean President Robert Mugabe through a highly unusual reduction in aid. After a flurry of articles in the international press, China vehemently denied that the total amount of its aid would be reduced. It later emerged that the amount going to economic programs China had deemed unsuccessful was being cut, while commensurate increases were being made in humanitarian aid. It is unclear why the change was made—whether it was a political message or a more technical decision relating to the efficacy of the use of development aid by Mugabe's government—and therefore whether it signaled a new willingness to use aid to press a recipient government to change its policies. But it is a noteworthy episode that should be further explored.

In international fora, China has been a marginally more cooperative player recently. It is increasingly inclined to abstain on, rather than veto, some international initiatives with which it is uncomfortable, such as the Security Council's referral of Darfur to the International Criminal Court or the Asia-Europe Meeting's communique harshly criticizing the Burmese junta. China is contributing larger numbers of troops to international peacekeeping efforts, including 1,000 to efforts in Lebanon, which shows a growing level of comfort with such initiatives.

What China Can Do Differently

Senior Chinese foreign policy makers' core beliefs remain largely unchanged, and it will be at least another decade until younger, more progressive diplomats come to the fore. Consequently, it is unlikely that China will significantly change its approach in the near future and embrace some of the practices most relied upon by other influential governments: international scrutiny, political pressure on abusive governments, sanctions, conditioned aid.

Yet there are some steps China can take that are consistent with its current world view which will help victims of human rights abuses. At a minimum, Beijing should reconsider its aid strategies. It is highly unlikely that China will begin "attaching strings," but it can at least suspend gratuitously inappropriate projects, such as the new presidential palace for Sudanese President Omar Bashir, and reallocate those funds to other projects that would help those most in need. In the direst circumstances, such as the crackdown in Burma in September 2007, it should suspend some aid to send a political signal. Should it fail to do so, the Chinese government must recognize that its actions will give others legitimate grounds to criticize its agenda and question its motives. Simply being more transparent about aid, particularly in countries with serious human rights issues, would also be a significant improvement.

China could also articulate the conditions under which it will set aside its insistence on sovereignty and non-interference, particularly with respect to human rights crises. Some argue persuasively that by ratifying legally binding international human rights treaties China's obligations are clear.[1] When in 2005 it signed up to the "responsibility to protect" at the UN, China agreed that member states are obliged to intervene when a government fails to protect its own population against serious human rights abuses. It is not yet clear under what circumstances China will endorse the doctrine's use—if it is serious, the discussion in China (and elsewhere) should move from *whether* to treat state sovereignty as an impregnable boundary to *how* it will join with other countries to intervene in the most egregious humanitarian crises when circumstances require. In order for the responsibility to protect to be implemented, the capacity to prevent and respond to mass atrocities must be created, both within countries and at the international level. For example, the UN secretary-general should have the ability to deploy human rights monitors if alerted to a developing situation which implicates the doctrine, and the UN should have a standby force ready to deploy immediately when mass atrocities loom. Chinese support for such measures would indicate true international responsibility.

Finally, China should be truer to its own rhetoric that it is a devoted friend of the developing world. It should see its foreign policy as not just about relations with other governments, but also about helping to improve the well-being of the people of those states. This would earn China the gratitude of people around the globe. But it will require a policy that accepts that human beings need civil and political rights as well as economic development. If it wants to be seen as a responsible power, China should be willing to act decisively when people suffer at the hands of their own governments. Putting human dignity at the core of Chinese foreign policy would indeed constitute revolutionary change for China and the rest of the world.

Sophie Richardson is Asia advocacy director at Human Rights Watch.

---

[1] As a member of the United Nations, China is expected to uphold the Universal Declaration of Human Rights (UDHR), but it is also a party to the Convention Against Torture (CAT), the Convention to Eliminate All Forms of Discrimination (CEDAW), the Convention on the Rights of the Child (CRC), and the International Covenant on Economic, Social, and Cultural (ICESCR) Rights. It has signed but not ratified the International Covenant on Civil and Political Rights (ICCPR).

Two Novembers: Movements, Rights, and the Yogyakarta Principles

By Scott Long

1992

In 1992 in Romania, repression was a vivid legacy, privation a lived reality, and intimacy of any kind had to survive in whatever privacy it could garner. That November in the city of Timisoara, Ciprian C., in the last year of high school, met Marian M., two years older. They were both men; they fell in love.[1]

In 1989 Timisoara had begun the revolution against Ceausescu's dictatorship; then, blood stippled the snow. Three years later, suspicion and the police remained. Ciprian's sister informed on the couple. Prosecutors charged them in January 1993 with "sexual relations with a person of the same sex."

> The investigators called me a "whore" repeatedly .... Marian admitted everything during the interrogation. I tried to deny it, until I was shown my diary, which had been brought to the police by my sister. Then I realized I would lose everything.[2]

Those were Ciprian's memories. Timisoara police gave their names and photos to the press, calling Ciprian a "peril to society":

> Looking at the facts and taking into account the age of the accused, you remain shocked by what they were capable of .... [When arrested], the two did not admit the incriminating act ... But after the investigation and the forensic report, it was established that this was a typical case of homosexuality.[3]

The two were jailed for months, separated, their families not allowed to visit. Inmates raped each repeatedly because the guards announced they were homosexual. Ciprian remembered that "once, during a religious service in the penitentiary, Marian kissed the cross, as a believer. On his return to the cell, his cellmates beat him for 'defiling the cross.'"

A court convicted the two in June 1993, but—partly through foreign pressure—their prison sentences were suspended.

Hate pursued them. Ciprian's school expelled him; Marian could find no job. In June 1995 Marian M. committed suicide. His mother only found his body weeks later. Ciprian left Romania and gained asylum in another country.

2006

Human rights are a system of law: treaties and jurisprudence, provision and precedent. Looking back six decades to the beginning of that system, with the Universal Declaration of Human Rights, its construction seems one of the major works of the twentieth century.

In 1948, though, few could have imagined the system would eventually acquire the full solidity of positive law. At the time the Declaration looked less like a set of legal norms than a utopian rebuke to existing injustices, with no enforcement or authority on its own. Only slowly did human rights principles harden into law, and assume the expectation that they would protect, not just critique.

In November 2006, 16 experts on international human rights law gathered in Yogyakarta, Indonesia to discuss sexuality, gender, and human rights. They included a special rapporteur to the United Nations Human Rights Council, four present and former members of UN treaty bodies, a member of Kenya's National Commission on Human Rights, and scholars and activists from—among others—Argentina, Brazil, China, and Nepal.

The result of the meeting is called the "Yogyakarta Principles on the Application of International Human Rights Law in relation to Sexual Orientation and Gender Identity."[4] It contains 29 principles adopted unanimously by the experts, along with recommendations to governments, regional intergovernmental institutions, civil society, and the UN itself.

Everyone understood the meeting was groundbreaking because of what it would cover. Yet the aim was normative, not utopian, to codify what was known: to set out a common understanding developed over three decades. The deliberations drew on precedent and practice by international human rights mechanisms and bodies, but also on national law and jurisprudence from the United States to South Africa.

There are models for such a process. In the absence of a single covenant setting out the rights of internally displaced persons, a body of experts in 1998 assembled guiding principles to spearhead human rights approaches.[5] A similar convening produced the 1998 International Guidelines on HIV/AIDS and Human Rights.[6] Such processes explore so-called "emerging issues" or "protection gaps." The gap is between what human rights law says and what it ought to be doing.

Necessary ghosts hover about such a gathering. Although no one mentioned Marian M. and Ciprian C., they were, in a sense, remembered. Behind what was said hung a history of failure: the ones for whom protections against torture, against arbitrary arrest, for health, for family, had not been sufficient. Two sets of questions constantly arose:

- Who has been left out of existing protections?

- How can those protections then be given real force? How can we expand their reach while acknowledging that their power depends on the idea that they are already "universal?"

The Principles look forward, laying out a program of action for states to ensure equality and eliminate abuse. They can be seen as encoding progress already achieved for lesbian, gay, bisexual, and transgender (LGBT) people, turning it into a new set of norms with the promise of becoming binding.

Yet looking back—toward 1992, or 1948—the experts also saw the modern history of human rights as one of gaps, in which standards never enjoyed stasis. Protections against torture, once solid, could threaten to erode. Moreover, the legal principle and the abstract norm needed constantly to be measured against experience. Protections meant nothing unless some pressure constantly kept forcing the question: did they protect enough? The drive behind the Principles, demanding whether existing understandings of law fitted the real shape of violations, was the drive that made human rights make sense. As South Africa's highest court wrote, "The rights must fit the people, not the people the rights. This requires looking at rights and their violations from a persons-centered rather than a formula-based position, and analyzing them contextually rather than abstractly."[7]

What bridged the gap between the norm and the need was the movement. Human rights movements are often seen only as an adjunct to human rights law, enforcers bringing up the rear. What made the Principles possible, however, was the steady press of movements representing lesbian, gay, bisexual, and transgender people, presenting violations and demanding that institutions act. They both established that law was not living up to its obligations, and pointed the way for it to do so.

So-called "social movements" are not just political actors, but repositories of experience, telling new kinds of stories that demand new responses from human rights systems, as well as governments and societies. One can see LGBT people's movements as opening "new conceptual space,"[8] producing previously unrecorded knowledge about how lives were lived and violations happened, thus reconfiguring both the ambit of rights and the expectations on them. The Yogyakarta Principles not only codify norms but condense what movements have learned. Even looking between the lines of a few Principles can show something of how lesbian, gay, bisexual, and transgender people moved human rights.

Denial and Recognition

Principle 3: *Everyone has the right to recognition everywhere as a person before the law. ... Each person's self-defined sexual orientation and gender identity is integral to their personality and is one of the most basic aspects of self-determination, dignity and freedom.*

"Recognition before the law" is principally a guarantee of judicial personality. It arose in Yogyakarta in the histories of people whom law or society refused to acknowledge because their given identity did not match their appearance or their gender as they lived it. In Nepal in 2007, for instance, Human Rights Watch spoke to many people who identified as *metis* (an indigenous term for those born male who reject being "masculine"): they could not get jobs, find homes, or sometimes even see doctors because the government denied them necessary IDs.

Many would recognize their situation as a symptom—not only of the economic and legal consequences of inequality, but of how governments, where sexuality and gender are concerned, can erase the idea of difference itself.

When Mahmoud Ahmadinejad visited the US in 2007, he made a stir by saying: "We in Iran ... we do not have homosexuals [*hamjensbaz*, a derogatory term] as you have in your country .... In Iran, absolutely such a thing does not exist as a phenomenon." The US press treated the statement as a strange outrage, but it was nothing new. Politicians had long been making comparable claims. Namibia's President Sam Nujoma blasted an interviewer in 2001 who raised the subject: "Don't repeat those words ["gay" and "lesbian"]. They are unacceptable here .... Those words you are mentioning are un-Namibian."9

Nujoma was defending Namibia's law prohibiting homosexual conduct. His tirade showed a syllogism which recurs around the subject.

- We do not have these people here;

- We need laws against them.

The paradox is vicious. Whenever southern African leaders said homosexuality was imaginary in their countries, real people suspected of it were beaten or arrested. The talk about terminology elides the jailed bodies, the broken bones, the eliminated lives involved. Ahmadinejad's statement seemed more shocking only because Iran's criminal code provides penalties, up to death, for homosexual conduct. His language described an absence. His laws enforce it.

However, the Yogyakarta Principles themselves are ambivalent about these words. They use "lesbian," "gay," "bisexual," "transgender," only sparingly. Their authors dealt in terms, not of identities, but status: "sexual orientation," "gender identity," all given as much space as possible to be "self-defined."

One could see this wordsmithing as ignoring common experience. Yet the experts hoped to capture that "experience" is never unproblematically "common."

No reasonable standard of "cultural authenticity" exists by which to judge that words or identities do not belong. There is, however, a standard of autonomy and dignity saying people should be able to determine who they themselves are in the course of their lives. In the US, a 2003 Supreme Court decision overturned laws against consensual homosexual conduct by citing "an autonomy of self that includes freedom of thought, belief, expression, and certain intimate conduct."[10] The European Court of Human Rights has called defining one's own gender identity "one of the most basic essentials of self-determination."[11]

The Yogyakarta Principles attempt to treat sexuality and gender in ways they have not usually been treated by the law: not as embarrassments better left alone, but as places where human beings do things that help define themselves. This implies a fuller notion of the "person" who is the subject of human rights. Her self becomes more capable, and more capacious. The Principles deepen the ordinary right to recognition as a person, finding in it not just legal subjectivity,[12] but personal self-determination. Recognizing this also means respecting that people will define themselves in diverse ways.

Ahmadinejad talks of *hamjensbaz*, a Farsi insult—derogating the thing he denies. Nujoma, for years, turned "lesbian" into a curse against all Namibian feminists. Laws likewise need to lump in categories in order to punish or repress. Ciprian C. and Marian M. became just "a typical case of homosexuality."

Meanwhile, people and movements group under different banners to talk back. "Lesbian," "gay," "transgender," are only some of the more familiar. In fact, there is no global "lesbian, gay, bisexual, and transgender movement," because it is fruitless to try to sum up people's experiences of gender and sexuality, and the violations they face, in one vocabulary. There are people and movements pursuing different goals, defining themselves in different relations to those terms. The Yogyakarta Principles seek space for the diverse ways people name themselves and form solidarities.

Yet they also try to get at something deeper. The Principles locate an elemental source of rights back where diversity as well as solidarity begins—the struggle for autonomy and self-determination.

Private and Public

Principle 6: *Everyone, regardless of sexual orientation or gender identity, is entitled to the enjoyment of privacy without arbitrary or unlawful interference .... The right to privacy ordinarily includes the choice to disclose or not to disclose information relating to one's sexual orientation or gender identity, as well as decisions and choices regarding both one's own body and consensual sexual and other relations with others.*

When Marian M. and Ciprian C. were arrested, over 100 countries around the world had laws against consensual sex between adult men, and sometimes between adult women. In some places the prohibitions were part of religious law or tradition. Most, though, were tied to modern state authority.

Romania's sodomy law, for instance, had appeared only 60 years before—in the 1930s, as the country moved toward fascism. In the 1960s, as Ceausescu's dictatorship tightened the screws, punishments for homosexual acts drastically increased. Simultaneously, draconian new laws banned all birth control as well as abortion, and subjected women to regular gynecological exams, all intensifying the policing of private life.[13]

Moral pretext blended into political purpose as the state turned totalitarian. In the twentieth century, many regimes used laws on "private" behavior to expand and secure their power. When Stalin's Soviet Union criminalized homosexual conduct, one of his prosecutors explained that the least permitted privacy could breed political dissent: "classless hoodlums" would "take to pederasty," and in their "stinky secretive little bordellos, another kind of activity takes place as well—counter-revolutionary work."[14]

In the United States since the 1960s, it has become a commonplace that sexual and reproductive rights need the judiciary to shelter them from the overreachings of majoritarian rule.[15] From that vantage, it is surprising how often, after the Berlin Wall fell, expressing the diversity of sexuality was connected to democracy.

It was not just a matter of rolling back the surveillance powers of dictatorships which had spread sodomy laws from Bucharest to Vladivostok. The totalitarian state had erased the line between public and private: campaigners for sexual rights created new knowledge about public and private spheres and how the two could relate.

They showed that the right to remain private was fused with the right to become public, the right to conceal with the right to disclose, intimacy with association and expression. In post-1989 Romania, defending privacy and dismantling the instruments of intrusion were critical. The struggle against the repressive sodomy law, however, had to be highly public.

For almost a decade after 1993, while allying with other victims of (ethnic and religious) inequality, the campaign brought something new to Romanian politics: evidence that an intimate fact could become a basis of community and action. In 2001 Parliament finally annulled the law that had allowed to jail Ciprian C. and Marian M.[16] In doing so it protected privacy and also, in a sense, broke down the prison walls around it. The Romanian movement attested that people cannot enjoy their privacies without public freedoms; securing democracy meant giving those interrelations institutional recognition.

Where democracy is fragile in post-1989 Eastern Europe, lesbians and gays have come under new attack. In Russia, assaults on peaceful Gay Pride marchers in 2006 and 2007 displayed the rollback in political rights. As police wielded nightsticks on the streets, politicians sneered that homosexuals should stick to freedom in the bedroom. "There is another way," one lesbian countered after she was released from jail. "I love my girlfriend, and I want to be allowed to say that in my own country."[17]

Equality and Politics

Principle 2: *Everyone is entitled to enjoy all human rights without discrimination on the basis of sexual orientation or gender identity .... Discrimination based on sexual orientation or gender identity may be, and commonly is, compounded by discrimination on other grounds including gender, race, age, religion, disability, health and economic status.*

As dictatorships fell in Europe and Latin America in the 1990s, sodomy laws went too. In 2007, though, over 85 still remain worldwide.[18] Almost all are a legacy of colonialism.

White colonizers legislated inequality, creating segregated categories with radically incommensurate rights. Colonial rulers saw "native" sexuality as feral, requiring constant restriction. Laws around it helped keep subjugated people under both stigma and surveillance.

Great Britain imposed a sodomy law on its Indian possessions in 1837.[19] The Indian Penal Code, a vast imperial experiment in making a conquered territory submit to codified Western law, criminalized "unnatural lust." The provision spread to other colonies; today, the Republic of India, Bangladesh, Singapore, Malaysia, Kenya, Uganda, and Tanzania are among its inheritors.[20] Other colonizers—French, Dutch, German—imposed their own penalties for homosexual acts.

Yet 50 years after anti-colonial struggles for liberation, the laws have stayed behind. Jamaican leaders defend an imported law on "buggery" as intrinsic to their culture. The Indian government still asserts in court that a Victorian paragraph remains relevant after viceroys have gone.[21] In many places, the old laws have offered post-colonial leaders a convenient prop for the state's rickety power.

And yet:

> A democratic, universalistic, caring and aspirationally egalitarian society embraces everyone and accepts people for who they are. ... Respect for human rights requires the affirmation of self, not the denial of self. ... At issue is a need to affirm the very character of our society as one based on tolerance and mutual respect.[22]

That was the South African Constitutional Court in 2005, mandating equal recognition of lesbian and gay relationships in law. The 1996 South African Constitution was the world's first to include sexual orientation as a protected status. This came through long campaigning by LGBT activists who were also veterans of the anti-apartheid movement. It came in a country where criminalizing sex—whether interracial or otherwise "deviant"—had been a foundation of apartheid rule.

South Africa's record since 1996 is full of failures to defend human rights (including LGBT rights) in international arenas, and failures to make them meaningful at home. The murders of three black lesbians in South African townships in 2007 point to prejudice's persistence in places where unresolved poverty turns to violence.

South Africa, though, still shows that sexual and gender rights are not a detour from the post-colonial path to self-determination. The confluence making its progressive constitution possible came partly from the length of its liberation struggle, and the way it engaged almost the whole society—so that liberation was accepted in many different meanings. The document had to take in compounded forms of discrimination, as well as economic and social injustices that limited the reach of rights on paper.

LGBT activists in the rest of the world like to point to the South African example as though the relevant parts can be detached and taken to Zimbabwe or the US, much as colonists carried their laws like baggage. That is not its lesson. Rather, it teaches about integrating rights struggles with one another: how one group's claims achieve greater meaning and reach in connection with another's. The interdependence of human rights is fully revealed in the politics of movements, in how they support one another but also learn from one another, and deepen the sense of the terms—"freedom" or "equality"—they use.

VI. Local and International

Principle 27: *Everyone has the right, individually and in association with others, to promote the protection and realisation of human rights at the national and international levels, without discrimination on the basis of sexual orientation or gender identity.*

"What are the lesbians doing here?" the journalist demanded:

> What can they ask for? Do they want now to inscribe their pathologic irregularity in the Charter of Human Rights? ... They have discredited this Conference and distorted the true purposes of woman's emancipation.[23]

He was describing participants at the World Conference on Women in Mexico City in 1975 who had formed an International Lesbian Caucus. When even the idea of crossing borders to advocate for human rights was relatively new, lesbians were there—and lesbian and bisexual women have steadily been at the forefront of international women's activism. LGBT people's movements, too, have continued to seek transnational alliances and demand action from the international community.

Activists have turned to international bodies despite lack of resources to get there, and lack of results when they go home. In 1995 women worldwide mobilized to support references to "sexual orientation" in the final document of the Fourth World Conference on Women in Beijing. On the meeting's last night, debate dragged on until the language was deleted. In 2004 dozens of national LGBT groups campaigned for a resolution introduced by Brazil before the Commission on Human Rights, on basic protections around sexual orientation. Brazil withdrew it at the last moment.

The reasons for persisting are not self-evidently practical. Mere visibility has not justified the expense and effort. To be sure, international institutions have furthered issues of sexual orientation and gender identity. International jurisprudence has established the reach of basic rights to both privacy and non-discrimination.[24] Many UN special rapporteurs have responded effectively to abuses against LGBT people. However, with the exception of the European Union and the Council of Europe (which have both made non-discrimination a clear, common standard), the political sides of international institutions have shown little will to address even grave abuses related to sexuality or gender identity. In the UN, neither the old Commission, the Human Rights Council, nor the Office of the High Commissioner for Human Rights have shaken loose the obstructionism of abusive states to affirm clear principles, or accepted the jurisprudence as a mandate to act. Now, with the efficacy of the UN's human rights institutions increasingly under fire, LGBT movements—still waiting for most of those bodies to give them simple recognition—are well qualified to join the firing squad.

The process leading to Yogyakarta began after the 2004 Commission resolution failed. The experts believed that if the UN's institutions could not say the obvious about how human rights applied to sexuality and gender, they would do so themselves. At the same time, they knew the movements in question were *not* going to join the firing squad. International solidarity and standards continue to be essential to how most LGBT activists see their future.

One reason is the intense opposition so many movements face from national governments—the bald insistence that LGBT people have *no* human rights, coupled with brutality. Fanny Ann Eddy, a lesbian activist from Sierra Leone, testified to the UN Commission in 2004 that "because of the denial of our existence,"

> we live in constant fear: fear of the police and officials with the power to arrest and detain us .... We live in fear that our families will disown us .... We live in fear within our communities, where we face constant harassment and violence from neighbors and others. Their homophobic attacks go unpunished by authorities, further encouraging their discriminatory and violent treatment of lesbian, gay, bisexual and transgender people.[25]

State denial leaves the international sphere the only place where many activists can be heard. And when some governments repeat by rote that LGBT people are not human, human rights seem like a last affirmation of humanity.

International pressure can bring significant success, from mitigating individual injustices such as Ciprian C.'s and Marian M.'s imprisonment, to forcing the repeal of intolerable laws. Sexual rights activists face the additional challenge, though, of building global connections that reflect the real diversity of identities they defend: a visible global movement broad enough to refute the discrediting slur that bodily autonomy and dignity are imported freedoms, "Western" or "Northern" concerns. Meanwhile, LGBT campaigners are likely to remain—for worse or better—internationalists caught between hope and desperation.

VII. Conclusion

At the UN Human Rights Council in September 2006, Nigeria, a member, scoffed at "the notion that executions for offences such as homosexuality and lesbianism is excessive": "What may be seen by some as disproportional penalty in such serious offences and odious conduct may be seen by others as appropriate and just punishment."[26]

At that time, Nigeria's government was trying to pass a draconian bill providing harsh criminal penalties for supporting the rights of lesbian and gay people, or for public display of a "same sex amorous relationship." Handholding could be criminalized. The bill failed in 2007, but could still be revived.

Dismissal abroad, discrimination at home: these point to the challenges ahead of LGBT lives, and of the Yogyakarta Principles. Where the most basic rights, including life, are threatened because of gender identity or sexual orientation, the UN's central human rights institution does little. The Human Rights Council has been widely criticized for reticence over major humanitarian crises such as Darfur. Another test of its credibility will be whether it can respond to the control of sexuality and gender underlying almost daily violence in every country. Inaction on the everyday violations, as on the exceptional ones, will undermine it.

In November 2007 Argentina, Brazil, and Uruguay cosponsored a panel on the Yogyakarta Principles at the UN in New York. Their representatives highlighted their governments' commitment to protecting sexual rights at national and international levels. More than 20 countries' diplomats attended; a Netherlands Foreign Ministry spokesman announced his government's intent to use the Yogyakarta Principles as a guide for anti-discrimination components of its foreign policy and aid. These indicate an awareness, arching across the latitudes, of the urgent necessity of action. The onus is on institutions to respond.

We talk of human rights as things, as possessions humans have, but they are strange ones. For the most part, people only declare they *have* a right at the moment they are denied it—the instant it is not theirs. We realize how vital rights are only in the lack of them. Human rights end as norms and laws, but they begin as human hurts, hopes, and needs felt in innumerable daily lives. The task of human rights movements is to turn those needs into viable claims, then into standards that bind. Their task also is to remind institutions when they are failing, by taking them back to the needs where the norms began. The Yogyakarta Principles are part of this double work. They help remember the Novembers when the law fell short. They point forward to where the law should go.

Scott Long directs the Lesbian, Gay, Bisexual, and Transgender Rights Program at Human Rights Watch.

1 The author investigated their case in January 1993, interviewing family members and police and prosecutors. He interviewed the two victims both before and after their trial, which he attended in June 1993.

2 Ciprian C., testimony before the International Tribunal on Human Rights Violations Against Sexual Minorities, organized by the International Gay and Lesbian Human Rights Commission (IGLHRC), October 17, 1995, at www.iglhrc.org/files/iglhrc/reports/Tribunal.pdf. Quotations from Ciprian C. that follow are from this source.

3 Gigi Horodinca, "Anuntul misterios," *Tim-Polis,* February 1993, quoted in Human Rights Watch and IGLHRC, *Public Scandals: Sexual Orientation and Criminal Law in Romania* (New York: Human Rights Watch and IGLHRC, 1997), pp. 19-20.

4 The experts' meeting, held at Gadjah Mada University, was organized by the International Service for Human Rights and the International Committee of Jurists. It was chaired by Sonia Onufer Correa of Brazil and Vitit Muntarbhorn of Thailand, and Prof. Michael O'Flaherty both served as rapporteur to the meeting and played an instrumental role in the development of the Yogyakarta Principles. Human Rights Watch along with ARC International were represented on a secretariat serving the experts and the convening. The principles are available online at www.yogyakartaprinciples.org. The document was later endorsed by eight other UN special rapporteurs, by jurists and human rights experts whose countries of origin included Botswana, Costa Rica, Pakistan, and South Africa, and by a former UN High Commissioner for Human Rights.

5 See Guiding Principles on Internal Displacement, at http://www.unhchr.ch/html/menu2/7/b/principles.htm.

6 "HIV/AIDS and Human Rights International Guidelines," at www.data.unaids.org/publications/irc-pub02/jc520-humanrights_en.pdf.

7 National Coalition for Gay and Lesbian Equality et. al. v. Minister of Justice et. al., 1999 [1] SA 6 (S. Afr. Const. Ct.), at 112-114.

8 Ron Eyerman and Andrew Jamison, *Social Movements: A Cognitive Approach* (New York: Polity Press), p. 55.

9 Quoted in Human Rights Watch and IGLHRC, *More than a Name: State-Sponsored Homophobia and its Consequences in Southern Africa* (New York: Human Rights Watch, 2003).

10 *Lawrence and Garner v. Texas,* Supreme Court of the United States, 539 US (2003).

11 *Van Kuck v. Germany,* 35968/97, European Court of Human Rights 285 (June 12, 2003), at 69.

[12] Manfred Nowak, UN Covenant on Civil and Political Rights: CCPR Commentary (Kehl: N. P. Engel, 1992), pp. 282-83.

[13] See Human Rights Watch and IGLHRC *Public Scandals*, and Gail Kligman, *The Politics of Duplicity: Controlling Reproduction in Ceausescu's Romania* (Berkeley: University of California, 1998).

[14] Quoted in Vladimir Kozlovsky, Argo russkoy gomoseksualnoy subkultury: Source Materials (Benson, Vermont, 1986), p. 154, cited in Human Rights Watch and the International Lesbian and Gay Association – Europe, "'We Have the Upper Hand': Freedom of assembly in Russia and the human rights of lesbian, gay, bisexual, and transgender people," June 2007.

[15] Opposition to "judge-made law" has been a focus of activism against reproductive rights in the US since the 1970s (as it was against the civil rights movement after *Brown v. Board of Education*), and after a Massachusetts court opened civil marriage to lesbian and gay couples in the state in 2004, identification of equal protection with "anti-democratic" judicial intervention has, if anything, intensified. However, it was an elected California legislature that twice passed a bill ensuring marriage equality for same-sex couples (the governor vetoed it in 2005 and 2007). See Human Rights Watch, "Letter Urging Gov. Schwarzenegger to Sign 'The Religious Freedom and Civil Marriage Protection Act,'" September 10, 2007.

[16] Sustained pressure from the Council of Europe, and especially from the European Union—which made repeal of the law an effective condition for Romania's accession—assisted the decision. However, the very fact that these institutions applied such pressure was partly due to advocacy by groups (especially ACCEPT, the main LGBT organization) within Romania.

[17] Quoted in Human Rights Watch and ILGA-Europe, "'We Have the Upper Hand.'"

[18] The most thorough survey is Daniel Ottoson, International Lesbian and Gay Association,"State-Sponsored Homophobia: A world survey of laws prohibiting same sex activity between consenting adults," 2007. However, because the application of many laws and the legal interpretation of their terminology remain unclear to outsiders and fluid at home, an exact number is impossible.

[19] This section draws gratefully on still-unpublished research for Human Rights Watch by Alok Gupta, now clerk to the South African Constitutional Court. See also Martin L. Friedland, "Codification in the Commonwealth: Earlier Efforts," *Criminal Law Journal,* Vol. 2 (1), 1990.

[20] English settlers in east Africa exposed the purpose of the code when it was introduced, protesting a policy of placing "white men under laws intended for a coloured population despotically governed." Friedland, "Codification in the Commonwealth," p. 13.

21 See Arvind Narrain and Brototi Dutta, Naz Foundation International, "Male-to-male sex, and sexuality minorities in South Asia: An analysis of the politico-legal framework," 2006, pp. 26-27.

22 Minister of Home Affairs and Others v. Fourie and Bonthuys and Others, Constitutional Court of South Africa, CCT 10/05, at 61 and 60.

23 Pedro Gringoire in *Excelsior,* July 1, 1975, quoted in Charlotte Bunch and Claudia Hinojosa, "Lesbians Travel the Roads of Feminism Globally," in John D'Emilio, William B. Turner and Urvashi Vaid, eds., *Creating Change: Public Policy, Civil Rights and Sexuality* (New York: St. Martin's, 2000).

24 The European Court of Human Rights, in a series of landmark decisions beginning in the 1980s, held that privacy rights were incompatible with the criminalization of consensual homosexual sex, and later established protections against discrimination based on both sexual orientation and gender identity. The UN Human Rights Committee in its landmark decision in Toonen v. Australia in 1994 found that "sexual orientation" should be understood as protected under the International Covenant on Civil and Political Rights; in successive decisions it has extended the implications of the conclusion.

25 "Testimony by Fanny Ann Eddy at the U.N. Commission on Human Rights," Item 14 – 60th Session, U.N. Commission on Human Rights, at http://hrw.org/english/docs/2004/10/04/sierra9439.htm. Eddy was murdered in her office, under unclear circumstances, later that year.

26 "Recognizing Human Rights Violations Based on Sexual Orientation and Gender Identity at the Human Rights Council, Session 2", ARC International (2006); also available on Human Rights Council Website, www.unhchr.ch.

THE BETRAYAL OF TRUST: VIOLENCE AGAINST CHILDREN

By Jo Becker

Millions of children around the world face violence on a daily basis—in their homes, in their schools, on the streets, in their workplaces, and in institutions such as orphanages and juvenile detention centers. Yet addressing these human rights abuses poses a particular challenge, as the perpetrators of this violence are often the very individuals who are responsible for children's care and protection—parents, guardians, teachers, caregivers, employers, police and security forces, and others.

Because of the intimate relationship between children and their abusers, many children never report violence. Many parents and guardians routinely beat children in the home, but children often are conditioned to believe that such treatment is "normal." Schoolgirls submit to sexual coercion from their teachers, fearing that if they refuse they will be given a failing grade. Child domestic workers may suffer repeated beatings, knowing that if they complain they may lose not only their employment, but also a place to live. Street children who are extorted and beaten by police officers may never report the crimes, because to do so means approaching the perpetrator's colleagues.

The child who experiences violence is often victimized twice—first by abuse from someone that they should be able to trust, and secondly by the failure of authorities to intervene. To end violence against children, states must take special steps to address this unique dynamic.

In 2006 the scale and scope of violence against children was brought to international attention through a comprehensive study conducted by Paulo Pinheiro, an independent expert to the United Nations secretary-general. The study was requested by the UN General Assembly in 2001 and was prepared through a global consultative process including governments, nongovernmental organizations (NGOs), academics, experts, and children themselves. In contrast to previous UN studies that focused on the impact of armed conflict on children, this study focused on violence against children in non-conflict situations.

The study found that children are subject to unconscionable violence on a scale that has rarely been acknowledged: An estimated 150 million girls and 73 million boys have experienced rape or other sexual violence, most often by members of their own family. Each year, between 133 million and 175 million children witness violence in their home. Between 20 and 65 percent of children in most countries report that they had been verbally or physically bullied in school in the previous 30 days. In at least 30 countries, sentences of whipping or caning are still legally imposed on children in penal systems.[1]

The scale of violence is well illustrated by a 2006 government survey of over 12,000 children in India, which found that more than half had been subjected to sexual abuse, most often by a person known to the child or in a position of "trust and responsibility," and that two of every three children had been beaten by their schoolteachers.[2] More typically, however, statistics are simply not known, demonstrating both the lack of effective monitoring mechanisms for violence against children, and the low priority that governments have placed on collecting such information.

Violence against children is often sanctioned by the state, and reinforced by societal attitudes that violent punishment of children is acceptable. Fewer than 20 states have prohibited all forms of violence against children in their national legislation, providing legal protection to only 2.4 percent of the world's children.[3] In most cultures it is still widely accepted that violence is an appropriate form of discipline of children, and given their immaturity, the only form that they will "understand." In the past, similar societal attitudes were used to justify violence against women, and legislation often allowed corporal punishment of wives, servants, slaves, and apprentices. Yet evolving norms generally now reject violence against women as unacceptable. Considering the particular vulnerability of children, it is ironic that in most parts of the world, violence that would be considered unacceptable and illegal if directed toward an adult is still condoned if directed toward a child.

Violence within the Family

Children are most at risk of violence by members of their own family. Fifty to 75 percent of murders of children under age 10 are committed by family members.[4]

According to epidemiological studies from 21 countries, relatives or step-parents are responsible for between 14 to 56 percent of sexual abuse of girls.[5] Corporal punishment by parents is also extremely common. In countries as diverse as Australia, Belize, Italy, Liberia, Peru, South Korea, and the United States, a significant majority (ranging from 65 to 90 percent) of parents believe that corporal punishment is acceptable or "necessary."[6]

The widespread acceptance of violence against children in the home contributes to violence in other settings. For example, in 2007 Human Rights Watch found that parents in Kenya frequently criticized the government's ban on corporal punishment in schools. Some parents even brought their children to school and caned them in front of teachers or asked the teachers to cane them in their presence.

Violence by Teachers

Schools are commonly believed to foster the healthy growth of children, and teachers are seen not only as educators, but also role models who shape the character and development of their pupils. However, for many children, their experience at school is one of fear and insecurity, influenced by bullying by their peers, sexual violence, or "discipline" imposed by their teachers that may be violent and at times arbitrary or discriminatory. The UN Study on Violence against Children found that violence in schools is a major contributor to absenteeism and drop-out.[7]

Some teachers demand sexual favors from girls or subject them to rape or other sexual assault. Yet students may be particularly reluctant about reporting sexual violence by their teachers. In one survey in Ghana, six percent of girls said that teachers blackmailed them, threatening to give them lower grades if they refused sex. Two-thirds of the girls had not reported the incidents, citing shame, advice from others to tolerate the abuse, or their belief that no action would be taken against the perpetrators.[8] This belief is well-founded: Human Rights Watch investigations of sexual violence in schools in Zambia and South Africa found that few teachers were penalized for sexual abuse of their students, and in many instances schools actively discouraged victims of school-based sexual violence from alerting anyone outside the school, or accessing the justice system.[9]

In over 80 countries around the world, corporal punishment in schools is allowed by law.[10] For example, in the United States alone, more than 270,000 students each year on average are subject to corporal punishment.[11] However, even in countries where it is legally prohibited, corporal punishment is often still practiced. Kenya prohibited corporal punishment in the schools in 2001, but in 2007, Human Rights Watch found that caning was still prevalent. In some countries, over 90 percent of children report being subject to caning, flogging, or other physical punishment in school.[12]

Violence by Employers

Much of Human Rights Watch's recent work on child labor has focused on child domestic workers, the sector of child labor that involves the largest number of girls. In millions of households worldwide, girls work as domestic servants, cooking, cleaning, doing laundry, providing child care, shopping, and performing other household duties, often for long hours and with no access to education. Their workplace is hidden from public view, rarely subject to government regulation or inspection, and often cut off from other workers or services in the community.

The isolation of child domestic workers reinforces their dependence on their employers and makes them particularly vulnerable to exploitation and abuse. Human Rights Watch investigations have found that girl domestic workers are often beaten by their female employers, and subject to sexual abuse by male members of the family. Girls often feel that they have no choice but to keep silent because to do otherwise can mean not only joblessness, but homelessness.

During a 2006 investigation of child domestic workers in Guinea, Human Rights Watch found that nearly all of the 40 girls interviewed had experienced physical violence from their employers and guardians. They described beatings with whips, belts, sticks, brooms, and other items. One 14-year-old girl described working 18-hour days, and said that when she tried to rest, her employer would often beat her with an electric cord. In tears, the girl said that she wanted to leave, but she had nowhere else to go.[13]

Violence by State Authorities

The dependent relationship between children and perpetrators of violence is by no means limited to schools or to private households. In many cases, children who are in the custody of the state—in detention facilities, centers for migrant and asylum-seeking children, or other institutions—are subjected to violence by the very individuals who are, often by law, responsible for their care and safety.

Each year an unknown number of children leave their home countries and seek asylum or better economic opportunities in other countries. Many are apprehended by authorities and placed in detention facilities or special centers while their cases are being determined. For some children these centers are a nightmare. In Spain's Canary Islands, for example, Human Rights Watch found in 2006 that children in centers for unaccompanied minors were often subject to violence not only by peers but by staff. In particular, children in one center described a "punishment cell," where children were beaten by staff and locked up for several days at a time.[14]

For many children, particularly those living and working on the street, police officers are not protectors, but the primary perpetrators of violence. Police officers may beat street children for their money, extort from them in exchange for protection, subject them to street sweeps as "undesirables," and force girls to submit to sex to avoid being arrested or taken into custody. In the Democratic Republic of Congo, Human Rights Watch found in 2006 that police officers approached street children, often at night, and demanded their money or articles of clothing, threatening them with their fists, batons, and boots. Police and soldiers raped and sexually assaulted street girls.[15] In Papua New Guinea we found that the vast majority of children who were arrested were severely beaten or tortured by members of the police.[16]

Based on such practices, it is no wonder that many children do not trust the police to look after their interests and are reluctant to approach the police for protection. In particular, children who have been victims of police violence feel that they have no avenues of recourse, as reporting the abuse typically entails approaching their perpetrator's fellow officers. As a result, the majority of cases of police abuse of children go undetected and unreported.

Lack of Complaints Mechanisms

In general, reporting rates related to violence against children are low. In the Indian study cited above, 70 percent of children who suffered sexual abuse reportedly told no one about their experience.[17] The fear of reprisal is only one part of the picture. In many situations children simply have no mechanisms of complaint available to them, nor knowledge of where they might turn for help.

In Rio de Janiero, Brazil, Human Rights Watch found that most juvenile detention centers had no meaningful complaint mechanism. When complaints were made, centers usually failed to conduct an investigation, and administrative sanctions were rarely imposed on perpetrators.[18] In Egypt Human Rights Watch found that the police routinely beat street children during arrest and detention, but under Egyptian law, only the Public Prosecution Office can initiate criminal investigations into allegations of police torture or ill-treatment. However, public prosecutors almost never visit police stations or question detained children about police abuse.[19]

Societal Attitudes

The failure to treat violence against children seriously is linked to persistent societal norms that condone violence against children and to the inferior status that children have in society generally. Children who make attempts to complain about violence often find that their accounts are disregarded or discredited. In South Africa Human Rights Watch found that schoolgirls who reported sexual abuse by their male classmates or teachers were treated by school officials with indifference, disbelief, and hostility. In the United States we heard numerous accounts of teachers and administrators who refused to act to protect lesbian, gay, bisexual, and transgender students from harassment out of the belief that they "get what they deserve." In Indonesia Human Rights Watch found that some government officials were reluctant to accept our documentation of abuses against child domestic workers; in some cases this seemed motivated by the fact that officials employed child domestic workers in their own households.

Although governments have an affirmative duty to protect children, many state authorities take the attitude that parents and guardians have the right to treat children as they like, and that it is not government's business to intervene. For example, in Saudi Arabia in 2006 Human Rights Watch interviewed several social workers and medical professionals who said it was nearly impossible to get police to intervene in cases of domestic violence unless the guardian filed the complaint. Often, however, it was the guardian who was the abuser.

Effective Responses to Violence against Children

The UN Study on Violence against Children features a range of recommendations to member states outlining steps to prevent violence against children and respond effectively when it occurs. The recommendations encompass overarching measures, including legal reform to prohibit all forms of violence against children; the creation of national action plans to address the issue; developing and strengthening complaints, investigation, and documentation systems; and public education campaigns. The study also includes detailed recommendations tied to the distinct settings considered by the study: the home and family, schools, care and justice institutions, the workplace, and the community.

However, the extent to which governments are willing to implement the recommendations remains in doubt. Although the study recommended the legal prohibition of all forms of violence against children, the 2006 General Assembly was unable—in its annual resolution on the rights of the child—to agree on wording calling for a prohibition on all corporal punishment, or even to prohibit the use of corporal punishment in schools.

Ending violence against children demands concerted efforts and greater attention from senior levels of government. However, success also depends on tailoring policies and programs to take into account the intimate relationship between child victims of violence and their perpetrators.

Legislative prohibitions: Very few governments have adopted legislation that clearly prohibits all forms of violence in all settings. Many states are particularly reluctant to legislate the use of "discipline," including corporal punishment, in the home, believing it to be a private matter outside the purview of the state. Legal prohibitions should not automatically be accompanied by criminal prosecutions against parents except when severe cases so warrant. However, failure to protect children from forms of violence that would be considered illegal assault if perpetrated against adults discriminates against children and reinforces attitudes that violence against children is acceptable.

Changing societal attitudes and promoting alternatives: In countries that have prohibited all violence against children, public education efforts have been effective in changing attitudes and behavior. For example, Sweden linked legal prohibitions on all violence against children to comprehensive public education. National studies subsequently found that between 1980 and 2000, the percentage of parents who said they had used corporal punishment during the previous year declined from 51 percent to 8 percent.[20] Efforts to eliminate physical punishment in schools in many countries can be strengthened by helping teachers learn alternative forms of discipline.

Creating and establishing support systems: Dealing with violence against children in the context of relationships of trust often requires stronger support systems for both caregiver and child, rather than punitive mechanisms. Violence against children by parents and guardians may be the result of poor parenting skills, and a reaction to stress. Studies have shown that providing families with access to social workers, trained volunteers, or community-based support centers, particularly for at-risk families, can serve a significant protective function and help provide caregivers with skills that can prevent violence in the home. In institutions, adequate staffing levels and supervision, together with training in child development and the appropriate treatment of children, can help establish safer, healthier environments for children.

Ensuring effective complaints mechanisms: Many children feel they have no avenues to report violence and fear negative repercussions if they make a complaint. Children need to know whom they can turn to, that their complaint will be taken seriously, that help is available, and that they will be protected from reprisals. In schools, institutions, and other facilities with children in their care, simple and accessible complaints mechanisms are essential. For children who are outside an institutional setting, including those in the home, foster care, or on the street, other avenues for complaint can include neighborhood drop-in centers or toll-free telephone helplines.

Effective oversight: The state should ensure regular independent monitoring of all institutions caring for children, whether privately-run or operated by the state, and develop systematic monitoring of children without parental care. For example, in some contexts, families employing children as domestic workers can be required to register with local neighborhood associations and allow the associations access to their employees to discuss their working conditions and treatment.

Addressing impunity: In too many cases, children who have suffered violence are further victimized by the failure of authorities to hold their perpetrators accountable. This failure not only betrays the child's trust, but also puts other children at risk. Teachers who have sexually assaulted their students continue to teach. Police officers who have tortured children, even in front of witnesses, remain on duty. Institution staff who have subjected children to extreme mistreatment and neglect continue to have children in their care. The failure to hold perpetrators accountable allows the violence to continue, discourages children from reporting violence, and reinforces societal attitudes that such violence is acceptable. Ending impunity demands that authorities investigate complaints thoroughly and in a timely fashion, treat children as credible witnesses, and when allegations are supported, take appropriate punitive action, including dismissal and criminal prosecution when warranted.

Conclusion

Children have the right to be protected from violence, and to rely on the individuals closest to them to protect their best interests and support their healthy development. When these individuals abuse their position of responsibility by subjecting children to violence, the state has an affirmative responsibility to respond. The intimate relationship between children and many perpetrators of violence creates unique challenges, but these are not insurmountable. By learning from successful models, putting in place effective support systems and monitoring mechanisms, and by refusing to tolerate impunity, states can take effective action to reduce violence against children and its devastating effects on families, communities, and society at large.

Jo Becker is children's rights advocacy director at Human Rights Watch.

1 Paulo Sérgio Pinheiro, *World Report on Violence against Children* (Geneva: United Nations Secretary-General's Report on Violence against Children, 2006), pp. 11-12.

2 Ministry of Women and Child Development, Government of India, "Study on Child Abuse: India 2007," 2007.

3 Global Initiative to End All Corporal Punishment against Children, "States with full abolition," http://www.endcorporalpunishment.org/pages/frame.html (accessed October 16, 2007).

4 Pinheiro, *Global Report on Violence against Children*, p. 51.

5 Ibid., p. 54.

6 Global Initiative to End All Corporal Punishment of Children, "Nature and Extent of Corporal Punishment – Prevalence and Attitudinal Research," June 2007, http://www.endcorporalpunishment.org/pages/pdfs/prevalence/PrevalenceResearch2007.pdf (accessed October 20, 2007).

7 Pinheiro, *Global Report on Violence against Children*, p. 130.

8 Ibid., p. 120.

9 See Human Rights Watch, *Scared at School: Sexual Violence against Girls in South African Schools* (New York: Human Rights Watch, 2001), http://www.hrw.org/reports/2001/safrica/; *Suffering in Silence: The Links between Human Rights Abuses and HIV Transmission to Girls in Zambia* (New York: Human Rights Watch, 2003), http://www.hrw.org/reports/2003/zambia/.

10 Global Initiative to End All Corporal Punishment of Children, "On-line Global Table: Legality of Corporal Punishment," http://www.endcorporalpunishment.org/pages/frame.html (accessed October 16, 2007).

11 United States Department of Education, Office for Civil Rights, "Civil Rights Data Collection 2004," http://vistademo.beyond2020.com/ocr2004rv30/wdsdata.html (accessed October 16, 2007).

12 Pinheiro, *World Report on Violence against Children*, pp 117-118.

13 See Human Rights Watch, *Bottom of the Ladder: Exploitation and Abuse of Girl Domestic Workers in Guinea* , vol. 19, no. 8(C), June 2007, http://hrw.org/reports/2007/guinea0607/.

[14] See Human Rights Watch, *Unwelcome Responsibilities: Spain's Failure to Protect the Rights of Unaccompanied Migrant Children in the Canary Islands*, vol. 19, no. 4(D), July 2007, http://hrw.org/reports/2007/spain0707/.

[15] See Human Rights Watch, *What Future? Street Children in the Democratic Republic of Congo*, vol. 18, no. 2(A), April 2006, http://hrw.org/reports/2006/drc0406/.

[16] See Human Rights Watch, *Making Their Own Rules: Police Beatings, Rape, and Torture of Children in Papua New Guinea* , vol. 17, no. 8(C), September 2005, http://hrw.org/reports/2005/png0905/.

[17] Ministry of Women and Child Development, Government of India, "Study on Child Abuse: India 2007."

[18] See Human Rights Watch, *Brazil – Real Dungeons: Juvenile Detention in the State of Rio de Janiero*, vol. 16, no. 7(B), December 2004, http://hrw.org/reports/2004/brazil1204/.

[19] See Human Rights Watch, *Charged with Being Children: Egyptian Police Abuse of Children in Need of Protection*, vol. 15, no. 1(E), February 2003, http://hrw.org/reports/2003/egypt0203/.

[20] Pinheiro, *World Report on Violence against Children*, p. 76.

MIND THE GAP: DIPLOMATIC ASSURANCES AND THE EROSION OF THE GLOBAL BAN ON TORTURE

By Julia Hall

Introduction

The United States has rightly attracted massive international criticism for its appalling and illegal conduct in the "war on terrorism." The abuses—Abu Ghraib, extraordinary renditions, secret prisons, enhanced interrogation techniques, Guantanamo Bay—are so dramatic and counterproductive, that they overshadow the fact that the Bush administration could not have "achieved" all this single-handedly. Allies and partners complicit in the US project to undermine the rule of law have provided airspace for illegal transfers, bases to house secret prisons, and intelligence support for operations that have led to torture and disappearances. None of these governments has a record to be proud of, either.

But the role of the British government raises particular concerns. In addition to the more evident transgressions—complicity in renditions, failure to criticize Guantanamo early and assertively, and an array of rights-abusive domestic anti-terrorism measures—it has offered a counterterrorism tool that is less obvious, allegedly more "human rights friendly," and thus uniquely insidious: diplomatic assurances against torture. The US government borrowed this handy device to justify renditions, and now many countries the world over are eager to try them out. The fact that promises of humane treatment from state torturers are inherently untrustworthy and have not worked in a number of cases does not seem to bother London. The goal is to deport terrorism suspects, no matter what—and if brokering unreliable, unenforceable agreements with states that torture is what it takes, then so be it.

Like the Americans, the British government obtains promises of fair treatment from countries where torture is a serious and enduring problem in an effort to get rid of foreign terrorism suspects. Like Washington, London tries to sell this policy as a genuine effort to square the needs of fighting international terrorism with its human rights obligations. But the British government's boast that it is committed to stopping torture cannot mask the fact that its promotion of empty promises of humane treatment will do irreparable damage to the absolute ban on torture.

The British government has sought assurances over the years from a veritable A-list of abusive regimes: Algeria, Egypt, Jordan, Libya, and Russia, to name a few. These countries have long histories and continuing records of torture, a fact that Whitehall readily acknowledges. What London fails to admit, however, is that despite compelling independent documentation of abuses, these governments routinely deny that torture takes place and usually fail to investigate allegations of abuse. And it fails to explain adequately why these governments—which continue to torture with impunity, despite international condemnation—would keep their promises not to torture a single individual.

The problems with these promises begin with the nature of torture itself. Torture is criminal activity of the most brutal sort, practiced in secret using techniques that often defy detection (for example, mock drowning, sexual assault, and the internal use of electricity). In many countries, medical personnel monitor the abuse to ensure that the torture is not easily detected. And detainees subjected to torture are often afraid to complain to anyone about the abuse for fear of reprisals against them or their family members. Occasional monitoring of a suspect's well-being after return in such circumstances is unlikely to protect him or her from abuse. Moreover, there is no formal enforcement mechanism to ensure a victim has recourse if he or she is abused.

It should therefore come as no surprise that UN High Commissioner for Human Rights Louise Arbour has opined that diplomatic assurances do not work, cannot stop torture, and should not be used. Her concerns are echoed by many human rights experts in the US, Europe, and elsewhere. With good reason: reliance on diplomatic assurances is growing in the US, Canada, and throughout Europe, and is spreading to other parts of the world.

It is bad enough that the British government has mounted a concerted campaign to gain the acceptance of assurances at the Council of Europe, the European Court of Human Rights, and in the European Union, proselytizing at every opportunity on the benefits of this counterterrorism tool. But abusive governments are also taking a leaf out of the UK and US book to rid themselves of unwanted terror suspects. The Russian government now readily accepts diplomatic assurances from Uzbekistan—a notorious practitioner of torture. Renditions are outlawed in the Philippines *unless* promises of humane treatment are secured first. Ironically, a draft anti-torture plan recently devised by the Georgian government includes acceptance of assurances to justify the deportation of terrorism suspects. The torture ban is being slowly but surely eroded—and the British government has helped lead the way.

Good vs. Bad Assurances

Seeking "diplomatic assurances" to protect human rights began as an earnest effort by European governments to protect the most fundamental right: the right to life. Governments in countries where the death penalty is outlawed have long asked for guarantees against capital punishment from states like the US, where such punishment is legal, before extraditing suspects. International law does not prohibit the death penalty, but capital punishment is outlawed in nearly all of Europe, and the United Nations and every major intergovernmental organization and nongovernmental human rights group condemn the practice. Nearly every bilateral and multilateral extradition agreement or treaty contains a provision requiring that an abolitionist state secure assurances against the death penalty from a state where that sanction remains legal.

Assurances against torture, however, came into being in the 1990s from what Swedish legal expert Gregor Noll calls "the silence of international law." International human rights law absolutely prohibits sending a person to a place where he or she is at risk of torture (the *nonrefoulement* obligation). No exceptions are allowed, even if a person poses a threat to national security. But the law says nothing about no-torture promises between states as a means of meeting that obligation.

The UK and other governments have capitalized on this gap in the law, applying the assurances regime to torture. But they fail to acknowledge the profound difference between the dynamic governing death penalty convictions and the dynamics of torture.

As repellant as it may be to many people, the death penalty is a legal sanction, a sentence handed down after a criminal trial, and often followed by a number of appeals if fairness has been compromised. Executions are generally scheduled well in advance. If a state fails to honor a promise not to seek the death penalty, it should be easy to monitor and protest a potential breach before an execution happens. According to the Washington-based Death Penalty Information Center, the US, for example, has never violated a formal death penalty assurance, lending credence to the claim that such promises can be trusted.

The Reality of Assurances against Torture

By stark contrast, torture is always illegal. It is a brutal criminal act, usually carried out secretly and robustly denied by the perpetrators. Torture is not scheduled in advance and made public like the execution of a death sentence. Any government that receives a diplomatic assurance against torture will be able to identify a breach of the promise only after the abuse has occurred.

As the cases involving the US, Canada, and Sweden below amply demonstrate, people sent back based on these empty promises have been tortured and ill-treated:

In December 2001, Egyptian asylum seekers Ahmed Agiza and Mohammed al-Zari were apprehended together and "roughed-up" by Swedish police, denied permission to contact their lawyers, driven to Bromma airport outside Stockholm, and handed over to hooded CIA agents. These operatives cut off the men's clothing, and blindfolded, hooded, and drugged them (by inserting suppositories), before transporting Agiza and al-Zari aboard a US government-leased Gulfstream jet to Cairo. The men were subsequently tortured, including with electric shocks, in Egyptian custody. Sweden defended its decision to permit the expulsions, claiming it had received diplomatic assurances from Egypt promising that the men would not be tortured. The UN Committee Against Torture and UN Human Rights Committee have both since ruled that Sweden violated the ban on torture as Stockholm should have known that assurances from Egypt could not be relied upon to protect the men.

Maher Arar, a dual Syrian-Canadian national, was deported from the US in 2002 and transported to Syria where he was held for nearly a year. The US government claimed that it had secured assurances of humane treatment from the Syrian authorities before sending Arar back, but failed to explain why he was not sent to Canada where he lived. After his release in late October 2002, Arar told a gruesome tale of abuse and torment that included severe beatings, incarceration in a tomb-like cell infested with rats, and psychological abuse. A specially convened Canadian inquiry ruled definitively in 2006 that Arar was not a terrorist; that he suffered a nightmare of abuse amounting to torture in Syrian custody; and that his case is a clear example of the problems inherent in relying on diplomatic assurances. Arar is now suing the US government for deporting him to torture.

The US government transferred seven Guantanamo Bay detainees to Russia in March 2004 in reliance on promises from Moscow to prosecute the detainees only on terrorism charges and to treat them humanely. Russia did neither. Some of the men were subsequently harassed and convicted on trumped up charges. Former detainee Rasul Kudaev, a resident of Kabardino-Balkaria in southern Russia, was detained after an armed uprising in the provincial capital in October 2005. According to photographs, medical records, court documents, and the testimony of lawyers and family members, Kudaev was repeatedly beaten in custody in an effort to compel him to confess to involvement in the uprising. The men's treatment illustrates how the "stamp of Guantanamo" can lead to ill-treatment, despite promises to the contrary.

Two former Guantanamo Bay detainees were sent home to Tunisia in June 2007 based on Tunisia's pledge to the US government that they would be treated humanely on return. Both men were incarcerated in Tunisian prison upon return and have told those who visit them that their treatment has been so poor they would rather be back in Guantanamo.

Promoting Assurances at Home

The UK first developed assurances in the early 1990s as a means of removing a Sikh activist labeled a threat to national security. The British government began efforts to deport Karamjit Singh Chahal to India in 1990. After much procedural wrangling, the UK issued a final deportation order in 1995, purporting to satisfy qualms about his safety upon return by producing two sets of diplomatic assurances against torture and ill-treatment from the Indian government. The British government argued that Chahal's high profile in the UK and India would guarantee him fair treatment (a claim that it and other governments continue to make).

The European Court of Human Rights, however, did not buy the British government's "all eyes are watching" defense and in a landmark 1996 decision ruled that the UK's public branding of Chahal as a "terrorist," coupled with the Indian government's lack of control over brutal security forces in Punjab, made him particularly vulnerable to torture and ill-treatment. This case set the standard in Europe for transfers of terrorism suspects: no balancing test between national security and the risk of torture is permitted; torture and ill-treatment are prohibited at all times, under all circumstances, even if a person has committed horrible crimes; and diplomatic assurances will not suffice from a country where human rights abuses are a "recalcitrant and enduring" problem.

Although the British tried to get assurances in a number of cases after the Chahal ruling, opposition within the government itself and court challenges appeared to sound the death knell for the practice. For example, throughout 1999, the Home Office and the Foreign and Commonwealth Office engaged in an unusual internal struggle against an effort led by then-Prime Minister Tony Blair to deport four Egyptian terrorism suspects, arguing that Cairo's assurances against torture could not be trusted. The Egyptian government eventually refused to give assurances and the deportations were halted.

In the aftermath of September 11, 2001, the British government took the opportunity to introduce new counterterrorism measures, including the shocking power to indefinitely detain foreign terrorism suspects whom the government refused to prosecute but who could not be sent home because they risked being tortured there. There was no talk at that time about diplomatic assurances against torture, which led many to believe that they might be off the table.

But the credibility of no-torture promises came under renewed scrutiny in 2003 when the Bow Street Magistrates' Court in London considered Russia's extradition request for the surrender of Akhmed Zakaev, an envoy for the Chechen government-in-exile, for alleged crimes committed in Chechnya. A Russian government minister traveled to London to assure the court that Zakaev would come to no harm in prison in Russia. But Zakaev's lawyers produced a credible witness who said he was tortured into giving Zakaev's name to the Russian authorities. The court rejected the Russian promises of fair treatment, relying on the fact that torture was widespread in Russia; that Chechens were particularly susceptible to torture; and that the Russian government didn't have effective control over the vast prison system.

By the time the House of Lords ruled in 2004 that the British government could not detain foreign terrorism suspects indefinitely without charge or trial, the government had already revived plans to use assurances as a solution. The UK went on to broker a series of "memorandums of understanding" (MoU) with Lebanon, Libya, and Jordan for the "deportation with assurances" (DWA) of terrorism suspects who are nationals of these countries. The agreements, which purport to systematize assurances, contain a new element: employing an "independent" local human rights group, funded and trained by the British government, to monitor an individual suspect's well-being post return. The British government argues that monitoring greatly reduces the chances that a returned suspect will be abused.

In fact, monitoring is no panacea. Its key deficiency is the lack of confidentiality. If monitors have universal access to all detainees in a facility, and are able to speak with all detainees, each in private, a single detainee can report torture or other abuse without fear that he will be identified by the authorities. The International Committee of the Red Cross (ICRC) makes universal access a condition of its monitoring for precisely that reason. Such confidentiality cannot be provided when only one detainee or small group is being monitored. The prison or detention facility authorities would know directly where the allegations of ill-treatment came from. Detainees would be too afraid of reprisals to report abuse. In a statement given after he was released from Syrian custody, Maher Arar had this to say about visits from Canadian consular officials:

> I could not say anything about the torture. I thought if I did, I would not get any more visits, or I might be beaten again ... The consular visits were my lifeline, but I also found them very frustrating. There were seven consular visits, and one visit from members of Parliament. After the visits I would bang my head

and my fist on the wall in frustration. I needed the visits, but I could not say anything there.

The British government has tried to argue that local human rights organizations can effectively monitor any abuse. To that end, it has provided thousands of pounds to support the Adaleh Center for Human Rights Studies, a small non-governmental organization in Jordan. But monitoring organizations, both local and international, often have trouble with open access to facilities. Local monitoring groups are particularly vulnerable to intimidation by their governments, which often control them via registration laws, if not by threats, outright harassment, and worse.

Monitoring by the ICRC at the infamous Abu Ghraib prison in Iraq was often frustrated by the actions of prison staff. In the past few years, the ICRC has suspended visits more than once to Jordanian detention facilities owing to problems of access to certain detainees. Human Rights Watch has spoken to numerous former detainees who claim they were hidden from the ICRC while in the custody of the Jordanian intelligence services. Official government monitors are even less capable of detecting torture, let alone preventing it: Ahmed Agiza and Mohammed al-Zari were both tortured in Egyptian custody, despite numerous visits from Swedish diplomats.

The British government's MoU policy is now being challenged in the courts. In February 2007 the Special Immigration Appeals Commission (SIAC), which hears appeals against deportation in national security cases, ruled that Omar Othman (better known as Abu Qatada), a recognized refugee and radical Muslim cleric accused of ties to al Qaeda, could be returned safely to Jordan under the terms of the UK-Jordan MoU. The court admitted that torture in Jordan is a serious problem, especially for terrorism suspects, and there is little accountability for those who perpetrate such abuse. But having raised those concerns, it ignored them, and simply relied on the British government's argument that the strength of ties between the two countries meant that Jordan would keep its word.

The policy suffered a setback in April, however, when the same court ruled that two Libyan terrorism suspects risked torture and a "complete" denial of due process if deported. Applying the same logic as in the Qatada case, it determined that ties between Libya and the UK were not sufficiently strong and enduring to overcome the Libyan government's routine use of incommunicado detention and torture against prisoners.

A second SIAC ruling on the Jordan MoU, in November 2007, again failed to engage with the substantive risk of torture, despite fresh documentation of Jordanian torture practices. In August 2007, Human Rights Watch interviewed numerous prisoners in several prisons in Jordan who complained of persistent abuse by prison guards, including hanging by iron cuffs in a large cage-like cell and beatings with cables. When we returned for a second time to speak to prisoners at one prison, they reported mass beatings by guards. There were evident signs of new injuries: bruises on backs, calves, and arms, and head wounds. The prison guards wore face masks and some wielded truncheons. A diplomat representing the British government before the SIAC in the case admitted in open court that these events were "frankly horrific."

Despite accepting these accounts as truthful and accurate, the court maintained that ties between London and Amman guaranteed that no such misfortune would befall any of the suspects returned under the agreement. The court skirted around the fact that the Human Rights Watch monitors—skilled independent researchers—were invited to inspect detention facilities and interview prisoners by the Jordanian authorities, but the abuse occurred anyway. How would a small local NGO with little experience, questionable independence, and virtually no power to hold the government accountable for torture abuses be able to ensure the safety of a person returned under the terms of the memorandum? That question went unanswered.

Setting a Bad Example

The British government promotes itself as a leader in the global effort to eradicate torture. It is true that the government has funded international anti-torture projects, and paid for publications like "The Torture Reporting Handbook"—a practical guide to identifying, documenting and reporting incidents of torture for doctors, lawyers, and human rights activists. The UK was one of the first states to ratify the Optional Protocol to the Convention Against Torture, which creates parallel international and domestic monitoring systems aimed at reducing torture and ill-treatment in detention, and has been active in pressing other governments to do the same.

All this deserves praise. But the government's relentless campaign to see "deportations with assurances" accepted throughout Europe reflects a more ambivalent attitude toward torture. In 2005-2006 it helped mount an effort to develop guidelines for the "appropriate" use of assurances at the Council of Europe, a regional intergovernmental human rights body comprising 47 member states. That effort was decisively rejected when a number of experts, including representatives from Belgium, France, Italy, and Switzerland expressed serious concern that promises from torturers could not be trusted and that any shift to reliance upon assurances would effectively gut the ban on transfers to torture.

It was not surprising that the UK then extended its direct advocacy effort on diplomatic assurances to the European Union. Although the vast majority of counterterrorism policy is set at the national level, the EU has taken up select issues for consideration and consensus, including the definition of terrorism and a regional arrest warrant. The UK is leading an effort, through the G6 group of interior ministers (France, Italy, Spain, UK, Poland, and Germany), for broader EU endorsement of the deportation with assurances policy. A UK government memorandum circulated in advance of a November 2007 meeting of EU interior ministers claimed that the expulsion of terrorism suspects is an effective tool to protect people from foreigners who threaten national security, adding that "the mechanism of seeking assurances, on a government-to-government basis" could be a "way forward."

It is also likely that the UK played a role in Italy's interest in using assurances in an effort to deport a Tunisian national security suspect. In June 2007 the Italian government argued before the Grand Chamber of the European Court of Human Rights that Nassim Saadi should be sent back to his home country with promises from the Tunisian authorities that he would not be tortured on return. The British government intervened in the Saadi case and made oral representations to the court in favor of a national security balancing test for returns to risk of ill-treatment. A decision is pending.

The Real Way Forward

The United Kingdom's post-Blair approach to combating terrorism appeared at first to offer some welcome relief. Prime Minister Gordon Brown wants to engage in the parallel battle of "winning hearts and minds" in Muslim communities. During the September 2007 Labour Party conference, Tony McNulty, the minister responsible for counterterrorism policy, said that Blair had got it wrong: the "rules of the game" have not changed and the response to terrorism should be "rooted in our civil liberties and human rights, with whatever slight tweaks at the top."

Apparently, sending people to places where they risk being tortured is simply a "slight tweak." In November 2007 Brown virtually boasted that new "memorandums of understanding" were being negotiated with a number of other countries. If these agreements are necessary, then the UK is acknowledging that these governments engage in torture, but London is willing to make a deal.

Accepting torture undermines the moral legitimacy of the British government around the world. And instead of winning hearts and minds, it damages the government's standing at home, especially with British Muslims, whose cooperation with the police and security services is so vital if the terrorist threat is to be addressed.

No person has been deported yet under an official British "memorandum of understanding." The UK government can act now to stop all deportations with assurances to countries where torture is practiced. That would send a simple but powerful message around the world: the British government does not bargain with torturers, and neither should you.

Julia Hall is senior counterterrorism counsel at Human Rights Watch.

CHAD

Early to War

Child Soldiers in the Chad Conflict

HUMAN
RIGHTS
WATCH

WORLD REPORT
2008

AFRICA

ANGOLA

Elections in Angola—the first since 1992—were postponed yet again in 2007. Legislative elections are now scheduled to take place in 2008 and a presidential election in 2009, but no specific dates have been announced.

Since the end of the civil war in 2002, increasing oil revenues, trade, and foreign investment, along with a greater role in international and regional affairs, have helped insulate Angola from international criticism regarding good governance and human rights. Despite the nation's strong economic growth—forecast to be the world's highest in 2007—the majority of Angolans continue to live in dire poverty. Since 2001 thousands of Angolans have been forcibly evicted from their homes by the government to make way for development projects. As of yet, most have not received compensation or alternative housing. The environment for civil society organizations and the media grew increasingly hostile in 2007, despite participation of civil society organizations in civic education and observation of voter registration.

Election Preparations

Voter registration ended on September 15, 2007, with approximately 8 million voters registered. In May the government cancelled the registration of expatriates, contrary to the electoral laws. The National Electoral Commission (CNE), which supervises the registration process, issued a resolution recommending that the government reverse the decision, to which the government has not responded.

Voter registration is carried out by the Inter-ministerial Commission for the Electoral Process (CIPE), coordinated by the Ministry for Territorial Administration under the supervision of the CNE. A delegation of the Parliamentary Forum of the Southern Africa Development Community (SADC) found in March 2007 that the division of responsibility between electoral bodies at both national and local levels lacks transparency. Under Angolan law, elections must be announced at least 90 days in advance, but the SADC delegation urged the government to announce the date as soon as possible, to leave sufficient time for political parties to campaign and civil society organizations to carry out voter education.

The CNE still lacks resources to carry out its mandate at national, provincial, and municipal levels. The president of the CNE is a Supreme Court judge. Since the Supreme Court reviews appeals of CNE decisions on complaints arising from the electoral process, his two functions may clash.

Cabinda

Since 1975, rebels in the oil-rich enclave of Cabinda have been fighting for independence from Angola. In August 2006 the government and the leader of the Cabindan Forum for Dialogue (FCD, a joint commission of the rebels and local civil society representatives) signed a Memorandum of Understanding that purportedly ended the conflict. However, a considerable part of local society claims the peace talks were not inclusive and the FCD signatory of the MOU was not a legitimate representative. Although the conflict has not reignited, armed clashes did occur in the territory in 2007.

Freedom of association and expression in Cabinda continue to be highly restricted. Mpalabanda, a human rights NGO and member of the FCD, was shut down by the government in July 2006. The group has appealed the decision, but has been unable to operate while the verdict is pending. Roman Catholic groups have continued to express dissatisfaction at the appointment of the current bishop of Cabinda, who for the first time is not a Cabinda native. On July 14, 2007, four men were arrested for demonstrating against the bishop. They were brought before the public prosecutor and formally charged on July 17—beyond the 48 hours required by Angolan law—and released on July 23, after summary procedures. One was released without charge, while the other three were given prison sentences that were converted into fines and suspended for two years.

Freedom of Expression

On May 15, 2006, a new Angolan press law came into force, but its specific implementing regulations have yet to be published. Consequently, provisions of the law that are crucial to ensuring freedom of expression and access to information cannot be implemented. For example, private radio stations still cannot broadcast nationwide and community radio stations are not in operation. This situation, in conjunction with the very limited circulation of private newspapers outside of the capital, seriously hinders the dissemination of diverse points of view in the pre-election period.

Several provisions of the press law, the electoral laws, the Law on Access to Administrative Documents, and the Criminal Code, are highly restrictive. Defamation is still criminalized and journalists can incur prison sentences of up to two years if found guilty. Many of the legal limitations on media freedom and access to information are vaguely formulated and can easily intimidate journalists and hamper their ability to criticize the government.

On October 3, 2007, the editor of the private weekly *Semanario Angolense* was sentenced for defamation and "injúria" of the former justice minister (and current ombudsman) to eight months' imprisonment and ordered to pay damages equivalent to US$250,000. The Supreme Court ordered him released on November 8 pending appeal.

Housing Rights and Forced Evictions

Human Rights Watch and the Angolan organization SOS Habitat have documented the forced eviction of an estimated 30,000 people between 2002 and 2006. Throughout 2007 Human Rights Watch continued to receive reports of residents whose houses were demolished without notice or compensation in Luanda and other cities. In August police evicted approximately 70 people, including street children, from an informal settlement in Lobito, Benguela province, without notice or stated reason or any provision for their relocation. The Public Prosecutor's Office initiated an investigation into allegations of police brutality connected to the eviction; the results of the investigation are still pending at this writing.

The legal framework for housing rights in Angola remains problematic. The Land Law and the Law on Urban Management do not explicitly forbid forced evictions and do not adequately ensure security of tenure. In 2007 the government announced further plans for an extensive development and infrastructure program in and around Luanda. Unless this and other projects are accompanied by strong measures to protect the right to adequate housing, forced evictions are likely to continue.

ANGOLA

"They Pushed Down the Houses"

Forced Evictions and Insecure Land Tenure for Luanda's Urban Poor

HUMAN
RIGHTS
WATCH

SOS Habitat - Acção Solidária
«pela plena cidadania e um habitat harmonioso»

Human Rights Defenders

The environment for civil society organizations worsened during 2007. In February a researcher from the international nongovernmental organization (NGO) Global Witness was arrested in Cabinda. She was detained for three days, and was not allowed to retain a lawyer of her choice but was assigned a court clerk to defend her. She was charged with violating state security under an "open norm" that allows for the criminal prosecution of "any act not foreseen within the law, which endangers or could endanger state security." Such "open norms" are contrary to basic criminal law principles. She was eventually released and allowed to leave Angola after providing assurances that she would return for court proceedings if necessary. At this writing, a trial date has not been set, but nor have the charges against her been formally withdrawn.

On July 10 the head of the government's Technical Unit for the Coordination of Humanitarian Aid (UTCAH), Pedro Walipi Kalenga, accused several national and international civil society organizations of carrying out illegal activities. In previous statements he had indicated that some organizations registered with UTCAH might even be shut down. The local groups named by Walipi all have strong records of defending human rights in Angola. None has ever been formally notified of any violation of Angolan law. Statements such as this amount to harassment and intimidation of human rights groups and are particularly worrying ahead of elections.

The Constitutional Law grants freedom of association. The Law on Associations and a decree-law enacted in 2003 regulate the activity of NGOs. Several provisions of the decree-law on NGOs impose obligations that may excessively restrict freedom of association, such as an extensive list of duties including reporting duties to government bodies, and provision for the government to order an NGO to be audited whenever the government sees fit. Local human rights groups claim the decree-law is also unconstitutional because it was enacted by the government whereas legislation on fundamental rights should only be enacted by the National Assembly. The government is currently revising the Law on Associations and has requested suggestions from a limited number of civil society organizations. However, the government has not so far disclosed the final draft.

Key International Actors

Throughout 2007 Angola continued to raise its profile in international and regional affairs. In May it was elected to the United Nations Human Rights Council and in August took over the presidency of the SADC's Organ on Politics, Defense and Security. Numerous high-level government and military officials from Africa and other regions, as well as international organizations, have visited Angola in the past year.

This increasing international role, along with major investment and trade opportunities mainly from the oil, diamond, and reconstruction sectors, has helped to insulate Angola from criticism on good governance and human rights. The World Bank and other donors have attempted to make lending to Angola conditional on transparency and good governance, but the government has been able to avoid these conditions by obtaining large unconditional loans from China.

Representatives of the UN Human Rights Office in Angola and the European Union have approached the government concerning harassment of human rights defenders but neither has issued a public statement of concern about it, nor has any foreign government or intergovernmental organization publicly condemned forced evictions. International partners have also generally failed to pressure Angola to set election dates.

BURUNDI

The political situation in Burundi is marked by efforts of the ruling National Council for the Defense of Democracy–Forces for the Defense of Democracy (CNDD-FDD) to monopolize power and by continuing impunity for severe human rights abuses. Despite its resounding electoral victory in 2005, the CNDD-FDD struggled with internal divisions and challenges from opposition parties that paralyzed legislative action for most of 2007. In August unidentified assailants threw grenades into the homes of five opposition political leaders, further embittering the political atmosphere.

The war between the government and the last active rebel group, the National Liberation Forces (FNL), had been halted by a September 2006 ceasefire, but on July 21, 2007, talks on implementation broke down and rebel leaders returned to the bush. Though there was international pressure to return to the talks, the FNL leadership refused to negotiate unless the South African mediator was replaced. In August fighting broke out near the capital Bujumbura between two FNL factions—one for and one against immediate implementation of the terms of the ceasefire—leaving 21 combatants and one civilian dead and causing hundreds to flee. Claiming responsibility for initiating the attack, the FNL leadership under Agathon Rwasa declared that the self-professed "dissident" faction favoring peace was a government creation. In September-October the FNL carried out several more attacks on this "dissident" group at sites protected by the Burundian military and in Bujumbura, killing a total of 12 "dissidents"; at least four Burundian soldiers have also been killed by the FNL since the ceasefire's breakdown. Mediators in Burundi's peace process are attempting to verify the status of those claiming to be dissident combatants.

Judicial Action against the Opposition

On January 15 the Supreme Court acquitted former President Domitien Ndayizeye, former Vice President Alphonse-Marie Kadege, and three others of plotting a coup in 2006, but convicted Alain Mugabarabona and Tharcisse Ndayishimiye. In September 2006 three of those eventually acquitted filed complaints of torture against intelligence agents, although no one was arrested for the alleged crime.

BURUNDI

Paying the price
Violations of the rights of children in detention in Burundi

HUMAN
RIGHTS
WATCH

In convicting Mugabarabona and Ndayishimiye, the court discounted claims that they had been forced to make the confessions that constituted the primary evidence against them. Three journalists who had been arrested in late 2006 for their coverage of the alleged coup were acquitted in early January 2007 in a separate trial, but the government filed an appeal which is pending at this writing.

Hussein Radjabu, president of the CNDD-FDD and once a dominant force in the government, was ousted by his party in February and was arrested in April, along with several supporters, on charges of endangering state security. Two of those detained were beaten and then released, and a third, Evariste Kagabo, was tortured. He and Radjabu remain detained and have not yet been tried. Jean-Bosco Ngendaganya, chief of staff at the National Intelligence Service (SNR) when Kagabo was tortured, was removed from his post and charges of assault were prepared against him, but he has not been arrested.

Human Rights Violations by Security Agents, Police, and Soldiers

Accusations of grave violations by security agents and soldiers declined in 2007, but impunity for cases of torture, unlawful killings, and war crimes continued to be the norm. There was no progress toward accountability in the case of the 31 people "disappeared" and presumed dead in July 2006 in Muyinga province, although three different judicial commissions investigated the crimes. An intelligence service agent arrested in September 2006 was released without trial in May 2007, and two soldiers arrested at the same time have not been tried. High-ranking civilian and military authorities admitted that an arrest warrant was issued against the former commander of the Fourth Military Region, Col. Vital Bangirinama, but was never executed. Colonel Bangirinama was removed from his post in Muyinga, but remains on active duty.

In October a special police brigade known as the Mobile Rapid Intervention Group (GMIR) was detached from Bujumbura to combat criminality and arms possession in Muramvya province. In collaboration with local police, the brigade established two clandestine jails where at least 20 individuals were illegally detained, tortured, and questioned about their alleged affiliation with the FNL.

Several victims pressed charges, but officials have yet to seriously investigate abuses or discipline offending officers, who remain in service.

In one positive development, judicial authorities arrested Lieut. Col. Léopold Ntibaruhisha for ordering the beating and kidnapping of a local resident near Buyengero military camp, Bururi province, in May 2007. Ntibaruhisha is awaiting trial at this writing.

Transitional Justice

Since 2006 the government has provisionally released thousands of prisoners accused of crimes connected to the assassination of President Melchior Ndadaye in 1993 and the subsequent 10-year civil war. Some had been detained for years without trial. In principle they will appear before a yet to be established truth commission. In June 2005 the United Nations Security Council directed the government to hold public consultations on transitional justice mechanisms to address crimes committed during the civil war. After long delays, consultations are tentatively scheduled to begin in early 2008. Under the supervision of the government, UN, and civil society representatives, some 6,000 Burundians will be asked their views on reconciliation and accountability, and the proposed truth commission and an associated special tribunal for serious violations of international law will be explained.

Despite this apparent progress, the government has yet to recognize the need for an independent prosecutor for the tribunal and the CNDD-FDD insisted that only cases in which reconciliation had failed would be brought to the tribunal. This position conflicts with international law principles, which hold that all serious crimes under international law must be prosecuted.

Juvenile Justice

Hundreds of children are imprisoned in Burundi, and three-quarters of them have never been tried or sentenced for their alleged crimes. Following increased public attention, the government released some categories of child detainees, but some 472 remained incarcerated as of late 2007. A penal reform bill that would raise the age of criminal responsibility from 13 to 15 and provide alternatives to incar-

ceration for juvenile offenders remains blocked in parliament since being introduced in the spring.

Burundians Expelled from Tanzania

During the 1990s hundreds of thousands of Burundians fled the civil war into
Tanzania. Many settled in local communities rather than enter refugee camps and
failed to register with the United Nations High Commissioner for Refugees
(UNHCR). In 2006 Tanzania began deporting these persons, arguing they had
never been recognized refugees. Tanzania also expelled some Burundians who
had become naturalized Tanzanian citizens. Tanzanian soldiers, police, and militia beat many expelled people, separated family members, and looted or
destroyed property. Following international protests, most blatant abuses
decreased, but in July 2007 the Tanzanian authorities once again announced that
all of the 150,000 Burundians who had taken refuge in Tanzania after 1993 and
were housed in UNHCR camps must return to Burundi by the end of 2007.
However, expulsions proceeded slowly, and at this writing the vast majority of
those refugees remain in Tanzania.

More than 36,000 Burundian refugees returned voluntarily in 2007, fewer than in
previous years. Refugee agencies attributed the decline to drought in eastern
Burundi, as well of lack of access to land and fear of renewed conflict.

Human Rights Defenders

Burundian human rights defenders are widely respected both nationally and
internationally. In May 2007 Pierre-Claver Mbonimpa, president of the Burundian
Association for the Promotion of Human Rights and Detained Persons (APRODH),
was summoned for interrogation by the prosecutor's office after denouncing the
delays in prosecuting the case of the 31 people "disappeared" in Muyinga, but he
was not detained. Mbonimpa was later awarded the prestigious Martin Ennals
Prize for human rights defenders.

Key International Actors

The UN withdrew peacekeepers at the end of 2006, and opened the UN Integrated Office in Burundi (BINUB) to assist in post-conflict development. The newly created UN Peacebuilding Commission, meant to monitor progress in countries recently emerged from war, chose Burundi as one of two beneficiary nations. The fund will administer a US$35 million grant, part of which is supposed to strengthen human rights. Commission members, however, saw no need to speak publicly about human rights concerns.

Regional governments tried to broker implementation of the ceasefire signed between the FNL and the government, with South Africa as the formal mediator. The African Union supported troops to provide protection to returning FNL leaders as well as combatants. In August the AU declared its concern about the deteriorating state of the negotiations and deadlock in the legislature.

In 2007 the Office of the UN High Commissioner for Human Rights documented abuses and brought human rights defenders and government agents together to discuss various cases. OHCHR also initiated regular briefings of representatives of donor nations on human rights concerns. In September the UN Human Rights Council extended the mandate of the independent expert on Burundi for one year. Since 2004 the expert has provided support to the government in its efforts to improve the human rights situation by monitoring, reporting, and making recommendations.

Donors made few public statements on human rights issues, but did privately press Burundian authorities to speed the trial of the journalists arrested in connection with the 2006 "coup plot" and to prosecute those accused of the Muyinga killings. When the abuses of children in prisons were publicized, the United Kingdom and Sweden agreed to fund legal assistance to accused juvenile offenders.

CENTRAL AFRICAN REPUBLIC

Since gaining independence in 1960, the poverty stricken Central African Republic (CAR) has experienced dictatorial rule, corruption, and severe political instability. François Bozizé, the current President, came to power in a March 2003 military coup and in May 2005 won a contested election organized to legitimate his administration.

Since 2005, the government of President François Bozizé has been facing two major rebellions. The Popular Army for the Restoration of the Republic and Democracy (Armee Populaire pour la Restauration de la Republique et la Democratie, APRD) is active in the northwestern provinces of Ouham, Ouham-Pende, and Nana-Grebizi. The Union of Democratic Forces for Unity (Union des Forces Democratiques pour le Rassemblement, UFDR) is most active in the remote northeastern provinces of Bamingui-Bangoran and Vakaga. Although the CAR borders the volatile eastern region of Chad and war-ravaged Darfur in Sudan, the roots and dynamics of rebellion within the country are largely local, rather than being "spill-over" from the crises in neighboring states. The grievances of the main rebel protagonists lie in part in the exclusion of former President Patassé (1993-2003) from the political process, and in part in economic and social disparities.

Both rebel groups have used child soldiers, have been responsible for widespread looting and the forced taxation of the civilian population in areas they control; and rebels in the northeast have committed killings, beatings, and rape. However, it is the government's Central African Armed Forces (Forces armees Centrafricaines, FACA) and elite Presidential Guard (Garde presidentielle, GP) that have been responsible for the majority of abuses—summary executions, unlawful killings, and village burnings—in northern CAR. Several hundred people have been killed and over 200,000 civilians have been displaced and now live in desperate conditions in the bush. Abuses by government forces often appear to have been committed in retaliation for rebel attacks. The perpetrators of violence and abuse, the vast majority of them government soldiers, have enjoyed total impunity for acts that include war crimes.

Government Abuses in Northwestern CAR

The political grievances of supporters of former President Ange Felix Patassé, who was toppled by the 2003 coup and barred from competing in the 2005 election, and the failure of CAR security forces to protect local communities from banditry, are both important elements behind the emergence of the APRD. Armed bandits, known as zaraguinas or coupeurs de route, regularly attack villagers, kidnap children for ransom, and kill civilians. Cattle-herders from the Peulh ethnic group in the northwest have been particularly targeted because of their valuable livestock. The APRD's professed aim is to improve the security situation.

In direct response to APRD activity in the area, the CAR security forces have committed serious and widespread abuses against the civilian population, including multiple summary executions and unlawful killings, widespread burning of civilian homes, and the forced displacement of hundreds of thousands of persons, instilling terror in the civilian population.

Evidence collected by Human Rights Watch suggests that hundreds of people have been killed by government security forces since 2005. In some cases dozens of civilians were killed in a single day, many suffering unspeakable brutality. For example, on February 11, 2006, a GP unit killed at least 30 civilians in more than a dozen separate villages located along the Nana-Barya to Bemal road. On March 22, 2006 this same GP unit beheaded a teacher in Bemal with a knife while he was still alive. Some victims are targeted simply for wearing amulets, a common accessory in the region. On January 27, 2007, FACA soldiers executed Roger Masamra, the son of the village catechist in Zoumanga, who was accused of being a rebel because he was wearing a traditional gri-gri amulet. On January 30, 2007, FACA forces executed an unidentified Chadian Christian merchant at the Kabo market, also because he was wearing protective gri-gri amulets, and had scars on his hands that the FACA soldiers claimed were old bullet wounds. According to a local humanitarian official the eyes of the victim had been gouged out. Other civilians have simply "disappeared" in military custody, arrested and not seen alive again.

Since December 2005, government forces, particularly the GP, have also been almost solely responsible for the burning down of more than 10,000 civilian homes in northwestern CAR. Hundreds of villages across vast swathes of northern CAR have been destroyed. Troops arrived in villages and indiscriminately fired into the civilian population, forcing them to flee before burning down their homes, sometimes looting them first. Over 100,000 civilians have been forced to abandon their road-side homes and live deep inside the bush, too fearful to return to their burned villages in case of repeat attack.

The displaced live in dire conditions with irregular access to clean water and food. Their widely dispersed shelters are beyond the reach of the humanitarian community. Educational facilities have been closed, and aside from mobile clinics run by international organizations in some areas, health care is non-existent.

Government Abuses in Northeastern CAR

The UFDR rebellion has its roots in the deep marginalization of northeastern CAR, which is virtually cut off from the rest of the country and is almost completely undeveloped. Elements from the Gula ethnic group, many of them trained militarily as anti-poaching units, are at the core of the rebellion, citing grievances such as discrimination against their community.

From October to December 2006, the UFDR rebel movement gained international attention by seizing military control of the major towns in the remote Vakaga and Bamingui-Bangoran provinces of northeastern CAR, right on the border of Sudan's Darfur region. The UFDR's bold military offensive led to French military intervention on behalf of the CAR government in December 2006, allowing the security forces to regain control of urban centers.

The rebellion has been accompanied by an increase in pre-existing anti-Gula sentiment among government officials, the military, and the general population. In late 2006, as CAR security forces were regaining control of northeastern urban centers occupied by the rebels, several suspected UFDR rebels were summarily executed, and numerous houses were burned down. Almost all of these abuses were committed against ethnic Gulas, causing virtually the entire Gula population to flee from towns and villages formerly occupied by the UFDR, including Ndele, Ouadda, Ouanda Djalle, and Birao.

CENTRAL AFRICAN REPUBLIC

State of Anarchy

Rebellion and Abuses Against Civilians

HUMAN
RIGHTS
WATCH

Rebel Abuses

APRD rebels in the northwest have engaged in widespread extortion, forced taxation, kidnappings for ransom, and beatings of civilians, particularly in the Batangafo-Kabo-Ouandago area of Ouham province. In that area, particularly on the Batangafo-Ouandago road, almost all villages have been systematically looted of all livestock, and village leaders have been regularly kidnapped for ransom. APRD rebels also have large numbers of child soldiers in their ranks, some as young as 12. Human Rights Watch documented one summary execution by the APRD in 2006.

UFDR rebels in the northeast have attacked villages and towns, often indiscriminately firing at fleeing civilians. UFDR rebels have also been responsible for summary executions of captured civilians. From October to December 2006, rebels carried out a massive looting campaign in areas they controlled. The UFDR also has child soldiers in its ranks, some of them forcibly recruited.

The Need for Accountability

Government abuses in northern CAR are no secret inside the country. Local newspapers and radio frequently report them, opposition parliamentarians have prepared public reports documenting the atrocities, and diplomatic envoys regularly raise their concerns with President Bozizé. However, even in the capital, Bangui, security forces carry out summary killings of suspected bandits and rebels with impunity.

In late 2007, following the publication of Human Rights Watch report in September, President Bozizé has publicly admitted that CAR forces have committed abuses and that those responsible will be held accountable. The Presidential Guard was temporarily withdrawn to Bangui. Despite this statement, the government has not investigated, prosecuted, or punished a single military officer and five civilians were reportedly killed by the Presidential Guard and the FACA in late October and early November 2007 in the northwestern region.

Key International Actors

For much of the year, the current conflicts and the human rights situation in CAR were hardly on the international agenda. The International Criminal Court (ICC) prosecutor's office announced in May 2007 that they would investigate crimes committed in CAR during the 2002-2003 fighting, and that they would continue to monitor the current conflict. In October, the ICC opened a new field office in Bangui.

A 19-person human rights unit in the office of the United Nations Peace-building Support Office in the Central African Republic (BONUCA) has not effectively monitored or reported on human rights abuses in the north. The head of BONUCA was replaced at the end of 2007 and it is anticipated that more senior staff will be appointed to the human rights unit.

Largely in response to the risk of spillover from conflict in CAR's neighbors, a multi-dimensional international force for Chad and the Central African Republic (MINURCAT) was authorized by United Nations Security Council Resolution 1778 in September. It is due to deploy in Birao in northeastern CAR to secure the area but will not operate in the northwestern region where most human rights abuses have been committed.

Later in 2007 the issue of protection of civilians and abuses in the north became a central part of international engagement in CAR. President Sarkozy of France— without whose direct military support the government of President Bozizé would not survive—has declared that he was expecting "efforts in improving human rights" in CAR from President Bozizé. France has decided to review and may reconsider its military cooperation agreements with CAR but has not publicly demanded accountability for the crimes committed there.

In September 2007 Human Rights Watch published a major report on the human rights situation in the northern war zones.

CHAD

Chad plunged into civil war shortly after it gained independence from France in 1960 and has been intermittently wracked by conflict ever since. The current round of internal conflict is in its third year and is complicated by the war in the neighboring Darfur region of Sudan. Khartoum increased its support to Chadian rebel groups based in Darfur in retaliation for Ndjamena's support to Sudanese rebels with bases in Chad. In late 2006 rebel offensives launched from Darfur nearly toppled the government of President Idris Déby, but by early 2007 Chad's security forces had managed to consolidate control over the volatile border zone. The Chadian government signed a peace accord with one of the most powerful rebel factions in December 2006 and agreed to preliminary peace terms with the four largest remaining factions in October 2007. However, the outlook for a sustained cessation of hostilities remains dim, with hundreds of combatants reported killed in renewed hostilities in late November.

The government of President Idriss Déby has failed to protect its citizens from armed violence and has been responsible for direct attacks against civilians suspected of complicity with rebel groups seeking Déby's overthrow. Militia attacks against Chadian civilians living along the border with Sudan reduced in number in 2007, but killings and other human rights violations continued to be reported.

Abuses in Counterinsurgency

The Chadian government has been responsible for human rights abuses against both combatants and non-combatants during military operations against Darfur-based rebel groups. In northern and northeastern Chad insurgents wounded or captured during a rebel offensive in late 2006 were subject to summary execution and torture at the hands of Chadian government soldiers. In the southeast civilians complain of extrajudicial killings, rape, beatings, arbitrary arrests, extortion and property theft in the wake of counterinsurgency sweeps conducted by government security forces, including government-backed militia groups. These violations have been met by near total impunity and have forced thousands of civilians into involuntary displacement, both internally and across the border into Sudan.

CHAD

"They Came Here to Kill Us"

Militia Attacks and Ethnic Targeting of Civilians
in Eastern Chad

**HUMAN
RIGHTS
WATCH**

The recruitment of child soldiers continues, even though the government signed a formal agreement in May 2007 to demobilize children from its forces.

Militia Attacks against Civilians

There were fewer militia attacks against civilians in 2007 compared to the year before, but eastern Chad continued to be violent and insecure. In March the adjacent villages of Marena and Tiero were attacked by a predominantly Arab militia; at least 200 people were killed, including women and children, and civilians attempting to flee the violence were hunted down and killed. The first wave of attackers was repulsed by a government-supported militia in Tiero, but village defenses were overwhelmed when Chadian rebel forces joined the fray.

Refugees and the Internally Displaced

More than 180,000 Chadians have been displaced by violence in the past two years in eastern Chad, which also hosts 230,000 refugees from Darfur. Chadian government security forces and allied paramilitaries regularly seek recruits, including children, from camps for refugees and displaced persons in eastern Chad, sometimes by force. In 2007, recruitment activities were reported at most of the large, well-organized displaced persons camps in southeastern Chad, including Gassiré, Gouroukoum, Habilé and Koubigou.

Under the UN's Guiding Principles on Internal Displacement, humanitarian assistance such as food, water, shelter and medical care should be provided in an equitable manner. However, many Arabs and members of allied non-Arab ethnic groups such as the Ouaddai and the Mimi displaced by the conflict receive almost no humanitarian aid. Part of the problem is that counterinsurgency attacks by Chadian government security forces lead many Arabs to avoid large towns where these forces—as well as authorities responsible for humanitarian assistance—are based. But even when Arabs are not geographically isolated, they rarely receive assistance as a group. In August 2007 Human Rights Watch found hundreds of internally displaced Arabs living at levels of subsistence verging on desperation, while in nearby camps thousands of others, nearly all non-Arab, were receiving a range of services, including food, shelter and medical care.

The Trial of Hissène Habré

The long-standing campaign to bring Chad's former dictator Hissène Habré to jus-tice reached a turning point in February 2007, when Senegalese President Abdoulaye Wade signed into law measures to remove the primary legal obstacles to the trial.

Habré was arrested in Senegal in February 2000 on charges of crimes against humanity and torture stemming from his 1982-1990 rule in Chad. In 2001 Senegal refused to prosecute him and in 2005 it refused to extradite him to face charges in Belgium. However, in 2006 Dakar agreed to abide by a 2006 African Union decision that Habré should be put on trial in Senegal. The 2007 legislation allows such a trial by permitting Senegal to prosecute cases of genocide, crimes against humanity, war crimes and torture, even when they are committed outside of the country.

Key International Actors

In September 2007 the UN Security Council authorized the deployment of an international civilian protection force for eastern Chad. The force comprises troops under European Union command working in conjunction with UN police officers as well as a UN civilian component. This EU military force is to operate for an initial 12 months, and a transition to a UN command will be assessed after six months.

The Sudanese government continues to provide safe haven and support to armed groups such as Janjaweed militias, which have been responsible for raids on Chadian border villages, and Chadian rebel groups, which for the first time in the current phase of anti-government insurgency have committed large-scale attacks against civilians.

France has been instrumental in pushing the Chadian government to take action on the problem of child soldiers and has been the driving force behind the deployment of the EU civilian protection force, to which it has pledged a substan-tial number of troops. France simultaneously provides support to the Chadian mil-itary, even though it has been responsible for some of the very human rights abuses the French initiatives are designed to mitigate. France has more than

1,000 troops permanently stationed in Chad and has provided military intelligence, logistical assistance, medical services and ammunition to the Chadian military.

Like France, the United States provides military support to Chad in spite of its human rights record. American diplomats have urged President Déby to undertake voluntary democratic reforms, but the United States could exert far more pressure, given the amount of military assistance it provides. In the US 2006 defense budget, Chad was one of roughly a dozen countries to receive at least $10 million in Section 1206 funding, intended to build counterterrorism capacity in foreign military forces. US Marines and Army Special Forces instructors organize and train brigades of elite counterterrorism commandos, some of whom have defected to the rebels. The sale of four American-made C-130 transport aircraft was pending at this writing.

CÔTE D'IVOIRE

The March 2007 signature of a new peace accord, the Ouagadougou Agreement, has brought a palpable decrease in political tensions in Côte d'Ivoire, and prospects for resolution of the five-year political and military stalemate look brighter than a year ago. At the same time, the prevailing culture of impunity threatens long-term stability and the prospects for peaceful elections in the future.

Compared to previous years, 2007 saw fewer politically motivated attacks on journalists, northerners, and others perceived to be associated with the political opposition or the rebellion. Politically motivated hate speech also decreased. In September Radhika Coomaraswamy, United Nations special representative for children and armed conflict, announced that recruitment of child soldiers had not been detected in the past year. But other chronic human rights abuses persist and go unaddressed: most notably, government security forces and New Forces rebels continue to engage in widespread extortion at checkpoints and, on a more limited scale than in previous years, sexual violence against girls and women.

Meanwhile, underlying problems that have fomented and sustained the Ivorian conflict—the question of citizenship eligibility for some three million immigrant residents, harassment by security forces of residents living without national identity papers, and competition for land resources between "indigenous" and immigrant communities in the volatile western region—remain largely unresolved.

Efforts to End the Political-Military Stalemate

Since the crisis erupted, France, the Economic Community of West African States (ECOWAS), the African Union, and the United Nations have all spearheaded initiatives to end the political-military stalemate in Côte d'Ivoire.

Following a series of unfulfilled peace agreements and the October 2005 expiry of the five-year constitutional mandate of President Laurent Gbagbo, the UN Security Council postponed elections for one year under Resolution 1633 (2005). Then-Prime Minister Charles Konan Banny's efforts to implement a "roadmap" to elections soon deadlocked, however, making elections before October 2006 impossible. In response, the Security Council adopted resolution 1721 (2006) extending the mandates of President Gbagbo and Prime Minister Banny for a further 12 months, and granting sweeping powers to the prime minister. Soon after its adoption, however, President Gbagbo made clear that he would not accept key provisions of resolution 1721.

In March 2007 Gbagbo and rebel leader Guillaume Soro signed a peace accord negotiated with the help of Burkina Faso President Blaise Compaoré. The Ouagadougou Agreement is the first to have been directly negotiated by the country's main belligerents on their own initiative and resulted in the appointment of Guillaume Soro as prime minister in a unity government. Implementation efforts following signature resulted in important, if thus far largely symbolic milestones in the peace process. A buffer zone between north and south Côte d'Ivoire, formerly patrolled by French and UN troops, was dismantled and President Gbagbo visited the rebel capital Bouaké for the first time since the conflict erupted.

The Ouagadougou Agreement sets forth an ambitious 10-month timetable, which, if followed, would lead to citizen identification, voter registration, disarmament, and presidential elections by early 2008. For many observers the Agreement is the nation's best hope yet of resolving the crisis. However, since signature, target dates for the completion of disarmament and the identification process have been pushed further and further back. In September 2007 the head of the Independent Electoral Commission (CEI) projected that presidential elections will not likely take place before October 2008, three years beyond the expiry of President Gbagbo's constitutional mandate.

Extortion and Racketeering

In the government-controlled south, members of the police, gendarmerie, army, customs, and the Security Operations Command Center (CECOS) continue to engage in systematic and widespread extortion, racketeering, intimidation, and even physical assault at hundreds of roadside checkpoints. Although few residents are fully spared such abuses, the problem is particularly acute for travelers with names from northern ethnic groups and for West African immigrants. In the north, New Forces rebels regularly extort money from civilians in areas under their control, most commonly at the hundreds of roadblocks they maintain.

CÔTE D'IVOIRE

"My Heart is Cut"

Sexual Violence by Rebels and Pro-Government Forces
in Côte d'Ivoire

HUMAN
RIGHTS
WATCH

Sexual Abuse

Although the scale of abuse has diminished since its peak during the armed conflict of 2002-2003, members of government security forces and New Forces rebels continue to sexually abuse women and girls with impunity. The problem is most acute at checkpoints manned by these groups, where women and girls are subject to invasive body searches and rape. Specialist medical and psychological services for victims are all but non-existent, and courts often fail to enforce laws relating to sexual violence.

In July the UN suspended a Moroccan peacekeeping unit following an internal investigation into allegations of sexual exploitation and abuse, including of minors of both sexes, by some of its soldiers.

Impunity for Crimes Committed by Pro-Government Groups

In May members of the Students' Federation of Côte d'Ivoire (FESCI), a violent pro-government student union, ransacked the headquarters of two prominent Ivorian human rights groups they suspected of supporting a teachers' strike. One of these attacks took place in the presence of police officers who failed to intervene. FESCI members regularly rob and extort merchants and taxi drivers in the vicinity of university campuses and dormitories, often in plain view of security forces.

Rule of Law

In the government-controlled south, striking deficiencies in the judicial system, including lack of independence of the judicial branch from the executive and widespread corruption, constitute a significant impediment to victims seeking justice and to rebuilding respect for the rule of law. Those unable to bribe judges and other officials are routinely denied justice. Some of these bribes take the form of sexual favors. In the north, where most judicial infrastructure was destroyed during the armed conflict of 2002-2003, many individuals accused of common crimes are arbitrarily held in prisons and informal detention centers for extended periods. There are also credible reports that New Forces officials increasingly use torture to extract confessions from those accused of common crimes.

Internal Displacement

Some 750,000 people have been displaced since the crisis began in 2002. Although many were able to return home in 2007, they continue to suffer dire economic hardship. In the west, resettlement of some groups, particularly Burkinabe, is sometimes accomplished through signature of locally administered reconciliation agreements in which "indigenous" inhabitants impose discriminatory conditions on displaced immigrant groups as a condition of return. For example, some formerly displaced immigrants are now prohibited from residing outside of what is deemed to be their "host" village, despite the fact that the areas where they lived and earned their livelihood before the crisis began are tens of kilometers away.

Accountability

Throughout 2007 neither the government nor the rebel leadership took significant steps to discipline, investigate, or hold accountable those responsible for recent crimes, much less atrocities committed during the 2002-2003 civil war. In April 2007 President Gbagbo signed an ordinance granting amnesty to soldiers who deserted to join the rebels in 2002, among others. Though the ordinance has several ambiguous provisions, Gbagbo has publicly stated that the amnesty does not apply to "crimes against human kind," reinforcing that the ordinance does not extend to serious crimes under international law, for which amnesties are in any event not permissible.

The UN Security Council has still not made public or discussed the findings of the UN Commission of Inquiry report into serious violations of human rights and international humanitarian law since September 2002, which was handed to the UN secretary-general in November 2004.

In September 2003 the Ivorian government accepted the jurisdiction of the International Criminal Court over serious crimes. However, in 2006 and 2007 it consistently undermined a planned ICC mission to assess the possibility of opening an investigation into such crimes.

Key International Actors

In 2007 efforts of regional actors to resolve the Ivorian crisis, most notably those of President Compaoré of Burkina Faso in his capacity as ECOWAS chairman, took center stage. At the same time, President Gbagbo used the success of the Ouagadougou Agreement to press for a reduction in the prominence of the role played by the UN. For example, in early 2007 Gbagbo successfully pressed for the departure of Pierre Schori as special representative for the UN secretary-general in Côte d'Ivoire. In addition, Gbagbo demanded the removal of the UN high representative for elections, and in July Security Council resolution 1765 (2007) terminated the post.

The signature of the Ouagadougou Agreement was soon followed by the withdrawal of 500 out of some 3,500 French peacekeepers. They back up approximately 8,000 UN peacekeepers.

DEMOCRATIC REPUBLIC OF CONGO

Despite widespread optimism following the 2006 elections, violence against civilians, political repression, and impunity has continued during Joseph Kabila's first year as the newly elected president of the Democratic Republic of Congo.

In eastern Congo, political agreements to integrate combatants loyal to renegade general Laurent Nkunda failed, and war continues. All sides in the conflict commit atrocities against civilians, especially women, and a further 350,000 people joined the hundreds of thousands already displaced. In western Congo, soldiers and police killed more than 100 persons protesting corruption in the Bas Congo provincial elections. In March the soldiers and bodyguards of opposition leader Senator Jean-Pierre Bemba clashed with government soldiers in the heart of Kinshasa, leaving hundreds of civilians dead. Law enforcement officials arbitrarily detained over 300 people linked to the opposition, including journalists and members of civil society, and brutally tortured some of them.

Few military or civilian authorities were held accountable for past crimes. Warlords and militia leaders continue to be awarded top army positions instead of facing justice for their abuses.

Ongoing Violence in Eastern Congo

The people of the eastern Congo, buffeted by years of war, endured more armed conflict and human rights abuses, including murders, rape, and the recruitment and use of child soldiers, despite political agreements meant to resolve conflicts in the eastern province of North Kivu. Early in the year combatants loyal to the renegade general Laurent Nkunda were integrated into the national army in a process called "mixage." The newly established mixed brigades killed scores of civilians and committed rapes and other abuses in their operations against the Forces for the Liberation of Rwanda (FDLR), a Rwandan rebel group based in eastern Congo. By August the political agreements had collapsed and many of Nkunda's former troops returned to his control; renewed clashes between Nkunda's troops and government soldiers followed.

Government policy towards the FDLR followed a confused and contradictory course, with the army sometimes supporting and sometimes attacking this group. The FDLR, composed largely of Rwandese combatants, is supposedly committed to overthrowing the current government of Rwanda, but in recent years its members have attacked Congolese civilians more than they have engaged the Rwandan military.

The shifting configurations of the conflict have variously seen all forces fighting each other. The Congolese government, backed by the international community, tried various measures to end the fighting, but failed to address its underlying causes. Although crimes by all parties constituted violations of international humanitarian law, virtually none has been investigated, let alone prosecuted.

Violence in Kinshasa

On March 22, government forces and bodyguards of disappointed presidential contender Bemba clashed for three days in Kinshasa, the third such incident since August 2006. Both sides used heavy weapons in densely populated residential areas without regard for the welfare of civilians. At least 300 persons—many of them civilians—were killed. No investigation has established a definitive death toll. Some of Bemba's bodyguards fled across the river to Brazzaville (Republic of Congo) or sought protection with United Nations peacekeepers. Others tried to hide in local homes, but many were found and detained by security forces who reportedly summarily executed dozens of persons, including civilians. Bodies found in the Congo River, some bound and blindfolded, substantiated allegations of execution by government forces. Government troops also seized and ransacked Bemba's party headquarters and his radio and television stations, forcing their closure for a number of months. In April, following the violence and government threats to try him on charges of treason, Bemba left the country.

Tens of thousands of street children continued to be at risk in Congo, subjected regularly to physical, sexual, and emotional abuse, often at the hands of police and military forces. The Congolese government has taken few steps to protect these children from abuses.

DEMOCRATIC REPUBLIC OF CONGO

Renewed Crisis in North Kivu

HUMAN
RIGHTS
WATCH

Political Repression in Western Congo

Throughout 2007 law enforcement officials and soldiers used violence and repressive tactics against perceived opposition supporters, including politicians, journalists, and persons from Equateur, the home region of opposition leader and former presidential candidate Jean Pierre Bemba.

On January 31 and February 1, soldiers and police used excessive force to quell demonstrations against corruption in the gubernatorial elections in Bas Congo. They fired indiscriminately into crowds armed with sticks but no firearms, killing more than 100 followers of the politico-religious group Bundu Dia Kongo (BDK). Soldiers and police officers even trailed injured persons into their hiding places and executed some. Congo's newly elected national assembly established a commission to investigate the incident, but its efforts were restrained by political leaders. As of nine months after the massacre, no assembly report had been issued and no soldier or police officer had been prosecuted for his conduct.

Threats to Journalists and Human Rights Defenders

Two journalists were killed and over 30 others critical of the government were detained, beaten, or otherwise harassed during the year. On June 13 Radio Okapi journalist Serge Maheshe was murdered in Bukavu. Two of his friends were later convicted of the crime in a trial marred with contradictions and irregularities. On August 8 freelance photojournalist, Patrick Kikuku Wilungula, was murdered in Goma by an unidentified gunman. On March 21, government troops seized and ransacked Bemba's radio and television stations, forcing their closure and driving nearly a dozen journalists and technicians into hiding. Security forces also raided at least five other radio and television stations in connection with their news coverage.

When, in July, activists from the human rights group Journaliste en Danger (JED) denounced attacks on journalists, the government information minister called them "unpatriotic" on national television and threatened to review their registration. When union members, including those from the teachers union (Syndicat des Enseignants du Congo, Syeco), used their freedom of expression and association to strike over pay and conditions, they were threatened by anonymous callers.

Justice and Accountability

Persons suspected of grave violations of international humanitarian law continued to enjoy near total impunity. Only a handful were arrested and prosecuted while dozens of others were promoted to senior positions in the army or the government. In one exceptional case the Ituri warlord Chief Kahwa Mandro was tried on charges of war crimes and crimes against humanity, but he was acquitted after an appeals process marred by irregularities.

The judicial process continued to be characterized by political interference and corruption. Since late 2006 some 300 people linked to the opposition—including women and children—have been arbitrarily arrested and imprisoned in Kinshasa. Many have been tortured at Kin-maziere police prison, at Tshatshi military camp, or elsewhere to try to force them to confess to coup plotting or insurgency. Few of them have been brought before the courts. In one exceptional case, former presidential candidate Marie Thérèse Nlandu and nine others were tried for organizing an insurgency. During proceedings closely observed by human rights monitors, the prosecutor failed to prove the charges, and all were acquitted on April 30. Shortly afterwards the presiding judge was removed from his post, and the state appealed the acquittal. Nlunda fled abroad.

The International Criminal Court (ICC) in the Hague provided some hope that perpetrators of human rights abuses in Congo would be held to account. In January judges at the ICC decided there was sufficient evidence against its first suspect in custody, Ituri warlord Thomas Lubanga Dyilo, charged with enlisting, subscripting, and using child soldiers. The trial, the first in the court's history, is scheduled to start in March 2008. On October 17 a second Ituri warlord, Germain Katanga, was transferred to the ICC and charged with war crimes and crimes against humanity for his involvement in killings, use of child soldiers, sexual enslavement, and pillaging.

Key International Actors

Apparently reluctant to criticize the leader chosen by an electoral process in which they invested so much political and financial capital, international donors have said little about human rights abuses under Kabila's government. Instead, they flocked to Kinshasa to sign agreements for economic development programs. Concern over the possible increase of influence from China was spurred by the Chinese loan of over US$5 billion to Congo's government in return for mining concessions.

Slow to react to the crisis in eastern Congo, UN leaders and representatives of the United States, the United Kingdom, France, Belgium, and South Africa finally acknowledged in September the risks of wider conflict and committed themselves to finding political solutions to the crisis.

The UN peacekeeping force in Congo, MONUC, had to redefine its role in the wake of elections and struggled to find the appropriate balance among contending political actors while still implementing its mandate to protect civilians. MONUC hesitated for months to speak openly about the human rights problems linked to conflict in eastern Congo, and it failed to publish two reports on human rights abuses that might have embarrassed the government. The UN high commissioner for human rights, the special rapporteur on violence against women, and the special representative of the secretary-general for children and armed conflict all visited Congo and contributed significantly to raising public awareness of human rights abuses among diplomats and the public in general.

In September the Human Rights Council (HRC) rescheduled for March 2008 its consideration of whether or not to keep or amend the mandate of the Independent Expert on the situation in the DRC.

Eritrea

The government of President Isayas Afeworki continues to maintain its totalitarian grip on the country. Arbitrary arrests and detention without trial are common. Prisoners are routinely tortured and kept for years in underground cells in isolation or crammed into shipping containers. Mass arrests and harassment of members of minority religious denominations continue. The government imposes such prolonged and repeated compulsory military service that thousands of young men have fled the country.

The constitution approved by referendum in 1997 remains unimplemented. No national election has ever been held and an interim parliament has not met since 2002. No political groups are permitted aside from the ruling People's Front for Democracy and Justice (PFDJ), of which Afeworki is executive secretary. The last session of the PFDJ party congress occurred in 1997. No media or civil society organizations exist outside those controlled by the PFDJ. Private enterprise has been severely curtailed, largely replaced by PFDJ-owned businesses.

Afeworki justifies his repressive rule by claiming that the country must remain on a war footing until a boundary dispute with Ethiopia is resolved. Ethiopia refuses to accept the 2002 demarcation decision by a Boundary Commission established under the 2000 cease-fire agreement ending the bloody two-year war between Ethiopia and Eritrea.

Suppression of Free Expression

Dissent is ruthlessly suppressed including within the PFDJ. Eleven PFDJ leaders arrested in September 2001 for questioning the president's leadership remain detained without charge or trial. The independent press remains closed—in 2001 all editors and publishers except those who managed to flee—were detained. In 2007, Reporters without Borders ranked Eritrea last of 169 countries on its Press Freedom Index. The government even cannibalizes its own media. In November 2006 it arrested nine state media employees after others fled the country. They were beaten while under arrest to obtain information about their email accounts and to discover possible escape plans. One of those arrested, Fetiha Khaled, is reported to have been forced to join the army. The others were released but were placed under surveillance and forbidden to leave Asmara. In July 2007, one of those released, Paulos Kidane, fell ill while trying to escape to Sudan and later died or was killed by security forces.

Government permits are required for gatherings of more than three to five persons. No domestic human rights organizations are allowed to exist; foreign human rights organizations are denied entry. All labor unions are PFDJ affiliates. In 2007, the regime released three PFDJ union leaders who had been arrested two years earlier after advocating for improved working conditions.

Prison Conditions and Torture

Incarceration of suspected political opponents without trial or rudimentary legal safeguards is routine. The political leaders and journalists arrested in 2001 remain in solitary confinement in a secret detention facility; nine of the 31 prisoners are reported to have died. Many other prisoners are packed into unventilated cargo containers under extreme temperatures or are held in underground cells. Torture is common, as are indefinite solitary confinement, starvation rations, lack of sanitation, and hard labor. Prisoners rarely receive medical care, even when severely injured or deathly ill. Death in captivity is common.

Prisoners are warned not to speak about their imprisonment after release, but some details have emerged. In 2006 one escapee, a former journalist, told a conference in Uganda that he had been beaten and kicked, had his feet tied to his hands behind his back, was later manacled, threatened with death, held in solitary confinement in a narrow underground dungeon, and prohibited from sending or receiving mail. He was released after almost two years, but then was conscripted into the army, where he was closely monitored, before managing to escape.

Military Conscription and Arrests

Men between ages 18 and 50, and women between 18 and 27, must serve 18 months of military service. However, as in previous years, men were rounded up in massive sweeps and house-to-house searches (*giffas*) for repeated periods of service far exceeding 18 months. As one young Eritrean noted in 2007, "there is no end to this service." Conscripts are used in labor battalions on public works and on projects benefiting military commanders personally. Pay is nominal and working conditions often harsh. Over a dozen conscripts were reported to have died in the summer of 2007 at the Wia military training camp near the Red Sea coast from intense heat, malnutrition, and lack of medical care. Conscientious objection is not recognized.

Refugee agencies report that approximately 120 young men fleeing conscription arrived in Sudan each week in 2006 and 2007 and that another 400 to 500 reach Ethiopia monthly, even though border guards reportedly have orders to "shoot-to-kill."

Since 2005, families of conscription evaders are fined at least 50,000 nakfa (US $3300), a massive sum in a country where yearly per capita income is less than $1000. Since late 2006, some family members have reportedly been conscripted to substitute for missing relatives.

Religious Persecution

Only Catholic, Evangelical Lutheran, and Orthodox Christian churches and traditional Islam are permitted to worship in Eritrea. Although four other denominations applied for registration in 2002, none were registered as of late 2007. Members of unregistered churches, especially Protestant sects, are frequently persecuted. Some 2,000 members of unregistered churches are incarcerated at any one time in shipping containers, underground cells, and military outposts. Many are beaten and otherwise abused to compel them to renounce their faiths. Some are arrested and released after a month or two but others are held indefinitely.

Even "recognized" religious groups have not been spared. In 2006, the government engineered the removal of the 79-year-old patriarch of the Eritrean Orthodox church and placed him under house arrest after he refused to interfere with a renewal movement within the church. In May 2007 he was evicted from his home after a replacement patriarch was "unanimously" confirmed by church authorities; his whereabouts are currently unknown. Members of the renewal movement have been arrested and abused in the same fashion as members of non-recognized churches.

The government has also interfered with the Catholic Church. In late 2006, the government demanded that Roman Catholic Church schools, health clinics, and other social service facilities be turned over to the Ministry of Social Welfare. In November 2007, it expelled 13 Catholic missionaries by refusing to extend their residency permits.

Relations with Ethiopia

Tensions with Ethiopia remain high. A September 2007 Border Commission meeting with the two countries to obtain agreement to demarcate the border ended in failure. Ethiopia subsequently announced it might terminate the armistice agreement altogether. In 2002, the commission had designated the border and directed that it be demarcated accordingly. Although Eritrea accepts the commission decision in full, Ethiopia refuses to permit demarcation of portions of the border that would award the village of Badme, the flashpoint of the war, to Eritrea.

An international peacekeeping force, the UN Mission in EritreaEthiopia (UNMEE), maintains 1,700 troops and observers in a 25-kilometerwide armistice buffer between the two countries. Since 2005 Eritrea has infiltrated thousands of troops into the buffer zone, and has prevented UNMEE from patrolling large parts of it and from engaging in aerial observation, all in violation of the armistice agreement. Eritrea ignores repeated Security Council resolutions demanding withdrawal of the troops and cooperation with UNMEE. As a result, heavily armed troops of both countries are within meters of each other. In March 2007, the government expelled the program manager of the UNMEE Mine Action Coordination Center, one of a series of expulsions of UNMEE personnel over the years.

Since 2006, Eritrea and Ethiopia have been engaged in a proxy war in neighboring Somalia. Eritrea allegedly provides logistical and military support to insurgent groups fighting with the Islamic Courts Union (ICU) against Ethiopian forces and the Somali transitional government. In 2007 it provided refuge to ICU leaders. A United Nations team monitoring the arms embargo on Somalia in July 2007 accused Eritrea of providing "huge quantities of arms," in late 2006 to the ICU. In April 2007 Eritrea suspended its membership in the regional Inter-Governmental Authority on Development (IGAD) because of the organization's support for Ethiopian intervention in Somalia.

Key International Actors

Relations with the United States, already strained, worsened in 2007. President Afeworki harshly criticized the United States for failing to pressure Ethiopia to comply with the boundary commission decision. In August 2007, the US threatened to place Eritrea on its short list of "state sponsors of terrorism" because of its alleged military support to the ICU and for sheltering ICU leaders whom the US labels terrorists. The US also ordered Eritrea to close its consulate in the US—in California—in response to interference with operations of the American embassy in Asmara.

Since the government ordered the USAID office to shut down in 2005, the US has provided no development assistance to Eritrea. For economic assistance, Eritrea now relies on China, Arab states, and the European Union, and remittances from the Eritrean diaspora. In 2007, China partially cancelled Eritrea's existing debt. It also agreed to provide assistance for construction of a college in Adi-Keyih. China's Export-Import bank agreed in 2007 to lend the government US$60 million to purchase a large minority interest in a gold mine project by a Canadian mining company at Bisha in western Eritrea. Still, currency flows remain decidedly in China's favor. In 2006, the last full year for which figures are available, China exported almost $38 million worth of goods to Eritrea and imported only $720,000-worth.

The European Union is in the final year of a US$119 million five-year development grant. In September, the EU expressed concern about "severe violations of basic human rights" by the government.

In July 2007, two British Council employees, were arrested, one of whom was released shortly thereafter. A visiting British diplomat was expelled for allegedly trying to install communications equipment without authorization at the council.

ETHIOPIA

The Ethiopian government's human rights record remains poor, both within the country and in neighboring Somalia, where since early 2007 thousands of Ethiopian troops have been fighting an insurgency alongside the Transitional Federal Government of Somalia.

Government forces committed serious human rights violations, including rape, torture, and village burnings, during a campaign against Ethiopian rebels in eastern Somali Region (Region 5). Abuses also took place in other parts of the country, notably in Oromia State where local officials carried out mass arrests, extrajudicial killings and economic sanctions.

In March and April 2007 in Mogadishu, Somalia, the Ethiopian military used heavy artillery and rockets indiscriminately, in violation of international humanitarian law, killing hundreds of civilians and displacing up to 400,000 people, as they fought an escalating insurgency.

In Addis Ababa, the government pardoned and released dozens of opposition leaders and journalists detained since the post-election crackdown in 2005. However, the press remains hobbled and local human rights organizations operate with great difficulty.

Abuses in Somali and Oromia States

In June, the Ethiopian military launched a major offensive in Somali region, the eastern third of the country inhabited by ethnic Somalis. The offensive was a response to increasing attacks by the Ogaden National Liberation Front (ONLF), a longstanding armed opposition movement demanding self determination for the region. In April the ONLF attacked an oil exploration site killing nine Chinese oil workers, 50 armed guards, and 28 nearby villagers; the group was also allegedly responsible for two bombings in May that indiscriminately killed 17 people, mostly civilians, and wounded dozens in Dhagabur and Jigjiga, the state capital.

In the five zones affected by the conflict, the Ethiopian military retaliated by razing entire villages, carrying out public executions, raping and harassing women and girls, arbitrarily arresting, torturing and sometimes killing suspects in military custody; and forcing thousands to flee their homes. They also imposed a commercial blockade on the affected region and confiscated livestock—the main asset in this largely pastoralist region—exacerbating food shortages.

In July, the government expelled the International Committee of the Red Cross and restricted access to the affected region by other international humanitarian agencies. Restrictions on humanitarian agencies were slightly eased in September and October, when the government permitted the UN to conduct an assessment and open regional offices in the affected area.

In Oromia, Ethiopia's most populous state, government authorities have used the fact of a long-standing insurgency by the Oromo Liberation Front (OLF) to imprison, harass, and physically abuse critics, including school children. Victims are informally accused of supporting the OLF, an outlawed rebel group, but supporters of the Oromo National Congress (ONC) and the Oromo Federalist Democratic Movement (OFDM), registered opposition political parties, suffer similar treatment. In early January, more than thirty students were arrested and at least one, a tenth-grader, died as a result of police beatings in Dembi Dollo, western Oromia. Other students were severely injured and hospitalized. Also in January, local police and militia members in Ghimbi shot two high school students dead, one as he and others were walking peacefully along, the other as he covered the body of the first with his own in order to protect him from further harm. In March security officials allegedly executed 19 men and a 14-year-old girl near Mieso in northeastern Oromia. Starting in August, federal and state security forces arrested well over 200 people in western Oromia, including three members of the executive committee of the Nekemte chapter of the Ethiopian Human Rights Council and OFDM members, on suspicion of links to the OLF. Some, including the EHRCO officials, were released under court order after the police failed to provide evidence against them but most were still detained as of early November. At least 25 were being held in defiance of court orders to release them.

Farmers in Oromia who fail to support the governing political party are denied fertilizer and other agricultural aids over which the government exercises monopoly control.

Abuses Relating to the Conflict in Somalia

Thousands of Ethiopian troops were deployed in Mogadishu and other parts of Somalia in late 2006 as part of the military campaign to oust the Islamic Courts Union (ICU) and install the Transitional Federal Government. In March and April 2007, the Ethiopian military indiscriminately bombarded large residential areas of Mogadishu with mortar shells, artillery, and "Katyusha" rockets, killing hundreds of people and causing up to 400,000 people to flee the city. Ethiopian forces made no apparent effort to distinguish between civilian and insurgent targets, and they shelled and occupied several key hospitals located in the frontline areas. (See Somalia chapter)

In collaboration with TFG forces, Ethiopian troops detained and sometimes beat hundreds of men in mass arrests in Mogadishu in June and July. Dozens of suspected ICU supporters who fled Mogadishu in December 2006 were detained by Ethiopian forces in Somalia or by Kenyan officials at the border, and rendered to Ethiopia in January and February, where they were held in incommunicado detention for months of interrogations, by US security agents, among others. At least 40 of the detainees were released in April and May—including more than a dozen women and children under the age of fifteen—but scores of others have disappeared.

Suppression of Free Expression and Attacks on Civil Society

An unknown number of people remain imprisoned without trial after election-related violence following events in June and November 2005, although in July 2007 the government finally released the leadership of the leading opposition party, the Coalition for Unity and Democracy (CUD) and six newspaper publishers.

In proceedings that became popularly known as "the treason trial," the government had accused the CUD leadership, journalists and others of using unlawful means to change the "constitutional order," obstruct the exercise of constitutional powers, promote armed rebellion, and impair "the defensive power of the state," as well as treason and genocide. In April 2007, the treason and genocide charges were dismissed, but some defendants were convicted of the other charges. The court also ordered three newspapers to be closed. Shortly after sentencing, most of the defendants were released and all charges against them were dropped after they submitted letters accepting some responsibility for the 2005 unrest. However, two civil society representatives, Daniel Bekele and Netsanet Demissie, who acted as mediators between the EPRDF and the CUD after the 2005 elections, refused to sign letters of regret and insisted on judicial exoneration. Despite flimsy government evidence against them, they remained incarcerated as of early December 2007, two years after their arrest, because of repeated court recesses.

Following the 2005 elections, the government has sharply reversed a liberalizing trend and subjected independent newspapers and their editors, publishers, and reporters to renewed harassment, intimidation, and criminal charges. Three journalists acquitted during the treason trial fled the country after their release from jail, citing multiple death threats from government security agents. The government and its allies own all electronic media. It blocks access to internet sites critical of its policies. In October, the government began jamming Deutsche Welle and Voice of America Amharic and Oromomifa language broadcasts, the principal source of news for the rural population.

The government has long tried unsuccessfully to outlaw the Ethiopian Teachers Association (ETA), the largest independent membership organization in the country. ETA's president, released from six years in prison in 2002, was tried in absentia in the treason trial; the chair of ETA's Addis Ababa branch was acquitted. Four ETA members were arrested in December 26, 2006, severely beaten, and otherwise tortured to coerce confessions that they were members of an armed opposition group, the Ethiopian People's Patriotic Front. Released in March 2007, they were rearrested in late May and early June.

Lack of Judicial Independence

The judicial system remains unable to assert independence in prominent cases. In the treason trial, for example, the trial judges showed little concern for defendants' procedural and constitutional rights and ignored claims of serious mistreatment by prison authorities. With exceptions, courts generally allow police protracted periods to investigate for evidence that might support the charges brought by prosecutors; in the meantime, defendants remain jailed without an opportunity for release on bail.

In January 2007 a court convicted Mengistu Haile Mariam of genocide in absentia, and sentenced him to life imprisonment. Mengistu, the leader of the former military government, lives in Zimbabwe under the protection of the Zimbabwe government. Several hundred former officials remain jailed awaiting trial, sixteen years after Mengistu's overthrow.

Mistreatment of Human Rights Defenders and Civil Society

The staff of Ethiopia's only nationwide human rights organization, EHRCO, is regularly subjected to government harassment and intimidation. One investigator who fled the country in 2005 was charged in absentia in the treason trial. Three members of the Nekemte executive committee were arrested and imprisoned for fifteen days (see above.)

The Oromo-focused Human Rights League, allowed to register in 2005 after years of litigation, remains inactive. Leaders of the traditional Oromo self-help organization Mecha Tulama, arrested in 2004, were released without trial in early 2007.

Key International Actors

Ethiopia remains deadlocked over a boundary dispute with Eritrea dating from the 1998-2000 war. The war in Somalia is another source of tension between the two countries.

International criticism of the Ethiopian government's human rights performance is muted. The United States and major European donor states view the government as an important ally in an unstable region. Ethiopia remains the largest beneficiary of US military and development aid in sub-Saharan Africa. The US provided logistical and possibly financial support for Ethiopia's invasion of Somalia in December 2006 and has not pressured Ethiopia to accede to the Eritrea boundary decision.

Ethiopia is also among the top African recipients of European Union aid. After the 2005 election violence, the UK suspended direct budget support to Ethiopia, but has since increased its aid to an annual GBP 130 million in 2007-2008.

China is an increasingly important trading partner. Chinese-Ethiopian trade has increased 17 percent since 2006, to US$660 million, and Chinese investment has reached $345 million from just $10 million four years ago, according to official figures.

In August 2007 the government expelled two thirds of the diplomatic staff of Norway, apparently for criticizing its human rights record and pressing too aggressively for acceptance of the Eritrea boundary commission decision.

GUINEA

2007 was a tumultuous year in Guinea, characterized by rising demands for political change, continued economic uncertainty, and brutal repression by security forces.

In January and February government security forces violently repressed a nationwide strike organized by Guinea's leading trade unions to protest widespread corruption, bad governance, and deteriorating economic conditions. The six-week crisis ended in late February when President Lansana Conté agreed to appoint Lansana Kouyaté as prime minister from among a list of candidates, as demanded by the trade unions, raising hopes of improvements in economic conditions and respect for human rights.

Amid the economic and political turmoil, state-sponsored violence has continued, including torture, assault, extortion, and theft by the very security forces responsible for protecting Guinean citizens. The government has so far failed to tackle the impunity that accompanies serious human rights abuses, particularly abuses committed by security forces.

Political Transition Brings Hope and Frustration

Prime Minister Kouyaté's government has managed to mitigate Guinea's spiraling inflation and restore the confidence of international donors, but the economic prospects for most Guineans remain bleak. Despite the country's abundant mineral resources and agricultural potential, basic foodstuffs and other essential commodities are beyond the means of many Guineans. Electricity blackouts and water shortages, even in the capital Conakry, are chronic, and impatience with the pace and progress of reforms has led again to growing discontent.

Impatience among ordinary Guineans is paralleled by rising discontent and fractiousness in Guinea's military, an institution thought to be deeply divided along both generational and ethnic lines. In April soldiers rioted in the streets of Conakry demanding back pay. Up to a dozen civilians were killed by stray bullets. The soldiers returned to their barracks when President Conté promised them money and promotions, but these have yet to materialize.

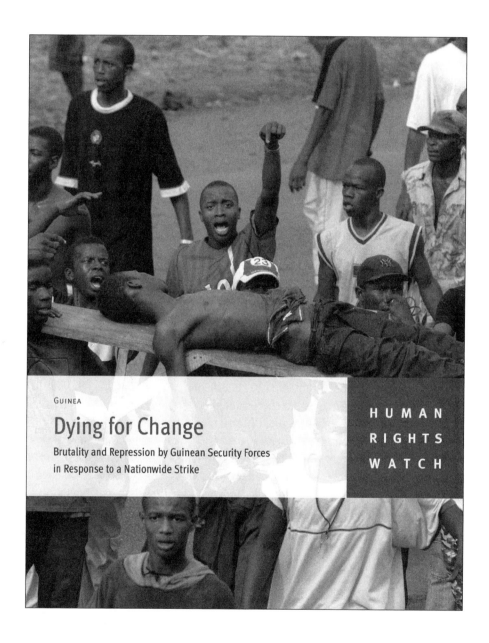

GUINEA

Dying for Change

Brutality and Repression by Guinean Security Forces
in Response to a Nationwide Strike

**H U M A N
R I G H T S
W A T C H**

Conté, age 73, is rumored to be gravely ill, and many observers suspect that if he dies before his current term ends in 2010 a military takeover is inevitable. Parliamentary elections, initially postponed from June to December 2007, appear unlikely before early 2008, mainly due to delays in setting up an Independent National Electoral Commission, a longtime demand of the opposition.

Excessive Use of Force and Other Strike-Related Abuses

The January-February crackdown resulted in at least 137 dead and over 1,700 wounded. Security forces, particularly the presidential guard, were involved in murder, rape, assault, and theft. Members of security forces fired directly into crowds of unarmed demonstrators and gunned down demonstrators trying to flee to safety. In what appeared to be well organized operations, security forces ransacked the offices of one of the trade unions that organized the strike, as well as those of a private radio station. In the course of these raids, trade union leaders and journalists were robbed, arbitrarily arrested, beaten, and threatened with death. In addition, scores of people, including women, children, and elderly men who had not participated in the protests, were severely beaten and robbed at gunpoint by security forces, often in their own homes.

In May the National Assembly unanimously adopted a law creating an independent national commission of inquiry into abuses committed during the January-February strikes. While the list of commissioners was finally announced in late September, there were concerns about the ability of the members to act independently given the politically sensitive nature of the crimes involved, and at this writing the commission has yet to become operational. The Guinean government has historically failed to adequately investigate abuses. For example, there have been no meaningful efforts to hold to account security forces responsible for murder, rape, assault, and robbery of unarmed demonstrators during a similar June 2006 strike.

Rule of Law

The judicial system in Guinea is plagued with deficiencies, including lack of independence of the judicial branch from the executive branch, inadequate resources, corruption, inadequately trained magistrates and other personnel, and insufficient numbers of attorneys, especially those specializing in criminal law. Many people are denied justice because they cannot afford to bribe judges, magistrates, and other officials. In 2006 the global anti-corruption organization Transparency International ranked Guinea Africa's most corrupt country.

Police Torture

Torture and mistreatment of criminal suspects in police custody, including children, is routine. During interrogation suspects are frequently bound with cords, beaten, burned with cigarettes, and otherwise physically abused until they confess to the crime of which they are accused. Failure to prosecute perpetrators remains the biggest single obstacle to ending these abuses.

Detention-Related Abuses

Prolonged pretrial detention remains a serious human rights issue, although in 2007 local human rights organizations were able to free some prisoners who had spent more time awaiting trial than the maximum sentence for the crime of which they were accused, and to secure a trial for others. Nevertheless, over 80 percent of those held in Guinea's largest prison in central Conakry are untried and many have been awaiting trial for two or more years.

Detention conditions throughout Guinea are grossly inadequate. In 2007 the largest prison housed close to 800 prisoners in a facility designed for up to 300. In violation of international standards, prison officials often fail to separate convicted and untried prisoners, or children from adults. Malnutrition and other health problems are rife, although fewer prisoners died from hunger in 2007 than in previous years because local and international civil society organizations are now providing food. Many prison guards, especially those serving on an unpaid "volunteer" basis, extort money from prisoners or sell them illegal drugs with impunity.

Child Labor

Domestic work is the largest employment category among children in Guinea, with tens of thousands of girls working as domestic laborers. Girls come from as far as Mali to work as maids, many of them victims of trafficking and forced labor. They are routinely denied education and health care and are forced to work up to 18 hours a day without pay. Beatings, sexual harassment, and rape at the hands of employers are frequent. Significant numbers of children are also employed in artisanal gold and diamond mines and granite quarries, where they perform back-breaking and dangerous work for little or no money. There is no functioning child protection system in Guinea. Although the government has created a special police unit to combat child prostitution, trafficking, and other abuses against chil-dren, perpetrators are rarely prosecuted.

Key International Actors

The brutal repression of unarmed demonstrators in January-February 2007 was roundly condemned by the United Nations, the African Union, the Economic Community of West African States (ECOWAS), the European Union (EU), the United States, and France. ECOWAS played a leading role in helping to diffuse both the January-February crisis and tensions that arose in its aftermath. However, no country or organization was able or willing to convince Guinea to hold those responsible to account by, for example, getting the independent national commis-sion of inquiry up and running, or addressing impunity for other more routine state-sponsored violence, such as torture.

In 2002 the International Monetary Fund, the World Bank, and the African Development Bank suspended economic assistance to Guinea due to poor eco-nomic and political governance. In 2003 the EU invoked Article 96 of the Cotonou Agreement to suspend all but humanitarian assistance to Guinea due to human rights concerns. Since his appointment in March, Prime Minister Kouyaté has been lobbying extensively for more donor assistance. At a Paris donors' confer-ence in July, the World Bank, the European Commission, and other donors com-mitted US$90 million in short-term emergency assistance. The European Commission and France have also announced programs to assist in reform of the judicial sector.

KENYA

Kenya's multiparty political system has developed considerably since the retirement of President Daniel Arap Moi in 2002. The new pluralism, though flawed and very fractious, has helped stabilize the country, along with economic growth, a less divisive executive style and increasingly independent media and legislature. In 2007, the human rights situation was shaped by the run-up to the December elections and the persistent corruption that has plagued the nation for decades. In addition, the escalating conflicts in neighboring Somalia and the Somali region of Ethiopia contributed to instability throughout the region, strengthening fears of further terrorist attacks in Kenya. Kenya's borders were closed to refugees and terrorism suspects fleeing Somalia were sent back, for rendition to Ethiopia.

A brutal police clampdown on a renegade criminal gang in Nairobi's slums resulted in the extrajudicial killings of hundreds of people.

In the Mount Elgon region, clashes among clans of the Kalenjin tribe left nearly 200 people dead and some 116,000 displaced.

Elections and Governance

Kenya's political climate has improved considerably since the 1990s, when elections were regularly marred by state-sponsored violence and harassment of journalists and human rights defenders.

The run-up to the December 2007 elections was far less violent than that of past election years, although, as of this writing, there were sporadic clashes in various parts of the country, and a series of attacks on women candidates in local and parliamentary elections threatened the prospects for fair elections in those areas.

Kenya has one of the most assertive, independent Parliaments in Africa today. Government frequently struggles to get its legislative initiatives enacted. In turn, President Mwai Kibaki has on occasion successfully vetoed bills passed by the legislature. During 2007, Kibaki rejected two publicly controversial bills passed by parliament—a restrictive media bill and a bill limiting the activities of the Kenya

Anti-Corruption Commission (KACC). Public outcry over the bills, and parliament's vote to award a huge pay rise to its own members coupled with ongoing revelations about corruption and patronage, made it likely that large numbers of parliamentarians would not retain their seats.

Mistreatment of Refugees from Somalia

In December 2006, Ethiopian forces with US assistance ousted the Union of Islamic Courts (UIC) and installed the Transitional Federal Government (TFG) in Mogadishu. Several terrorism suspects believed to have been responsible for the 1998 bombing of the US Embassy in Nairobi and the 2002 Mombasa hotel bombing were alleged by the US to be living in Somalia under UIC protection.

In an attempt to stem the flow of refugees, the Kenyan government closed the border with Somalia in January 2007 and only gradually opened up limited cross-border access for humanitarian relief convoys as the year progressed. In January and February 2007 Kenyan security forces, including the Anti-Terrorism Police Unit, held scores of individuals who fled Somalia in incommunicado detention for weeks. At least 85 individuals were then expelled from Kenya to Somalia on several flights, and were subsequently rendered to Ethiopia, where they were held for several months without charge.

Among the group detained in Kenya and rendered to Ethiopia were Kenyan citizens and more than twenty women and young children, most of them under the age of fifteen. Several individuals were deported from Kenya in the midst of pending habeas corpus applications in the Kenyan courts. At least 40 individuals, including the women and children, were released from Ethiopian custody between April and June, but the whereabouts of scores of others, including the alleged Kenyan citizens, remain unknown.

The Mungiki Sect and Subsequent Police Crackdown

In June 2007 Kenyan police launched a crackdown on the Mungiki sect, a quasi-religious Kikuyu criminal gang responsible for a spate of recent attacks in Nairobi's shanty towns, especially Mathare.

The Mungiki sect engages in mafia-like economic and political activities and claims to have connections to the nation's political elite, although the group is not connected to the state. Its members raise funds through protection rackets, and by levying extra charges on public transportation as well as water and electricity connections. Those who are not able or refuse to pay have not only been denied services but have in some cases have also been kidnapped, tortured, and, in several notorious cases, beheaded. The victims to date include several policemen and tourists.

The brutality of the police crackdown matched or even exceeded that of the Mungiki itself. Police searching for weapons ransacked homes and shops and carried out brutal interrogations of suspects involving torture and beating. In November, the Kenya National Commission on Human Rights reported that there had been over 450 extrajudicial police killings related to the Mungiki violence. Many of the victims were found with a bullet in the back of the head. The police denied responsibility for the killings, but many slum dwellers corroborated the report's claims.

Media Freedom

Press freedom has improved considerably in Kenya since the elections of 2002. However, there have been some instances of official intolerance of political criticism. In March 2006 the Standard newspaper published an article describing a secret meeting between President Kibaki and an opposition politician. The government ordered the police to raid the newspaper's offices, as well as the office of their broadcast affiliate, KTN channel. The case drew international condemnation, and there were no similar incidents in 2007. However, certain controversial issues, such as the Mount Elgon clashes (see below) and the rounding up and rendition of individuals fleeing Somalia in Kenya are seldom reported on, perhaps due to wariness about the government's reaction.

In September, President Mwai Kibaki rejected legislation that included a controversial amendment introduced by a member of his own party, requiring journalists to reveal their sources. The move was greeted with widespread relief by the human rights community.

Corruption

Action to address Kenya's longstanding problems with corruption continue to be desultory. The Kenyan Anti-Corruption Commission—established after the 2002 elections—has arrested numerous chiefs, policemen, taxi touts, and others on charges of bribery. However, since the first KACC head John Githongo fled the country in 2005, claiming he had been threatened, no effort has been made to recover the vast sums of government money—which some estimates place in the billions of dollars—that have been lost in major scandals such as Anglo-Leasing and Goldenberg. Many senior politicians and judges are alleged to have been involved, and some officials did resign when these allegations came to light.

In September 2007, parliament passed the Statute Law (Miscellaneous Amendments Bill) permitting the Anti-Corruption Commission to investigate only offenses committed after 2003. Since the most serious scandals date from before that time, this was seen as a move to protect many parliamentarians from prosecution. President Kibaki rejected the legislation.

Women's and Children's Rights

In 2007, Parliament passed a new Sexual Offenses Bill that broadens the definition of sexual and gender-based violence and imposes harsher penalties on perpetrators. Women's rights groups are now actively working to implement the bill.

Kenya also made considerable progress in expanding access to free AIDS treatment services for the approximately six percent of the population living with HIV. At present, these programs tend to prioritize adults over children, however. Poverty and lack of information also prevent many children and adults with AIDS from obtaining services to which they are entitled.

Human Rights Defenders

Most human rights groups functioned without interference in 2007. However, Maina Kiai, the head of the Kenya National Commission on Human Rights (KNCHR) was investigated by the Kenya Anti-Corruption Commission. Independent non-governmental human rights monitors have claimed the charges may have been related to KNCHR investigations of corruption on the part of the Kenyan government, including the purchase of a fleet of expensive cars for government officials, and the use of public funds for by-election campaigns. A full investigation of the allegations against Kiai is still pending.

In the Mount Elgon region, fighting among clans of the Kalenjin tribe left nearly 200 people dead and around 116,000 displaced. Human rights groups, journalists and even the International Committee of the Red Cross were temporarily barred by Kenyan security services from entering the area.

In August, a legal protest against the extremely generous raises that Parliament voted for itself was violently disrupted by police using tear gas. Many of the demonstrators were rounded up, beaten and held overnight in police cells. They were all released the next day.

Key International Actors

Foreign donors, originally optimistic that President Kibaki would crack down more vigorously on corruption, have lowered their expectations and generally remained silent about Kenya's human rights performance. For the US, Kenya is a frontline state in counterterrorism efforts, and since 2001 US military aid to Kenya has increased eight-fold, most of it for weapons and training.

Kenya derives only seven percent of its budget from foreign aid, so donor leverage on human rights issues may be more limited than in other countries in the region. The World Bank and IMF, which pulled out of Kenya during the Moi regime, have begun lending again, especially in the areas of public sector management, fighting corruption and simplifying the legal procedures for starting a business or selling land.

Despite the nation's ongoing struggle with corruption, the World Bank has praised Kenya's economic reforms and Kenya has also been commended, both locally and internationally, for its Universal Primary Education Program and for expanding access to primary health care.

LIBERIA

Throughout 2007 the government of President Ellen Johnson-Sirleaf made tangible progress in rebuilding Liberia's failed institutions, fighting corruption, and promoting the rule of law. However, longstanding deficiencies within the judicial system and security sector continue to undermine basic human rights. Meanwhile, there have been few efforts to pursue justice for the egregious human rights violations committed during Liberia's 14 years of armed conflict that finally came to an end in 2003.

Ongoing Insecurity and Abuses in Law Enforcement

The 2003 Peace Agreement was followed by the deployment of 15,000 United Nations peacekeepers. In 2007 this force, along with some 1,200 international civilian police, appeared to have little impact on Liberia's escalating rates of violent crime including armed robbery, rape, and murder. Lack of funding for transportation and for essential forensic and communications equipment severely undermined the effectiveness of the national police, especially in rural areas. Of the over 3,500 police vetted and trained by the United Nations Mission in Liberia (UNMIL), fewer than 700 have been deployed outside the capital, Monrovia. Liberian police have also continued to engage in unprofessional and sometimes criminal behavior including extortion, soliciting bribes from detainees, and excessive use of force. There were several reports of detainees being subjected to physical abuse by policemen, including torture and male rape. While a few of these cases resulted in internal police investigations and suspension from duty, there was little effort to hold those involved accountable for their alleged crimes.

Performance of the Judiciary

Persistent deficiencies within the judicial and corrections systems also resulted in human rights abuses. Some weaknesses were attributable to insufficient judicial personnel including prosecutors and public defenders, and limited court infrastructure, particularly outside Monrovia. However, unprofessional and corrupt practices by judicial staff, such as chronic absenteeism and the release of criminal suspects in exchange for bribes, also occurred. Lack of public confidence in the judicial system led to incidents of vigilante justice, resulting in at least one death.

Even so, some improvements were evident including the deployment of state prosecutors to most courts outside the capital and the renovation and reconstruction of several court houses and detention facilities. UNMIL in particular has trained judicial and corrections personnel, improved judicial infrastructure, and subsidized the salaries of prosecutors and public defenders.

Prisons and detention centers nevertheless remain severely overcrowded and lack basic sanitation and health care for detainees. In 2007 hundreds of people were held in prolonged pretrial detention, including some children, who were held with adult detainees in violation of international standards. Of the some 1,000 individuals detained in Liberia's prisons at this writing, fewer than 50 had been duly tried and convicted of a crime. Insufficient numbers of and unprofessional conduct by corrections officers led to numerous jailbreaks and disturbances in prisons and detention facilities.

Harmful Traditional Practices

Serious abuses resulting from harmful traditional practices continued to occur in 2007, due in part to the absence or distrust of judicial authorities. These included the killing of alleged witches and "trials by ordeal," in which suspects are forced to swallow the poisonous sap of the local sassywood tree or endure burning or other forms of pain—their alleged guilt or innocence is determined by whether they survive. These local practices often involve extortion, extracting statements under torture, and other forms of physical and sexual assault. In February 2007 then-Minister of Justice Frances Johnson-Morris instructed all county attorneys to arrest and prosecute anyone caught engaging in "sassywood" ordeals, but the practice has continued.

Women's and Children's Rights

According to government figures there were some 1,000 recorded female rapes in 2007, up from 568 in 2006. The 2006 Rape Amendment Act, which imposes heavier penalties for the most serious cases, appeared not to reduce the incidence of rape, prompting calls by Liberian civil society and others to establish specialized police units and a dedicated rape court.

Poor working conditions and child labor on rubber plantations were reported in 2007. Substandard conditions within dozens of Liberian orphanages—including inadequate food, water, bedding, clothing, and heath care—continued, yet resulted in few closures by the Ministry of Health and Social Welfare.

Corruption

Corruption involving public monies has long been endemic, and is widely recognized as having contributed to Liberia's political instability and failure to provide the country's most vulnerable with basic services such as education, water, and health care.

Throughout 2007 the government and its international partners took concrete steps to reduce corruption and improve economic governance. President Johnson-Sirleaf had numerous senior government officials dismissed for corrupt practices, and some 7,000 "ghost workers" removed from the payroll. In addition, Liberia's attorney general brought charges for the embezzlement of several million dollars against two former high-ranking public officials, one of them Charles Gyude Bryant, the former chairman of the 2003-2005 National Transitional Government of Liberia.

The Governance and Economic Management Assistance Program (GEMAP), a three-year anti-corruption plan drafted and imposed by key donors as a condition for development aid, continued to make progress in economic governance despite resistance from some government officials. Meanwhile, in July Liberia became the 14th African country to join the Extractive Industries Transparency Initiative (EITI).

The Truth and Reconciliation Commission and Accountability

Since its creation in 2006 the Liberian Truth and Reconciliation Commission (TRC) has been plagued with leadership and operational problems including lack of transparency and proper process in hiring staff, awarding contracts, and other fiscal matters; lack of strategic leadership by the commissioners; and an inadequate workplan and budget. In January 2007 these problems led to the suspension of funds and grounding of operations, including public hearings scheduled to commence that month. In October, after a joint working group comprising members of the International Contact Group on Liberia and the TRC drew up a revised workplan and budget, approximately US$100,000 of pledged donor funds were released. However, at this writing the work of the commission remains extremely hindered by lack of funds and it remains unclear whether donor confidence will be fully restored.

The TRC is mandated to investigate gross human rights violations and economic crimes that occurred between January 1979 and October 14, 2003, and is empowered to recommend for prosecution the most serious abuses of human rights. For a variety or reasons including the 2006 surrender of former Liberian President Charles Taylor to the Special Court for Sierra Leone (where he is currently on trial for war crimes and crimes against humanity committed during Sierra Leone's armed conflict), debate was much reduced in 2007 within Liberian civil society and among Liberia's partners about the ongoing need to hold accountable perpetrators of war crimes and crimes against humanity committed during Liberia's wars. Yet questions remain about whether prosecutions should take place during or after the completion of the TRC's work; whether TRC commissioners would act on their power to recommend individuals for prosecution; and whether the Liberian judicial system would be able and willing to try these crimes.

Liberian Army

Since 2004 the United States has taken the lead in recruiting and training a new Liberian army of some 2,000 soldiers, all of whom will be vetted for past abuses. However, the exercise is running months behind schedule, and by late 2007 only 600 recruits had completed basic training. Local human rights groups expressed concern that excessive expenditures on army barracks and equipment may be occurring at the expense of civic and human rights education for recruits.

Disarmament of Former Combatants

Since the end of the war in 2003, 101,000 former combatants have been disarmed. All but 9,000 have received vocational training or education but most remain unemployed. During 2007 disgruntled ex-combatants staged several demonstrations protesting inadequate reintegration opportunities. Fears about the potential risks posed by unemployed ex-combatants were raised in July when two former commanders were arrested and charged with planning to destabilize the government.

Key International Actors

Throughout 2007 the top priorities of Liberia's international partners were the creation of mechanisms to fight corruption and ensure proper management of Liberia's natural resources. Donors are also helping to rebuild Liberia's judicial system and strengthen the rule of law.

The United States, Liberia's leading bilateral donor, committed $252 million for 2006-2007 to support democratization, security, and reconstruction efforts. In February 2007 the US announced the cancellation of $391 million in bilateral debt under the Heavily Indebted Poor Countries Initiative.

Since the end of the armed conflict, Liberia's government has also received support from the European Commission including almost €100 million for peace support operations and post-conflict rehabilitation and institution building. China is also increasingly involved in Liberia's development and reconstruction.

In April 2007 the UN Security Council voted unanimously to lift a ban on Liberian diamond exports. The ban, imposed in 2001, was intended to prevent the export of "conflict diamonds" whose proceeds were fuelling the civil war. In May 2007 Liberia was admitted to the Kimberly Process Certification Scheme and in September the first consignment of diamonds was shipped abroad. UN and European Union arms and travel bans on associates of former President Charles Taylor, and an asset freeze against Taylor and his top officials, remain in place.

NIGERIA

Widespread government corruption, political and intercommunal violence, police torture and other abuses continue to deny ordinary Nigerians their basic human rights. During 2007 Nigerian government actors including the police, military, and elected officials committed serious and persistent abuses against Nigerian citizens with near-complete impunity. Hopes for improvement in the human rights situation were dashed when the April 2007 presidential and parliamentary elections were marred by fraud, violence, and intimidation so pervasive as to destroy all confidence in the results. The declared victors were Umaru Yar'Adua as president, and the ruling People's Democratic Party with a landslide parliamentary majority.

The violence and fraud surrounding elections reflected entrenched patterns of corruption and human rights abuse that have long pervaded Nigeria's political system. The country has earned well over US$223 billion in oil revenues since the end of military rule in 1999, but millions of Nigerians still lack access to basic health and education services because so much of the money has been lost to corruption and mismanagement. A process of electoral reform embarked upon in 2007 shows signs of promise but cannot succeed unless underlying patterns of impunity and criminality in the political system are addressed.

Rule of Law and Impunity

Politically powerful individuals and members of Nigeria's security forces who stand accused of serious human rights abuses and other crimes are seldom held to account. Numerous powerful ruling party politicians have been implicated in mobilizing armed gangs responsible for election-related violence and also in orchestrating the open rigging of the 2007 elections, but no investigation has been undertaken. Nor have federal authorities taken any action to ensure accountability for past atrocities such as the Nigerian military's complete destruction of the Bayelsa state town of Odi in 1999 or its massacre of several hundred civilians in Benue state in 2001.

Nigeria's judiciary has won widespread respect for its increasing independence, ruling against the government in numerous politically-charged cases related to the elections. But all too often the federal government has impeded rather than supported those efforts. The judiciary itself is flawed, especially the criminal justice system: magistrates and judges routinely accept confessions extracted under torture and allow spells of extended pretrial detention that may last for months or even years.

Law enforcement agencies have also subverted the rule of law. Police openly and routinely torture criminal suspects and others, and have killed more than 8,000 Nigerians in the past eight years; the police carried out 785 largely unexplained killings of alleged "armed robbers" during the current inspector general's first 90 days in office in 2007. At the same time, police have refused to investigate prominent politicians implicated in political violence and other human rights abuses.

Intercommunal and Political Violence

While large-scale massacres like those in Kaduna in 2002 and Yelwa in 2004 did not occur in 2007, intercommunal violence remained common. Since the end of military rule, more than 11,000 Nigerians have died in over 500 violent sectarian and political clashes. The underlying causes of this strife are varied and complex, since the ethnic, religious, and other tensions that provoke it often overlap with and exacerbate one another. Many government policies discriminate against individuals not deemed to be ethnic "indigenes" (descendants of the original inhabitants) of their communities and this has made issues of local citizenship increasingly contentious. Many Nigerians believe the government's failure to combat the nation's grinding poverty lies at the heart of many conflicts that appear to be ethnic or religious in nature, as competition for scarce economic resources becomes increasingly desperate.

Security forces have generally failed to prevent or suppress political violence, most notably before and during the April elections, a period that witnessed well over 100 incidents of election-related violence that left some 300 people dead. When voters were driven away from polling areas by gangs of thugs employed by politicians, the police very often turned a blind eye.

NIGERIA

Criminal Politics

Violence, "Godfathers" and Corruption in Nigeria

HUMAN
RIGHTS
WATCH

Conflict and Poverty in the Niger Delta

Nigeria's oil-rich Niger Delta has become increasingly militarized and insecure. Scores of civilians were murdered by armed gangs and security forces in 2007, and the violence further impeded the impoverished region's development. Numerous armed groups have risen to prominence in the Delta. Many of these groups claim to be fighting for greater local control of the region's oil wealth, while simultaneously engaging in various forms of violent criminal activity including the kidnapping for ransom of more than 200 expatriate oil workers and a handful of locally prominent Nigerians.

Much of the insecurity that plagues the Delta is directly related to failures of governance at all levels. Despite massive budget increases due to rising oil prices, federal, state, and local governments have made no effective effort to address the grinding poverty and environmental degradation that lies at the heart of political discontent in the region. Instead, many regional political figures have been directly implicated in sponsoring and arming militia groups that have carried out violent abuses.

After the April elections, fighting between armed gangs linked to prominent Rivers state politicians engulfed the state capital Port Harcourt, claiming dozens of civilian lives. A military intervention in August resulted in more civilian deaths. Politicians whose gangs rigged the elections in 2003 and 2007, laying the foundation for the crisis, have not been held to account.

Human Rights Concerns in the Context of Sharia

Since 2000, Sharia (Islamic law) courts have had jurisdiction over criminal cases in 12 of Nigeria's 36 states. Sharia has provisions for sentences that amount to cruel, inhuman, and degrading treatment, including death sentences, amputations, and floggings. Although capital sentences have been thrown out on appeal or simply not carried out, Sharia courts continue to hand down death sentences.

Many trials in Sharia courts fail to conform to international standards and do not respect due process even as defined by Sharia legislation: defendants rarely have access to a lawyer, are not informed about their rights, and judges are often poorly trained. The manner in which Sharia is applied discriminates against women,

NIGERIA

Chop Fine

The Human Rights Impact of Local Government Corruption and Mismanagement in Rivers State, Nigeria

HUMAN RIGHTS WATCH

particularly in adultery cases where standards of evidence differ based on the sex of the accused. State governments in northern Nigeria have continued to enforce oppressive Sharia laws targeting gay and lesbian Nigerians. In August, 18 men were arrested under suspicion of participating in a "gay wedding" ceremony in Bauchi state. The federal government has abandoned its obligation to combat such discriminatory laws, and backed repressive anti-gay legislation of its own in early 2007, though this has not been passed.

Freedom of Expression and Attacks on Civil Society

Nigerian civil society and the country's independent press are generally free to criticize the federal government and its policies, and a vibrant public debate exists around such issues. However, many local media outlets enjoy considerably less freedom than their national counterparts, and some have been subjected to intimidation or harassment by state and local authorities. In June 2007 authorities in the Federal Capital Territory demolished the new offices of Africa Independent Television (AIT), a move that was widely seen as a reprisal for AIT's critical coverage of the 2007 elections and of former President Olusegun Obasanjo's failed bid to secure a third term in office. In March prominent human rights campaigner Anyakwee Nsirmovu, director of the Institute for Human Rights and Humanitarian Law in Port Harcourt, received death threats and was attacked by a gang of armed men. The assault and threats were likely a reprisal for his outspoken criticism of corrupt state and local government officials in Rivers state.

Key International Actors

Because of Nigeria's political significance and its status as a major oil producer, key governments—notably the United Kingdom and the United States—and organizations such as the African Union and the Commonwealth have been unwilling to exert meaningful pressure on Nigeria over its human rights record. Observer missions fielded by the European Union and various US-backed organizations issued reports that were highly critical at the conduct of the April 2007 polls. But beyond this, none of Nigeria's foreign partners has strongly condemned the ongoing patterns of corruption and abuse put on display then. Nor have international partners demanded meaningful human rights improvements from the new government.

Multinational oil companies operating in the Niger Delta have been central, if often unwilling participants in the region's conflicts and dysfunctional political dynamics. The companies have largely failed to meet their basic responsibilities toward the communities impacted by their operations. They have done little to prevent human rights abuses committed by security forces assigned to protect their operations, and

have not done enough to curb environmentally harmful gas flares and oil spills caused by ageing and poorly-maintained infrastructure.

RWANDA

The Rwandan government continues to struggle with the consequences of the genocide that killed about three-quarters of the Tutsi population in 1994.

In 2001, Rwanda established a system of community-based *gacaca* courts to try all but the most egregious genocide-related crimes. In many jurisdictions faulty judicial performance undermined trust in the system. As the number of persons accused of genocide soared to 818,000, the government in March 2007 reformed the *gacaca* jurisdictions for the third time, seeking to expedite the trials.

In 2006 and 2007 several survivors of the genocide and judges involved in *gacaca* jurisdictions were murdered, and others suffered property damage. Officials began holding local residents collectively responsible for alleged offenses against survivors, arbitrarily imposing fines and even beating people in communities where survivors had been harassed.

Police officers killed at least 20 detainees since late 2006, claiming they were trying to escape. Asked to explain the deaths, a police official said the detainees—even those charged with ordinary crimes like theft of electrical cable—had shown "genocidal ideology."

Rwanda's prison population reached a high of 97,000 in July 2007, before authorities released some 20,000 people. In Kigali city officials reopened an irregular detention facility, closed in 2006, where children, women, and others rounded up by police are again being kept in harsh conditions.

Officials forced one human rights group to change its name and mandate in order to obtain legal recognition and repeatedly harassed journalists critical of the government. In February 2007 a journalist was severely beaten by assailants and another fled the country.

After a UN Development Program study documented growing inequality beneath Rwanda's apparently successful economic development, the government denounced the research and publicly criticized its authors. Meanwhile, farmers in at least one district had crops uprooted when they refused to follow a new policy on land use.

Extrajudicial Executions, Collective Punishment, and Arbitrary Detention

By mid-2007 Rwanda National Police officers had killed at least 20 detainees in apparent extrajudicial executions. The frequency of such killings began to increase in late 2006, following publicity surrounding the killings of several genocide survivors and others involved in the *gacaca* jurisdictions.

Faced with demands for increased protection of survivors, officials ordered collective punishments, including beatings and fines, for persons living in neighborhoods where survivors and others involved in *gacaca* had suffered property loss or damage. Those punished were not tried but were held responsible for the alleged offenses merely because they lived in the vicinity.

In 2006 Kigali city officials closed an irregular detention center after Human Rights Watch reported that people were being detained there in harsh conditions, without legal procedure, sometimes for months at a time. However, early in 2007 officials reopened the facility, again detaining scores of children and others picked up from city streets.

Gacaca Jurisdictions

The *gacaca* law was amended in May 2007 to increase the number of *gacaca* courts in order to speed trials of an estimated 818,000 persons accused of genocide. The law also changed the categorization of crimes, so that more suspects will be referred to *gacaca* jurisdictions, rather than to conventional courts. Previously *gacaca* courts could impose no sentence longer than 30 years but the amended law authorizes them to impose life imprisonment. As before, accused persons have no right to counsel in *gacaca* jurisdictions. The amended law also provides for suspended sentences and for more use of community service as an alternative to incarceration.

By October some 47,000 persons were sentenced to community service and some 10,000 were carrying it out, including breaking rocks for road construction or terracing agricultural land. At this writing authorities continue to insist that *gacaca* courts would finish trials by early 2008, although tens of thousands of cases remain outstanding in late 2007.

Popular trust in *gacaca* appears to have declined as numerous cases of faulty procedure, judicial corruption, and false accusations became known. In August, a *gacaca* appeals court upheld the 19-year prison sentence of human rights activist Francois-Xavier Byuma, even though his original trial was marred by grave procedural errors. The trial judge was known to have a prior conflict with Byuma but had refused to recuse himself, as law required and Byuma requested. Byuma, head of an association for the defense of childrens' rights, had previously investigated allegations that the judge had raped a minor. The judge also failed to accord Byuma the right to defend himself fully.

Justice

In a prominent trail known as "the media case", the appeals court of the International Criminal Tribunal for Rwanda (ICTR)—the international court trying genocide and other crimes committed in 1994—upheld in part the conviction of Jean-Bosco Barayagwiza, Ferdinand Nahimana, and Hassan Ngeze for inciting genocide, but reduced Baragwiza's sentence by three years and the sentence of the others, from life to 30 years and 35 years in prison respectively. The ICTR is due to end trials in 2008 but several cases will likely not be heard before the deadline and may be transferred to national jurisdictions. In November 2007 the ICTR transferred two cases to French courts for trial. In an effort to assure that cases would be transferred to its courts, Rwanda created special prison facilities and assured the ICTR judges that fair trials would be held.

In July Rwanda abolished the death penalty, a requirement for Rwandan courts to receive cases from jurisdictions that prohibit it, including the ICTR. Death sentences were commuted to life imprisonment; persons convicted of genocide, like others found guilty of particularly brutal crimes, may be sentenced to serve their terms in solitary confinement.

In April President Paul Kagame pardoned former president Pasteur Bizimungu, imprisoned for 15 years on charges of forming a criminal association and inciting rebellion after he attempted to form a political party to rival the dominant

Rwandan Patriotic Front. Former minister Charles Ntakirutinka, imprisoned for 10 years on the same charges, remained in jail. The two were detained for two years before being convicted in April 2004 in a trial that fell short of international standards.

Human Rights Defenders and Journalists

Mindful of harsh official repression in 2004, most human rights organizations practiced some measure of self-censorship, but the League for the Defense of Human Rights of the Great Lakes (LDGL) spoke out on some sensitive issues, including the police shooting of detainees. It also criticized the lack of civil society participation in the African Peer Review Mechanism (APRM) process that evaluates political space for opposition and civil society.

Officials had previously refused to recognize the Community of Indigenous Peoples in Rwanda (CAURWA), which defends the rights of the Batwa minority (some 30,000 people), claiming its name and purpose were "divisionist" and therefore illegal. After the African Peer Review experts criticized Rwanda's hostility to diversity among its citizens, the government accorded legal status to the organization, but only after it changed its name. The group no longer refers to its members as "indigenous people" but as potters, because many Batwa are, or used to be, potters.

Officials repeatedly chastised journalists for irresponsible reporting and in September 2007 one minister suggested in a televised debate that several of them were colluding with regional rebel groups. President Kagame regularly held press conferences but sometimes responded angrily to probing questions. In February, shortly after journalist Jean-Bosco Gasasira raised harassment of the press by intelligence agents in one such press conference, assailants attacked and beat him with iron bars. A suspect in the attack has been linked with senior military intelligence officials. He has not been brought to trial.

Throughout the year journalists were interrogated, detained without charge for several days or dismissed from their jobs after criticizing the government. In October high-ranking civilian and police officials twice warned journalists that they faced serious consequences if press criticism were to continue. One journalist feared for his life and left the country.

Recruitment of Child Soldiers in Rwanda

In early 2007 Congolese Tutsi refugees, some of them children, were recruited in refugee camps in Rwanda and taken for military service in the forces of rebel general Laurent Nkunda, fighting against the Congolese government. Rwandan authorities at first denied all knowledge of the recruitment but later agreed to a UNHCR proposal to curb such activity.

Growing Inequality and Land-Related Abuses

The United Nations Development Program (UNDP) reported that Rwandan economic growth, praised by the international community, was promoting large, growing, and potentially destabilizing inequalities between classes, regions, and between men and women. The cabinet angrily forced the minister who had approved the report to disavow it. Government employees involved in producing the report were sanctioned and one of its Rwandan authors was denounced publicly by an official.

Officials began implementing a new land policy that, among other measures, requires farmers to plant a single crop designated for their region. In Musanze District an RPF leader who headed the local cooperative obliged farmers to uproot crops to plant potatoes. The farmers then had to sell the potatoes to the cooperative at a price they judged unfair.

Key International Actors

Donors, generally satisfied with Rwanda's apparent economic growth and less aggressive stance in the DRC, said little publically about Rwanda's human rights performance. But several, including the United States and the United Kingdom, which are major supporters, intervened privately on at least two occasions to protest police killings of detainees and to inquire about increased killings of survivors and others. No further killings by police have been reported since their intervention. Belgium, a major donor to *gacaca* jurisdictions, and the UK also raised questions about several blatantly unfair *gacaca* cases. The European Union acknowledged that criticisms of *gacaca* were justified and expressed concern about the proposed hasty completion of trials.

Sierra Leone

Sierra Leone is making some political progress as the country begins to put behind it the legacy of the 11-year civil war that ended in 2002, but still faces fundamental challenges to ensuring the consolidation of respect for human rights. Despite hundreds of millions of dollars of development aid, rampant corruption and gross public financial mismanagement persist, along with major deficiencies in the justice system.

Democratic Processes

The presidential and parliamentary elections held on August 11, 2007 were a crucial and largely successful recent test of stability. The ruling Sierra Leone People's Party (SLPP) lost the presidency and its majority in parliament, and new president, Ernest Bai Koroma of the All People's Congress (APC), assumed power on September 17. The ousting of the ruling party was widely viewed as a success for democracy and as a referendum on the government's failure to deliver on postwar reconstruction.

Pre- and post-election violence between rival parties—including house burnings and street clashes—left at least one person dead and dozens injured. However, both domestic and international observers agreed that the polls themselves were generally free, fair, genuinely contested, and well organized. The National Electoral Commission was deemed competent, neutral, and independent. The police and army—once seen as organs of the ruling party—acted professionally to quell violence generated by all sides.

Legal Protection

The government has taken various steps to improve legal protection. During 2007, for example, four important bills were passed by parliament aimed at ensuring greater legal protection for women and children. The National Child Rights Bill, passed in June, prohibits early marriage, military conscription of children, and child trafficking. Three other bills—the Registration of Customary Marriages and Divorce Act, the Domestic Violence Act, and the Devolution of Estates Act—create a legal framework criminalizing domestic violence, ensuring women's property rights, setting the minimum age for customary marriage at 18, requiring such marriages have the consent of both parties, and recognizing rights to inheritance without interference from extended family.

Corruption

Public and private corruption remains a major obstacle to development. The Anti-Corruption Commission (ACC) established in 2000 largely at the behest of donors, refers cases for prosecution to the president-appointed attorney general. So far it has referred only low-level cases for prosecution. As in previous years, 2007 saw few convictions, and none involving high level government officials. A UK assessment of the ACC found that it had "little or no impact" on corruption, and as a result withdrew its financial support for it.

Efforts to Establish the Rule of Law

Defects in the judicial system persist, including extortion and bribe-taking by court officials; insufficient numbers of judges, magistrates, and prosecuting attorneys; little representation for the accused; absenteeism by court personnel; inadequate remuneration for judiciary personnel; and extended periods of pre-trial detention. In 2007 some 90 percent of prisoners lacked any legal representation during their trials.

On November 1, three men arrested in January 2006 on treason charges, including former Revolutionary United Front (RUF) Spokesman Omrie Golley, were released from prison for lack of evidence after 22 months in custody. The move followed a commitment by newly elected President Koroma to conduct a review of all detainees held on politically motivated charges. The trial of the three men was marked by a failure to respect basic legal norms, including the alleged fabrication of evidence and the lack of an arrest warrant.

At this writing, 20 individuals, including one woman, remain on death row, 10 of whom following a December 2004 conviction for treason in connection with a 2003 coup attempt; their case is under appeal.

The only legal system accessible to some 70 percent of the population is a network of "customary" courts controlled by traditional leaders and applying customary law, which is often discriminatory, particularly against women. Local court officials frequently abuse their powers by illegally detaining persons and charging high fines for minor offenses, as well as by adjudicating criminal cases beyond their jurisdiction.

Police and Army Conduct

The Sierra Leone police continue to engage in unprofessional and often illegal conduct, despite a Commonwealth-run training program from 1998 to 2005, and current efforts by the British government and the United Nations. This has included widespread extortion from civilians, requiring victims of crimes to pay the police to file reports or conduct investigations, and, in a few cases, sexual abuse of female detainees.

Since 1999, the UK-led International Military Advisory and Training Team (IMATT) has been working to reform the Republic of Sierra Leone Armed Forces (RSLAF). In 2007, there were a few reports of abuses and indiscipline by members of the army, but the RSLAF leadership demonstrated their commitment to penalize and sanction soldiers for offenses committed.

Detention Conditions

Numerous prisoners, including several children, are held in extended pre-trial detention. At least 16 people died in detention in 2007, a consequence of the overcrowding and lack of adequate food, clothing, medicine, hygiene, and sanitation in Sierra Leone's prisons. In August, then-President Kabbah ordered the release of 50 prisoners convicted on minor offences in an effort to relieve overcrowding, but the population of the country's largest detention facility, designed for 350 detainees, still stands at over 1,000.

Truth and Reconciliation Commission

The 2005 report of Sierra Leone's Truth and Reconciliation Commission (TRC) attributed the civil war largely to decades of corrupt rule by the political elite and recommended abolishing the death penalty, repealing laws that criminalize seditious libel, increasing the transparency of the mining industry, improving good governance, and establishing a reparations fund for war victims. The government has either ignored or been slow to implement the recommendations, and openly rejected some of them, including the abolition of the death penalty.

National Human Rights Commission

In October 2006 parliament approved five commissioners to lead a National Human Rights Commission (NHRC), charged with investigating and reporting on human rights abuses and pushing for the implementation of the TRC recommendations. However, lack of government funding has undermined the ability of the NHRC to fully carry out its mandate.

Accountability for Past Abuses

The United Nations-mandated Special Court for Sierra Leone has made progress on achieving accountability for war crimes. The Special Court for Sierra Leone, established after the war to bring justice to victims of atrocities, handed down its first five judgments in 2007. In June, three members of the rebel Armed Forces Revolutionary Council (AFRC) were convicted for, among other things, the recruitment and use of child soldiers, the first such conviction by an international tribunal. The judge noted that the three—Alex Tamba Brima, Brima Bazzy Kamara, and Santigie Borbor Kanu—were "responsible for some of the most heinous, brutal, and atrocious crimes ever recorded in human history." In August, two members of the Sierra Leonean Civil Defense Forces (CDF) were convicted of war crimes including murder and pillage. A third CDF indictee, former interior minister Sam Hinga Norman, died in custody in February.

The trial of former Liberian president Charles Taylor—charged with 11 counts of war crimes and crimes against humanity for supporting Sierra Leonean rebel groups—started in June 2007, but was postponed after Taylor boycotted the trial and dismissed his lawyers. Taylor was appointed new counsel and the trial is expected to resume in January 2008. For security reasons it will take place at The Hague.

While several states, including the UK, US, the Netherlands, and Canada, made additional contributions to the Special Court for Sierra Leone, which relies primarily on voluntary funding, the court continued to suffer from serious financial shortfalls.

Key International Actors

Sierra Leone's key international partners, in particular the UK, have been playing an important role in supporting the transition to democracy and the rule of law, but have seldom publicly denounced government corruption and other problems. In September, the Executive Representative of the UN Secretary General, the UK and Nigerian High Commissioners, and the US Ambassador pressured the then-ruling SLPP to concede after it sought an injunction to restrain the National Electoral Commission from releasing the results of the second round of voting in the presidential election.

Since 2002, international donors have provided millions of dollars in assistance to Sierra Leone. In 2006, the government agreed to benchmarks for reducing corruption, but still refuses to publish audited accounts of government spending.

Following the complete withdrawal of UN peacekeepers in December 2005, the UN Security Council approved a peacebuilding mission—the UN Integrated Office for Sierra Leone (UNIOSL)—to address weak governance and rule of law. Sierra Leone is on the agenda of the UN Peacebuilding Commission, created in December 2005 to bridge the gap between peacekeeping and the consolidation of peace.

SOMALIA

2007 was a bleak and turbulent year for Somali civilians, particularly in the volatile south-central region of the country, following the December 2006 invasion by Ethiopian forces in support of the Transitional Federal Government (TFG), which ousted the Islamic Courts Union (ICU) from Mogadishu. The TFG was formed in 2004 following extensive negotiations between Somali factions and clans mediated by the Inter-Governmental Authority on Development (IGAD) in Kenya. Before the government was able to impose its authority in Somalia, in 2006 the Islamic Courts emerged as a powerful political force in Mogadishu and surrounding areas, disarming warlords and bringing about unprecedented local stability. Their emergence threatened the existence of the TFG, and their links with Eritrea and Ethiopian opposition groups triggered Ethiopian military intervention.

Since January 2007, Ethiopian forces deployed in Mogadishu have become increasingly embroiled in a violent counter-insurgency campaign. In one of the world's most ignored human rights and humanitarian crises, residents of Mogadishu have been indiscriminately attacked by all of the warring parties, leaving hundreds dead and more than 500,000 displaced according to UN estimates. Escalating attacks on Ethiopian and TFG forces precipitated a massive Ethiopian bombardment of residential neighborhoods in the capital in March and April 2007 that failed to quell the insurgency, but took a heavy toll on civilians. As part of the crackdown, Ethiopian and TFG forces also harassed and arbitrarily detained civilians. Tens of thousands of people suffered widespread looting, sexual violence, and lack of access to humanitarian relief while fleeing the clashes in Mogadishu, which escalated again in November and show no sign of abating.

The violence and lawlessness of Mogadishu is extending to other regions. The southern port town of Kismayo remains in the hands of clan militias opposed to the TFG. Another port town, Merka, located 100 kilometers south of Mogadishu, witnessed growing fighting in October between two rival groups affiliated to the TFG. Two formerly peaceful regions, Somaliland and Puntland, clashed over Las Anod, a town on the border which is claimed by both regions. Puntland is reportedly regrouping after Somaliland forces took the town on October 15.

But Mogadishu remains the focal point for the country's seemingly endless cycle of violence. There, representatives of the media and civil society are increasingly under threat from all the warring parties, particularly the TFG, which has repeatedly tried to suppress independent reporting of events in Mogadishu.

Violations of International Humanitarian Law in Mogadishu

Since January 2007, a coalition of insurgent groups including the extremist Al-Shabaab militia has waged almost daily attacks on Ethiopian and TFG forces, including several suicide bombings, and killed TFG civilian officials. In March, members of the insurgency summarily executed and mutilated the bodies of several captured TFG soldiers. Hit and run attacks by insurgency forces using remotely detonated roadside devices, small arms, and heavy weaponry have also killed and injured many civilians. The insurgency has repeatedly launched mortar attacks from urban neighborhoods, further jeopardizing civilian security.

The Ethiopian and Somali government have responded to the insurgency by besieging entire neighborhoods with heavy weaponry and conducting mass arrests and detentions. Ethiopian forces launched two major offensives on large areas of Mogadishu in March and April 2007. Densely populated neighborhoods perceived to be insurgent strongholds were indiscriminately bombarded with "Katyusha" rockets, artillery, and mortar fire, with no apparent effort to distinguish between insurgents and civilians. On several occasions Ethiopian troops have occupied hospitals, looting them of desperately needed medical equipment.

The Ethiopian military was mainly responsible for the bombardment and civilian casualties in March and April, but TFG officials failed to provide effective warnings to civilians in combat zones and also looted property, impeded relief efforts for displaced people, and mistreated dozens of people detained in mass arrests.

Many of those arrested have been transferred to known and secret detention centers where they are held without charge for long periods. The Ethiopian and TFG forces have not disclosed the number of people detained—believed to be in the hundreds—or their whereabouts. Although dozens of people were released in late June 2007 after the TFG offered an amnesty, hundreds more have been detained since then and many people have disappeared.

The ongoing mayhem has crippled the economy. Tens of thousands of displaced people remain in desperate circumstances without sufficient food, water, or medical supplies, and have become easy prey to extortion and abuse by the warring parties and by other armed groups outside the capital.

Threats to Freedom of Expression

The environment for journalists and independent media outlets in Mogadishu, already difficult under the Islamic Courts Union, worsened dramatically with the intensifying conflict. The TFG repeatedly closed major independent media outlets such as Shabelle Media Network, HornAfrik, and other smaller radio stations serving Mogadishu, claiming the broadcasts incited violence. Several journalists were detained for long periods without charge, apparently in an effort to suppress independent reporting.

At least eight journalists were killed in the course of the year, making it the most dangerous year for Somali journalism since 1991. On the morning of August 11, Mahad Ahmed Elmi, a talk show host with HornAfrik radio, was shot in the head by two men armed with pistols. Just a few hours later, Ali Iman Sharmake, one of the owners of HornAfrik, was killed in a roadside explosion as he returned from his colleague's funeral. On October 19, the acting manager of Shabelle Media Network, Bashir Nur Gedi, was shot dead at close range outside a cafe in Mogadishu. Several high profile journalists from Shabelle Media Network and HornAfrik fled the country after the killings.

Threats to the media continued with a series of brief detentions of journalists and raids on local radio stations. On September 16, Somali government troops fired on the Shabelle Media compound and briefly detained 16 staff members, alleging that a grenade was thrown from the building, which Shabelle vehemently denied. The following day, government troops besieged the station with gunfire, allegedly injuring one staff member slightly and damaging equipment. Shabelle radio was closed for two weeks and returned to the air on October 2, after government troops withdrew from the area. On November 12, TFG forces again closed Shabelle radio without any explanation.

Attacks on Human Rights Defenders and Civil Society

Human rights defenders and members of civil society organizations also came
under increasing attack in 2007. On March 14, Isse Abdi Isse, a founder of KISIMA,
a non-governmental organization based in Kismayo, was shot dead at close range
in Mogadishu by unknown assailants.

In September, a well-known lecturer at the Somali Institute of Management and
Administration Development, Professor Mohammed Ahmed Hussein, was gunned
down as he walked through Mogadishu's central Bakara market. Professor
Hussein had played a significant role in reviving higher education in the city following the collapse of public services in the early 1990s.

On June 18, TFG and Ethiopian troops raided the offices of SAACID-Somalia, one
of the largest nongovernmental organizations in the south-central region. Several
SAACID staff members, including the director, were arrested and briefly detained.
The soldiers smashed doors and windows, destroyed office equipment, and confiscated property.

On August 18, TFG officials raided the office of the Somali Red Crescent in Bal'ad
town, 30 kilometers north of Mogadishu, temporarily closing the office and
detaining a staff member. The staff member was released and the office reopened
two days later.

In October the TFG ordered the closing of one of Somalia's oldest human rights
organizations, Elman Human Rights, citing "security reasons."

Key International Actors

Somalia's internal crisis is exacerbated both by the ongoing tension between
Eritrea and Ethiopia, and by US counterterrorism initiatives in the region. The failure to resolve Ethiopian-Eritrean tension has led to each country supporting
opposing sides in Somalia: Ethiopia, backed by the US, supports the weak, but
internationally-recognized TFG, while supporters of the ICU reportedly rely on substantial military and financial support from Eritrea.

SOMALIA

Shell-Shocked

Civilians Under Siege in Mogadishu

H U M A N
R I G H T S
W A T C H

US policy on Somalia is dominated by counterterrorism concerns, including the presence in Mogadishu of several allegedly high-level suspects wanted for involvement in the 1998 US embassy bombings in Kenya and Tanzania. US backing for Ethiopia's December 2006 offensive became obvious when US aircraft launched several airstrikes in southeastern Somalia in January 2007 and again in Puntland in June 2007. US intelligence agents also participated in interrogations of some of the dozens of people rendered from Kenya and Somalia to Ethiopia in early 2007 (see Ethiopia chapter).

While most key government and international institutions ignored or downplayed the serious crimes committed in Mogadishu in 2007, some policymakers have recognized the urgent need to replace the Ethiopian forces with a neutral force. The African Union sent 1,500 Ugandan troops to Somalia in March as part of a proposed 8,000-member African Union mission known as AMISOM. However, by year's end the force remained at only 1,700 members, with most African states reluctant to provide further forces in the volatile context.

On August 20, the United Nations Security Council voted to extend the AMISOM Mission in Somalia by six months and approved contingency planning for a possible UN takeover of the mission. However, few observers anticipate that a UN mission will materialize in the short term.

SOUTH AFRICA

Emerging from a history of institutionalized racial inequality, South Africa has made admirable progress in transforming the state and society to ensure respect for fundamental rights, including freedom of expression, an independent judiciary, and free and fair elections. Nevertheless, widespread poverty, unemployment, persistently high levels of violent crime, and gender inequality continue to inhibit the full enjoyment of human rights.

Poverty in South Africa has a strong rural dimension: the rural poor suffer from higher unemployment rates, lower educational attainment, and lower access to essential services. South Africa's Bill of Rights provides for binding and justiciable rights for all South Africans to education, housing, health care, food, water, and social security. A priority concern for the nongovernmental human rights sector in South Africa is to ensure that the government continues to address the progressive realization of socioeconomic rights and to hold the government accountable to fulfill these rights as binding obligations rather than programmatic aspirations.

Socioeconomic Rights

Under South Africa's constitution, every child has the right to basic education. Serious concerns persist regarding the quality of rural education: many farm schools are staffed by unqualified teachers, and lack resources and infrastructure. State schools are required to waive fees for families that are unable to afford them, yet some local administrators refuse to do so. This contributes to de facto discrimination against very poor children and those from families affected by HIV/AIDS, who may consequently be excluded from attending school.

South Africa has undertaken commendable housing and land initiatives, including national housing subsidy schemes. However, many people continue to live in poor conditions in informal settlements, without access to basic services. In 2007 urban evictions were carried out without due warning or provision for relocation or compensation. Commercial farm workers remain particularly vulnerable to eviction. In September the South African Human Rights Commission conducted public hearings to assess land tenure security for farm workers on commercial farms.

Access to public healthcare services and the quality of care provided remain inadequate, despite policy and legislation governing this sector. Many provincial hospitals in South Africa are dilapidated and lack sufficient trained staff, drugs, and supplies. In September Dr. Nokuzolo Ntshona, superintendant of Cecilia Makewane hospital in the Eastern Cape, was dismissed by the Eastern Cape Department of Health for "breaching protocol" after her investigation into, subsequent public criticism of, and letter to the president about appalling conditions and high infant mortality rates in Frere hospital. Her actions were followed by national media investigation and widespread publicity. The South African Medical Association affirmed that her whistleblowing about hospital conditions was an ethical and responsible intervention. South Africa's Protected Disclosures Act, 2000, is intended to protect whistleblowers from retaliation in both the public and private sectors.

Inequitable access to antiretroviral treatment (ART) and lack of support services for people with HIV/AIDS, particularly for prisoners and people in rural areas, remain inadequately addressed by the government. The majority of prisons are unauthorized to distribute ART on-site. In 2006, after a protracted legal struggle and a hunger strike by hundreds of HIV-positive inmates, Westville Prison authorities were ordered by a High Court judgment to provide HIV testing and ART to prisoners in need. The prison was subsequently accredited by the Department of Health as an ART distribution site.

Refugees and Migrants

Many asylum seekers in South Africa continue to encounter procedural obstacles and administrative delays throughout the refugee status determination process and face arbitrary arrest, detention, mistreatment, and extortion by immigration and police officers. In August 2007 South Africa's parliamentary committee on home affairs condemned conditions in the country's largest refugee reception centre, Marabastad, in Pretoria, reporting that the center was filthy, overcrowded, and understaffed. The government subsequently agreed to upgrade this center, and has recognized the need to address corruption and expedite the administrative process for asylum applications.

Political repression and the economic crisis in Zimbabwe continue to cause a significant number of Zimbabwean nationals to seek entry into South Africa. Officials at the Lindela repatriation centre, situated near a South Africa-Zimbabwe border post in Limpopo province, are detaining illegal immigrants in overcrowded detention facilities and deporting large numbers of Zimbabweans without screening for refugee status. South Africa's Department of Home Affairs maintains that most Zimbabweans entering South Africa are economic migrants and cannot be classified as refugees as they are not facing persecution in their own country. Human rights groups dispute this.

Large numbers of Zimbabwean and Mozambican migrants continue to seek seasonal work in South Africa's commercial agricultural sector. Although South Africa's employment law affords rights to foreign migrant workers, many farmers openly disregard the minimum wage, do not pay overtime, and make unlawful deductions from workers' wages. Undocumented migrants are also frequently harassed by police and immigration officials and are subject to assault and extortion during farm raids.

Women's Rights

Strong women's organizations in South Africa continue to challenge the patriarchal attitudes that persist in society and to pressure the government to address gender-based abuses and discrimination. At the 2007 Women's Parliament, South Africa's deputy president acknowledged the need for government to create partnerships with civil society to expedite the implementation of the country's progressive legislation.

Rape and other forms of gender-based violence continue to be under-reported and complaints often receive inadequate response by police officials. The government has established 52 specialized sexual offenses courts throughout the country, which have had relative success in improving conviction rates. In close proximity to these courts, the government has also established Thuthuzela Care Centers where survivors of rape are able to report the crime, access specialist investigators and prosecutors, and obtain medical care and counseling.

On May 22, Parliament passed the Sexual Offences and Related Matters Amendment Bill, which acknowledges the high incidence of sexual offenses committed in South Africa, broadens the definition of rape, and acknowledges the link between rape and HIV infection. The bill provides for victim-initiated compulsory HIV testing for rape perpetrators; compels test results to be made available to the victims; and entitles victims to receive, at state expense, post-exposure prophylaxis (PEP), a course of antiretroviral drugs that can reduce the risk of contracting HIV by up to 80 percent if taken within 72 hours of exposure. However, although the bill mandates designated public health facilities to provide rape survivors with PEP, it does not mention other treatment or counseling services and makes access to PEP dependent on the survivor laying criminal charges. Important recommendations by the South African Law Reform Commission that would have improved conviction rates by improving the court experiences of claimants have not been included in the bill.

Children's Rights

The Children's Act (2005) remains to be enacted, although certain parts of the Act came into effect in July 2007, including provisions that grant children from age 12 the right to access medical services for HIV testing and treatment and that allow children to acquire contraceptives without parental consent. The Act prohibits child trafficking, for which South Africa continues to be a source and destination country, and makes the UN Protocol to Prevent Trafficking in Persons applicable as part of South African law. Delays in passing the Act have been caused by parliamentary debate over the complementary Children's Amendment Bill (2007), which was passed on November 6 and is currently being reviewed by the National Council of Provinces. The bill scales up delivery of social welfare services for children, provides for well resourced strategies to facilitate child protection in instances of abuse and neglect, and provides greater integrated support to child-headed households, as determined by a vulnerability criterion.

Sexual violence, corporal punishment, bullying, gang-related activities, and occasional murders continue to occur in some South African schools. In September Parliament proposed that legislation to curb violence in schools be included in the Education Laws Amendment Bill, currently under consideration.

Lesbian, Gay, Bisexual, and Transgender Rights

Although South Africa's constitution outlaws discrimination based on sexual orientation, and same-sex marriage has been legalized, gay and lesbian people remain vulnerable. In 2007 a spate of homophobia-induced murders of lesbians prompted the South African Human Rights Commission to develop a program of action to combat escalating hate crimes and determine whether South Africa needs legislation in this regard. The commission recommended concerted action from the criminal justice system. Nongovernmental organizations have recommended that diversity sensitization should be part of a preventative curriculum in schools.

International Role

South Africa continues to play a prominent role in international affairs. It actively supported the establishment of the African Court on Human and Peoples' Rights, which began its first session in September 2007, and has been involved in conflict mediation in the DRC, Western Sahara, Côte d'Ivoire, and other countries. In March the Southern African Development Community mandated South Africa to mediate in the Zimbabwean crisis, where it has focused on encouraging dialogue between the Zimbabwean government and the main opposition party. South Africa continues to contribute to peacekeeping efforts in the DRC, Burundi, Sudan, and along the Ethiopian-Eritrean border.

South Africa's voting record during its first year as a non-permanent member of the United Nations Security Council has been criticized. In January it opposed a resolution condemning human rights abuses by the military junta in Burma, on the grounds that domestic human rights violations in Burma do not constitute a threat to international peace and security and, therefore, that the matter does not fall within Security Council jurisdiction. In the UN Human Rights Council South Africa has been criticized by Council members and the international media for attempting to block discussion of human rights abuses in Zimbabwe and for voting to end monitoring of rights abuses in Iran and Uzbekistan.

SUDAN

The dynamics of conflict in Darfur in western Sudan became increasingly complex during 2007 as militia and rebel factions proliferated. Peace talks in Libya towards the end of the year were hampered by key groups refusing to participate. Meanwhile, delays to the implementation of the Comprehensive Peace Agreement (CPA), signed in January 2005 to end 21 years of north-south conflict, threatened to derail the consolidation of peace in the south. The delays both result from and contribute to deteriorating relations between the two ruling parties, the National Congress Party (NCP) and the Sudan People's Liberation Movement (SPLM), prompting fears of renewed conflict in southern Sudan.

Abuses also occurred in other parts of the Sudan. Security forces killed and injured seven people involved in protests against two dam projects in northern Sudan, and injured and arrested many others. Restrictions on freedom of expression persist, along with arbitrary arrests and detention of journalists, activists and others.

The Conflict in Darfur

The proliferation of rebel groups, which clashed with each other as well as with government military and allied forces, not only challenged peace initiatives but also created an increasingly unpredictable situation on the ground for civilians, peacekeepers and humanitarian agencies. Throughout the year, parties on all sides of the conflict committed atrocities against civilians.

The Sudanese government played a central role in fomenting the chaos, both continuing to carry out direct attacks on civilians and failing to rein in or hold accountable individuals responsible for abuses. In July the government finally consented to the deployment of a joint African Union-United Nations "hybrid" peacekeeping force for Darfur. However, throughout the rest of the year progress towards deployment was dogged by Sudanese government obstruction, bureaucratic delays, and the slow pace of military contributions to the force.

The government made no genuine efforts to address the impunity with which abuses have been carried out. On April 27, 2007, the International Criminal

Court's (ICC) Pre-Trial Chamber issued arrest warrants for Sudan's state minister for humanitarian affairs Ahmed Haroun and the Janjaweed militia leader "Ali Kosheib." The Sudanese government publicly refused to cooperate with the ICC, and instead of handing Haroun over to the court, in September 2007 it appointed him co-chair of a committee authorized to respond to human rights complaints, including on Darfur. Kosheib, who had been arrested in connection with other crimes was, according to Sudan's Foreign Minister, released from custody in October.

In late 2006 the government renewed bombing, striking areas under rebel control in North Darfur on an almost daily basis. Government-backed militias also attacked the civilian population throughout Darfur, even in camps for internally displaced persons. Prior to peace talks in October 2007 there was once again an increase in violence, including major attacks on the towns of Haskanita and Muhajariya.

In May 2006 Sudan Liberation Army (SLA)-Minawi rebel leader Minni Minawi signed the Darfur Peace Agreement with the government and was subsequently appointed Special Assistant to the President, but residents of North Darfur increasingly complain about abuses carried out by his forces. These abuses—and clashes between rebel groups and SLA-Minawi fighters—caused thousands to flee from the Korma and Tawila areas of North Darfur to displaced persons camps. Since January 2007 fighting among Arab groups has also left more than 200 people dead and forced thousands more to flee. More than 250,000 civilians were newly displaced in the first nine months of 2007 alone, bringing the total displaced population in Darfur to more than 2.2 million.

While large scale attacks drive people into IDP camps, ongoing violence keeps them there. The camps themselves are becoming increasingly violent with no guarantee of safety. Sexual violence in particular continues to be a feature of everyday life for women and girls.

The African Union Mission to Sudan (AMIS) has also come under attack. On September 30, 2007 unidentified forces attacked an African Union base in Haskanita, South Darfur, killing 10 AMIS peacekeepers.

After almost five years of conflict, more than four million people—two thirds of the population of Darfur—depend on humanitarian assistance. However, humanitarian operations continue to be hampered by insecurity. The UN estimated that in June 2007 one in every six relief convoys that left provincial capitals was attacked, either by Janjaweed, rebels, or bandits. Twelve humanitarian workers were killed in the first nine months of 2007.

South Sudan and Political Reforms

Implementation of the CPA continues to fall behind schedule as key deadlines, such as the start of a national census and the establishment of the National Civil Service Commission, pass without progress.

The government's handling of the Darfur conflict is one source of contention between the NCP and the SPLM. The SPLM has become more involved in attempts to resolve the conflict and supports UN deployment to the region, contrary to the policy of the NCP. Other issues include the refusal of the NCP to make information available to enable the SPLM to calculate the oil revenue to which they were entitled; failure to withdraw Sudanese Armed Forces from southern Sudan by the agreed deadline of 9 July 2007; and ongoing disagreement over the status of the border area of Abyei. Matters came to a head in October 2007 when the SPLM suspended its participation in the Government of National Unity (GNU), highlighting the vulnerability of the CPA.

With national elections due in 2009, the development of a legislative framework to support them is well behind schedule. Several key pieces of legislation are yet to be tabled at the National Assembly, including the Elections Act as well as the National Land Commission and the National Security Act.

Security is essential to enable refugees and other displaced persons to return to their homes in southern Sudan. However, there has been only limited progress on disarmament and violent inter-tribal clashes left hundreds dead in 2007. In May 54 people were killed following clashes over cattle between Didinga and Toposa community members in Eastern Equatoria. In July 56 people were killed following violent inter-tribal clashes between Nuer and Murle in Jonglei State.

Merowe and Kajbar Dams

In northern Sudan the government moved forward with construction of two major dams in Merowe (also known as Hamadab) and Kajbar, despite protests from local communities and human rights campaigners. Currently scheduled to be completed in 2008, the Merowe dam is expected to displace more than 50,000 people, while Kajbar will affect more than 10,000.

In April 2006 security forces killed three people and injured and arrested dozens of others when community leaders organized a peaceful protest against the construction of Merowe dam. Local community protests against Kajbar dam were also violently dispersed by police and security in June 2007. Four people were killed at the scene and more than eight people were injured when security forces used tear gas and live ammunition to scatter the protesters.

Some journalists attempting to report on the dam protests were arrested without charge and allegedly tortured. In Dongola, capital of Northern State, four journalists and three lawyers, along with their driver were arrested on their way to the Kajbar dam site. More than ten more people were arrested in Khartoum and Dongola in the following days; all were later released.

Arbitrary Arrests and Detentions

There has been a notable increase in cases of arrest and incommunicado detention of journalists and political activists in Khartoum, often without charge. Articles 31 and 33 of Sudan's National Security Act allow for detention without charge for up to nine months, in violation of international standards.

In July 17 people were arrested in Khartoum on suspicion of plotting to overthrow the government. Most remain in detention without charge, including retired army generals and members of the Umma Party Reform and Renewal splinter group, including its leader Mubarak al-Mahdi.

Freedom of Expression and Human Rights Defenders

Journalists in Sudan use the term "red line" to describe issues they cannot report on for fear of reprisals by the government authorities. "Red line" issues include

Darfur, the ICC, and the July detention of the 17 alleged "coup plotters," including Mubarak al-Mahdi, leader of the Umma Party (Reform and Renewal). Newspapers risk confiscation of their publications or closure if they report on these issues, and journalists risk harassment and arrest.

Following passage of the Voluntary Work Act in 2006, several organizations, especially human rights groups, have been harassed and intimidated, for instance by being summoned to national security for questioning. Lengthy new registration procedures connected to the Voluntary Work Act have forced some to suspend their activities for months.

Key International Actors

In 2007 international efforts on Darfur focused mainly on the deployment of peacekeepers. In July the Sudanese government consented to the deployment of a new peacekeeping force for Darfur, and the UN Security Council passed resolution 1769 authorizing a "hybrid" AU-UN force of up to 26,000 troops and police. However, there was no sign that Sudan was prepared to change its policy of supporting the Janjaweed militia or its refusal to cooperate with the ICC. Resolution 1769 does not mention Sudan's obligation to turn over the two suspects wanted by the ICC.

The UN, EU, US, UK, and France have consistently decried the violence in Darfur. However, such condemnations have largely failed to translate into concrete political action. It is clear that the government of Sudan has consistently failed to fulfill its obligations under international law, including those imposed by various Security Council resolutions. It continues to carry out attacks on civilians, has failed to take action to reign in the Janjaweed militia, and has refused to cooperate with the ICC. However, to date, the United Nations has imposed targeted sanctions on only four low-level individuals, none of whom are senior government policymakers.

Draft language that would have threatened additional sanctions in the event of Sudanese government obstruction of UNAMID was deleted from resolution 1769 prior to its adoption, apparently at the insistence of China and other Council members. Divisions among Security Council members appear to make additional targeted sanctions unlikely.

On May 29, 2007, the United States unilaterally placed targeted economic sanctions on two Sudanese government officials, a rebel leader, 30 companies owned or controlled by the Sudanese government, and one company alleged to have violated the UN arms embargo on Darfur.

Although the European Union and individual EU leaders have also indicated willingness to adopt targeted sanctions, and have even threatened to do so, they have not done so as of yet. European contributions to peacekeeping in the region have mainly focused on the EU force in Chad (see Chad); offers of support to UNAMID from Scandinavian countries were rejected by the Sudanese government.

China continues to have an important partnership with the Sudanese government and is believed to have played a key role in influencing Khartoum to consent to the hybrid force. Sudan was among the African countries visited by Chinese President Hu Jintao on his first visit to the continent in February, and in May a new Chinese Special Envoy was appointed, with a special focus on Darfur.

In December 2007 the Human Rights Council is due to receive the final report of the Group of Experts on Darfur. Many of the recommendations compiled by the Group of Experts, which provide a framework of indicators that the Government of Sudan should account for, have not been implemented by the Sudanese authorities. In the same month the Human Rights Council is due to debate the future of the mandates of both the Group of Experts on Darfur and the Special Rapporteur on Sudan.

UGANDA

Throughout 2007, the impending Commonwealth Heads of Government Meeting (CHOGM) held in the Ugandan capital Kampala in November had the effect of a creating a particular context for government action on human rights. The government engaged in talks with the Lord's Resistance Army (LRA), which yielded relative peace in northern Uganda and hopes for an end to over 20 years of conflict. Attempts to make Kampala an international showcase, however, led officials to permit mass arrests of alleged vagrants and criminals. In a continuing effort to hobble the political opposition, security agents interfered with the judiciary as they had done in 2005 and used heavy-handed police tactics in dealing with demonstrations. Soldiers engaged in law enforcement operations in the northeastern region of Karamoja improved their performance after international criticism of human rights abuses, but nonetheless committed grave violations in 2007.

The War in Northern Uganda

Intermittent peace talks between the government of Uganda and the LRA in Juba, Sudan, which began in July 2006, continue at this writing, although reports of LRA leader Joseph Kony's murder or arrest of his second-in-command Vincent Otti cast an uncertain shadow over the talks' prospects at year's end.

The parties signed a significant agreement on "accountability and reconciliation" in June 2007. The agreement sets out a framework for justice, providing formal prosecution in Ugandan courts of those who "bear particular responsibility for the most serious crimes," and traditional justice mechanisms for as yet unspecified crimes in addition to trials.

The parties left the details of implementation to as yet undrafted protocols and then adjourned the talks for much of the rest of the year to permit national consultations on them. Warrants issued by the International Criminal Court (ICC) for four LRA leaders in 2005 remain an important step towards justice being done. The ICC's statute allows national trials of its cases where possible. However, judges of the ICC will have the final say in deciding whether national trials are an adequate alternative.

Relative peace held in northern Uganda, although the LRA reportedly engaged in raids into southern Sudan in early 2007. With improved security, the Ugandan government closed two internally displaced people's (IDP) camps. A relatively small number of the displaced returned home in the areas most affected by the conflict. A larger number moved to interim settlement sites that offer fewer services but allow easier access to farmland.

Access to justice for the civilian population in camps remains a serious problem. The government assigned greater numbers of civilian police in the north to encourage residents to return home, but most were junior police aides with only one month of training instead of the usual nine.

Disarmament in Karamoja

Soldiers of the national army continued to commit human rights violations during law enforcement operations in the impoverished Karamoja region, primarily in connection with a "cordon and search" disarmament campaign launched in May 2006.

Eyewitnesses told Human Rights Watch that between September 2006 and January 2007 soldiers fired on children, killing three; used armored personnel carriers to crush two homesteads; and, on several occasions, severely beat and arbitrarily detained men in military facilities to force them to reveal the location of weapons. Dozens of soldiers were also killed by Karamojong during armed confrontations or ambushes.

The government imposed stricter controls on its soldiers in late 2006 and early 2007, after which fewer military abuses were reported. Government officials claimed that soldiers had been held to account for past abuses, but provided few substantiating details.

Judicial Independence

In March 2007 security agents forced their way into a court building in an effort to prevent the release on bail of persons accused of supporting the rebel People's Redemption Army. The detainees—co-defendants of opposition Forum for

Democratic Change President Dr. Kizza Besigye—were bailed after a stand-off of several hours, but were re-arrested as they left the court and held on fresh charges of murder. The Uganda judiciary went on strike for a week to protest judicial interference and demonstrators took to the streets where they encountered extensive police deployment. It is the second time in as many years that security forces were used to derail judicial process in the case.

Freedom of Expression

In the first half of 2007, police used the supposed failure to obtain authorization to hold rallies as the pretext for breaking up demonstrations by opposition parties in Kampala and other towns, sometimes using tear gas against demonstrators. Police banned all rallies in Kampala's Constitutional Square and central business district.

On April 12, 2007, environmental activists joined parliamentarians and supporters of various opposition parties in demonstrating against government plans to permit an Indian-owned company to plant sugar in the Mabira Forest nature reserve. The organizers had obtained authorization but sought to depart from the prescribed route. When police prevented them from doing so, the demonstration turned violent and protestors set upon persons of Asian origin, beating one to death. Police shot in the air and used tear gas to end the demonstration.

In the following days, police detained demonstration organizers, including two members of parliament, on suspicion of inciting violence. Supporters of six opposition parties then marched from a joint press conference to the central police station where the detained parliamentarians were being held. In full view of security personnel who did not intervene, a group of men wielding identical sticks attacked the demonstrators. Police and security agencies subsequently disclaimed responsibility for the "stick brigade" as it was dubbed by the media, but President Museveni praised its actions. Police arrested other opposition activists during the following week, in some cases because they had joined other demonstrations.

Mass Detentions and Removals

On several occasions during 2007 police swept up alleged vagrants and criminals, predominantly Karamajong and non-Ugandan nationals. According to police comment in the press, cleaning up the city this way was meant to ready Kampala for the international visitors expected at the Commonwealth meeting.

Detained children were held in facilities meant for juvenile offenders and were, in some cases, separated from their adult caregivers. Some 700 persons, mostly women and children, were sent from Kampala to Karamoja in early 2007, in some cases suffering ill-treatment on the way. Some returned to their homes but others remained in resettlement sites without adequate food, shelter, and medical care.

In August 2007 the Rapid Response Unit of the Uganda Police Force (formerly the Violent Crimes Crack Unit, accused of torturing detainees by Human Rights Watch, the Uganda Human Rights Commission and others) detained forty-one persons, many of them non-Ugandan in origin, and held them in overcrowded cells for five days. There are reports that at least three detainees were tortured.

Government security personnel removed thousands of Rwandan nationals from Uganda in October 2007 in a sudden, unannounced operation.

Human Rights Defenders

Officials intimidate or otherwise seek to restrict free expression by activists supporting lesbian, gay, bisexual or transgender (LGBT) rights. In August 2007 activists, some wearing masks for fear of reprisals, organized a rare demonstration in support of LGBT rights in Kampala. Immediately afterwards, the ethics and integrity minister and deputy attorney general denounced LGBT people and called for the use of the criminal law against homosexuals. Also in August, the Uganda Broadcasting Council, a government regulatory body, suspended a radio presenter at Capital FM for interviewing a lesbian human rights activist, supposedly in violation of "minimum broadcasting standards." Meanwhile, officials took no action against the tabloid *Red Pepper* when it printed the first names, workplaces, and other identifying information of 39 allegedly homosexual men in September 2007.

In spite of generally high regard for the quality of its monitoring, the Uganda Human Rights Commission (UHRC), a government body, failed in 2007 to take a strong stand on human rights abuses during the Karamoja disarmament operations. The commission chaired two investigations of the abuses in August 2006 and April 2007, but no report was published of either one. An independent human rights expert who participated in the second investigation said publicly that it had been biased in favor of the government.

At least two Ugandan human rights organizations, as well as a coalition of other civil society groups, condemned the March court raid by security agents.

Key International Actors

In February 2007, sixteen diplomatic missions in Kampala joined together to encourage resumption of the stalled talks between the LRA and the Ugandan government, and a UN special envoy also helped keep the peace talks moving forward. UN and government actors, including the United States and United Kingdom, have stressed the need for justice in northern Uganda. But no government has arrested any of the four LRA leaders in implementation of the ICC warrants.

Visits by international partners to northern Uganda, as well as reports on abuses by the Uganda office of the UN High Commissioner for Human Rights, helped prompt government efforts to reduce abuses by soldiers.

Commonwealth leaders assembled in Kampala in November 2007 for their biennial summit studiously avoided public comment on their host's human rights record, even as police force was used to keep opposition supporters confined to a designated area outside of the city center.

ZIMBABWE

In 2007, Zimbabwe descended further into political and economic chaos as President Robert Mugabe's Zimbabwe African National Union—Patriotic Front (ZANU-PF) intensified its stranglehold on power. With annual inflation reaching 8,000 percent in September, life for ordinary Zimbabweans had become a struggle to meet basic needs. The government continues to severely restrict the political opposition, media, and nongovernmental organizations. Torture in police custody is common, as is the harassment and arrest of journalists and human rights defenders.

The arrest and brutal assault of over 50 opposition and civil society activists during a prayer meeting on March 11, 2007, marked yet another low point in the country's seven-year crisis. There has been renewed international concern, but continuing divisions and lack of decisive leadership from regional powers, has done little to help improve the human rights situation in the country.

While there has been considerable concern that presidential and parliamentary elections scheduled for March 2008 might not be free and fair, ZANU-PF and the two factions of the opposition Movement for Democratic Change (MDC) reached an agreement over proposed constitutional changes to the election laws in September 2007 during South African-led mediation talks.

Freedom of Assembly

In 2007, hundreds of civil society activists and opposition members were arbitrarily arrested during routine meetings or peaceful protests against social, economic and human rights conditions.

On February 21, 2007, in response to opposition attempts to hold rallies launching their election campaigns, the government imposed a three-month ban on political rallies and demonstrations in Harare. Police argued that the rallies would lead to a breakdown in law and order and political violence. Then, on March 11, 2007, police violently prevented a prayer meeting in Highfields township organized by the MDC and the Save Zimbabwe Campaign—a broad coalition of church and civil society organizations. More than 50 opposition members and civil society activists were arrested on their way to the meeting, including the leaders of the two MDC factions, Morgan Tsvangirai and Arthur Mutambara. Many were beaten in police custody, sustaining severe injuries including fractured skulls, broken bones and severe bruising that required hospitalization. The government has done little to address torture in Zimbabwe's prisons and police cells, and such incidents are rarely investigated.

Freedom of Expression and Information

Intimidation, arbitrary arrest, and criminal prosecution of journalists continue to seriously limit freedom of expression and information. Several of the journalists who tried to report on the events of March 11, 2007 and its aftermath were arrested, including independent journalist Gift Phiri, who was reportedly tortured in police custody. He was released on bail after four days, and charged with practicing without a license and "abusing journalistic privilege." On the day of the March prayer meeting itself, police assaulted photojournalist Tsvangirai Mukhwazi and held him in custody for three days, even though he had the required media accreditation. Four days later, police severely beat another photographer and his brother in Glenview, Harare when they attempted to take pictures of a group of people at a shopping mall mourning the death of an opposition activist.

In August 2007, the government introduced the Interception of Communications Act which threatens to further restrict the rights of Zimbabweans to privacy, information and expression. The law allows the government to intercept emails; and monitor telephone calls, the internet and postal communications. There are serious concerns that the law could be used to target human rights activists, journalists, trade unionists, and other government critics.

Police Use of Excessive and Lethal Force

On several occasions police have used tear gas to disperse demonstrations, beaten protestors with batons and rifle butts and even fired on peaceful protestors. In 2007 MDC member Gift Tandare was killed when police opened fire on unarmed demonstrators during clashes with the police in the immediate aftermath of the March 11 prayer meeting. The following day, police opened fire on mourners at Tandare's funeral and two MDC supporters were seriously injured. On April 7,

2007, armed police reportedly stormed the home of opposition member Philip Katsande and shot him three times in the arms and chest.

After the shootings, Philip Alston, United Nations Special Rapporteur on Extrajudicial, Summary or Arbitrary Executions, called on the government to immediately halt the use of lethal force against unarmed political activists. So far, the police have not investigated any of the shootings.

Human Rights Defenders

Human rights defenders, especially lawyers, are often subjected to intimidation, death threats, arrest and beatings by the police and intelligence officers. For example on May 4, 2007, human rights lawyers Alec Muchadehama and Andrew Makoni were arrested and held for three days after submitting papers to the High Court on behalf of an opposition activist.

On May 8, 2007, a group of lawyers, including Beatrice Mtetwa, president of the Zimbabwe Law Society, gathered outside the High Court in Harare to protest the unlawful arrest of Muchadehama and Makoni. Mtetwa and several others were arrested, forced into a police truck, driven to a secluded area and beaten with batons.

Police assaulted lawyer Harrison Nkomo on March 11 when he tried to secure the release of an opposition member who had been arrested in connection with the March prayer meeting.

Impunity

Government officials implicated in rights violations have by and large escaped prosecution. On several occasions in 2007 police failed to comply with judicial orders to investigate allegations of torture and other abuses committed by their own personnel. In any case, there is currently no independent mechanism within the police force to deal with such allegations. Political manipulation of the police and judiciary and the obstruction of human rights organizations have also con- tributed to a climate of impunity.

Elections

Parliamentary and presidential elections are scheduled for March 2008. In September 2007, the government tabled the Constitution of Zimbabwe Amendment No. 18 Bill, which, among other things, harmonizes parliamentary and presidential elections, sets the election date, establishes a presidentially-appointed human rights commission, and provides for an electoral college consisting of the Senate and House of Assembly to elect a successor in the event that a President resigns, dies or is removed from office.

At first, the opposition contested the Bill, arguing that it would merely deliver an electoral advantage to the ruling party. However, during South African-led negotiations in Pretoria, both factions of the MDC accepted the proposed amendments in the bill. At this writing, South African-led negotiations between the two parties over other aspects of the elections, including further reform of electoral laws and the political climate, were ongoing.

Even so, there are serious concerns over whether the forthcoming elections will be free and fair. Impunity that perpetrators of political violence enjoy in Zimbabwe conveys the message that violence in the run-up to and the aftermath of the 2008 elections will also go unpunished. During the 2005 parliamentary elections, Human Rights Watch documented numerous abuses, including widespread political intimidation, the use of repressive laws to limit voters' rights to freedom of expression, association and assembly, and electoral irregularities.

Key International Actors

International actors are divided over how to address the Zimbabwe crisis. The United States, the European Union and Australia have consistently condemned the human rights situation, but many African governments have refrained from doing so publically, stating that they are exerting pressure through quiet diplomacy. However, this does not appear systematic and sustained, or to be securing a response from President Mugabe's government that improves human rights. So far Mugabe appears to have largely managed to persuade regional governments that his government has been the victim of excessive and selective western attention. African governments are also critical of western assertions that the situation in Zimbabwe amounts to a threat to international peace and security, and have objected to Zimbabwe's situation being addressed at the UN Security Council.

The arrest and beating of the opposition leadership and civil society activists on March 11, 2007, has drawn widespread public condemnation from western governments including the United States and the United Kingdom. UN Secretary-General Ban Ki-moon also criticized the government's actions. African leaders were typically less vocal, although some, such as President John Kufour of Ghana expressed concern at the mounting political unrest. A statement from the chairperson of the commission of the African Union (AU) Alpha Oumar Konare, also called for the respect for human rights in Zimbabwe.

The Southern Africa Development Community (SADC), which is well positioned to exert pressure on the government of Zimbabwe, has so far extracted no concrete concessions on human rights from Mugabe's government. On March 28, 2007, SADC member states convened an extraordinary summit in Dar es Salaam, Tanzania to address the Zimbabwe crisis. Despite high hopes, the summit's final communique made no mention of the arrests and beatings of opposition members and supporters, civil society activists and ordinary Zimbabweans. Instead, SADC mandated President Thabo Mbeki of South Africa to mediate talks between the ruling party and the opposition.

The abuses have continued, and at the SADC annual summit in August 2007, leaders once again failed to establish concrete measures for addressing the human rights crisis in Zimbabwe. The degree to which South Africa's and SADC's response to the situation leads to improvements in respect for human rights is a significant test for the effectiveness of regional leadership in support of international human rights standards.

Meanwhile, in February 2007 the EU extended its travel sanctions on President Mugabe. In September British Prime Minister Gordon Brown threatened to boycott a December EU-AU Summit in Portugal—which currently holds the EU presidency—if President Mugabe was invited and allowed to travel to Portugal. The AU on the other hand, insisted that all African Presidents should be invited to the summit, and threatened a similar boycott if President Mugabe was not invited. In October, German Chancellor Angela Merkel appeared to back the AU position.

She described the situation in Zimbabwe as "disastrous," but insisted that it was necessary to discuss the matter "in the presence of each and everyone."

At a Germany/European partnership with Africa conference in November, Nigerian president Umaru Yar'Adua reconfirmed the AU's stance, arguing that President Mugabe's attendance at the EU-AU summit should not be made an issue. However, President Yar'Adua went on to express concern at the human rights situation in Zimbabwe stating that what was taking place in the country was "not in conformity with the rule of law."

COLOMBIA

Maiming the People

Guerrilla Use of Antipersonnel Landmines
and other Indiscriminate Weapons in Colombia

HUMAN
RIGHTS
WATCH

WORLD REPORT
2008

AMERICAS

ARGENTINA

Argentina has taken important steps to bring to justice former military and police personnel accused of having committed grave human rights violations during the country's "dirty war." Since the Supreme Court struck down the "Full Stop" and "Due Obedience" laws in 2005, two former police officers and a Roman Catholic priest have been convicted.

Inmates are held in deplorable conditions in Argentina's overcrowded prisons. Inmate violence and brutality by guards are a continuing problem.

In October 2007 Senator Cristina Fernandez de Kirchner, President Néstor Kirchner's wife, was elected to succeed him as president. She was to take office on December 10.

Confronting Past Abuses

Since 2003 Argentina has made significant progress in prosecuting military and police personnel responsible for "disappearances," killings, and torture during its last military dictatorship (1976-1983). President Kirchner forcefully encouraged these prosecutions, reinforcing what began as a legal challenge to impunity in the courts. According to the Attorney General's Office, there are currently more than 250 people in jail facing charges for these crimes.

Several important cases were reopened in 2003 after Congress annulled the 1986 "Full Stop" law, which forced a halt to the prosecution of all such cases, and the 1987 "Due Obedience" law, which granted automatic immunity in such cases to all members of the military, except those in positions of command. In June 2005 the Supreme Court declared the laws unconstitutional, and in 2006 two police officers were convicted for "disappearances." In October 2007 Fr. Christian Von Wernich, a chaplain for the Buenos Aires police during the dictatorship, was sentenced to life imprisonment for his involvement in dozens of cases, including murders, torture, and abduction.

The security of witnesses in human rights trials has become a serious concern since the disappearance in September 2006 of a torture victim who had testified in one of the cases that concluded that year. Jorge Julio López, age 77, who vanished from his home in La Plata the day before he was due to attend one of the final days of the trial, remains missing.

Since 2005 several federal judges have struck down pardons decreed by President Carlos Menem in 1989 and 1990 of former officials convicted or facing trial for human rights violations. In July 2007 the Supreme Court declared unconstitutional the pardon in favor of Gen. Santiago Omar Riveros, arguing that pardon cannot be granted when someone is accused of committing crimes against humanity.

Prison Conditions

Overcrowding, abuses by guards, and inmate violence continue to be serious problems in Argentine prisons. In a landmark ruling in May 2005 the Supreme Court declared that all prisons in the country must abide by the United Nations Standard Minimum Rules for the Treatment of Prisoners.

Although there have been slight improvements in the province of Buenos Aires, the situation remains severe. During 2006-2007 there was a small reduction in overcrowding. The number of detainees held in police lockups—which for years have absorbed the overflow from the prison system—also decreased. However, one of the causes of overcrowding is the high proportion of criminal suspects sent to prison to await trial, who make up over 70 percent of the prison population. The government has built new prisons, but they do not comply with international standards. Although the number of such incidents continued to decrease, prisoners still die as a result of preventable inmate violence.

In November 2007, in one of the deadliest incidents in the Argentine prison system, a fire in a jail in Santiago del Estero province, caused by prisoners who were reportedly trying to escape, killed over 30 inmates.

Freedom of Expression and Information

Defamation of public officials remains punishable by criminal penalties. After being under debate for several years, a bill to decriminalize defamation has not advanced. In September 2007, as a consequence of a complaint initiated by the governor of Salta, a journalist was convicted of criminal slander for mentioning in his news program allegations of government corruption.

Additionally, a bill giving Argentine citizens the right to information held by public bodies made no progress for a third consecutive year. The lower house approved the bill in May 2003, but the Senate voted for a much-weakened version. In November 2005 the bill was dropped altogether from the parliamentary agenda.

Some provincial governments discriminate in the distribution of official advertising by rewarding local media that provide favorable coverage and punishing those with a critical editorial line. In 2003 the newspaper *Rio Negro* filed a writ with the Supreme Court alleging that the provincial government of Neuquen had drastically reduced its advertisements in reprisal for the newspaper's coverage of a bribery scandal that indirectly implicated the governor. In September 2007 the Supreme Court ruled against the provincial government, stating it had failed to justify why it had abruptly limited official advertising in this newspaper. According to the Court, although there is no right to receive official advertising, a government that grants it may not apply discriminatory criteria in granting or withdrawing it.

Access to Legal Abortion

Women and girls in Argentina face arbitrary and discriminatory restrictions on their reproductive decisions and access to contraceptives and abortion, while sexual violence goes unpunished at times.

Therapeutic abortions and abortions for mentally disabled rape victims are legal, but women face obstacles even when their right to an abortion is protected by law. For example, doctors in Santa Fe province would not perform a therapeutic abortion for a 20-year-old woman with cancer, and in May 2007, after she had a cesarian section when she was over 22 weeks pregnant, both mother and baby died. A mentally disabled 19-year-old who became pregnant after being raped could not find a doctor who would perform an abortion, even after the highest court in the province of Entre Rios authorized it in September 2007. The abortion was carried out in another province, after the national health minister intervened.

Key International Actors

In proceedings before the Inter-American Commission on Human Rights in 2005, the Argentine government formally accepted partial responsibility for failing to prevent the 1994 bombing of the Jewish Argentine Mutual Association, and for subsequently failing to properly investigate the crime, in which 85 people died. In October 2006 an Argentine special prosecutor accused Iran of planning the attack, and Hezbollah of carrying it out. The following month, a federal judge issued an international warrant for the arrest of former Iranian president Ali Akbar Hashemi-Rafsanjani and eight other Iranian former officials. In September 2007 President Kirchner held before the UN General Assembly that Iran had not collaborated with the Argentine justice system, and in November 2007 the Interpol General Assembly voted to issue six arrest notices.

In August 2007 the government of Argentina admitted its international responsibility before the Inter-American Court of Human Rights in the case of Eduardo Kimel, a journalist who had been sentenced to one year in prison, suspended, and ordered to pay 20,000 pesos (US$20,000 at that time) in damages for defamation. Kimel had criticized the work of a judge investigating a massacre committed during the last military government. At this writing the case is pending before the Court.

The Inter-American Court continued to monitor the performance of the government in implementing provisional measures ordered by the Court to protect the lives and physical security of prisoners held in the province of Mendoza. In August 2007 the Court held that existing provisional measures remained in place.

BRAZIL

Police violence continues to be one of Brazil's most intractable human rights problems. Faced with high levels of violent crime, especially in urban centers, some police engage in abusive practices rather than pursuing sound policing policies. Prison conditions are abysmal. In rural regions, violence and land conflicts are ongoing, and human rights defenders suffer threats and attacks. And, while the Brazilian government has made efforts to redress human rights abuses, it has rarely held accountable those responsible.

Police Violence

Brazil continues to face major problems in the area of public security. The country's metropolitan areas, and especially their low-income neighborhoods (*favelas*), are plagued by widespread violence perpetrated by criminal gangs, abusive police, and—in the case of Rio de Janeiro—militias reportedly linked to the police. Every year roughly 50,000 people are murdered in Brazil.

In Rio, criminal gangs launched a series of coordinated attacks against police officers, buses, and public buildings in December 2006, killing 11 people, including two officers. Reacting to the attacks, police killed seven people whom they classified as suspects. Earlier in 2006, in Sao Paulo state, a criminal gang's coordinated attacks on police and public buildings led to clashes between police and gang members that left more than 100 civilians and some 40 security agents dead. A preliminary investigation by an independent committee found evidence that many of the Sao Paulo killings were extrajudicial executions.

According to official figures, police killed 694 people in the first six months of 2007 in Rio de Janeiro in situations described as "resistance followed by death"— one-third more than in the same period in 2006. The number includes 44 people killed during a two-month police operation aimed at dismantling drug trafficking gangs in Complexo do Alemão, Rio de Janeiro's poorest neighborhood. Violence reached a peak on June 27, 2007, when 19 people were killed during alleged confrontations with the police. According to residents and local nongovernmental organizations, many of the killings were summary executions. In October at least

12 people were killed during a police incursion in Favela da Coreia, including a four-year-old boy.

Police violence also remained common in Sao Paulo state, where officers killed 201 people in the first half of 2007, according to official data. Fifteen officers were killed during the same period.

Torture remains a serious problem in Brazil. There have been credible reports of police and prison guards torturing people in their custody as forms of punishment or intimidation, and for extortion.

Abusive police officers are rarely sanctioned, and abuses are sometimes justified by authorities as an inevitable by-product of efforts to combat Brazil's very high crime rates.

Prison Conditions

The inhumane conditions, violence, and overcrowding that have historically characterized Brazilian prisons remain one of the country's main human rights problems. According to the National Penitentiary Department, Brazilian prisons and jails held 419,551 inmates in June 2007, exceeding the system's capacity by approximately 200,000 inmates.

Violence continues to plague prisons around the country. In the first four months of 2007, 651 persons were killed while in detention, according to a parliamentary commission investigating problems in the country's prisons. The commission was formed in August after 25 inmates burned to death during a riot in a prison in Minas Gerais. In September detainees in a prison in Manaus also rioted, killing two men. Riots also ended in deaths in overcrowded prisons in Recife and Abreu e Lima, in the state of Pernambuco.

At Urso Branco prison, in Rondônia, one prisoner died and at least seven were injured during an uprising in July. Since November 2000, at least 97 inmates have reportedly been killed at the facility. The Inter-American Court of Human Rights on four occasions since 2002 has ordered Brazil to adopt measures to guarantee the safety of inmates in Urso Branco, but Brazil has failed to do so.

Overcrowding, rats, diseased pigeons, poor water quality, and a lack of medication were among the problems reported by the Sao Paulo state public defender's office at Sant'Ana female penitentiary in Sao Paulo. The office has repeatedly urged the closing of the facility, where five inmates died between December 2006 and June 2007.

Although children and adolescents are granted special protection under Brazilian and international law, they are subjected to serious abuses by the juvenile detention system. Young inmates are subject to violence by other youths or prison guards.

Forced Labor

The use of forced labor continues to be a problem in rural Brazil, despite government efforts to expose violations. Since 1995, when the federal government created mobile units to monitor labor conditions in rural areas, approximately 26,000 workers deemed to be working in conditions analogous to slavery have been liberated. From January to August 2007, Brazil's Ministry of Labor and Employment liberated over 3,400 workers, including a record 1,064 people freed in a single operation on a farm in Para in July.

Yet, according to the Pastoral Land Commission, a Roman Catholic Church group that defends the rights of rural workers, the number of reports that it receives of laborers working under slave-like conditions remains constant at 250 to 300 a year, involving between 6,000 and 8,000 workers, but the government investigates only half of these cases. As of August 2007, no one had been punished for maintaining workers in slave-like conditions, according to the head of the public prosecutor's division responsible for combating slave labor.

Rural Violence and Land Conflict

Indigenous people and landless peasants face threats, violent attacks, and killings as a result of land disputes in rural areas. According to the Pastoral Land Commission, 39 people were killed and 917 were arrested in rural conflicts throughout the country in 2006. Two indigenous people were killed in Mato Grosso do Sul state in 2007, allegedly by militiamen working for landowners, according to the Missionary Indigenous Council (CIMI), a Roman Catholic Church group that defends the rights of indigenous peoples. In September a member of the Movement of Landless Rural Workers (MST) was shot and killed in Goias state by two unidentified men.

Among other human rights defenders facing threats and intimidation, Dom Manoel João Francisco, a bishop working for indigenous rights in Chapeco (Santa Catarina state), received death threats in June 2007, according to CIMI. CIMI also reported that several of its missionaries were driven to leave Mato Grosso state after receiving threats from landowners.

Impunity

Human rights violations in Brazil are rarely prosecuted. In an effort to remedy this, the Brazilian government passed a constitutional amendment in 2004 that makes human rights crimes federal offenses. It allows certain human rights violations to be transferred from the state-level to the federal justice system for investigation and trial. The transfer, however, can only happen if requested by the federal prosecutor general and accepted by the Superior Tribunal of Justice. To date, there have been no such transfers.

In a positive step, the trial for the 2005 murder of Dorothy Stang, a missionary who fought for agrarian reform, resulted in the conviction and sentencing of three men in May 2007. Because two of them received sentences greater than 20 years' imprisonment, however, they had the right to new trials. At this writing one of them has already been retried, convicted, and sentenced to 27 years' imprisonment.

Brazil has never prosecuted those responsible for atrocities committed in the period of military rule (1964-1985). An amnesty law passed in 1979 pardoned government agents and members of armed political groups who had committed abuses.

The Brazilian federal government released in August 2007 a report on the results of an 11-year investigation by the national Commission on Political Deaths and Disappearances to determine the fate of government opponents who were killed or "disappeared" by state security forces between 1961 and 1988. The commission was unable to clarify important aspects of these crimes, including the whereabouts of the majority of the "disappeared," because the Brazilian armed forces have never opened key archives from the military rule years. In September 2007 the Superior Tribunal of Justice ordered the armed forces to open secret files and reveal what happened to the remains of Brazilians who died or "disappeared" when the government sent troops to fight the Araguaia guerrilla uprising in 1971.

Key International Actors

In 2006 the Inter-American Commission on Human Rights found Brazil responsible for violating the rights to equality before the law, judicial protection, and fair trial in the racial discrimination case of Simone André Diniz. It also deemed six cases against Brazil admissible. In one of them, the country is accused of violating the rights to life, humane treatment, fair trial, and judicial protection of inmates at the Urso Branco prison. In June 2007 the Commission agreed to review the Castelinho case, in which police officers reportedly ambushed a bus of prisoners in Sao Paulo in 2002, killing 12.

CHILE

Since the death of former dictator Gen. Augusto Pinochet in December 2006, Chilean judges have continued to prosecute and convict former military personnel accused of committing grave human rights violations under the military government. The Supreme Court's criminal chamber, which issues final verdicts in these cases, has begun to rule that neither amnesties nor statutes of limitations may block trials or punishment for these crimes.

In September 2007 a landmark Supreme Court criminal chamber ruling ordered the extradition of former Peruvian president Alberto Fujimori to stand trial in Peru on charges of human rights violations and corruption.

Prosecutions for Past Human Rights Violations

In the pursuit of accountability for human rights abuses under military rule, as of July 2007, 458 former military personnel and civilian collaborators were facing charges for enforced disappearances, extrajudicial execution, and torture; 167 had been convicted; and 35 were serving prison sentences.

At the time of his death from a heart attack while he was under house arrest, Pinochet was facing criminal prosecution for torture, enforced disappearances, tax evasion, and forgery. The courts had closed three previous human rights cases against him after deciding that mild dementia rendered him unfit to stand trial. However, Chile's judges had come increasingly to doubt that assessment: two judges who interrogated Pinochet in August and November 2005 in connection with more than 125 secret bank accounts found the 90-year-old general to be lucid. In October 2007 the court investigating that case indicted Pinochet's widow, their five children, and 17 close military and civilian collaborators, for embezzlement of public funds. However, the Supreme Court's criminal chamber later struck down the charges against four of the children on grounds that embezzlement only applies to government officials.

Chilean courts have almost overcome legal obstacles to human rights trials, including an amnesty law in force since 1978 whose purpose was to shield state agents from prosecution for human rights abuses. In March 2007 the Supreme

Court's criminal chamber unanimously overturned a court decision applying the amnesty to former Brig. Víctor Pinto Pérez, who was facing charges for the murder in 1973 of an army reservist. It stated unequivocally that the amnesty is inapplicable where any war crime or crime against humanity is involved, and that such crimes cannot be subject to a statute of limitations. However, in November 2007 the Court applied a statute of limitations and absolved an army colonel who had been convicted for killing three peasants in 1973.

President Michelle Bachelet announced in October 2006 that she would present a bill to prevent the amnesty law from being applied in cases of grave human rights abuse. Her announcement came in response to a ruling of the Inter-American Court of Human Rights that the law was incompatible with the American Convention on Human Rights. However, the bill has been delayed by differences of opinion on its necessity given the advances in the courts and the possibility that legislation might be challenged in the Constitutional Court.

The ruling in the Supreme Court's criminal chamber approving a Peruvian request for the extradition of former President Fujimori was the first time anywhere in the world that a former president has been extradited to stand trial in his home country for human rights violations.

A bill to ratify the Rome Statute of the International Criminal Court stalled when the Constitutional Court, ruling on a petition by a group of opposition senators, declared it unconstitutional. A bill to reform the constitution to allow ratification of the Rome Statute has been in the Senate since April 2002.

Prison Conditions

Chile has more prisoners per capita than any other country in South America, and the prison population continues to grow by 8 percent a year. Despite the opening of six new privately contracted prisons (three of them in 2007), overcrowding remains a serious problem. In the older prisons, which house 80 percent of Chile's prisoners, sanitation and hygiene are often deplorable, there are insufficient doctors and medicine, and food is poor.

Military Justice

Even though Chile has completely overhauled its criminal justice procedure in recent years and reinforced due-process guarantees, military courts still have wide jurisdiction over civilians and also over human rights abuses committed by the uniformed police, Carabineros, which is part of the armed forces.

In June 2007 the government presented a bill to Congress to undertake initial reforms of the system of military justice. It also set up a commission to prepare more comprehensive reforms for presentation in 2008. However, the bill leaves the most serious problems unchanged: if approved as written, military courts will continue to deal with assaults by civilians against police (the most common use of military courts at present) as well as abuses committed by the police against civilians while carrying out orders or on military premises.

Non-Discrimination

As of November 2007 a bill that would establish measures against discrimination was under congressional consideration. It creates a specific civil action for acts and omissions considered "arbitrary discrimination," and includes a broad and detailed range of categories of social and individual characteristics for which non-discrimination must be assured. There are concerns, however, that due to pressure from religious groups, the Senate might strike sexual orientation from among the categories for protection, leaving the bill incomplete in its goal to protect all people against discrimination.

Access to Public Information

Since the restoration of democracy in 1990 Chile has passed laws, including a constitutional reform, protecting the right of access to public information. However, officials continue to use the wide powers they have to deny requests for information. The current government has undertaken to increase transparency in public administration. A bill presented by the government in December 2006 guaranteeing access to public information proposes the creation of an independent Council for Transparency, which would be empowered to order officials to make information available to the public, as well as to impose sanctions if they fail to do so. As of November 2007 the bill was in the final stages of debate in the legislature.

Key International Actors

The special rapporteur for women of the Inter-American Commission on Human Rights visited Chile in September to observe and receive information on the situation of women's rights, in particular their right to be free from discrimination.

The United Nations Working Group on the Use of Mercenaries visited Chile in July. The working group collected information on the recruitment of Chileans to work with private security companies in Iraq. It noted that, although contracted as security guards, the recruits were given military training in the United States, Jordan, or Iraq and eventually performed military functions not covered in their contracts.

COLOMBIA

Colombia's internal armed conflict continues to result in widespread abuses by irregular armed groups, including both left-wing guerrillas and paramilitaries who remain active. Targeted killings, forced disappearances, use of antipersonnel landmines, recruitment of child combatants, and threats against trade unionists, human rights defenders, and journalists remain serious problems. Due to the abuses, Colombia has the second largest population of internally displaced persons in the world.

Colombia's public security forces also engage in abuses, and in recent years there has been an alarming increase in reports of extrajudicial executions of civilians by the military.

Most cases involving violations of human rights and international humanitarian law are never solved. Thanks to investigations by its Supreme Court, Colombia has begun to make progress in uncovering longstanding links between paramilitaries and high-ranking national political figures. Nonetheless, on several occasions in 2007 the administration of President Álvaro Uribe took steps that threatened to undermine this progress.

Paramilitary Influence in the Political System

Dozens of Congressmen from President Uribe's coalition, including the president's own cousin, Senator Mario Uribe, came under investigation by the Supreme Court in 2007 for their alleged collaboration with paramilitaries responsible for widespread atrocities. At this writing, 17 congressmen were under arrest. One of them is the brother of former Foreign Minister Maria Consuelo Araújo, who resigned as a result.

President Uribe's former intelligence chief from 2002 to 2005, Jorge Noguera, is also under investigation for links to paramilitaries.

The government has provided funding to the court and spoken of the need for full investigations. However, President Uribe has repeatedly lashed out against the court, accusing it of suffering from an "ideological bias" and personally calling one Supreme Court justice to inquire about ongoing investigations.

In April 2007 President Uribe announced a proposal to release from prison all politicians who are convicted of colluding with paramilitaries. After it became evident that the proposal would be an obstacle to ratification of the US-Colombia Free Trade Agreement, he tabled it.

Demobilization of Paramilitary Groups

The Colombian government continues to claim that, thanks to its demobilization program, paramilitaries no longer exist.

Both the Organization of American States and the Office of the UN High Commissioner for Human Rights in Colombia reported in 2007 that mid-level paramilitary commanders continue to engage in criminal activity and recruitment of new troops.

The Inter-American Commission on Human Rights noted in a 2007 report that while over 30,000 individuals may have gone through demobilization ceremonies, some may not have been paramilitaries at all, but persons who played the role to access government stipends.

Thanks to a 2006 ruling by Colombia's Constitutional Court, paramilitary commanders and others who have applied for reduced sentences under Law 975 of 2005 (known as the "Justice and Peace Law") are legally required to confess and turn over illegally acquired assets. However, confessions moved slowly in 2007, in part due to a lack of sufficient prosecutors and investigators assigned to the unit of the attorney general's office charged with interrogating the commanders.

Several paramilitary leaders are temporarily in prison, but government officials have publicly stated that they will eventually be allowed to serve their reduced sentences on "agricultural colonies" or farms.

Guerrilla Abuses

Both the FARC and ELN guerrillas continue to engage in abuses against civilians. The FARC's widespread use of antipersonnel landmines has resulted in a dramatic escalation in new reported casualties from these indiscriminate weapons in recent years. The FARC also continues regularly to engage in kidnappings. In June 2007, the FARC announced that 11 congressmen from the state of Valle del Cauca that it had been holding for more than five years had been shot to death while under their control.

The government announced in June that it was unilaterally releasing hundreds of FARC members, as well as Rodrigo Granda, a senior FARC leader, from prison to encourage the FARC to release hostages. At this writing, the FARC had not moved to release any hostages.

Military Abuses and Impunity

Reports of extrajudicial executions of civilians by Colombia's army have increased substantially in recent years, according to the UN High Commissioner for Human Rights as well as local groups, including the Colombian Commission of Jurists.

Colombia continues to suffer from rampant impunity for human rights abuses. The authorities' failure to effectively investigate, prosecute, and punish abuses has created an environment in which abusers correctly assume that they will never be held accountable for their crimes.

The problem is particularly acute in cases involving military collaboration with paramilitaries. Low-ranking officers are sometimes held accountable in these cases, but rarely is a commanding officer prosecuted.

In one positive development, prosecutors in 2007 continued to make progress in investigating the "disappearance" of 10 people during security force operations in 1985 to retake Colombia's Palace of Justice (which housed the Supreme Court), after its invasion by the M-19 guerrilla group.

Violence against Trade Unionists

Colombia has the highest rate of violence against trade unionists in the world. The National Labor School, a Colombian labor rights group, has recorded over 2,500 killings of trade unionists in Colombia since 1986.

The number of yearly killings has dropped since 2001. However, the situation remains critical. The National Labor School reports that 72 trade unionists were killed in Colombia in 2006. The government reports 58 killings in 2006. At this writing, final statistics for 2007 were unavailable.

The overwhelming majority of these cases have never been solved. In 2007, a specialized sub-unit of the attorney general's office reopened some cases, but it remains to be seen whether the unit will produce concrete results.

Threats against Human Rights Defenders, Journalists, and Victims of Paramilitaries

Human rights monitors, journalists, politicians, and victims of paramilitary groups continue to be the subjects of frequent threats, harassment, and attacks for their legitimate work. Investigations of these cases rarely result in prosecutions or convictions.

In 2007 President Uribe once again made statements attacking the media for its coverage of public issues. In October, journalist Gonzalo Guillén fled Colombia due to the numerous death threats he received after Uribe accused him of making false claims about the president. Another prominent journalist, Daniel Coronell, who had only recently returned to Colombia after nearly two years in exile, also received a death threat after Uribe publicly accused him of being a "liar."

Victims of paramilitaries who speak about their experiences are also threatened and sometimes killed. Mrs. Yolanda Izquierdo, for example, a mother of five who led a group of 700 paramilitary victims who were demanding the return of land that paramilitaries had stolen from them, requested government protection after receiving repeated threats to her life. The protection was never provided. In February, 2007, she was shot to death in front of her house.

The Colombian Ministry of Interior has a protection program, established with US funding, for journalists, trade unionists, and others who are under threat. The program does not cover victims of paramilitaries who present claims in the context of the demobilization process. In October 2007 the government announced that, pursuant to a Supreme Court ruling, it would create a victim protection program.

Discrimination against Same-Sex Couples

On May 14, 2007, the UN Human Rights Committee found that Colombia had breached its international obligations when it denied a gay man's partner pension benefits. In June, the Colombian Senate voted down a law that would have guaranteed same-sex couples equal access to welfare benefits. Colombia's Constitutional Court, however, issued decisions advancing equal rights: in February, it recognized same-sex civil partnerships and in October it recognized the right of same-sex partners to participate in the health plans of their partners.

Key International Actors

The United States remains the most influential foreign actor in Colombia. In 2007 it provided close to US$800 million to the Colombian government, mostly in military aid. Twenty-five percent of US military assistance is formally subject to human rights conditions.

The United States also provides financial support for the paramilitary demobilization process, subject to Colombia's compliance with related conditions in US law.

In 2007 the US Congress updated and strengthened the conditions in US law on military assistance and support for the demobilization process. In April 2007, the US Congress froze $55 million in US assistance due to concerns over the increase in reports of extrajudicial executions by the military and lack of adequate progress in reducing impunity in major cases involving military-paramilitary links.

The Democratic leadership in the US House of Representatives announced in June 2007 that it would not support a Free Trade Agreement with Colombia until there is "concrete evidence of sustained results on the ground" with regard to impunity for violence against trade unionists and the role of paramilitaries.

In 2007 the US Department of Justice announced a US$25 million settlement with Chiquita Brands in a criminal proceeding over the multinational corporation's payments to paramilitaries in the banana-growing region of Colombia. The AUC paramilitaries, as well as FARC and ELN guerrillas, are on the US Department of State's list of Foreign Terrorist Organizations.

The United Kingdom provides military assistance to Colombia, though the full amount is not publicly known. The European Union provides social and economic assistance to Colombia, and has provided some aid to the government's paramilitary demobilization programs.

The OAS Mission to Support the Peace Process in Colombia, which is charged with verifying the paramilitary demobilizations, issued reports in 2007 highlighting the presence of new, re-armed, or never demobilized groups. The Inter-American Commission on Human Rights also released a report raising numerous concerns over implementation of the demobilizations.

The Office of the UN High Commissioner for Human Rights (UNHCHR) is active in Colombia, with a presence in Bogota, Medellin, and Cali. In 2007 the UNHCHR announced that the government had extended the office's full mandate, with no changes.

CUBA

Cuba remains the one country in Latin America that represses nearly all forms of political dissent. There have been no significant policy changes since Fidel Castro relinquished direct control of the government to his brother Raul Castro in August 2006. The government continues to enforce political conformity using criminal prosecutions, long-term and short-term detentions, mob harassment, police warnings, surveillance, house arrests, travel restrictions, and politically-motivated dismissals from employment. The end result is that Cubans are systematically denied basic rights to free expression, association, assembly, privacy, movement, and due process of law.

Legal and Institutional Failings

Cuba's legal and institutional structures are at the root of rights violations. Although in theory the different branches of government have separate and defined areas of authority, in practice the executive retains control over all levers of power. The courts, which lack independence, undermine the right to fair trial by severely restricting the right to a defense.

Cuba's Criminal Code provides the legal basis for repression of dissent. Laws criminalizing enemy propaganda, the spreading of "unauthorized news," and insult to patriotic symbols are used to restrict freedom of speech under the guise of protecting state security. The government also imprisons or orders the surveillance of individuals who have committed no illegal act, relying upon provisions that penalize "dangerousness" (estado peligroso) and allow for "official warning" (advertencia oficial).

Political Imprisonment

In July 2007 the Cuban Commission for Human Rights and National Reconciliation, a respected local human rights group, issued a list of 240 prisoners who it said were incarcerated for political reasons. The list included the names of 12 peaceful dissidents who had been arrested and detained in the first half of 2006, five of whom were being held on charges of "dangerousness." Of 75 political dissidents, independent journalists, and human rights advocates who were summarily tried in April 2003, 59 remain imprisoned. Serving sentences that average nearly 20 years, the incarcerated dissidents endure poor conditions and punitive treatment in prison.

While the number of political prisoners has decreased in the last year, this decrease cannot be attributed to leniency or policy change on the part of the government. The political prisoners who were released had already served out their full sentences. In September 2007, approximately 30 activists were arrested and held for 24 hours. According to one of the released prisoners, Jorge Luis Garcia Perez—who was released from prison in May 2007 after serving out a 17-year sentence—the prisoners endured beatings, strip searches, and threats of future arrest.

Travel Restrictions and Family Separations

The Cuban government forbids the country's citizens from leaving or returning to Cuba without first obtaining official permission, which is often denied. Unauthorized travel can result in criminal prosecution. In May 2006 Oswaldo Payá, the well known Cuban human rights advocate, was awarded an honorary doctor of laws by Columbia University in New York City in recognition of his work. However, he was denied an exit visa by the Cuban authorities and could not receive the degree in person.

The government also frequently bars citizens engaged in authorized travel from taking their children with them overseas, essentially holding the children hostage to guarantee the parents' return. Given the widespread fear of forced family separation, these travel restrictions provide the Cuban government with a powerful tool for punishing defectors and silencing critics.

Freedom of Expression and Assembly

The Cuban government maintains a media monopoly on the island, ensuring that freedom of expression is virtually nonexistent. Although a small number of independent journalists manage to write articles for foreign websites or publish underground newsletters, the risks associated with these activities are considerable. According to Reporters Without Borders, 25 journalists were serving prison terms in Cuba as of July 2007, most of them charged with threatening "the national independence and economy of Cuba." This makes the country second only to China for the number of journalists in prison.

Access to information via the internet is also highly restricted in Cuba. In late August 2006 the dissident and independent journalist Guillermo Fariñas ended a seven-month hunger strike in opposition to the regime's internet policy. He began the strike after the Cuban authorities shut down his email access, which he had been using to send dispatches abroad describing attacks on dissidents and other human rights abuses.

Freedom of assembly is severely restricted in Cuba and political dissidents are generally prohibited from meeting in large groups. This was evident in mid-September 2006 during the 14th summit of the Non-Aligned Movement in Havana, when the Cuban government issued a ban on all gatherings that might damage "the image" of the city.

Prison Conditions

Prisoners are generally kept in poor and abusive conditions, often in overcrowded cells. They typically lose weight during incarceration, and some receive inadequate medical care. Some also endure physical and sexual abuse, typically by other inmates and with the acquiescence of guards.

Political prisoners who denounce poor conditions of imprisonment or who otherwise fail to observe prison rules are frequently punished with long periods in punitive isolation cells, restrictions on visits, or denial of medical treatment. In October 2006, Juan Carlos Herrera Acosta, who was sentenced to 20 years in prison following the government's 2003 crackdown on dissidents, was beaten and placed in a cell infested with rats and insects after demanding the right to telephone his family. Some political prisoners have carried out long hunger strikes to protest abusive conditions and mistreatment by guards.

Death Penalty

Under Cuban law the death penalty exists for a broad range of crimes. It is difficult to ascertain the frequency with which this penalty is employed because Cuba does not release information regarding its use. However, as far as is known, no executions have been carried out since April 2003.

Human Rights Defenders

Refusing to recognize human rights monitoring as a legitimate activity, the government denies legal status to local human rights groups. Individuals who belong to these groups face systematic harassment, with the government impeding their efforts to document human rights conditions. In addition, international human rights groups such as Human Rights Watch and Amnesty International are barred from sending fact-finding missions to Cuba. Cuba remains one of the few countries in the world to deny the International Committee of the Red Cross access to its prisons.

Key International Actors

In June 2007, bowing to political pressure, the UN Human Rights Council terminated the mandate of the UN expert charged with reporting on human rights conditions in Cuba.

The US economic embargo on Cuba, in effect for more than four decades, continues to impose indiscriminate hardship on the Cuban people and to block travel to the island. An exception to the embargo that allows food sales to Cuba on a cash-only basis, however, has led to substantial trade between the two countries.

In an effort to deprive the Cuban government of funding, the United States government enacted new restrictions on family-related travel to Cuba in June 2004. Under these rules, individuals are allowed to visit relatives in Cuba only once every three years, and only if the relatives fit the US government's narrow definition of family—a definition that excludes aunts, uncles, cousins, and other next-of-kin who are often integral members of Cuban families. Justified as a means of promoting freedom in Cuba, the new travel policies undermine the freedom of movement of hundreds of thousands of Cubans and Cuban-Americans, and inflict profound harm on Cuban families.

In January 2005 the European Union decided to temporarily suspend the diplomatic sanctions that it had adopted in the wake of the Cuban government's 2003 crackdown against dissidents. In June 2006, and again in June 2007, the EU decided to renew the suspensions, but not lift the sanctions outright. It offered to resume discussions with the Castro government, stipulating that if it were to accept the invitation, the Cuban government must be willing to discuss human rights, political prisoners, and democracy. In response, the Cuban foreign ministry indicated that Cuba would not participate in talks unless the sanctions were fully dropped. Nevertheless, representatives of the EU and Cuba held "informal, exploratory talks" at the United Nations in September 2007 and agreed to meet again in early 2008.

GUATEMALA

More than a decade after the end of Guatemala's brutal civil war, impunity remains the rule when it comes to human rights violations. Ongoing acts of intimidation threaten to reverse the little progress that has been made toward promoting accountability in recent years.

The country continues to face high levels of violence associated with both electoral politics and common crime. Guatemala's weak and corrupt law enforcement institutions have proven incapable of containing the powerful organized crime groups that, among other things, are believed responsible for continuing attacks on human rights defenders.

Impunity

Guatemala continues to suffer the effects of an internal armed conflict that ended in 1996. A truth commission sponsored by the United Nations estimated that as many as 200,000 people were killed during the 36-year war and attributed the vast majority of the killings to government forces.

Guatemalans seeking accountability for these abuses face daunting obstacles. The prosecutors and investigators who handle these cases receive grossly inadequate training and resources. The courts routinely fail to resolve judicial appeals and motions in an expeditious manner, allowing defense attorneys to engage in dilatory legal maneuvering. The army and other state institutions fail to cooperate fully with investigations into abuses committed by current or former members. The police do not provide adequate protection to judges, prosecutors, and witnesses involved in politically sensitive cases.

Of the 626 massacres documented by the truth commission, only two cases have been successfully prosecuted in the Guatemalan courts. In 1999, a Guatemalan court sentenced three former civil defense patrol members to prison for the murders of two of the 177 civilians massacred in Rio Negro in 1982. In addition, in October 2005, the Supreme Court of Justice upheld the 2004 sentencing of a lieutenant and 13 soldiers to 40 years in prison for the 1995 Xaman massacre in which 11 civilians were killed.

By contrast, the prosecution of former military officers allegedly responsible for the 1982 Dos Erres massacre, in which at least 162 people died, and the trial of six other civil defense patrol members, alleged to be complicit in the Rio Negro massacres, have been held up for years by dilatory defense motions.

The few other convictions obtained in human rights cases have come at considerable cost. In the case of Myrna Mack, an anthropologist who was assassinated in 1990, it took more than a decade to obtain the conviction of an army colonel, Valencia Osorio, for his role in orchestrating the killing. During that time, a police investigator who gathered incriminating evidence was murdered, and two other investigators—as well as three witnesses—received threats and fled the country. Osorio, meanwhile, escaped police custody and has not served his sentence.

In April 2007, Guatemala's Constitutional Court confirmed the lower courts' sentencing of Colonel Byron Disrael Lima Estrada, Captain Byron Lima Oliva, and priest Mario Orantes Nájera to 20 years in prison on charges of being accomplices in the 1998 murder of Bishop Juan Gerardi Conedera.

The July 2005 discovery of approximately 70 to 80 million documents of the disbanded National Police, including files on Guatemalans who were murdered and "disappeared" during the armed conflict, could play a key role in the prosecution of those who committed human rights violations during the conflict. Yet there is no legal framework in place to ensure adequate long-term management of the archive, nor to regulate public access to its files.

In July 2007, a Guatemalan appellate court ordered the declassification of military documents from the 1980s. These documents may also provide crucial evidence for use in future human rights trials.

Impunity remains a chronic problem with common crimes as well. According to the National Civilian Police, 5,885 people were murdered in 2006. This is the highest number of murders reported in the last 10 years. The Guatemalan Human Rights Ombudsman's Office estimates that convictions are only obtained in approximately 6 percent of all criminal cases; the conviction rate drops to less than 3 percent in cases involving murders of women and children.

On February 19, 2007, three Salvadoran representatives from the Central American Parliament and their driver were murdered near Guatemala City. On February 22, four Guatemalan policemen were arrested as suspects in the crime, but were murdered several days later while in prison awaiting legal proceedings. At this writing, no trial date had been set for the suspects arrested in either of these two cases.

Frustration with the lack of justice in Guatemala has undoubtedly contributed to acts of vigilantism in the last several years. Public lynching is a common problem, with 40 lynching cases reported between January and August 2007. The majority of lynching victims were suspected of having committed a crime, but there have also been lynching cases in the past few years which were motivated by other factors, such as disputes over land or water.

Electoral Violence

The September 9, 2007, presidential, congressional, and municipal elections and the November 4 run-off presidential election were preceded by a wave of violence against political candidates and members of political parties. The Guatemalan Human Rights Ombudsman's Office reported 55 attacks and threats against political candidates and members of political parties in 2007, resulting in 26 deaths.

Excessive Use of Force

Members of the national police still sometimes employ excessive force against suspected criminals and others. The perpetrators are often poorly trained police officers. In addition, the UN Special Rapporteur on extrajudicial, summary, or arbitrary executions has reported that there is "strong evidence" that members of state security forces have engaged in acts of social cleansing, including the execution of gang members, criminal suspects, and other social "undesirables."

Human Rights Defenders

Attacks and threats against human rights defenders remain commonplace. In February 2007, for example, an employee of the Center for Legal Action in Human Rights (Centro para la Accion Legal en Derechos Humanos, CALDH) was briefly kidnapped and several other members of CALDH's legal team received written and oral threats in connection with their work for the organization. Members of the Guatemalan Foundation for Forensic Anthropology (Fundacion de Antropologia Forense de Guatemala, FAFG) continued to receive death threats in 2007 in connection with their work exhuming bodies buried in clandestine cemeteries throughout the country.

Others involved in human rights prosecutions are also routinely threatened or attacked, including justice officials, forensic experts, plaintiffs, and witnesses. Journalists, labor activists, and others who have denounced abuses by the authorities are also subject to violence and intimidation. Guatemalan human rights organizations report that 158 such acts of violence or intimidation were reported between January and August 2007.

There is widespread consensus among local and international observers that the people responsible for these acts of violence and intimidation are affiliated with private, secretive, and illegally armed networks or organizations, commonly referred to in Guatemala as "clandestine groups." These groups appear to have links to both government officials and organized crime—which give them access to considerable political and economic resources. The Guatemalan justice system, which has little ability even to contain common crime, has so far proven no match for this powerful and dangerous threat to the rule of law.

Key International Actors

In September 2007 the UN secretary-general appointed a former Spanish prosecutor and judge to lead the newly-created Commission Against Impunity in Guatemala (Comision Internacional de Investigacion contra la Impunidad en Guatemala, CICIG). The commission will be composed of international and national experts, who will work in conjunction with the Guatemalan Attorney General's Office to investigate, prosecute, and dismantle the "clandestine groups" responsible for ongoing violence against human rights defenders.

In a landmark ruling, Spain's Constitutional Court held on September 26, 2005, that in accordance with the principal of "universal jurisdiction," cases of alleged genocide committed during Guatemala's internal armed conflict could be prosecuted in the Spanish courts, even if no Spanish citizens were involved. On July 7, 2006, Spanish Judge Pedraz issued international arrest warrants for eight Guatemalans and the Spanish government requested their extradition in late 2006. Although Guatemalan courts have authorized the arrests of four of the accused, at this writing only Germán Chupina Barahona, the former director of the National Police, and Ángel Aníbal Guevara Rodriguez, the former minister of defense, are in police custody in Guatemala. Extradition proceedings have been delayed due to the defendants' numerous appeals.

The UN High Commissioner for Human Rights opened an office in Guatemala in 2005 to provide observation and technical assistance on human rights practices. In February 2007 the office issued a report on Guatemala, expressing its concern over human rights violations and urging the government to take a number of steps in order to combat violence and impunity, such as providing the National Civilian Police with human rights training and with the human and financial resources required to function effectively.

The Inter-American human rights system continues to provide an important venue for human rights advocates seeking to press Guatemala to accept responsibility for past abuses.

Haiti

Haiti made important progress in restoring democratic rule in 2006, electing President René Préval after two years of postponed elections. Yet in 2007 internal conflicts within Haiti's electoral council led to the postponement of legislative elections originally scheduled for November.

President Préval's government continues to face entrenched lawlessness and chronic human rights problems, including pervasive police abuse, corruption, inhumane prison conditions, and violence against journalists.

Violence, Lawlessness, and Instability

Violent crime remains rampant in Haiti. Gang violence, for example, resulted in 29 deaths in the Port-au-Prince neighborhood of Martissant in January 2007. Kidnappings for ransom remain a serious problem, although they have decreased considerably since 2006 when there were more than 400 reported cases, according to the United Nations independent expert on human rights in Haiti. Lynching cases have become increasingly common, with reports of 60 people killed by lynching and 28 maimed or seriously injured in attempts during the first six months of 2007.

The UN stabilization mission in Haiti (known by its French acronym, MINUSTAH) and the Haitian National Police (HNP) have collaborated to infiltrate criminal-gang strongholds and successfully regained state control over some of Haiti's most violent neighborhoods. Yet, according to the UN Security Council, "the security situation remains fragile."

Police lawlessness continues to contribute to overall insecurity. The HNP is largely ineffective in preventing and investigating crime. HNP members are responsible for arbitrary arrests, as well as excessive and indiscriminate use of force. They also face credible allegations of involvement in criminal activity, including drug trafficking, as indicated by the arrest of five HNP officers in a cocaine seizure in May. Although the HNP has participated in some training sessions, the police continue to suffer from severe shortages of personnel and equipment. Police perpetrate abuses with impunity.

Justice and Accountability

Haiti's highly dysfunctional justice system is plagued by corruption, politicization, and a lack of personnel, training, and resources. According to Transparency International's Corruption Perceptions Index (CPI), which serves as a recognized standard for international corruption comparisons, Haiti ranked as the most corrupt of the 163 countries surveyed in 2006.

Accountability for past abuses remains out of reach. For example, no one has been successfully prosecuted for the killing of civilians in La Scierie, Saint-Marc in February 2004.

Prison Conditions

Severe overcrowding plagues Haiti's prison system, with more than 6,000 detainees being held in prisons with a combined total capacity of only 1,088 inmates. Conditions in those facilities are dire, with prisoners held in dirty and overcrowded cells often lacking sanitary facilities. Violations of the right to health abound, as reportedly 90 percent of inmates suffer from some form of scabies or chronic itching. In Gonaives prisoners must take turns sleeping and standing due to a lack of beds, and numerous prisoners attest that they do not receive daily meals.

Arbitrary and long-term pretrial detention of suspects is commonplace. As of July 2007 fewer than 20 percent of prisoners had actually been tried and convicted for the alleged crimes for which they were detained.

Attacks on Human Rights Defenders and Journalists

Haitian human rights activists and journalists remain targets of acts of violence and intimidation. Freelance photojournalist Jean-Rémy Badio was gunned down in January 2007 in Martissant, where he lived and had photographed gang conflicts. Johnson Edouard, a correspondent for a Haitian weekly was shot dead while sleeping in his home in Gonaives in April. Alix Joseph, a radio station manager and host, was shot dead in Gonaives in May. A week later another radio show host, François Latour, was kidnapped at gunpoint in Port-au-Prince and later shot dead.

In August two gang members were sentenced to life in prison for the July 2005 abduction and murder of Jacques Roche, cultural editor for the Haitian daily *Le Matin*. Police made arrests in July for the murder of Joseph and in October for another suspect in the murder of Roche.

In August 2007 a well known human rights advocate, Lovinsky Pierre-Antoine, was abducted. At this writing his whereabouts remain unknown.

Key International Actors

MINUSTAH has been heavily involved in efforts to support and train the local police force to carry out its security functions. The UN Security Council voted unanimously in October 2007 to extend MINUSTAH until October 2008. At the end of August 2007 the force, which was created by a Security Council resolution in April 2004, included 7,054 troops and 1,771 police. The new resolution provides for 7,060 troops and 2,091 police, as part of the gradual shifting of stabilization capacity from the international forces to the Haitian police.

MINUSTAH conducted 19 security operations with the HNP in the Cité Soleil and Martissant neighborhoods of Port-au-Prince between December 2006 and February 2007. Six peacekeepers were injured in this process, continuing a history of clashes between gangs and the joint United Nations and Haitian security forces. Two peacekeepers from the Jordanian battalion of MINUSTAH were shot and killed near Cité Soleil in November 2006.

With the agreement of the Government of Haiti, the UN Human Rights Council in September 2007 decided to renew the mandate of the independent expert appointed by the secretary-general on the situation of human rights in Haiti.

The United States is Haiti's largest donor and in 2007 made a new pledge of US$106 million, to be allocated over a one-year period to aid Haiti's economic recovery. Canada, Haiti's second-largest donor, continues in its efforts "to re-establish security and stability" in the country. Canadian civilian police officers are currently part of MINUSTAH, and Canada has pledged more than C$550 million to the country to be distributed between 2006 and 2011. The European Union signed an agreement granting €26 million in 2008-2009 to supplement the €233 million already allocated through 2012.

In February 2007 a US federal court judge in Miami ordered Carl Dorélien, a former Haitian army colonel, to pay $4.3 million in damages—mostly out of the $3.2 million he won from the Florida lottery—to a former labor leader for torture and to a widow for the death of her husband in the 1994 Raboteau massacre.

In May 2007 a New York state supreme court judge rejected a plea bargain in the case of Emmanuel "Toto" Constant, a former leader of Haiti's notorious FRAPH death squad, held liable in 2006 in New York for $19 million in damages for rape and torture committed by paramilitary forces under his command in Haiti from 1991 to 1993, and who currently faces criminal charges for mortgage fraud in the US.

Mexico

Mexico's criminal justice system continues to be plagued by human rights problems. Persons under arrest or imprisoned face torture and ill-treatment. Law enforcement officials often neglect to investigate and prosecute those responsible for human rights violations, including those committed during Mexico's "dirty war" and abuses perpetrated nowadays during law enforcement operations. Mexico lacks adequate legal protections for women and girls against violence and sexual abuse.

Criminal Justice System

The criminal justice system routinely fails to provide justice to victims of violent crime and human rights violations. The causes of this failure are varied and include corruption, inadequate training and resources, and abusive policing practices.

Torture remains a widespread problem within the Mexican criminal justice system. One perpetuating factor is the acceptance by some judges of evidence obtained through torture and other mistreatment. Another is the failure to investigate and prosecute most cases of torture.

Over 40 percent of prisoners in Mexico have never been convicted of a crime. Rather, they are held in pretrial detention, often waiting years for trial. The excessive use of pretrial detention contributes to prison overcrowding. Prison inmates are also subject to abuses including extortion by guards and the imposition of solitary confinement for indefinite periods. Foreign migrants are especially vulnerable to such abuses.

In March 2007 President Felipe Calderon presented a constitutional reform proposal aimed at strengthening the ability of prosecutors to combat organized crime. The proposal creates serious exceptions to basic due process guarantees, including allowing prosecutors to adopt precautionary measures—such as administrative detention, home searches, and phone tapping—without previous judicial authorization. At this writing the proposal is being debated in Congress.

A major shortcoming of the Mexican justice system is that it routinely leaves the task of investigating and prosecuting army abuses to military authorities. The military justice system is ill-equipped for such tasks: it lacks the independence necessary to carry out reliable investigations and its operations suffer from a general absence of transparency. The ability of military prosecutors to investigate army abuses is further undermined by a fear of the army, which is widespread in many rural communities and which inhibits civilian victims and witnesses from providing information to military authorities.

Abuses by Security Forces

Mexican police forces routinely employ excessive force when carrying out crowd-control operations. In July 2007 a protest march ended in a violent confrontation with police in Oaxaca's state capital. The police fired teargas canisters, and marchers and police attacked each other with stones. Human Rights Watch received credible reports that police carried out arbitrary arrests, including pulling people from passing cars and buses, and beat those in custody. These events followed sporadic violent clashes that began in June 2006 in connection with a teachers' strike; during those clashes state and federal police forces used force excessively.

Over the past year Mexican soldiers have committed egregious abuses while engaged in law enforcement activities. According to the national human rights ombudsman, in May 2007, for example, soldiers arbitrarily detained 65 people in Michoacán state, holding some incommunicado at a military base, beating many of the detainees, and raping four minors. That same month soldiers in Michoacán arbitrarily detained eight people, keeping them incommunicado at a military base where they beat and covered the heads of four of them with plastic bags. In June soldiers opened fire on a truck in Sinaloa, killing five people, including three children, and injuring three others.

Impunity for "Dirty War" Crimes

In March 2007 President Calderon officially closed the Special Prosecutor's Office that former President Vicente Fox had established to address abuses committed during the country's "dirty war" in the 1960s, '70s and '80s. During its five-year existence the office made very limited progress in investigating and prosecuting these crimes. Its initial advances—such as the 2003 Supreme Court ruling authorizing prosecution of decades-old "disappearance" cases—were offset by significant failures. It did not obtain a single criminal conviction. Of the more than 600 "disappearance" cases, it filed charges in 16 cases and obtained indictments in nine; the office determined the whereabouts of only six "disappeared" individuals. At this writing only the genocide charge against former President Luis Echeverria for his responsibility in the 1968 massacre of student protestors remains pending before the courts.

Reproductive Rights, Domestic Violence, and Sexual Abuse

Mexican laws do not adequately protect women and girls against domestic violence and sexual abuse. Some laws on violence against women run directly counter to international standards, including provisions of Mexican law that define sanctions for some sexual offenses with reference to the "chastity" of the victim, and penalize domestic violence only when the victim has been battered repeatedly. Legal protections that do exist are often not enforced vigorously. Girls and women who report rape or violence to the authorities are generally met with suspicion, apathy, and disrespect. As a result, victims are often reluctant to report crimes and such underreporting in turn undercuts pressure for necessary legal reforms. The net effect is that sexual and domestic violence against women and girls continues to be rampant and shrouded in impunity.

In April 2007 the Mexico City legislature legalized abortion in the first 12 weeks of pregnancy. Abortion continues to be criminalized in the rest of Mexico, though every federal state in the country allows abortion in certain specific circumstances, including after rape. Yet pregnant rape victims who seek to terminate their imposed pregnancy are often thwarted from doing so by the dismissive and even hostile treatment they receive from authorities, in disregard for their rights to non-discrimination, due process, and equality under the law.

Freedom of Expression

Journalists, particularly those who have investigated drug trafficking or have been critical of state governments, have faced harassment and attacks. In April 2007 a journalist was shot dead in Acapulco, another in Sonora received death threats and was beaten unconscious, and a third in Chihuahua was kidnapped and found dead a week later. In October three media workers from a newspaper in Oaxaca were shot and killed. Five Mexican journalists have gone missing since 2005, including four who had reported on drug trafficking or organized crime.

In March 2007 the Mexican Congress passed a law that decriminalizes defamation, libel, and slander at the federal level. However, at the state level defamation laws continue to be excessively restrictive and tend to undermine freedom of expression. Besides monetary penalties, journalists are subject to criminal prosecution for alleged defamation of public officials.

Access to Information

A 2002 federal law on transparency and access to information increased avenues for public scrutiny of the federal government. However, there is still considerable risk that secrecy will reassert itself in the future: the federal agency in charge of applying the law to the executive has not been granted autonomy from the executive branch, remains vulnerable to political interference, and has encountered resistance from several key government agencies. Progress made in promoting transparency within the executive branch has not been matched in other branches of government nor in the autonomous state institutions.

Labor Rights

Legitimate labor-organizing activity continues to be obstructed by collective bargaining agreements negotiated between management and pro-management unions. These agreements often fail to provide worker benefits beyond the minimums mandated by Mexican legislation. Workers who seek to form independent unions risk losing their jobs, as inadequate laws and poor enforcement generally fail to protect them from retaliatory dismissals.

Right to Education

A chronic concern in Mexico is the government's failure to ensure that tens of thousands of rural children receive primary education during the months that their families migrate across state lines to work in agricultural camps. A large number of parents decide to take their children to work with them in the fields rather than have them attend school during these months. This decision is largely due to economic conditions, and to the government's failure to enforce child labor laws. Although there is a federal program to provide primary schooling in the agricultural camps, the classes are generally offered in the evening, when children are too exhausted from their work to study.

Key International Actors

The United Nations High Commissioner for Human Rights maintains an in-country office that, in December 2003, produced a comprehensive report documenting ongoing human rights problems and providing detailed recommendations for addressing them. The office is now working on an assessment of human rights problems in Mexico City and the state of Guerrero.

In August 2007 the Inter-American Commission on Human Rights held that Mexico was responsible for the detention, torture, and subsequent "disappearance" of Rosendo Radilla, carried out by members of the Mexican army in Guerrero in 1974. It stated Mexico had failed to inform Radilla's family of his whereabouts, and to adequately investigate the case and prosecute those responsible.

PERU

Justice for past abuses continues to be a leading human rights concern in Peru. While authorities have made some progress in holding accountable those responsible for abuses committed during its 20-year armed conflict (1980-2000), most perpetrators continue to evade justice. Investigations of massacres and "disappearances" by government forces have been held up in part by lack of military cooperation.

The efforts of Peruvian prosecutors to bring former President Alberto Fujimori to justice in Peru finally bore fruit in September 2007, when the Chilean Supreme Court, in a landmark decision, authorized his extradition on charges of human rights abuse and corruption.

A law endangering the autonomy of nongovernmental organizations (NGOs) was approved by Congress in 2006 but declared partially unconstitutional in 2007 by the Constitutional Court.

Confronting the Past

The government Truth and Reconciliation Commission estimated in 2003 that almost 70,000 people died or "disappeared" during the armed conflict. Many were victims of atrocities committed by the Shining Path and another insurgent group, and others of human rights abuses by state agents.

At this writing, former president Fujimori was imprisoned in Lima, awaiting trial. He had been in self-imposed exile in Japan for five years, before traveling to Chile, where he was arrested in November 2005. The crimes for which he faces prosecution in Peru include his alleged involvement in the extrajudicial execution of 15 people at a barbecue in the Barrios Altos district of Lima in November 1991 and the forced disappearance and murder of nine students and a teacher from La Cantuta University in July 1992.

Efforts have been underway to investigate and prosecute former officials and military officers implicated in scores of other killings and "disappearances" dating from the beginning of the armed conflict. For example, at least 50 alleged members of the Colina Group, the death squad directly responsible for the human rights crimes for which Fujimori was extradited, have been on trial in Lima since August 2005. Yet, at this writing, only 17 former military officers and civilians had been convicted for abuses attributed to state actors by the truth commission.

Lack of cooperation by the armed forces has hampered the investigations of these cases. The military has often failed to provide information needed to identify potentially key witnesses who served in rural counterinsurgency bases during the conflict. It has also declined to identify military officials known to witnesses only by their aliases.

Attacks on Journalists

Journalists who publicize abuses by local government officials are vulnerable to intimidation in some parts of the country. In March 2007, Miguel Pérez Julca, who worked for a news program on a local radio station in Jaén, Cajamarca province, was shot twice in the head by two gunmen in front of his wife, who was also injured, and two sons. He died while being rushed to hospital. Pérez had been reporting on police corruption and problems of public security in the city. Four days after Pérez's murder, three other journalists from Jaén received death threats in text messages on their cell phones. Pérez was the third Peruvian journalist killed in similar circumstances since 2004.

Torture

Torture and ill-treatment of criminal suspects continues to be a problem in Peru. The Human Rights Commission (Comisión de Derechos Humanos, COMISEDH)—an NGO that represents torture victims in court proceedings—recorded 78 complaints of torture between January 2005 and October 2007. In recent years, Peruvian courts have made some progress in holding accountable police who abuse detainees. Since 2000, the Supreme Court has confirmed prison sentences against 15 police officers, military agents, and prison guards for torture in seven cases. In July 2007, two policemen received eight-year and four-year sentences for a beating that led to the death of Ricardo Huaringa Félix in 2004. In September 2006, Peru ratified the Optional Protocol to the Convention against Torture and Other Cruel, Inhuman and Degrading Treatment or Punishment.

Death Penalty

The death penalty in Peru is restricted to cases of treason in wartime, and has not been applied since the 1970s. However, following an armed attack in Ayacucho in December 2006 in which eight people were killed, President Alan García presented a bill to Congress to reintroduce the death penalty for terrorist crimes. The constitution already contemplates the death penalty in such circumstances, but it has not been incorporated into the Criminal Code. In January 2007, a bill to do so was defeated in Congress by a substantial majority.

Human Rights Defenders

In November 2006, President Alan Garcia supported legislation that would allow the government to "supervise" the activities of Peruvian NGOs that receive foreign funding. After strong protests by civil society groups, an amended version of the bill was passed that limited its application to organizations that receive government funding or tax benefits. Privately-funded NGOs would still be required to register their activities and expenditures with the government aid agency. In September 2007, the Constitutional Court ruled that this requirement to report expenditures was unconstitutional.

Key International Actors

In November 2006, the Inter-American Court of Human Rights ruled on a case involving the indiscriminate killing in 1992 of 41 Shining Path prisoners at the Miguel Castro Castro prison in Lima. The court ordered the government to pay compensation of about $20 million to the families of the dead and to individuals tortured during the operation. President García said that he could not accept paying compensation to "terrorists," and said he would ask the court for "interpretation" of its decision.

VENEZUELA

After repeatedly winning elections and referendums, and surviving a coup d'etat in 2002, President Chávez and his supporters have sought to consolidate power by undermining the independence of the judiciary and the press, institutions essential for the protection and promotion of human rights.

State interference in trade union elections has weakened the right to free association. The government has failed to tackle widespread police abuse, and prison conditions remain among the worst on the continent. In 2007 fundamental due process rights, including fair trial rights, were threatened by proposed constitutional reforms allowing the indefinite suspension of rights during states of emergency. The reforms were defeated in a national referendum in December.

Independence of the Judiciary

The governing coalition in the Venezuelan National Assembly dealt a severe blow to judicial independence in December 2004 when it packed the country's Supreme Court by adding 12 new justices. A law passed earlier that year expanded the court from 20 to 32 members. The law also gave the National Assembly the power to remove judges from the Supreme Court by simple majority, rather than the two-thirds majority required under the constitution.

Since the 2004 court-packing law, the Supreme Court's judicial commission has fired hundreds of provisional judges and granted permanent judgeships to around a thousand others.

Freedom of Expression

While Venezuela enjoys vibrant public debate on political issues, laws passed since late 2004 have created dangerous restrictions on the media that pose a serious threat to freedom of expression. The Law of Social Responsibility in Radio and Television, which went into effect in December 2004, establishes detailed regulations for the content of television and radio programs. For example, stations deemed to "condone or incite" public disturbances or publish messages "contrary to the security of the nation" are subject to heavy fines and can be ordered to suspend broadcasting for 72 hours. Key terms in the law, such as those quoted above, are ill-defined, inviting politically-motivated applications. The National Commission of Telecommunications (CONATEL) may issue "precautionary measures" that prohibit the transmission of outlawed content.

Government officials have regularly threatened opposition media with sanctions under the Law of Social Responsibility, though no station has in fact been sanctioned to date for its coverage of events or expressing its political views. During student protests in May and June 2007, for example, the Directorate of Social Responsibility (the government body that investigates infractions of the law) warned stations about transmitting messages that incite hatred and law-breaking, and announced that the directorate was in permanent session monitoring media coverage of the protests.

President Chávez has repeatedly responded to critical coverage by threatening television stations that they would lose their broadcasting rights as soon as their concessions expired. In the case of Radio Caracas Television (RCTV), he carried out the threat, announcing at a nationally broadcast military ceremony in December 2006 that RCTV would not have its concession renewed because of its support for the 2002 coup. Neither the accusation about the station's role in the April 2002 events nor its alleged breach of broadcasting standards were ever proven in a proceeding in which RCTV had an opportunity to present a defense.

RCTV was removed from the public airwaves when its 20-year concession expired on May 27, 2007. Several days earlier, in compliance with a Supreme Court order, the military took control of RCTV's transmission facilities across the country, enabling them to be used by TVes, a newly created state channel. RCTV has since renewed broadcasting as a cable channel.

The government's administration of broadcasting concessions lacks transparency and is strongly influenced by political considerations. Other private stations which have requested permission to extend their frequencies and coverage from the government broadcasting authority, CONATEL, have had their requests turned down or ignored for years, while new stations recently created by the state, such as Vive, Telesur, and TVes, have quickly been approved for national coverage.

In March 2005 amendments to the Criminal Code came into force which extended the scope of Venezuela's *desacato* (disrespect) laws, and increased penalties for criminal defamation and libel. At least eight journalists faced charges in 2007 for *desacato*, libel, defamation, and related offenses.

In contrast to its efforts to restrict private media, the government has actively promoted the growth of nonprofit community broadcast media, and has given substantial financial backing to new community media ventures. The regulations include safeguards to protect pluralism and prevent intervention by the government or political parties in community media. In June 2007 more than 270 community radio stations and more than 30 community television outlets were licensed and operating across the country, according to CONATEL.

Freedom of Association

An article of the 1999 Constitution which authorizes the National Electoral Commission (Comision Nacional Electoral, CNE) to organize trade union elections is a serious obstacle to freedom of association and collective bargaining rights. The Ministry of Labor has frequently denied unions the right to represent their workers because of delays in the authorization of elections.

Police Killings

Extrajudicial killings by security agents remain a frequent occurrence in Venezuela. Thousands of extrajudicial executions have been recorded in the last decade. Impunity remains the norm. Between January 2000 and February 2007, the attorney general's office registered 6,068 alleged killings by the police and National Guard. Of 1,142 officials charged, only 204 were convicted.

Following several egregious murders implicating police agents, a long overdue police reform process began in June 2006 when then-Minister of the Interior and Justice Jesse Chacón convened the National Commission for Police Reform. After months of broad public consultations and debate, in January 2007 the commission published recommendations for remodeling public security institutions and strengthening police oversight. The reforms, however, had yet to be implemented at this writing.

Prison Conditions

Venezuelan prisons are among the most violent in Latin America. Venezuelan Prison Watch (Observatorio Venezolano de Prisiones), a Caracas-based group that monitors prison conditions, reported 370 violent prison deaths and 781 injuries in the first eight months of 2007. With a homicide rate of more than 20 per 1,000 prisoners, the risk of violent death is greater inside than outside prison walls. Weak security and corruption of guards allow armed gangs to effectively control prisons. Overcrowding, deteriorating infrastructure, and poorly trained security personnel contribute to the brutal conditions. Despite much fanfare, government plans to "humanize" the penitentiary system have not resulted in any notable improvements.

Constitutional Reform Proposals

In 2007 President Chávez and his supporters in the National Assembly proposed far-reaching reforms to the Venezuelan constitution. The reforms, which included 69 amendments covering a wide range of issues, would have enhanced executive powers during states of emergency to allow the suspension of due process rights (including essential guarantees like the right to fair trial and the presumption of innocence), removing constitutional time-limits on emergencies, and eliminating the Supreme Court's power to review decrees that suspend rights.

A positive aspect of the reforms was the proposed modification of the constitution's nondiscrimination guarantee to include sexual orientation and political views.

The proposed reforms were narrowly defeated in a national referendum in December.

Human Rights Defenders

Although human rights advocacy groups operate in Venezuela without legal restrictions, the government often questions their legitimacy and tries to block their participation in international human rights fora, typically on grounds that their work is political or that they receive US or other foreign funding. In

December 2006 the comptroller general wrote to the Organization of American States (OAS) objecting to the publication on the OAS website of a report by the Venezuelan branch of Transparency International about Venezuela's implementation of the Inter-American Convention against Corruption. Due to government objections, Transparency Venezuela was not allowed to present its report at a meeting of an expert panel of the OAS in June 2007.

Some human rights defenders continue to face threats and intimidation. They include María del Rosario Guerrero Gallucci and her husband, Adolfo Segundo Martínez Barrios, members of a human rights group in the state of Guarico that seeks justice for victims of police killings. The two were shot and wounded by a police agent in April 2006, and reportedly have been subject to repeated death threats. In July 2006 the Inter-American Court of Human Rights ordered Venezuela to take special measures to protect their lives and physical integrity.

Key International Actors

In July 2007, the Inter-American Commission on Human Rights (IACHR) transmitted a live hearing on the case of seven people killed during protests that culminated in the April 11, 2002 coup attempt against President Chávez. At this writing, Venezuela has still not set a date for a mission by the IACHR, which has not visited the country since 2002. The government has conditioned the visit on a public mea culpa by the commission for what officials consider its failure to condemn the coup in forthright terms.

In May 2007 the presidency of the European Union issued a statement expressing concern about the non-renewal of RCTV's broadcasting concession. The senates of Chile, Brazil, and the United States issued similar resolutions, while Cuba, Bolivia, Ecuador, and Nicaragua endorsed the decision.

BURMA

Crackdown

Repression of the 2007 Popular Protests in Burma

HUMAN
RIGHTS
WATCH

WORLD REPORT
2008

ASIA

AFGHANISTAN

Life for the average Afghan remains short, miserable, and brutal. Average lifespan for men and women hovers at around 45 years. According to the United Nations, nearly a third of all Afghans, some 6.5 million people, suffer from chronic food insecurity. Afghans face escalating violations of their human rights at the hands of a variety of abusers: the Taliban and other anti-government insurgent groups, including Gulbuddin Hekmatyar's Hezb-e Islami and tribal militias, criminal groups and local warlords (many with government affiliations), and, increasingly, the Afghan government itself. The insurgency in the south undermines development and reconstruction in the comparatively peaceful north, and as predicted, destabilizes neighboring Pakistan. The United Nations' assessment of areas considered "most dangerous" and thus out of bounds for nearly all aid workers doubled in 2007 to cover one-third of Afghanistan.

Where there are signs of development and economic progress, much of it is driven by a narcotics industry that is burgeoning, despite more than a billion dollars from the United States and the United Kingdom for counter-narcotics efforts. Afghanistan produces some 95 percent of the world's total supply of heroin. The narcotics industry penetrates ever more deeply into all areas of the Afghan economy and political system, weakening the rule of law and perverting the political process.

Nevertheless, there were a few bright spots where international assistance allowed Afghans to improve their living conditions, for instance by allowing hundreds of thousands of children to return to school if they were not hampered by security, indicating that helping Afghanistan does not pose an intractable problem.

Violence and Insecurity

2007 was a bloodier year than any since the US-led forces ousted the Taliban in 2001. Casualty rates were at least 25 percent higher than the previous year. Civilians were increasingly caught in fighting between anti-government forces and government forces and their international supporters. Anti-government forces also routinely violate the laws of war by launching attacks from civilian areas, or

AFGHANISTAN

The Human Cost

The Consequences of Insurgent Attacks in Afghanistan

H U M A N
R I G H T S
W A T C H

retreating to such areas, knowingly drawing return fire. NATO and US-led Coalition forces killed more than 300 civilians, although it is possible that the number is higher, given the difficulty of Western forces in distinguishing combatants from civilians and their extensive use of airpower. The Taliban began using anti-personnel mines in Helmand province again, complicating efforts to eradicate mines from one of the most mine-infested countries in the world.

Stymied by NATO from establishing clear control over more territory, in particular larger urban centers, anti-government groups carried out a record number of suicide bombings and attacks on civilian targets, destabilizing parts of the north and west of the country—including areas adjacent to Kabul—which had previously been relatively quiet. At this writing, such attacks have killed 374 Afghan civilians in 2007 and injured at least 631 civilians.

The Taliban increasingly relied on public executions to terrorize and rule populations living in areas under their influence. They carried out at least 28 beheadings, several of them filmed and broadcast on the internet. For instance, in April the Taliban distributed video footage of a clearly prepubescent boy beheading Ghulam Nabi, a Pakistani militant accused of betraying a top Taliban official killed in a December airstrike. The Taliban targeted humanitarian aid workers, journalists, doctors, religious leaders, and civilian government employees, condemning them as spies or collaborators. In June they publicly hanged four elders in Helmand province because they were perceived as cooperating with NATO forces. Insurgent groups killed at least 34 aid workers in Afghanistan in 2007.

At this writing, anti-government groups have kidnapped at least 41 Afghan civilians in 2007 and killed at least 23 of them, including journalist Ajmal Naqshbandi and driver Sayed Agha in Helmand. Anti-government groups also targeted foreign aid workers. The Taliban claimed responsibility for killing a German national whom they had taken hostage. In July the Taliban abducted a group of 23 South Koreans affiliated with a Christian organization. The Taliban killed two of the hostages before eventually releasing the rest.

Government Abuses and Failures

The Afghan government continues to lose public legitimacy because of widespread corruption, failure to improve living standards, and lack of progress in establishing the rule of law even in areas under its control.

In a troubling sign, President Hamid Karzai's government did very little to implement the Action Plan for Peace, Reconciliation and Justice, a five-year plan for implementing transitional justice in Afghanistan, which is part of the Afghanistan Compact and which he officially initiated on December 12, 2006. The warlords and criminals entrenched in the Afghan parliament attempted to pass several pieces of legislation designed to curtail human rights. In a highly controversial move, a group led by Abdul Rabb al Rasul Sayyaf, Burhanuddin Rabbani, and Taj Mohammad, all of whom have been implicated in war crimes and other serious human rights abuses, attempted to pass a blanket amnesty law. Facing unprecedented public opposition, the bill was amended to allow individuals to file criminal and civil cases against perpetrators, though these provisions are unlikely to be effective because of a lack of political will and severe threats and intimidation against witnesses and complainants. President Karzai did not sign the legislation and its legal status remains unclear.

The Afghan parliament made other attempts to restrict human rights. On May 21 the lower house of parliament voted to suspend parliamentarian Malali Joya, one of Afghanistan's most outspoken defenders of human rights, for her televised criticism of her colleagues. The parliament also attempted to enact significant limits on the freedom of the press, but in the face of strong pressure from Afghan and international journalists the parliament eased some of the proposed restrictions. The legislation has not been enacted as of this writing.

Unable to stem the growing crime wave associated with increasing militia activity and narco-trafficking, Karzai bowed to pressure from ultra-conservative groups and authorized the execution of 15 criminals in October by firing squad at the Pul-i Charkhi high security prison outside Kabul.

The National Directorate of Security, recipient of significant financial and operational support from the US, increasingly abuses prisoners. Many of them, including some originally detained by NATO forces, are held in unofficial or secret prisons.

Women

Afghan women and girls rank among the world's worst off by most indicators, such as life expectancy (46 years), maternal mortality (1,600 deaths per 100,000 births), and literacy (12.6 percent of females 15 and older). Women and girls still confront significant barriers to working outside the home and restrictions on their mobility; for example, many still cannot travel without an accompanying male relative and a burqa.

Children

As part of their campaign of terrorizing the civilian population, the Taliban target schools, and in particular girls' schools—the government reported that insecurity shut down 450 schools throughout the country, including 40 percent of schools in the south. On June 12, Taliban killed two schoolgirls in front of a girls' school in Logar, near Kabul, and injured three others and a teacher. The United Nations Children's Fund (UNICEF) said these incidents stalled or reversed the progress achieved in female education since the fall of the Taliban regime, and had already caused a significant drop in attendance in secondary schools. While the number of girls in school increased quickly after the Taliban's ouster in 2001, only one-third of school-age girls attended school in 2007.

According to the Afghan Independent Human Rights Commission, child labor was widely prevalent throughout the country and ranked alongside insecurity as one of the top reasons for children not attending school.

Refugees and Displacement

Insecurity and armed conflict continued to cause new displacement and deter millions of Afghans from returning to their homes. Tens of thousands of Afghans in the southern provinces of Helmand, Kandahar, Oruzgan, and Farah left their homes to escape fighting, leaving them particularly vulnerable to malnutrition and disease and with very limited access to humanitarian aid.

Nearly two million Afghan refugees have returned to their country, mostly from Pakistan. But the United Nations continues to report the presence of three to four million Afghan refugees in Pakistan and Iran. Between April and June the Iranian government forcibly deported nearly 100,000 registered and unregistered Afghans living and working in Iran (see Iran chapter).

Key International Actors

Despite a strong UN mandate, Afghanistan's chief international supporters continue to dither over their role and responsibilities in Afghanistan. The existing military, political, and economic resources are poorly coordinated. There is no coherent mechanism for assisting civilians injured or displaced by NATO forces. One sign of this is that, five years after the United Nations Assistance Mission in Afghanistan (UNAMA) was created, there are not nearly enough UNAMA human rights monitors.

Taking into account Afghanistan's population and size, the 40,000 NATO and US-led coalition forces in the country are a small fraction of the security forces deployed in other recent post-conflict areas like the Balkans and Timor-Leste. Many are limited by national laws to comparatively safe areas in Afghanistan or cannot act to protect ordinary Afghans adequately. Despite significant overlap between NATO and the European Union, the international security effort in Afghanistan has been hobbled by insufficient resources and the failure to effectively address the security concerns of the Afghan population. For instance, the 160 police trainers fielded by the EU were too few to train the needed number of officers, resulting in a police force rife with corruption and lacking in public legitimacy.

The US military operates in Afghanistan without an adequate legal framework, such as a Status of Forces Agreement with the Afghan government, and continues to detain hundreds of Afghans without adequate legal process. In a singular exception to an otherwise poor record of accountability, on February 13, 2007, a US federal court sentenced David Passaro, a CIA contractor found guilty of assault in the beating death of Abdul Wali in June 2003, to eight-and-a-half years in prison.

BANGLADESH

A military-backed caretaker government was installed in January 2007 and ruled Bangladesh under a state of emergency for the rest of the year.

The caretaker government announced police and judicial reforms and promised to set up a National Human Rights Commission. It was initially welcomed by most Bangladeshis, civil society activists, and the international community in the hope that it would stamp out corruption, build the rule of law, and restore democracy.

However, as the year progressed there was increasing concern in Bangladesh and internationally about the lack of progress on election preparations, the increasingly visible role of the army as the main power in the country, and the large numbers of arbitrary arrests, cases of torture, and custodial killings by security forces acting with impunity under emergency rules.

As part of its "minus two" policy of removing the leaders of the two main parties from the political process, the government arrested former prime ministers Khaleda Zia, leader of the Bangladesh Nationalist Party, and Sheikh Hasina, leader of the Awami League, as well as other senior politicians and government officials, and charged them with corruption. In the name of sorting out political gridlock and preparing credible national elections, the government banned all political and trade union activities and imposed new limits on press freedoms.

Political Developments

In December 2006, widespread protests over alleged fraudulent election preparations led to deepening political instability. Several people were killed and hundreds were injured in the violence. On January 11, 2007, after the United Nations and European Union announced that plans for elections were so compromised that they would not send observers, then-President Iajuddin Ahmed announced that elections would be postponed and declared a state of emergency. He also resigned as chief advisor, and on January 12, a new army-backed "caretaker government" headed by Fakhruddin Ahmed was brought in.

(Under Bangladesh's constitution, a caretaker government is appointed for a period of three months immediately prior to elections to ensure they are carried out in a neutral and impartial manner. Since October 2006, President Iajuddin Ahmed had served as "chief advisor"—in effect, prime minister—of such a caretaker government. On January 11, the old caretaker government was dissolved and a new one established the following day, with Fakhruddin Ahmed as chief advisor.)

Although Fakruddin Ahmed promised reforms and a quick return to democracy, elections were soon put off until December 2008. Immediately upon being installed, the caretaker government issued the Emergency Power Rules, still in effect at this writing, which dramatically dilute constitutional protections for basic rights.

Anti-Corruption

Pervasive corruption has caused widespread disillusionment with the political parties running the country. Bangladesh has for many years ranked at or near the bottom of Transparency International's index of corruption. On April 18, 2007, the caretaker government announced the Anti-Corruption Commission (Amendment) Ordinance aimed at rooting out high level corruption and stopping the influence of organized crime over politics. It acceded to the UN Convention against Corruption, replaced senior bureaucrats with persons perceived to be more honest, and forced some officials in key statutory and constitutional positions—such as the attorney general and heads of the Anti-Corruption Commission and Election Commission—to resign and be replaced by officials considered to have greater integrity. These moves proved highly popular.

The Anti-Corruption Ordinance, however, also empowers Anti-Corruption Commission officials, with retroactive effect, to arrest suspects without warrants, confiscate property without court orders, and detain suspects for thirty days without a warrant. Many suspects have been held for 30 days while evidence of their alleged offenses is collected. The special tribunals set up for these cases often fail to meet international fair trial standards because of limits on access to counsel, flawed evidentiary requirements, and lack of judicial independence.

State of Emergency and Suspension of Rights

Tens of thousands of people were reportedly arrested in the weeks following the declaration of a state of emergency in January 2007. The government has not published accurate statistics on detainees, access to official places of detention has been restricted, and the security forces have used unofficial sites, such as the headquarters of the Directorate General of Forces Intelligence (DGFI, or military intelligence) in Dhaka, making it impossible to know exactly how many people were arrested or how many are still being held.

Most arrests under the state of emergency have taken place without warrants. Security forces have told detainees that they do not need such authorization under emergency rules. Evidence used to make arrests often has not been transparent or available to detainees or their lawyers. Credible reports suggest that many arrests have been based on coerced statements from others or have been the product of "score-settling." Many offenses have been deemed "non-bailable" under emergency rules, resulting in indefinite detention even for minor charges.

Bail orders or habeas corpus decisions in favor of detainees often have been ignored or overturned by politicized appellate decisions. On August 30, the United Nations Special Rapporteur on the independence of judges and lawyers expressed concern at alleged irregularities in the trial of Sigma Huda, the United Nations Special Rapporteur on trafficking in persons, who was convicted by the Special Anti-Corruption Court of Bangladesh and sentenced to three years' imprisonment on extortion charges, citing reports that the "right to legal representation and the independence of the court were severely affected during her trial."

Torture

Torture in custody, a longstanding problem in Bangladesh, continues to be routine. The use of unofficial places of detention for interrogation by the DGFI and others has exacerbated this problem, as such sites are beyond the scrutiny of the courts, lawyers, family members, and the media.

Professor Anwar Hossan, a Dhaka university professor, was taken into custody for his alleged involvement in inciting August campus protests against the army. He was taken to an unofficial detention center run by DGFI, where he remained for

BANGLADESH

Judge, Jury, and Executioner

Torture and Extrajudicial Killings by Bangladesh's
Elite Security Force

HUMAN
RIGHTS
WATCH

two days without being brought before a judge. When he was later produced in court, he said that he had not been allowed to sleep, was questioned constantly, and was slapped.

Similarly, Tasneem Khalil, a *Daily Star* reporter, CNN representative, and Human Rights Watch consultant, was taken to an unofficial place of detention by DGFI on May 11, where he was interrogated, tortured, and coerced into making a false confession. After international pressure, he was released but later had to seek asylum in Sweden.

Extrajudicial Killings

The paramilitary Rapid Action Battalion (RAB) and the police continue to engage in extrajudicial killings of suspected criminals and others. The security forces euphemistically call these "crossfire" killings, falsely suggesting they are carried out in self defense. Such killings continued under the caretaker government. Odhikar, a Dhaka-based human rights monitoring organization, said that 126 people were killed by security forces during the first 210 days of emergency. Of them, 82 were allegedly killed in "crossfire," while at least 23 others were allegedly tortured to death. The most brutal was the March torture and killing of Choles Ritchil, a well known rights activist. Although eyewitnesses identified some of the perpetrators, the government failed to bring them to justice.

Freedom of Expression, Assembly, and Association

Section 5 of the Emergency Power Rules bans the use of the internet or other electronic or print media to publish "provocative" editorials, feature articles, news items, talk shows, or cartoons. Violations lead to confiscation of equipment and jail terms ranging from two to five years.

In 2007, many journalists and NGO workers continued to receive anonymous phone calls from persons claiming to be members of DGFI, the army, or RAB, warning them against defaming the army or government. Others were summoned to military intelligence headquarters and delivered warnings. Some, such as Tasneem Khalil, were tortured, sending a chilling message to all journalists.

Security forces use mass arrests as a means to suppress demonstrations. Curfew was imposed after protests erupted in August when a squabble between soldiers and Dhaka university students spread into demonstrations against the emergency restrictions and de facto army rule. Many began to question whether the military would be willing to give up power.

Soon after the August demonstrations, two television channels—Ekushey Television (ETV) and the CSB news network—received a written notice from the Press Information Department warning them not to broadcast "provocative" news. Several journalists were arrested and some were beaten up while they were covering the protests.

Human Rights Defenders

The activities of nongovernmental organizations (NGOs) were also restricted by the army. In July 2007, a notice was issued by the NGO Affairs Bureau asking all voluntary organizations to spend at least half of their foreign grants on visible development works such as roads and canals. Human rights defenders, including the head of Odhikar, were threatened for highlighting abuses by troops.

Key International Actors

While governments such as the US, UK, and India expressed concern about the slow pace of election preparations, few expressed concern over the country's poor human rights situation. Most cheered reforms while turning a blind eye to the human rights violations that accompanied mass arrests and continuing reports of torture and illegal killings. Although the army already had effectively taken power in January when it installed the second caretaker government, no international actors publicly called on the army to return full powers to a civilian government.

The Bangladeshi army continues to receive assistance and training from several foreign governments including the US and UK, which are concerned about Islamic militancy in Bangladesh. The army remains a large contributor to UN peacekeeping operations and is thus susceptible to pressure from the UN and others to restore civilian rule and enforce basic rights. At this writing, international actors had not used this leverage.

BURMA

Burma's deplorable human rights record received widespread international attention in 2007 as anti-government protests in August and September were met with a brutal crackdown by security forces of the authoritarian military government, the State Peace and Development Council (SPDC). Denial of basic freedoms in Burma continues, and restrictions on the internet, telecommunications, and freedom of expression and assembly sharply increased in 2007. Abuses against civilians in ethnic areas are widespread, involving forced labor, summary executions, sexual violence, and expropriation of land and property.

Violent Crackdown on Protests

Poor economic conditions sparked a series of demonstrations and arrests from February onward. Protests were directly related to declining living standards, limited access to health services and education, and poor electricity supplies. Despite booming revenues from natural gas exports, the government raised fuel prices sharply and without warning on August 15, which had an immediate and adverse effect on the civilian population.

Small-scale protest marches were conducted in Rangoon by members of the "88 Generation Students" and members and supporters of the National League for Democracy (NLD), calling for improved living standards and dialogue with the government on political reforms. Demonstrations were broken up by police and members of the Union Solidarity and Development Association (USDA), a pro-government "social welfare" organization with a nominal national membership of 23 million, and Swan Ar Shin, a civilian paramilitary group. Over 150 political dissidents were arrested and dozens went into hiding in August.

Demonstrations by Buddhist monks and civilians spread to other towns such as Mandalay, Sittwe, and Pakkoku in September. Following the beating of monks in Pakkoku, public demonstrations increased. In late September marches by monks in Rangoon became larger, and political activists, artists, and other civilians gradually joined in the daily processions. On September 22 over 1,000 monks and supporters were permitted to march to the home of Nobel Peace Prize laureate Daw Aung San Suu Kyi.

On September 26, demonstrations in Rangoon were violently dispersed by riot police, supported by regular army soldiers, who used teargas, rubber bullets, and automatic weapons against unarmed civilians. Following brutal nighttime raids on monasteries and homes, demonstrations continued the next day in Rangoon, Mandalay, Mytikina, Pegu, Sittwe, and Pakkoku, and were met with more violence by security forces. Small demonstrations continued for the next several days, as the police and army arrested and detained an estimated 3,000 monks in Rangoon. An estimated 100 civilians were killed in the demonstrations in Rangoon; there are unverified reports of protester deaths in other locations throughout Burma. Official SPDC figures claim that 15 people were killed and over 3,000 arrested. The SPDC claims to have released over 2,000 detainees; there are fears several hundred remain incarcerated.

The SPDC made no concessions to international condemnation, staging mass rallies of the USDA and Myanmar Women's Affairs Federation throughout the country, condemning foreign interference in Burma, and blaming unrest on foreign media reports and exile radio broadcasts inciting protests.

Lack of Progress on Democracy

Burma's long-running National Convention concluded on September 3, after years of haphazard sessions since 1993. Participation by political parties, ethnic groups, and other non-military delegates was sharply circumscribed and alternative proposals routinely ignored. Criticism of the Convention was expressly forbidden by law. A list of "Detailed Basic Principles" has been finalized and this will form the basis of an eventual national constitution. Many of these provisions are designed to entrench military control over an envisaged civilian parliament, restrict citizens' freedoms and rights, and provide the future president with sweeping emergency powers in the event of a threat against national sovereignty.

Human Rights Defenders

The SPDC continues to imprison an estimated 1,100 political prisoners including Daw Aung San Suu Kyi, whose house arrest was extended in May for another year. In addition, political dissidents arrested in August and September, including Min

Ko Naing and leaders of the "88 Generation Students" remain in detention at unknown locations.

Other attacks against human rights defenders included the beating in April of two members of the Human Rights Defenders and Promoters group by USDA forces, north of Rangoon. Authorities detained Phyu Phyu Tin, a leading HIV/AIDS educator, between May 21 and July 2, for protesting against the lack of access to anti-retroviral drugs in government hospitals.

The SPDC appointed the deputy labor minister, Maj. Gen. Aung Kyi, as official liaison to Daw Aung San Suu Kyi. The two sides have already conducted preliminary meetings on establishing regular dialogue.

Continued Violence against Ethnic Groups

In ethnic areas of the borderlands human rights violations are widespread, involving forced labor, summary executions, sexual violence against women and girls, land confiscations, and the use of landmines to disrupt civilian food production. The ongoing military offensive in northern Karen state has displaced an estimated 40,000 civilians since early 2006, with an estimated 150 civilians killed by Burmese army attacks and landmines. Forty-three new Burmese army bases have been built in the area, using convict and forced civilian labor; local civilians were also forced to supply construction materials. An estimated 500 convict porters were killed as a result of Burmese army abuses, including through the practice of "atrocity de-mining"—forcing civilians to act in effect as human minesweepers. The use of landmines by the Burmese army and non-state armed groups is widespread.

Abuses by Burmese military units are commonplace against civilians also in Karenni, Chin, and Shan states. The army continues to use sexual violence with impunity in ethnic areas. For example, in February four teenage girls were raped by four Burmese army officers in Putao, Kachin state.

Since January 2006 the International Committee of the Red Cross (ICRC) has not been permitted to conduct prison visits. During 2007 they gradually closed several field offices in the countryside due to restrictions on their activities. In a rare public statement issued in June, the ICRC voiced concerns that "repeated abuses committed against men, women and children living along the Thai-Myanmar [Burma] border violate many provisions of international humanitarian law."

Child Soldiers

Recruitment of children into the government armed forces continues as a result of high desertion rates and chronic understaffing. Recruiters and civilian brokers used coercion, threats, and physical force to recruit children as young as 10. Former soldiers indicated that in many training camps children constituted 30 percent or more of new recruits.

Several non-state armed groups also continue to recruit children as soldiers, although in numbers far lower than the Burmese army.

Humanitarian Concerns, Internal Displacement, and Refugees

Burma's humanitarian crisis worsened in 2007 as government restrictions on United Nations and international development agencies' activities continued, including close monitoring and restrictions of movement. A United Nations Development Programme household living conditions survey issued in June showed that one-third of civilians in Burma live below the poverty line.

Despite official figures released by the SPDC and UNAIDS that argued that the country's HIV/AIDS epidemic had decreased, there are concerns that the extent of the crisis might be underestimated because of limitations on travel and access to healthcare facilities by foreign nongovernmental organizations. The "Three Diseases Fund" began operations in 2007 with two rounds of grant disbursals to address the epidemics of HIV, malaria, and tuberculosis in Burma. A major report on health and human rights released by US research institutes in June argued that epidemics of malaria, tuberculosis, HIV, and other diseases, many of them developing drug resistant strains, in Burma's border areas were exacerbated by government healthcare expenditures that are a fraction of state military expenditure.

There was little change in the plight of the estimated half a million internally displaced persons (IDPs) in eastern Burma during 2007. Estimating the number of

displaced people in other areas, including urban displacement, is difficult. International humanitarian organizations are denied access by the SPDC to IDP settlements in Shan and Karen states beside the border with Thailand.

Thousands of civilians fleeing fighting in Karen state are prevented from moving to camps in Thailand by the Thai authorities. Refugees from Shan state are routinely denied sanctuary in Thailand, and there were incidents of refugees being forced back to Burma in 2007. An estimated 2,500 Rohingya Muslims from western Burma and Bangladesh arrived in southern Thailand from November 2006 to May 2007 and were arrested by Thai security forces. In several incidents, Rohingya men were subject to refoulement to Burma by Thai authorities.

Some 150,000 refugees remain in 14 refugee camps along the border with Thailand. Since 2004 an estimated 40,000 refugees have been resettled to third countries such as the United States, Canada, Norway, Australia, and Sweden. Thai authorities have all but stopped their Provincial Admissions Board mechanism for ascertaining asylum seeker claims, and regularly threaten to send back unregistered camp residents to IDP settlements inside Burma.

Restrictions on migrant workers from Burma in Thailand increased, with a curfew invoked in several provinces on migrant workers and a ban on their use of mobile phones and motorbikes. Burmese migrant workers and refugees continue to be subject to harassment, arbitrary arrest, and abuses in detention in India, Malaysia, and Singapore.

Key International Actors

Responding to the August-September events, the UN secretary-general's special envoy to Burma, Ibrahim Gambari, visited Burma twice, meeting with the senior SPDC leadership and Daw Aung San Suu Kyi. He reported back to the Security Council on October 5 that there were "continuing and disturbing reports of abuses being committed by security and non-uniformed elements." Despite international calls for Gambari to have access to detainees, this was not permitted by the SPDC, who tightly controlled his schedule during the visits.

A special session of the UN Human Rights Council was convened on October 2, issuing a statement that "strongly deplores the continued violent repression of peaceful demonstrations in Myanmar, including through beatings, killings, arbitrary detentions and enforced disappearances." After four years of being denied access by the SPDC, the UN special rapporteur on the situation of human rights in Burma, Paulo Sergio Pinheiro, was permitted to visit and went in November.

International condemnation of the violent September crackdown included foreign ministers of the Association of Southeast Asian Nations (ASEAN) issuing a statement expressing their "revulsion" at the use of force. The United States imposed targeted financial sanctions on the 14 top leaders of the SPDC. The EU reinforced their Common Position on sanctions to Burma, and Japan suspended some aid projects. The reaction from China, India, and Russia was muted, as officials called on the SPDC and demonstrators to exercise restraint, but refused to issue strong statements denouncing the use of violence by the SPDC.

Throughout 2007 ASEAN increased its criticism of the SPDC, expressing exasperation over the slow pace of reform and unwillingness to consult with regional partners, although it permitted Burma to sign the ASEAN Charter in November.

The EU continued to invite Burmese officials to multilateral meetings such as the Asia-Europe Meeting in May, despite EU Common Position provisions banning attendance without progress on human rights.

China, India, Russia, and Ukraine continued to sell large numbers of weapons to the SPDC, and in May Russia announced the sale of a nuclear test reactor to Burma.

Foreign investment in Burma's natural energy sector increased, with natural gas exploration contracts signed with companies from China, India, South Korea, Thailand, and Malaysia. Natural gas sales from the Yetagun and Yadana fields accrued an estimated US$2.16 billion to the SPDC in 2007.

In February the International Labour Organization (ILO) reached an agreement with the SPDC on a mechanism for reporting cases of forced labor for a year from March 2007. The ILO stated in July that despite the mechanism there was still widespread use of forced labor in Burma.

UN Special Representative on Children and Armed Conflict Radhika Coomaraswamy, visited Burma in June and secured agreement from the SPDC to set up a mechanism on reporting the use of child soldiers.

Cambodia

Ten years after the 1997 coup, in which Prime Minister Hun Sen ousted his then co-Prime Minister Norodom Ranariddh, impunity for human rights violations in Cambodia remains the rule. 2007 was marked by ongoing illegal confiscation of farmers' land, forced evictions of urban poor, and attacks on rights defenders, as well as the murders of a trade union leader, a community forestry activist, and a monk. The judiciary continued to operate at the behest of the executive, and no progress was made to address rampant corruption or widespread plundering of natural resources. More than halfway through its three-year mandate, the Khmer Rouge Tribunal faced serious allegations of corruption and government interference.

Commune council elections, held in April with less political violence than in the past, were won by Hun Sen's ruling Cambodian Peoples Party (CPP). Ranariddh remained abroad, and in March was sentenced in absentia to 18 months' imprisonment for breach of trust over the sale of his former party's headquarters.

Suppression of Freedom of Expression, Association, and Assembly

The government continues to control all television and most radio stations, with media that criticized the government subject to suspension or threats of legal action. In June 2007 the government banned dissemination of a report by the international nongovernmental organization (NGO) Global Witness that alleged complicity of top government officials in illegal logging. Journalists who covered the report and people who helped prepare it received anonymous death threats. The French-language newspaper Cambodge Soir suspended publication in June after a staff strike protesting a reporter's dismissal for covering the report.

In August a reporter in Pursat was the victim of two attempted arson attacks on his home, which the commune police chief attributed to the reporter's logging coverage. Community activists involved in forest protection who came under attack included Seng Sarom, murdered in July in Stung Treng, and Sath Savuth, forced to flee his Oddar Meanchey home after a grenade was thrown at it in July.

In July the government-controlled Cambodian Bar Association claimed that lawyers cannot be legally employed by NGOs or provide legal services unless the NGO has signed an agreement with the Association. In June Finance Minister Keat Chhon's sister, Keat Kolney, filed a complaint with the Association against nine legal aid lawyers, accusing them of "inciting" villagers to file complaints against her in a Ratanakiri land dispute.

On February 24 Hy Vuthy, president of the Free Trade Union of Workers in the Kingdom of Cambodia (FTUWKC) at the Suntex factory in Phnom Penh, was shot dead. He was the third FTUWKC official to be killed in three years. In May riot police dispersed 1,000 striking workers from a factory in Kandal protesting the firing of workers organizing a union there.

Authorities continue to disperse or reject requests for many demonstrations. In October the government approved a demonstrations law that requires organizers to give local authorities five days' notice and holds organizers responsible for any misconduct that occurs.

Crackdown on Kampuchea Krom Monks

On February 27, 2007, heavily armed police dispersed a demonstration near the Vietnamese Embassy in Phnom Penh by Kampuchea Krom (ethnic Khmer originally from Vietnam) monks. They were protesting religious and ethnic persecution in Vietnam. That night one of the protesting monks, Eang Sok Thoeun, was found dead in his pagoda. Police labeled it a suicide, ordered his immediate burial, and prohibited monks from conducting funeral proceedings. On April 20 Phnom Penh police forcefully dispersed another Kampuchea Krom protest in which counter-demonstrators physically attacked the monks. In June Cambodia's Supreme Buddhist Patriarch Tep Vong and the Ministry of Cults and Religion issued an order banning monks from participating in demonstrations.

On June 30, Cambodian officials defrocked Kampuchea Krom monk Tim Sakhorn, a Cambodian citizen who was the representative of the Khmer Kampuchea Krom Federation (KKF) in Takeo, and escorted him to the border. Tep Vong alleged that Sakhorn had conducted propaganda harming Cambodia-Vietnam friendship by allegedly distributing leaflets about the KKF. In November Sakhorn was sentenced in a Vietnamese court to one year's imprisonment on charges of undermining national unity.

Rule of Law

In June 2007 the National Assembly passed a long-awaited Criminal Procedures Code, but it lacked safeguards regarding pretrial detention, rights of suspects after arrest, and extradition. In July the Constitutional Council ruled that Cambodia should consider its commitments under the Convention on the Rights of the Child when sentencing children.

Despite new eyewitness statements, in April the Appeals Court upheld the conviction of Born Samnang and Sok Sam Oeun for the murder of labor leader Chea Vichea in 2004. The original trial and appeals court decision were criticized for failing to meet fair trial standards by United Nations officials and rights groups.

Land Confiscation

The rural and urban poor continue to lose their land to illegal concessions awarded to foreign firms, government officials, and those with connections to government officials. Hun Sen failed to implement a public pledge made in March 2007 to dismiss CPP members involved in land grabs. On several occasions police used excessive force in evictions, such as in November when soldiers and police shot dead two unarmed villagers during a forced eviction of 317 families in Preah Vihear.

Khmer Rouge Tribunal

Five senior Khmer Rouge (KR) officials were placed in a detention facility at the Khmer Rouge Tribunal during 2007: Kaing Khek Iev (Duch), the former chief of S-21 (Tuol Sleng) prison; Pol Pot's deputy, Nuon Chea; former KR Foreign Minister Ieng Sary; former KR Social Affairs Minister Ieng Thirith; and former KR head of state Khieu Samphan. They were all charged with crimes against humanity and war crimes, except for Ieng Thirith, who was charged only with crimes against humanity.

Problems with the work of the tribunal included serious allegations of mandatory kickbacks by Cambodian staff to government officials in exchange for their positions. In February, after the Open Society Justice Initiative (OSJI) called for an investigation of these corruption allegations, government officials threatened to bar OSJI staff from the tribunal's premises and expel their international staff from Cambodia. International pressure caused the government to back down.

The tribunal has yet to establish satisfactory victims' support and witness protection units. Trials are expected to start in April 2008.

Refugees and Asylum Seekers

Cambodia continues to violate its obligations under the Refugee Convention by forcibly returning dozens of Vietnamese Montagnards before they could apply for asylum with the UN High Commissioner for Refugees (UNHCR). As of September 2007 there were 360 Montagnards under UNHCR protection. In April three Cambodians in Ratanakiri who helped Montagnard asylum seekers make contact with UNHCR were arrested on human trafficking charges for allegedly accepting money from Montagnards. Charges were later dropped.

Key International Actors

In June 2007 international donors, whose aid covers half Cambodia's national budget, increased their annual pledge to US$690 million, with China's pledge for the first time included as part of the formal donor package. Top donors were Japan, China, and the European Union. In June the International Monetary Fund criticized Cambodia's "high cost of informal fees" and failure to pass an anti-corruption law. In August the World Bank, which froze some funding for Cambodia in 2006 because of corruption by Cambodian officials, pledged $70 million for poverty reduction projects.

In August an announcement by the United States that it would increase its counterterrorism cooperation with Cambodia coincided with Cambodia awarding US petroleum giant Chevron an offshore mining contract. In February the US lifted a ban on aid to the Cambodian government instituted after the 1997 coup. New aid included Foreign Military Financing for the Cambodian military to purchase non-lethal "excess defense articles" and International Military Education and Training funds. In April the US Federal Bureau of Investigations (FBI) hosted National Police Chief Hok Lundy for counterterrorism discussions in Washington, despite Lundy's alleged involvement in political violence, drug smuggling, and human trafficking.

In March Cambodia endorsed the Oslo Declaration, which bans cluster munitions.

CHINA

Despite China's official assurances that hosting the 2008 Olympic Games will help to strengthen the development of human rights in the country, the Chinese government continues to deny or restrict its citizens' fundamental rights, including freedom of expression, freedom of association, and freedom of religion.

The government's extensive police and state security apparatus continues to impose multiple layers of controls on civil society activists, critics, and protesters. Those layers include professional and administrative measures, limitations on foreign travel and domestic movement, monitoring (covert or overt) of internet and phone communications, abduction and confinement incommunicado, and unofficial house arrests. A variety of vaguely defined crimes including "inciting subversion," "leaking state secrets," and "disrupting social order" provide the government with wide legal remit to stifle critics.

Human Rights and the 2008 Olympics

Despite temporary regulations in effect from January 1, 2007, to October 17, 2008, that give correspondents freedom to interview anyone who consents, foreign journalists continue to be harassed, detained, and intimidated by government and police officials. The temporary regulations do not extend to Chinese journalists or foreign correspondents' Chinese assistants, researchers, and sources, who continue to risk reprisals for violating government directives on taboo reporting topics.

Official efforts to rid Beijing of undesirables ahead of the Olympics have accelerated the eviction of petitioners—citizens from the countryside who come to the capital seeking redress for grievances ranging from illegal land seizures to official corruption. In September-October the Beijing municipal government demolished a settlement in Fengtai district that housed up to 4,000 petitioners.

The countdown to the Olympics has also sparked a construction boom. An estimated one million migrant construction workers are integral to this effort, yet their labor conditions are harsh and unsafe, and workers are often unable to access public services. When a subway tunnel under construction collapsed in

March, trapping six workers, the first step the employer took was to prevent workers from reporting the accident by confiscating their mobile phones.

Freedom of Expression

In 2007 the Chinese government stepped up its efforts to control increasingly vibrant print and online forms of expression, and sanctioned individuals, journalists, and editors for failing to conform to highly restrictive but inconsistently implemented laws and regulations.

China's system of internet censorship and surveillance is the most advanced in the world. Filtering, blocking, and monitoring technologies are built into all layers of China's internet infrastructure. Tens of thousands of police remotely monitor internet use around the clock. The elaborate system of censorship is aided by extensive corporate and private sector cooperation—including by some of the world's major international technology and internet companies such as Google, Yahoo, and Microsoft. Writers, editors, bloggers, webmasters, writers, and journalists risk punishments ranging from immediate dismissal to prosecution and lengthy jail terms for sending news outside China or posting articles critical of the political system. For example, Zhang Jianhong, former editor-in-chief of the Aegean Sea website, was sentenced to six years' imprisonment on March 19 for "inciting subversion."

The countdown to the Beijing Olympics has seen the threshold lowered for internet content considered "sensitive" by China's censors and prompted closure of access to thousands of websites in 2007, including popular international sites such as Wikipedia and Flickr. The government has expanded its traditional criteria for internet censorship from topics including references to the 1989 Tiananmen Massacre, the outlawed Falungong "evil cult," and content perceived as sympathetic to "separatist" elements in Tibet, Xinjiang, and Taiwan, to include "unauthorized" coverage of everything from natural disasters to corruption scandals that might embarrass the Chinese Communist Party (CCP). By official estimate the government shut down more than 18,000 individual blogs and websites since April 2007, and in August censors widened their focus to include shutting down numerous internet data centers. Official measures to filter or remove "sensitive" content from domestic websites sharply accelerated in the run up to the 17th CCP Congress in October.

Chinese journalists continue to risk severe repercussions for pursuing stories that touch on officially taboo subjects or threaten powerful private interests. Miao Wei, former executive editor of *Sanlian Life Weekly*, confirmed in April that he had been demoted in connection with a cover story on the aftermath of the Cultural Revolution (1966-1976). Lan Chengzhang, a reporter with *China Trade News,* was murdered in January while investigating an illegal coalmine in Datong, Shanxi province. In mid-August five journalists, including a reporter from the party mouthpiece *People's Daily*, were interviewing witnesses to the Fenghuang bridge collapse in Hunan province when plainclothes thugs interrupted the interviews and kicked and punched the journalists, who were then detained by police.

Legal Reform

Legal reforms proceeded at a fast pace in 2007 in order to achieve the CCP's over-riding goal of making the rule of law "the principal tool to govern the country." New legislation was adopted on a wide range of issues such as property rights, labor contracts, administration of lawyers, access to public records, and the handling of emergencies. But the party's continued dominance over, and interference with, judicial institutions, as well as weak and inconsistent enforcement of judicial decisions, means that overall the legal system remains vulnerable to arbitrary interference.

Ordinary citizens face immense obstacles to accessing justice, in particular over issues such as illegal land seizures, forced evictions, environmental pollution, unpaid wages, corruption, and abuse of power by local officials, a situation that fuels rising social unrest across the country. The authorities have stopped disclosing figures about the number of riots and demonstrations after they announced a decline from over 200 incidents per day in 2006, but large-scale incidents were reported in 2007 in almost all of China's 34 province-level administrative units. Several demonstrations involved tens of thousand of people, such as in Yongzhou (Hunan) in March 2007 and Xiamen (Fujian) in June. In speeches and articles top security officials acknowledged the heightening of social conflicts, but remained defiant toward greater independence of the judiciary, blaming

CHINA

"You Will Be Harassed and Detained"

China Media Freedoms Under Assault Ahead of the 2008 Beijing Olympic Games

HUMAN

RIGHTS

WATCH

"hostile" or "enemy forces" for trying to use the nation's legal system to undermine and westernize China. A string of lawyers defending human rights cases have been suspended or disbarred under a yearly licensing system that acts as a general deterrent to taking cases viewed as "sensitive" by the authorities.

The rights of criminal defendants continued to be sharply limited and violated by law enforcement agencies. Defense lawyers face chronic difficulties including accessing defendants in custody, consulting court documents, and producing exculpatory evidence before the court. Despite the reiteration by the Supreme People's Court in September that judges ought to "pay more attention to evidence and treat confessions with more skepticism," torture, especially at the pretrial stage, remains prevalent. The Public Security Bureau continues to make wide use, including for political and religious dissidents, of the reeducation-through-labor system, which allows detention for up to four years of "minor offenders," without trial.

Human Rights Defenders

Chinese human rights defenders, seizing on the official promise of lawful governance, are becoming more assertive and skillful at documenting abuses and mounting legal challenges. But the authorities, who have never tolerated independent human rights monitoring, have retaliated with harassment, unlawful detention, forced disappearances, and long prison sentences, often on trumped-up charges.

Authorities have targeted a small, loosely-organized network of lawyers, legal academics, rights activists, and journalists, known as the *weiquan* movement, which aims to pursue social justice and constitutional rights through litigation. The movement focuses on the protection of ordinary citizens in matters such as housing rights, land seizures, workers' rights, and police abuse. Yang Chunlin, a land rights activist, was arrested in July and charged with subversion for his role in organizing a petition titled "We want human rights, not the Olympics." Lu Gengsong, a former lecturer turned activist who documented illegal eviction cases and official collusion, was arrested in August on suspicion of subverting state power. Both are awaiting trial. The same month environmental activist Wu Lihong was sentenced to three years' imprisonment under ill-defined business fraud charges; his wife reported he had been tortured while held incommunicado. Yang Maodong, a Guangzhou-based land rights activist arrested in September 2006 and still awaiting trial, also reported that he had been repeatedly tortured in detention.

Defenders who document and report abuses against other activists are particularly vulnerable. In September lawyer Li Heping was abducted in broad daylight, held for six hours, severely beaten, and told he should leave Beijing. Li Jianqiang, a renowned human rights lawyer, was disbarred without reason. The human rights monitor Hu Jia has been kept under extralegal house arrest in Beijing for most of the year. Yuan Weijing, the wife of the blind activist Chen Guangcheng who is currently serving a three-year sentence for exposing family planning abuses, was prevented from traveling abroad to collect a human rights prize on his behalf.

Labor Rights

Chinese workers continue to be forbidden to form independent trade unions, as the government maintains that the party-controlled All-China Federation of Trade Unions (ACFTU) adequately protects workers' rights. This restriction on legally-sanctioned labor activism coupled with increasingly tense labor disputes in which protesting workers have few realistic routes for redress have contributed to increasing numbers of workers taking to the streets and to the courts to press claims about forced and uncompensated overtime, employer violations of minimum wage rules, unpaid pensions and wages, and dangerous and unhealthy working environments.

Workers who seek redress through strike action are often subject to attacks by plainclothes thugs who appear to operate at the behest of employers. In July a group of 200 thugs armed with spades, axes, and steel pipes attacked a group of workers in Heyuan (Guangdong), who were protesting over not having been paid for four months; they beat one worker to death.

Children's Rights

Under "Work and Study" programs regulated by the Ministry of Education, schools in impoverished areas are encouraged to set up income-generating activities to make up for budgetary shortfalls. According to the ministry, nationwide more than 400,000 middle and junior high schools, for children ages 12 to 16, are running agricultural and manufacturing schemes. Overly vague program regulations and poor supervision have led to chronic abuse by schools and employers alike: some of the programs interfere with children's education, lack basic health and safety guarantees, and involve long hours and dangerous work. Children as young as 12 have been employed in heavy agricultural and hazardous construction work. Others have been dispatched to local factories for weeks or months of "summer employment." Some schools have turned into full-fledged workshops to produce local handiwork or foodstuff while relegating teaching to a few hours a week.

Women's Rights

Gender-based discrimination and violence remain entrenched problems in China. Despite slowly increasing attention to domestic violence, public awareness and access to services in rural areas are especially low. Strong son preference contributes to sex-selective abortions, differential care of girls leading to significantly higher rates of female infant mortality, and in extreme cases female infanticide or sale to human traffickers.

HIV/AIDS

A senior central government official in September described China's HIV/AIDS situation in several provinces as "very serious" due to drug trafficking and illegal blood sales. But despite government assurances that it had prioritized all possible measures to contain the spread of HIV/AIDS, activists and grassroots organizations continued to come under attack in 2007 by local officials and security officials.

Dr. Gao Yaojie, a doctor who helped expose the Henan province HIV-contaminated blood sales scandal, was barred in February from going to the United States to receive a human rights award until an international outcry forced the government to reverse that decision. In August the government forced the cancellation of two meetings of HIV/AIDS activists in Guangzhou (Guangdong) and Kaifeng (Henan). On August 15 Henan Public Security Bureau officials also ordered, without explanation, the temporary closure of two provincial offices of the nonprofit China Orchid AIDS project.

The government's announcement in September that it would introduce compulsory screening of all blood products beginning on January 1, 2008, to prevent the transmission of HIV and other blood-borne diseases through transfusions and pharmaceutical products is an important step forward in official efforts to help control the spread of HIV/AIDS.

Freedom of Religion

The Chinese government recognizes the right to believe, but limits worship to a state-controlled system of registered and controlled churches, congregations, mosques, monasteries, and temples.

The official registration process requires government vetting and ongoing scrutiny of religious publications, seminary applications, and religious personnel. The government also closely monitors the membership and financial records of religious institutions and the personnel they employ, and retains the right to approve or deny applications for any group activities by religious organizations. Those who fail to register are considered illegal and are liable for criminal prosecution, fines, and closure.

Reprisals against non-registered religious organizations have primarily focused on arrests of Protestants who attend "house churches," for Bible study meetings and training sessions. The majority of those arrested are rapidly released, some after paying fines, but leaders of such underground churches are sometimes held on fabricated charges including "illegal business practices." The freedom of belief of certain groups designated by the government as "evil cults," including Falungong, continues to be severely restricted.

Involuntary Resettlement Programs

The growing scale of forced resettlement projects across China to make way for infrastructure, environmental, and urbanization projects in 2007 continued to be marked by widespread irregularities, including lack of consultation, forced evictions, embezzlement, and corruption. China announced in October plans to relocate up to 4 million more people from areas surrounding the Three Gorges Dam— the world's biggest hydroelectric power project.

Multiple programs to remove indigenous populations from environmentally fragile areas, such as on the Tibetan plateau, appear to be motivated, at least in part, by an integrationist agenda aimed at weakening minority cultural distinctiveness and extending Chinese control over their lives. An official policy of forcibly relocating ethnic Tibetan herders in Tibet, Gansu, Qinghai and Sichuan to urban areas is seriously disrupting traditional lifestyles and has put under threat the livelihoods of approximately 700,000 such people already resettled. In September the Chinese government announced that it would resettle another 100,000 nomads from Qinghai province alone.

Tibet

The Chinese government accuses the Dalai Lama, in exile in India since 1959, of being the linchpin of alleged plots to separate Tibet from China. It views Tibetan Buddhism as complicit in those efforts. The government lodged strong objections to meetings between the Dalai Lama and US, Australian, Austrian, and German leaders in 2007.

Widespread and numerous instances of repression target ordinary citizens, monks, nuns, and even children in an effort to quash alleged "separatism." Seven Tibetan boys in Gansu province were detained for over a month in early September after they allegedly wrote slogans on the walls of a village police station and elsewhere calling for the return of the Dalai Lama and a free Tibet. Ronggyal Adrak was detained and charged under state security offenses by police on August 1 after he called for the Dalai Lama's return at a horse race festival in Sichuan province. He is awaiting trial.

The Chinese government has failed to bring to justice those responsible for the shooting death by People's Armed Police officers of a 17-year-old nun, Kelsang Namtso, while trying to cross the border into Nepal on September 30, 2006.

Xinjiang

Drastic controls over religious, cultural, and political expression of Muslim populations remained in place in 2007 in the Uighur Autonomous Region of Xinjiang—aside from Tibet, the only province of China where the ethnic Chinese population is not the majority, despite in-migration of over a million people from other parts of China in the past decade. The government only tolerates religious activities in state-controlled religious venues, conducted by state-appointed clerics. Minors are prohibited from participating in religious activities and, in some localities, barred from entering mosques.

In June Xinjiang authorities started confiscating Muslims' passports in an apparent bid to prevent them from making non-state-approved pilgrimages to Mecca. Civil servants, teachers, and clerics are subjected to intense indoctrination against the "three evil forces"—separatism, religious extremism, and terrorism. Eighteen people were killed and 17 arrested in January in a raid on what the government described as a "terrorist training camp" of the East Turkistan Islamic Movement, a group whose existence independent analysts have been questioning since 2001. In November five of them were sentenced to death, and one to life imprisonment under various terrorism charges.

There is widespread evidence that the government uses isolated incidents to conflate any expression of public discontent with terrorism or separatism. Chinese officials have labeled the exiled activist Rebiya Kadeer—a Nobel Peace Prize nominee—a terrorist, and in April 2007 Ablikim Abdiriyim, her son, was sentenced to nine years' imprisonment for "having spread secessionist articles over the internet." Another son, Alim Abdiriyim, was sentenced in November 2006 to seven years' imprisonment for tax evasion. Huseyincan Celil, a former political prisoner who had fled China in 2000, was forcibly returned by Uzbek authorities to China in 2006, and sentenced to life imprisonment in April 2007. China refused to recognize his Canadian citizenship and did not allow Canadian diplomats to attend his trial.

Hong Kong

The government of the Hong Kong Special Administrative Region has failed to clearly indicate how it will fulfill two requirements of the Basic Law (the territory's mini-constitution) that have crucial human rights implications: the direct election of the chief executive and the drafting of anti-subversion legislation under article 23. Despite an adequate legal framework to uphold freedom of expression, Hong Kong journalists denounced the self-censorship prevalent in the media, particularly with respect to the coverage of mainland issues.

Key International Actors

China continues to describe itself as a "responsible power." Yet its resistance to the United Nations Security Council's and the Human Rights Council's taking decisive action to respond to serious human rights violations and hold individual countries accountable for their human rights records contradicted that label. China increasingly uses its leverage to minimize criticism in international institutions, most notably by forcing the World Bank in June to remove information about the consequences of pollution in China from a draft report. It continues to resist requests for cooperation with key UN offices, including the special rapporteur on North Korea, and the United Nations High Commissioner for Refugees (UNHCR), regarding the status of North Koreans in China.

Largely in response to considerable international pressure, China took more concrete and public steps to help ameliorate the human rights crisis in Darfur, Sudan. It appointed a new special envoy on Darfur and agreed to contribute peacekeeping troops, but it continued to enable Khartoum's brutality by consistently blocking international efforts to impose sanctions. In addition, while China consented to some critical UN Security Council language following the August-September repression in Burma, it refused to speak strongly itself or take steps to end the crisis, such as suspending all military aid and cooperation.

INDIA

India claims an abiding commitment to human rights, but its record is marred by continuing violations by security forces in counterinsurgency operations and by government failure to rigorously implement laws and policies to protect marginalized communities. A vibrant media and civil society continue to press for improvements, but without tangible signs of success in 2007.

India faces serious insurgencies and armed political movements in several states. Armed groups have been responsible for attacks on civilians, killings, torture, and extortion. In response, however, Indian security forces have repeatedly engaged in abusive tactics. The government has yet to root out the policies responsible for the violations, and continues to grant virtual impunity to perpetrators. Despite signing a new United Nations treaty to combat forced disappearances in February 2007, the Indian government is yet to launch a credible independent investigation into alleged disappearances and fake "encounter killings" throughout the country.

There is continuing failure to protect the rights of women, children, Dalits, tribal groups, religious minorities, and those living with HIV/AIDS. Authorities have introduced significant legal and policy reforms in many of these areas, but implementation has lagged, exacerbating popular discontent over widening economic and social disparities.

Armed Conflicts and Security Force Impunity

India's diverse ethnic and regional identities, coupled with deeply rooted economic and social grievances, have fueled violent insurgencies and armed campaigns. Militants often target civilians and engage in torture and extortion. While a number of regional conflicts pose serious threats, counterinsurgency operations by Indian security forces have led to large-scale violations including arbitrary detention, torture, and extrajudicial killings. Perpetrators are rarely prosecuted and the Indian government has not acknowledged or addressed institutional shortcomings that foster such impunity.

Conflict in Jammu and Kashmir

While the violence which began in 1989 has abated slightly since talks were initiated between India, Pakistan, and some separatist groups in 2005, abuses by all parties continue.

In February 2007, police investigations into a "missing persons" case in Jammu and Kashmir exposed a problem long alleged by human rights groups: people were being killed in custody by security forces who constructed fake armed encounters, staging executions to look like acts of defense.

In April 2007, a working group on Jammu and Kashmir recommended the repeal of laws sanctioning impunity, such as the Armed Forces Special Powers Act, but the government has failed to act.

Violence in the Northeast

Ethnic separatist tensions in some northeastern states ignited again in 2007. Based on newspaper reports, the South Asia Terrorism Portal recorded 640 deaths in 2006; as of November 2007, 880 people had already died.

In Assam, alleged members of the United Liberation Front of Asom (ULFA), a militant group, attacked and killed scores of Hindi-speaking migrants, most of them from Bihar state. Over 200 civilians had been killed in the violence as of late November.

Manipur remains among the most violent states in the northeast, with militants blamed for widespread extortion and targeted killings and security forces accused of violations such as torture, arbitrary detention, and custodial killings.

Combating Maoist Extremists

An ongoing campaign by leftwing extremists called Maoists or Naxalites has gained momentum in several Indian states. The Maoists find support among the rural poor, who feel left out by India's modernization process and surging economic growth. Unfortunately, these same vulnerable groups also suffer at the hand of the Maoists because of the latter's illegal taxes and demands for food

INDIA

Hidden Apartheid

Caste Discrimination against India's "Untouchables"

Shadow Report to the UN Committee on the Elimination of Racial Discrimination

center for human rights and global justice
nyu school of law

**H U M A N
R I G H T S
W A T C H**

and shelter. Succumbing to such extortion puts civilians at risk of retaliation by security forces.

According to the Ministry of Home Affairs, 950 people died in 2006 in Maoist-related violence and as of November 2007, according to data gathered by the South Asia Terrorism Portal, more than 550 people had died, including 200 civilians.

Violent attacks, whether perpetuated by the Maoists or security forces, take place in remote areas, making it difficult to independently monitor the situation.

Justice for Past Abuses in Punjab

In 2007 there was still no progress in investigating thousands of secret cremations in the northern state of Punjab. Following a spate of violent attacks by Sikh militants starting in the early 1980s, security forces illegally detained, tortured, executed, or "disappeared" thousands of people during counterinsurgency operations. None of the security officials who bear substantial responsibility for these violations has been brought to justice. The National Human Rights Commission in 2007 prepared for final hearings to determine compensation in a small number of cases, but the government still has not investigated how people died and who was responsible.

Failure of Relocation and Rehabilitation Policies

Tremendous economic growth and plans for industrial development and infrastructure building have uprooted millions of traders, farmers, and landless laborers. Protests by affected groups are ignored and often brutally curbed through excessive use of force.

On March 14, violence in Nandigram in West Bengal state during protests against state-sponsored land acquisition claimed at least 14 lives. In November, the ruling Communist Party of India (Marxist) (CPM) allowed its cadre to forcefully evict the Nandigram protestors. The National Human Rights Commission, political parties, and civil society activists condemned the violence that followed. The state

INDIA

Protecting the Killers
A Policy of Impunity in Punjab, India

HUMAN RIGHTS WATCH

Ensaaf
END IMPUNITY. ACHIEVE JUSTICE.
ਇਨਸਾਫ਼

government, which had advance notice of the evictions, failed to deploy adequate security forces to ensure law and order.

There have also been protests in several other states including Maharashtra, Uttar Pradesh, and Orissa.

Rights of Dalits and Indigenous Tribal Groups

In March 2007, the Committee on the Elimination of Racial Discrimination (CERD) urged the government to take effective measures to protect Dalits and tribal groups. Dalits and indigenous peoples (known as Scheduled Tribes or *adivasis*) continue to face discrimination, exclusion, and acts of communal violence. Laws and policies adopted by the Indian government provide a strong basis for protection, but are not being faithfully implemented by local authorities. Instead of addressing these concerns, the Indian government insists that caste is not the same as race and therefore discrimination based on caste and tribe falls outside the mandate of CERD.

Legacy of Communal Violence

A number of attacks occurred on places of religious worship in 2007, including a bomb blast at the revered Sufi shrine in Ajmer in October. The Indian government succeeded in preventing communal riots following this and other attacks. The Indian government, however, has failed to prosecute most of those who instigate or participate in religious mob violence.

Despite national and international condemnation, the Gujarat state government continues to protect those responsible for the killing of Muslims during the 2002 riots.

After more than a decade of hearings, a special court convicted 100 people for their involvement in the 1993 serial bomb attacks in Mumbai. However, the individuals believed responsible for attacks upon Muslims in January 1993 which preceded the bomb blasts are yet to be prosecuted and punished.

Despite promises made by the prime minister in 2005, there was also no progress in justice for victims of the 1984 anti-Sikh riots.

Death Penalty

There were no executions in 2007 but the death penalty remains on the books. Over 40 people were sentenced to death for the 1993 Mumbai bombings.

Human Rights Defenders

In Chattisgarh state, which experienced more Maoist violence than any other state in 2007, civil society organizations have come under attack in a classic example of "punishing the messenger." Prominent human rights defender Dr. Binayak Sen was detained for his alleged contact with the Maoist groups. Several journalists and other human rights activists said that they had been threatened by government officials.

Failure to Protect Children's Rights

Despite a scheme launched three years ago to provide universal education, millions of children in India still have no access to education and work long hours, many as bonded laborers. Many children continue to be forced into becoming soldiers in areas where there are armed conflicts, or are trafficked for marriage, sex work, or employment. Others languish in substandard orphanages or detention centers. In 2007, the National Children's Commission began operations to ensure protection of children's rights.

Rights of Those Living with HIV/AIDS

New estimates of people living with HIV/AIDS place the number at around 2.5 million, excluding children under age 15. Children and adults living with HIV/AIDS, as well as those whose marginalized status puts them at highest risk—sex workers, injection drug users, and men who have sex with men—face widespread stigmatization and discrimination, including denial of employment, access to education, orphan care, and healthcare. A promised law that would ban discrimination against people living with HIV had still not been presented to parliament at this writing, and sodomy laws have not been repealed. Although the number of people on anti-retroviral treatment increased, including over 6,000 children, India at this writing still fell short of the 100,000 people that a government minister promised to put on treatment in 2002.

Rights of Women

India has a mixed record on women's rights: despite recent improvements in legal protections, gender-based discrimination and violence remain deeply entrenched. The low status of women and girls is revealed by the skewed sex ratio of 933 females for every 1,000 males and the high rate of preventable maternal deaths, with one woman dying in childbirth every five minutes.

Key International Actors

India claims that its growing economic power should give it more clout in global diplomacy, seeking a permanent seat on the UN Security Council and a leading role in the Commonwealth and the Non Aligned Movement. However, it has yet to show that it can play a serious global role in pushing for greater adherence to international human rights standards.

While India has strong economic and strategic ties with the United States and the European Union, it has refused to engage in constructive dialogue on its own failures in protecting human rights. Governments have been reluctant to challenge India in part because they do not want to risk upsetting relations with an important economic and trade partner.

India's regional policies are often determined by strategic concerns over China's increasing influence in South Asia, and this often contributes to decisions by officials to avoid proactive engagement on human rights issues.

While India has continued peace talks with Pakistan to settle Kashmir and other disputed issues, it has failed to actively promote democracy and human rights in response to crises in Sri Lanka, Burma, Bhutan, and Bangladesh.

India has been engaged in discussions to encourage a political settlement in Sri Lanka and says it has privately expressed concern about human rights abuses by government forces. However, India has yet to urge the government of Sri Lanka to take positive steps to ensure greater protection of civilians, including agreeing to the deployment of a United Nations human rights monitoring mission.

Over 100,000 Bhutanese remain refugees in Nepal because of the Bhutanese government's discriminatory policies against its citizens of Nepali origin. In 2007, the United States offered to resettle 60,000 of the refugees, a step which many believe will allow Bhutan to continue its policy of exclusion. The Indian government has not publicly encouraged the Bhutanese government to end these discriminatory polices and allow the repatriation of the refugees.

After the Burmese junta's brutal crackdown on pro-democracy activists in September 2007, India simply issued statements calling for a peaceful settlement of the issue. India at this writing had not used its military sales and business dealings with the junta to press for accountability and respect for human rights standards.

INDONESIA

Two Constitutional Court decisions and efforts toward accountability for the murder of human rights defender Munir Said Thalib marked good progress on human rights in Indonesia.

However, threats and intimidation against human rights defenders significantly increased in Papua and West Papua, while efforts at military reform stalled. The killing of four civilians by marines in East Java exemplified continuing human rights violations associated with security force involvement in private business activity.

Impunity

Some progress was made in addressing human rights crimes of the Soeharto era. In December 2006 Indonesia's Constitutional Court declared unconstitutional a law establishing a Truth and Reconciliation Commission (TRC) in Indonesia. The law empowered the TRC to award amnesties to perpetrators of past crimes and barred victims from taking any future legal action against them. Reparations to victims were made contingent upon victims signing formal statements exonerating the perpetrators. The Court declared that provisions of the TRC law violated Indonesia's international obligations and domestic laws. The decision came after two years of legal challenges by Indonesian human rights groups.

In July 2007 prosecutors filed a civil suit against former Indonesian dictator Soeharto, seeking return of US$440 million allegedly stolen from the state during his 32 years in power and seeking US$1.54 billion in damages. The suit claims that the former president funneled money from the state to his own accounts through the Supersemar Foundation. In September the United Nations and the World Bank placed Soeharto at the top of a global list of political leaders accused of stealing state assets.

Military Reform

The government has not completed key military reforms. It has yet to end military business practices, as required under a 2004 law, or ensure accountability for abuses. In May 2007, 13 marines shot and killed four civilians of whom two were women, and wounded eight in Pasuruan, East Java. The incident was sparked by a long-running dispute over land that a Navy cooperative, jointly with an Indonesian company, wanted to develop into a plantation against the wishes of local residents. Military chief Air Marshal Djoko Suyanto defended the marines' actions, claiming self defense. These assertions were disputed by media, witnesses, and a subsequent investigation by the national human rights commission, Komnas HAM.

Aceh

In December 2006 Irwandi Yusuf, a former spokesperson for the Free Aceh Movement (GAM), won the gubernatorial election in Aceh. His running mate for vice-governor was Muhammad Nazar, a former political prisoner and head of the Aceh Referendum Information Center (SIRA), which campaigned on a referendum for Aceh independence. Irwandi and Nazar were installed in office on February 8, 2007.

The December 11, 2006 polls (district and provincial) were the first-ever direct local elections in Aceh, and first elections after the August 2005 Helsinki peace agreement between the Indonesian government and GAM, and the first in Indonesia allowing independent (non-party affiliated) candidates to stand.

To date there is no progress on accountability for past human rights violations in Aceh. The 2006 Law on Aceh Governance set out to establish a TRC and an ad hoc court to look at crimes committed after the August 2005 peace agreement. In 2007 there was little movement toward either, and since the national TRC was declared unconstitutional the status of the Aceh branch remained uncertain.

Papua and West Papua

Peaceful political activists in Papua and West Papua continue to be classified as separatists, facing arrest and criminal conviction for their activities. In the central highlands both army troops and police units, particularly mobile paramilitary police units, engage in largely indiscriminate village "sweeping" operations to pursue suspected militants. Excessive, often brutal force is used against civilians.

In 2007 Col. Burhanuddin Siagian was appointed as regional military commander in Papua. Colonel Siagian has been indicted by the United Nations for crimes against humanity in East Timor, including forming militias responsible for human rights violations.

Death Penalty

In August 2007 Indonesia's Supreme Court threw out a final appeal against the death penalty for Amrozi, one of the convicted 2002 Bali bombers. Verdicts for the other two Bali bombers on death row, Imam Samudra and Mukhlas, are still pending at this writing.

In April an Indonesian man was executed by firing squad for a 1999 murder conviction in Kalimantan. At least 90 other people remain sentenced to death in Indonesia.

Freedom of Expression and Press

In July the Constitutional Court declared unconstitutional legal provisions prohibiting free expression. Articles 154 and 155 of Indonesia's Criminal Code criminalize the "public expression of feelings of hostility, hatred or contempt toward the government" and prohibit "the expression of such feelings or views through the public media." Despite the ruling, those sentenced to prison under these provisions remained there, and no progress was made on removing the articles from Indonesia's new draft criminal code.

In April the court case against the editor-in-chief of *Playboy Indonesia*, Erwin Arnada, for violating indecency provisions of the criminal code was dismissed.

In August Indonesia's Supreme Court awarded Soeharto one trillion Rupiah (US$106 million) in damages for a defamation lawsuit brought against US-based *TIME* magazine over a May 1999 article alleging he had amassed a fortune in overseas bank accounts. Press associations criticized the ruling as a violation of media freedom, asserting that the *TIME* article had been fair, with Indonesia's Press Council declaring the decision an "evil omen" for local journalists covering corruption stories.

INDONESIA

Out of Sight

Endemic Abuse and Impunity in Papua's Central Highlands

**HUMAN
RIGHTS
WATCH**

In March 2007 Indonesia's attorney general banned a number of history books over their presentation of the events surrounding the 1965 coup in which Soeharto came to power. This was on the grounds that the books did not mention the alleged role of the PKI, the Indonesian Communist Party.

Freedom of Religion

Religious extremists forcibly closed more places of worship of religious minorities, with little response from local authorities. On June 3 a large group of people stormed a Sunday school session of a Christian congregation in Soreang, West Java, assaulting the pastor's wife and a teenager, and destroying church property. A week later the same group attacked a church in Garut, forcing the pastor and his congregation to flee for safety to another village.

In September in Malang, East Java, 41 people were convicted of blasphemy against Islam and each sentenced to five years' imprisonment. The defendants had been arrested in May for making a videotape denouncing the Quran. Those convicted were all members of the Lembaga Pelayanan Mahasiswa Indonesia, a mainly student organization active in disaster relief.

Child Domestic Workers in Indonesia

An estimated 700,000 to 1 million children, mainly girls, work as domestic workers in Indonesia, representing up to one-fifth of the country's domestic workers. Typically recruited between the ages of 12 and 15, often on false promises of decent wages and working conditions, girls may work 14 to 18 hours a day, seven days a week, and earn far less than the prevailing minimum wage. In the worst cases, child domestics are paid no salary at all and are physically and sexually abused.

As informal workers, domestics are not protected by traditional labor laws. At this writing, draft legislation that would mandate an eight-hour work day, a weekly day of rest, and an annual holiday remained under discussion in government and had not yet been presented to parliament. The current draft contains no sanctions against employers or recruiting agencies that violate its provisions.

Indonesian Migrant Workers

Approximately two million Indonesians work abroad, of whom the vast majority are women. Many migrate as domestic workers to the Middle East and other parts of Asia, where they are subject to a wide range of labor abuses (see Saudi Arabia and Malaysia chapters). Poorly monitored labor recruiters often deceive workers about their jobs abroad and impose excessive recruitment fees, placing these migrants at risk of trafficking and forced labor.

Migrants' groups protested against the continued operation of "Terminal 3" at Soekarno-Hatta Airport in Jakarta, where returning migrant workers are diverted to a separate terminal and subject to inflated charges and extortion.

Human Rights Defenders

Three years after the assassination of leading human rights defender Munir Said Thalib, no one has been convicted for murder. Following the acquittal of Pollycarpus Priyanto, a Garuda Airways pilot linked to intelligence officials, for Munir's murder, in April police arrested two new suspects, Indra Setiawan (former president-director of Garuda Indonesia) and Rohainil Aini (former secretary to the chief pilot for Garuda). Their trial for murder started in October. In August the Attorney General's Office filed new evidence to the Supreme Court and requested a review of Priyanto's acquittal.

In May a Jakarta civil court found Garuda guilty of negligence for failing to take adequate action to prevent Munir's death. The court ordered $73,800 damages to his widow, who nevertheless appealed seeking stiffer penalties and an apology.

In Papua and West Papua human rights defenders face increasing intimidation including death threats, arbitrary detention, and surveillance by Indonesian security forces. The head of the Papua branch of Indonesia's national human rights commission, Alberth Rumbekwan, was subjected to such intimidation throughout the second half of 2007.

In June the UN Secretary-General's Special Representative on Human Rights Defenders Hina Jilani visited Indonesia including Aceh and Papua. She noted that while prospects for promoting human rights had considerably improved, there remained resistance and little commitment to eliminate impunity for past and ongoing human rights violations. Of particular concern was the lack of protection for those engaged in socially sensitive issues such as the rights of lesbian, gay, bisexual, and transgender persons or public awareness on HIV/AIDS.

Key International Actors

In addition to Hina Jilani, UN High Commissioner for Human Rights Louise Arbour visited Indonesia for five days in July. Both Jilani and Arbour expressed concern about the Munir case and the lack of progress in dealing with past human rights violations. In November UN Special Rapporteur on Torture Manfred Nowak visited Indonesia. In May Indonesia was elected for a second term on the UN Human Rights Council.

US Congressman Eni Faleomavaega, chairman of the House Foreign Affairs Subcommittee on Asia, the Pacific and the Global Environment, led a delegation to Indonesia in July to investigate conditions in Papua. The Indonesian government denied him permission to the province but he met several Papuan leaders in Jakarta, as well as President Yudhoyono and other government officials.

In efforts to decrease its perceived over-reliance on US military cooperation, in April Indonesia ratified a security agreement with India. The agreement paved the way for the joint production of military equipment and cooperation on issues including combating terrorism and piracy.

The Indonesia-Timor-Leste bilateral Truth and Friendship Commission extended its mandate in June for a further six months. In July UN Secretary-General Ban Ki-moon effectively enforced a UN boycott of the Commission by stating that UN staff would not testify unless the amnesty provision of the Commission's mandate was changed to not include perpetrators of serious crimes. In September the Commission held its fifth and final public hearing in Dili.

MALAYSIA

Malaysia continues to confound hopes that human rights progress will parallel the country's strong economic growth. Basic rights such as freedom of expression, assembly, and association are subject to burdensome and unjustified restrictions. A series of stringent and outdated laws and regulations, such as the Internal Security Act (ISA) and Emergency Ordinance (EO), continue to undermine basic due process rights. Routine censorship threats target bloggers; new rules impede workers' right to organize; and indigenous communities face loss of communal land. The government has resisted widespread calls to establish an Independent Police Complaints and Misconduct Commission, as recommended in May 2005 by a Royal Commission.

Detention without Charge or Trial

Malaysian officials use the ISA and EO to indefinitely detain, without charge or trial, alleged terrorists and those suspected of organized criminal activities. Authorities have used the law against members of several Islamic groups, including the Jemaah Islamiah (JI), Kampulan Militan/Mujaahiddim Malaysia, and Darul Islam, as well as criminals engaging in human smuggling and passport and ID forgery. The inspector general of police stated in June 2007 that "there is no JI movement here in Malaysia."

According to Suaram, a respected Malaysian nongovernmental organization (NGO), as of September 2007, 87 suspects remained in ISA detention. In June 2007, four alleged JI members held for more than four years were released but sent, under the 1933 Restricted Residence Act, to remote districts where they are required to report regularly to local police.

The Malaysian government has not responded to a request for a visit by the UN Special Rapporteur on the promotion and protection of human rights while countering terrorism, nor has it responded to his request for information related to ISA detention.

The government has insisted on retaining the EO, saying it needs the law to impede the activities of criminal gangs, despite the fact that it violates constitutional due process requirements. In October 2006, in a blow to the rights of suspects, a federal court ordered that once the internal security minister signs a detention order, any prior police abuse or other misconduct may no longer be challenged in court. The court reasoned that when court-ordered release of a suspect is followed by a new detention order, a not uncommon occurrence in Malaysia, appeal of the original order is "rendered academic."

Migrant Workers, Refugees, and Asylum Seekers

Malaysian officials reported in 2007 that there were nearly 1.9 million documented migrants in the country. Although there is no official count of undocumented migrants, estimates suggest the total is 700,000 or more. Some 150,000 people are believed to be either refugees or asylum seekers, only a third of whom have been registered by UNHCR.

In July 2007, the government began one of its periodic roundups, seeking to deport those who had entered Malaysia illegally. Some 10,000 were apprehended during the first month of operation. In addition to deportation, those in violation of the law face up to five years' imprisonment and six strokes of the cane, as provided for by the Immigration Act 1959/63. Such round-ups, which fail to differentiate between people in need of international protection and other migrants, frequently involve violence by the authorities or their agents.

The almost half million strong Peoples Volunteer Force (RELA) is empowered by the Emergency (Essential Powers) Act 1979, as amended, to arrest and detain "undesirable persons" and suspected illegal migrants. Force members, authorized to enter and search any public or private premise without a warrant, have raided migrant housing in the middle of the night, beating up residents, confiscating valuables, and, at times, destroying the ID cards of legal migrants to justify the raids.

For example, on April 5, 2007, RELA volunteers arrested some 20 Burmese refugees and asylum seekers in downtown Kuala Lumpur. At least five had been recognized as refugees by the office of the UN High Commissioner for Refugees (UNHCR). On June 25, 2007, at 2:00 a.m., Malaysian Immigration officials and RELA volunteers raided the Chin Refugee Centre and Chin communities at Jalan

Imbi and Jalan San Peng, Kuala Lumpur, arresting 228 asylum seekers and refugees from Burma, most of whom UNHCR had recognized as refugees.

The migrant work force includes some 300,000 domestic workers, primarily Indonesian. They confront a wide range of abuses, including forced confinement in the workplace, excessively long work hours, lack of rest days, withheld wages, and physical and sexual abuse. Domestic workers not only are excluded from key provisions of Malaysia's Employment Act of 1955, but their work permits tie them to a particular employer, making it difficult to report abuse for fear of deportation. While Malaysia has imposed some penalties on agencies and employers following a 2006 agreement with Indonesia, the agreement does not extend many basic labor law protections to domestic workers. Criminal prosecutions of abusive employers are rare. Nirmala Bonat, whose employer burned and brutally beat her, has remained in the Indonesian embassy since 2004 while the trial of her employer continues.

In violation of the Convention on the Rights of the Child, which Malaysia has ratified, children of migrants with temporary residence are not entitled to free public education.

Police Abuse

Complaints directed against Malaysia's police force include allegations of routine physical abuse of detainees. In June 2007, Suhakam, the official Human Rights Commission of Malaysia, said police responded to only 16 of the 34 cases of police brutality brought to their attention over a one-and-a-half-year period. Prison abuse at times includes beatings so severe that hospitalization is required. The police also often rely on a policy of "remand first, investigate later." As a result, suspects spend days in detention, often without access to family members or a lawyer, greatly increasing the risk of mistreatment.

Freedom of Expression

In 2007 Malaysian officials cautioned private media outlets against abusing their privileges, advised newspapers to be wary of repeating blog criticisms of the government, and warned webmasters and bloggers to use their power cautiously.

Critical bloggers have been sued for defamation, a powerful tool long used in Malaysia by the government to stifle dissent.

The Internal Security Ministry sent warnings in March and July 2007 to newspapers not to publish cyber-induced speculation on "sensitive" issues. The circular reminded journalists that publishers are required to "always comply with directives issued by the ministry." The 1984 Printing Presses and Publications Act (PPPA) requires that newspapers renew their licenses every year.

On July 13, the police used section 8 of the Official Secrets Act (OSA) to arrest Nathaniel Tan, a staffer at the opposition People's Justice Party, on suspicion of possessing documents related to government corruption. Tan was held on remand for four days before being released on bail. The OSA is a broadly-worded law according to which any public officer can declare any material an official secret, a certification which cannot be questioned in court. The act allows for arrest and detention without a warrant, and substantially reverses the burden of proof.

Freedom of Religion

Islam is the official state religion, but the constitution protects freedom of religion for non-Muslims. Discussions in July 2007 as to whether Malaysia was an Islamic or a secular state grew contentious after Deputy Prime Minister Najib Abdul Razak declared it an Islamic state. The internal security minister then banned further media discussion, but ruled that statements by Prime Minister Badawi and Deputy PM Razak could be aired.

In a landmark ruling, Lima Joy, a Muslim covert to Christianity, lost her six-year battle to have the word "Muslim" removed from her identity card. She had argued she was entitled to freedom of religion under article 11 of the constitution. The top secular court ruled that only the Sharia court had jurisdiction.

Human Rights Defenders

The NGO community, the Malaysian bar, lawyers, and some opposition politicians are active in defense of human rights despite the serious personal and professional risks entailed.

In June 2007, during a rally in Johor Bahru organized to protest rising crime rates, police arrested two activists from the NGO Suaram for attempting to distribute leaflets supporting the proposed Independent Police Complaints and Misconduct Commission. The Johor Bahru Magistrate Court remanded the two for 24 hours.

In October, the Putrajaya district police requested the Malaysian Bar Association president, vice-president, and secretary to appear to discuss the September 26, 2006 "Walk for Justice." The 2,000 strong march to the prime minister's office delivered a memorandum urging the government to set up a Royal Commission of Inquiry to investigate apparent corruption in the appointment of justices. In November, police refused to issue a permit for a rally and march by the Coalition for Clean and Fair Elections (Bersih). When some 40,000 Malaysians defied the ban, police used chemical-laced water and tear gas to disperse peaceful participants. Tear gas and water cannons were also used against participants in a Hindu Rights Action Force November 25 rally. A total of 99 organizers and marchers were charged in the aftermath. Prime Minister Badawi threatened to use the Internal Security Act to prevent further unauthorized street demonstrations.

Key International Actors

As a key ASEAN member, Malaysian officials initially urged Burma to agree to talk with opposition leader Aung San Suu Kyi without preconditions and even suggested that Burma could be expelled from ASEAN following its violent crackdown on monks, students, and other protesters in September 2007. However, by November 19, 2007, Malaysian Foreign Minister Syed Hamid Albar had backed away from public denunciation of Burma's human rights record and was defending ASEAN's failure to take any steps to censure Burma.

Despite its own lack of enthusiasm and concern over protracted negotiations, Malaysia has pressed reluctant ASEAN members to support a regional human rights body.

Malaysia has not ratified any key UN conventions other than the Convention on the Rights of the Child and the Convention on the Elimination of All Forms of Discrimination against Women.

New US ambassador to Malaysia James Keith noted a "greater congruence between the interests of America and Malaysia," especially related to counterterrorism, during his May confirmation hearing before the US Senate. US-Malaysia negotiations on a free trade agreement, however, appeared stalled at this writing, in part because of a new Malaysian labor law rescinding key worker rights.

NEPAL

Implementation of the November 2006 Comprehensive Peace Agreement (CPA) to end the 1996-2006 civil war progressed with the promulgation of an interim constitution, and establishment of an interim parliament in January 2007, but withdrawal of the Communist Party of Nepal–Maoists (CPN-M) from government in September was a blow to plans for elections to a constituent assembly. There was considerable progress on the human rights situation, though concerns remain about a lack of political will to address accountability for past and ongoing human rights abuses. The CPN-M also continues to stall the verification process of cantoned combatants, which means that an unknown number of child soldiers remain in their ranks.

Unresolved grievances and issues of representation make the Terai region in the southern plains—home to almost half of Nepal's population—the most critical area for continuing instability. The security situation is steadily worsening in the Terai, as strikes and protests disrupt daily life, and abductions, killings, and other violence by armed groups sharply increases.

Implementing the Comprehensive Peace Agreement

The interim parliament's 330 members comprise representatives from the CPN-M, from political parties elected in 1999 to the previous parliament, and civil society nominees. On April 1, 2007, the Seven Party Alliance (SPA) and CPN-M formed an interim government under Prime Minister Girija Prasad Koirala, in which the CPN-M held five out of 22 cabinet positions. However, the CPN-M withdrew from the government on September 18, a month after announcing 22 preconditions for its continuing participation. These included the demand to immediately declare a republic, establish a commission on enforced disappearances, release all detained Maoist cadres, and begin security sector reform.

The withdrawal led the SPA on October 5 to declare planned constituent assembly elections suspended. In early November intense negotiations by the CPN-M led to a special session of parliament adopting two non-binding motions calling on the government "to make arrangements to turn Nepal into a federal democratic republic," and to adopt a system of fully proportional representation for constituent assembly elections, two main demands being put forward by the Maoists to participate in elections. However, at this writing the elections remain postponed indefinitely.

"People's courts" and other parallel government structures have been mostly dismantled. A number of individuals who had been "sentenced" to long periods of forced labor or captivity by "people's courts" were released or handed over to the police. However, cadres of the Young Communist League (YCL), the CPN-M youth wing, have not been fully reined in since the CPA came into force, and were responsible in 2007 for extortion, threats, intimidation, physical assault, ill-treatment sometimes amounting to torture, forced labor, disruption of rallies and meetings ,and destruction of property.

Some prospective improvements were made in securing better political representation for women. The Constituent Assembly Members' Election Act (2007) allots women half the seats in the proportional representation system and a third of candidates across the board.

Truth and Justice

Security sector reform, which would strike at the heart of the problem of impunity, has been resisted by the army and neglected by the political establishment.

The International Committee of the Red Cross estimates there are 1,042 cases of enforced disappearances attributable either to the Nepalese Army or CPN-M forces. There has been almost no progress on resolving these. The CPA committed the government and Maoists to make public the whereabouts of "disappeared" people within 60 days of its signing, a deadline that came and went with little action. On June 1 the Supreme Court called for setting up a commission of inquiry to investigate enforced disappearances, and commissioners were appointed by October, but at this writing the commission has yet to start work.

In June a draft Truth and Reconciliation Commission bill was tabled. It proposes establishing a commission with a mandate to investigate gross violations of human rights and crimes against humanity committed during the civil war. More than 12,000 people were killed in the conflict, many of them civilians.

In the draft bill, amnesties can be granted even for gross human rights violations if these acts had a political motivation, if the perpetrator made an application indicating regret, or if victims and perpetrators agree to a reconciliation process. Such a mechanism could result in protection from criminal prosecution for even the gravest of crimes. Thus the draft bill fails to reflect international standards as established by the United Nations Basic Principles and Guidelines on the Right to a Remedy and Reparation for Victims of Gross Violations of International Human Rights, adopted in 2005. These standards draw together international legal obligations, including specific treaties Nepal has ratified. The government's consultation with Nepalese civil society and victims has been insufficient on all issues relating to the commission.

Violence in the Terai

Denial of citizenship prior to November 2006 and state monolingualism contributed substantially to the marginalization and under-representation of the Madhesi community, an ethnic group that makes up nearly 40 per cent of Nepal's population of 27 million. Madhesis occupy less than 12 percent of posts in the judiciary, executive, legislature, political parties, industry, and civil society. Madhesis are also poorer and have lower education and health indicators than hill communities. Madhesis argue they are systematically under-represented in the electoral system, since the number of parliamentary seats for the Terai does not reflect its population.

Promulgation of the interim constitution sparked 21 days of protests by the Madhesis in January-February 2007. On January 16 leaders from the political party Madhesi Janadhikar Forum (MJF) were arrested in Kathmandu for burning copies of the constitution. Three days later MJF activists protesting the arrests in Lahan, Siraha district, clashed with Maoists, who shot dead Ramesh Kumar Mahato, a young MJF activist. Mahato's killing sparked prolonged agitation; Madhesi activists called for a general strike in the Terai and organized widespread protests, to which the government responded with curfews and an increased police presence. On January 25 the MJF announced it would continue the protests indefinitely until the interim constitution was amended. Activists looted government offices, police posts, banks, mainstream parties' district offices, and media organizations. The state response was harsh: police shot dead more than 30 demonstrators and wounded 800 in the following days.

On August 31 the government signed a 22-point agreement with the Madhesi People's Rights Forum (MPRF). Despite this, sporadic violent incidents continue to occur. The September 16 killing of Mohit Khan, leader of the Democratic Madhesi Front, by an unknown group in Kapilvastu sparked riots against hill people. Three simultaneous bomb explosions in Kathmandu on September 2 killed several people and injured others. These bomb attacks were the first in the capital and the most serious anywhere in the country since the end of the civil war.

Child Soldiers

The CPA includes provisions committing the parties not to use or enlist children in any military force and to "immediately rescue and rehabilitate" such children.

Children continued to be actively recruited by the CPN-M after the April 2006 ceasefire. The United Nations documented 154 children forcibly recruited from May to September 2006, of whom 72 were recruited into the People's Liberation Army (PLA) and 82 into other CPN-M-affiliated organizations, including militias. Reports since December 2006 indicate the enrolment of children into the YCL after the signing of the CPA. At the end of February the UN's Monitoring and Reporting Mechanism Task Force, set up within the framework of Security Council Resolution 1612, documented 1,995 children then serving with the CPN-M and its affiliates.

In January 2007 a newly established United Nations Mission in Nepal (UNMIN) with the assistance of other UN agencies started a programme of registration and verification of Maoist army combatants. Progress in identifying children was delayed due to disagreement between the UN and the CPN-M about the interpretation of the findings.

Refugees and Internally Displaced

A United States offer to resettle 60,000 or more Bhutanese refugees gave hope to many of the 106,000 refugees living in Nepal since the early 1990s. But some

refugees see the resettlement offer as undercutting the prospects for repatriation and have increasingly resorted to threats and violence to prevent other refugees from advocating for solutions other than return to Bhutan. In May 2007 Nepalese police shot and killed a Bhutanese refugee involved in a violent clash between refugees living in the camps. The Police killed a second refugee during a demonstration for repatriation to Bhutan.

Fear of Maoist action continues to prevent many internally displaced persons (IDPs) from returning to their homes particularly in northwestern Nepal. Often only those who support or have close affiliation with the Maoists have been able to return to their properties, while a large number of IDPs, particularly in the midwestern region, are unable to repossess their farms, livestock, and houses that were seized by the Maoists.

Human Rights Defenders

Human rights defenders, particularly women, continue to face attacks. In the Terai region in particular, where most of the recent violence in the country has occurred, there have been at least a dozen incidents where those defending the rights of women—including documenting violence against women—and the rights of Dalits were attacked and on occasion beaten. In August members of a Dalit community group, the Badi Women Human Rights Defenders, were beaten and arrested by the Nepal police in Kathmandu.

Key International Actors

India, the United Kingdom, the United States, and the European Union remain strongly committed to assisting the peace process and are keen to ensure that constituent assembly elections get back on track.

The presence of the UN Office of the High Commissioner for Human Rights (OHCHR) has contributed vastly to improving the human rights situation in Nepal. Enforced disappearances by the security forces came to a halt, and the CPN-M released a number of people it had taken hostage. The OHCHR presence encourages space for public debate and helps to create a climate for a political solution to the conflict. The OHCHR has responded to the Madhesi violence by addressing social exclusion.

UN Secretary-General Ban Ki-moon has reiterated the need for an inclusive peace process. In his December 2006 report to the Security Council, he recommended that the government invite the special representative for children and armed conflict to undertake a mission to Nepal in the near future. The visit was scheduled to take place in August 2007 but has been postponed by the UN.

NORTH KOREA

Human rights conditions in the Democratic People's Republic of Korea (North Korea) remain abysmal. Authorities continue to prohibit organized political opposition, independent news media, and civil society activities. Arbitrary arrests, lack of due process, and executions remain of grave concern.

The government denies citizens the right to leave the country. In 2007 authorities increased border patrols and repeatedly warned of harsher punishments for those who attempt to leave without state permission, which is virtually impossible to obtain. Nevertheless, many North Koreans continue to risk escaping to China in search of food and work, a trend exacerbated in 2006 and 2007 by massive summer flooding which damaged crops and homes.

While access to the country is strictly limited and reliable evidence is hard to obtain, some recent escapees told Human Rights Watch of an increase in underground Christian religious activity by individuals and families. Escapees also described seeing denunciations of allegedly corrupt local officials written on walls in some border cities. Such developments would have been unthinkable prior to the famine of the mid-1990s, when the leadership lost its aura of invincibility and some of its ability to control citizens' everyday lives.

Right to Food

North Korea is still recovering from the 1990s famine, which is believed to have killed about a million people and left many children permanently stunted. The government continues to provide state food rations to elites—including high-ranking members of the Workers' Party and the security and intelligence forces—before all others. Several non-elite North Koreans told Human Rights Watch that they had not received adequate food rations since the early 1990s, and blamed the preferential treatment given to elites as well as corruption among food distribution officials. Many say they receive rations only a few times each year, typically on major national holidays such as Kim Jong Il's birthday.

Rice, corn, and potato prices continued to rise through 2007. Many attribute the ongoing food shortage to South Korea's suspension of fertilizer and food aid in

2006, and to flooding in the summers of 2006 and 2007. North Korean intervie-
wees describe seeing more homeless people at train stations and markets,
including whole families living on the street after trading their homes for food as
a last resort.

South Korea resumed humanitarian aid, including food aid, in anticipation of the
inter-Korea summit on October 2-4, 2007.

North Koreans in China

Since the mid-1990s, hundreds of thousands of North Koreans have fled to China.
Many still live in hiding there because the Chinese government categorically
labels them illegal economic migrants and routinely repatriates those it arrests. In
doing so China violates its obligations to consider them refugees and offer them
protection.

The trafficking of North Korean women and girls in China persists, especially near
the border. Many are abducted or duped into marriage, prostitution, or sexual
slavery. Some North Korean women live with Chinese men in de facto marriages,
though doing so does not ensure legal residence for them or their children and
they remain vulnerable to arrest and repatriation. In 2007 officials of a small district in northeast China reportedly granted some North Korean women formal permission to reside within the district, but the policy apparently has not been
adopted elsewhere.

Refugees and Asylum Seekers Outside China

A relatively small number of North Koreans fortunate enough to avoid being repatriated from China have managed to reach other countries in the region, including
Cambodia, Laos, Mongolia, Thailand, and Vietnam. Most are seeking ultimately to
reach South Korea, Japan, or the United States. At this writing, hundreds of North
Koreans remained in overcrowded immigration detention centers in Bangkok,
awaiting transfer to South Korea or the United States.

South Korea accepts all North Korean asylum seekers as citizens, under its constitution that defines the entire Korean Peninsula as South Korean territory. In the

past decade, it has admitted around 10,000 North Koreans. The US, under the North Korea Human Rights Act of 2004, has granted refugee status to a few dozen North Koreans. Japan has accepted over 100 North Koreans, mostly individuals who lived in Japan in the 1960s and 1970s. In Europe, Germany, the United Kingdom, Ireland, the Netherlands, and Denmark collectively have granted refugee status to more than 300 North Koreans in recent years.

Treatment of Suspects and Prisoners

Leaving North Korea without state permission is considered treason and is punishable by heavy penalties. North Korean police interrogate and sometimes torture individuals returning from China, asking why they left, who they met, and what they did.

Some North Koreans report that the treatment of "illegal" border crossers and other criminal suspects improved in 2007, citing less verbal and physical abuse. They also note that suspects occasionally have been visited by, though not defended in court by, state-appointed defense lawyers. One person, for example, said an attorney had visited him once, asking whether his human rights had been violated since his arrest. It was not clear whether such changes were due to the discretion of regional state officials, or a reflection of a new central government policy.

However, many prisoners are still routinely subjected to inhuman and degrading treatment. Lack of food and medicine in detention facilities lead to illness and sometimes death. There are still reports of public executions, although not as frequently as in the 1990s. The death penalty appears to apply to treason, sedition, and acts of terrorism, as well as to lesser crimes such as selling illegal substances or stealing state property (everything from electrical cables to coal is deemed state property).

North Korean Workers at Kaesong Industrial Complex

The United States and South Korea signed a Free Trade Agreement in June 2007, which at this writing had not yet been ratified by the congress of either country. An annex to the agreement opened the possibility that products made in North

Korea's Kaesong Industrial Complex (KIC)—where over 15,000 North Korean workers produce watches, shoes, clothes, kitchenware, car parts, and other items for South Korean businesses—would be exported to the United States duty free. The US signed the agreement even though the law governing working conditions in the KIC falls far short of international standards on freedom of association, the right to collective bargaining, sex discrimination and harassment, and harmful child labor.

Key International Actors

In February 2007, North Korea agreed to disable its main nuclear reactor and reveal all nuclear weapons related activity in return for humanitarian aid, heavy fuel oil, and other economic benefits. The agreement was followed by six-party talks on implementation involving the two Koreas, the United States, Japan, China, and Russia.

On October 2-4, 2007, North Korea's leader Kim Jong Il and South Korea's President Roh Mu-hyun held the second-ever inter-Korea summit. They discussed humanitarian aid, economic cooperation, and ways to secure lasting peace on the Korean Peninsula.

China, Russia, and a number of European and Middle Eastern countries have hosted North Korean workers pursuant to agreements with North Korean state companies. In some of those countries, local human rights activists and journalists have expressed concern for the workers' basic rights, including restrictions on their freedom of movement, the constant presence of minders, and indirect payments under which a large chunk of their salaries is allegedly taken by middlemen or the North Korean government. In response to such criticism, the Czech Republic government, for example, stopped issuing work visas for North Korean workers in 2006. Human Rights Watch has recommended that host countries improve protection of worker rights instead of sending workers back home. According to media reports, North Koreans are also working in Bulgaria, Hungary, Iraq, Kuwait, Mongolia, and Poland.

South Korea says 485 of its citizens, abducted by North Korean agents, remain in North Korea against their will. North Korea has rejected repeated requests from the abductees' families to confirm their existence and return them home, or, if they have died, to return their remains. Japan's relations with North Korea also remain strained over the issue of abductees. While North Korea has admitted that it abducted 13 Japanese (it returned five of them in 2002), it claims that the other eight died and that no other Japanese citizens were abducted. Japan says that several more of its citizens have been abducted.

North Korea has not responded to repeated requests for dialogue from Vitit Muntarbhorn, who has been the UN's special rapporteur on human rights in North Korea since 2004.

PAKISTAN

General Pervez Musharraf's military-backed government, in office since a 1999 *coup d'etat*, declared a state of emergency on November 3, 2007, suspending the constitution and dismissing two-thirds of the country's senior judges including the chief justice of the Supreme Court, Iftikhar Muhammad Chaudhry. A swift crackdown followed, with Pakistani authorities arresting thousands of lawyers, judges, and opposition activists and violently suppressing peaceful protests.

Prominent human rights defenders were among those detained or placed under house arrest, including the chairperson of the independent Human Rights Commission of Pakistan and a UN Special Rapporteur, Asma Jahangir. Some of those detained were questioned by Pakistan's feared Inter-Services Intelligence (ISI) agency and Military Intelligence (MI) agency, known for using torture against opponents of the government. With the declaration of martial law, Musharraf imposed sweeping censorship rules on the media, closing down private television channels and international media agencies.

Following the suspension of the constitution, Musharraf issued a series of decrees that muzzle the media, allow the military to detain, charge, and try any civilian, and allow courts to revoke lawyers' licenses to practice law. The constitution was then amended so that these and other such measures will remain "legal" even after the constitution is restored.

On November 28, Musharraf retired as army chief and the following day he took the oath of office as president under the suspended constitution for a five-year term. Though Musharraf claims to be transitioning to civilian rule, his election was widely regarded as illegal and the country remains effectively under military control.

Ongoing concerns at this writing include arbitrary detention, lack of fair trials, mistreatment, torture, and enforced disappearances of terrorism suspects and political opponents; harassment, intimidation, and censorship of the media; increasing unrest amid military operations in the tribal areas bordering Afghanistan; and legal discrimination and mistreatment of religious minorities.

Judicial Independence Undermined

2007 saw a movement for judicial independence borne out of the events of March 9, when General Musharraf first tried to dismiss Supreme Court Chief Justice Iftikhar Muhammad Chaudhry for alleged "misuse of office." Justice Chaudhry refused to resign, triggering nation-wide protests against Musharraf. Authorities violently suppressed the movement, led by Pakistani lawyers, to restore the chief justice, beating lawyers, opposition activists, and media personnel covering unfolding events. On May 12, 42 people died in violence led by activists of the Mutahedda Qaumi Movement (MQM), a major coalition partner in the Musharraf government, trying to stop Chaudhry from entering Karachi to address the Sindh High Court Bar Association. In the face of relentless country-wide protests, Musharraf backed down temporarily and the Supreme Court restored the chief justice to office on July 20.

In November the Supreme Court was due to decide on the legality of Musharraf's presidential election which had occurred in October. However, the court never ruled because of the imposition of the state of emergency on November 3. Attempts by Supreme Court judges to bar the government from proclaiming emergency rule and urging government officials not to implement emergency orders were thwarted as the judges were summarily fired and detained. Justice Chaudhry was dismissed and placed under house arrest along with his family, including a seven-year-old son and a teenage daughter. Overall, almost two-thirds of 97 senior judges declined to accept emergency rule and were dismissed, many placed in detention or under house arrest. They were replaced by Musharraf loyalists and, on November 19, a "puppet" Supreme Court quickly dismissed the legal challenges to Musharraf's reelection as president.

On November 10, Musharraf issued a presidential decree allowing military trials of civilians for certain offences previously under the purview of the judiciary. The amendments were made retroactive to January 1, 2003, effectively sanctioning impunity of the army for detention and "disappearances" of civilians since that time. Until the sacking of most of its judges, the Supreme Court had been investigating some 400 cases of "disappearances" of Musharraf's political opponents and terrorism suspects.

Opposition Leaders Return

Two exiled opposition leaders, Benazir Bhutto and Nawaz Sharif, returned to Pakistan in 2007. Under pressure from the US, Benazir Bhutto, a former prime minister, was allowed to return to Pakistan unhindered on October 18. Bhutto's welcoming procession was targeted by suicide bombers killing 139 people and injuring several hundreds. Bhutto and her husband have claimed that members of the government and elements within the security services may have been complicit in the attack.

On November 25, Nawaz Sharif, another former prime minister, was finally allowed to return to Pakistan. Earlier, on September 10, Pakistan and Saudi Arabia had flouted international law by forcibly transferring Sharif into exile in Saudi Arabia as he attempted to end seven years of exile by returning to Pakistan. The Pakistani government's actions were in direct contravention of a Supreme Court ruling that Sharif had an inalienable right to enter and remain in the country.

Thousands of political activists from the parties headed by Bhutto and Sharif, as well as smaller political groups, have been arrested in order to prevent post-emergency protests. Bhutto herself has been intermittently placed under house arrest to prevent her from leading demonstrations in the aftermath of the crackdown on lawyers and activists.

Freedom of Expression

Concerted and increasing attempts by the Pakistani government to muzzle the media continued throughout 2007. Journalists faced persistent pressure and threats from the government to tone down their coverage of the anti-government protests. Media offices were physically attacked and closely monitored by the security forces. Reporters working for local, regional, national, and international media faced torture, kidnapping, illegal detention, beatings, and coercion.

On March 16, riot police attacked the Islamabad offices of the Jang Group, which houses the newspapers *Jang*, *The News*, and Geo TV. Police broke into the offices, damaging property and terrorizing journalists while the media attempted to cover an anti-government protest underway outside.

On May 22, the Mohajir Rabita Council (MRC), an affiliate of the MQM, issued a statement naming 12 eminent Pakistani journalists as "enemies." On May 29, journalists working for the Associated Press (AP) and the Agence France-Presse (AFP) wire services found identical envelopes, each containing a 30mm bullet, planted in their cars. Two of these journalists were named in the MRC statement. The MQM has a long record of political harassment, extortion, torture, and targeted killings, but Musharraf took no action in response, failing even to press the MQM to discipline its affiliate and ensure that such threats cease.

Throughout the year, several privately-run TV channels, including Aaj TV, ARY, and Geo TV, reported their transmissions were taken off air by cable operators because they were transmitting footage of violence by state authorities.

Since the November imposition of martial law, Musharraf has imposed sweeping curbs on the media through two presidential decrees and hundreds of journalists have been threatened, beaten, attacked, and detained. Some international journalists were expelled and many private and international television stations were removed from the air for several weeks. They were restored after they accepted government restrictions including bans on journalists and programming deemed objectionable by the government. Country-wide protests against curbs on the media have been violently suppressed on multiple occasions.

Unrest in Balochistan

Political unrest in the southwestern province of Balochistan continued in 2007. Though the dispute in Balochistan is essentially political, centered on issues of provincial autonomy and exploitation of mineral resources, the Pakistani military and Baloch tribal militants have increasingly sought a military solution to their disagreements. The Pakistani military has arbitrarily detained, tortured, and "disappeared" militants and political opponents; Baloch militants have continued to target civilians and use landmines in sporadic retaliatory attacks.

Counterterrorism

Serious violations of human rights continue to accompany Pakistan's large-scale counterterrorism operations. Terrorism suspects are frequently detained without charge or, if charged, are often convicted without proper judicial process. Human Rights Watch has documented scores of illegal detentions, instances of torture, and "disappearances" in Pakistan's major cities. Counterterrorism laws also continue to be misused to perpetuate personal vendettas and as instruments of political coercion.

It is impossible to ascertain the number of people "disappeared" in counterterrorism operations because of the secrecy surrounding such operations. Until the imposition of the state of emergency, the Supreme Court—investigating 400 cases of enforced disappearances—had been maintaining pressure on the government, publicly stating that it had overwhelming evidence that Pakistan's intelligence agencies were detaining terror suspects and other opponents and repeatedly urging the authorities to free such individuals or process them through the legal system. In response to pressure from the Supreme Court, scores of those who "disappeared" were freed or charged, and some foreign or dual citizens were deported to their countries of origin.

Torture and ill-treatment of such individuals in custody remains a serious concern. Rangzieb Ahmed, a British citizen of Pakistani origin was held in illegal custody for over a year during which time he alleges he was severely tortured by Pakistani intelligence agents. He was deported to the UK in September after Pakistan's Supreme Court ordered his release. The British government failed to intervene to prevent the torture though they admit having access to Ahmed during his incarceration. Ahmed was arrested at London's Heathrow airport upon arrival.

A peace agreement between the government, tribal leaders, and militants closely allied with the Taliban signed in September 2006, collapsed within months. As a result, the Pakistan Army continues to engage in aggressive counterterrorism operations in Pakistan's Federally Administered Tribal Areas along the Afghan border, with efforts particularly focused on the Waziristan region. Hundreds of Pakistani troops are being held hostage by pro-Taliban militants. In October 2007 Pakistani authorities launched a major offensive in north Waziristan. Reports indicate the offensive has been accompanied by civilian displacement, extrajudicial executions, house demolitions, arbitrary detentions, and harassment of journalists.

Armed groups in Pakistan's tribal areas continue to engage in vigilantism and violent attacks, including murder and public beheadings. Selective military operations aside, the government has done little to apprehend, let alone prosecute, Taliban and militant leaders guilty of committing serious human rights abuses across the border in Afghanistan, and increasingly in Pakistan.

Throughout November 2007 Taliban attacks and operations spread into settled areas of the North West Frontier Province. Battles during this month between pro-Taliban militants and security forces in the Swat valley saw hundreds killed and thousands of civilians displaced.

Gender and Religious Discrimination

Legal discrimination and persecution on grounds of gender and religion continued in 2007. As in previous years, violence against women and girls, including "honor killings," rape, domestic violence, and forced marriages, remained serious problems. According to the Human Rights Commission of Pakistan, honor killings continued to rise in 2007 and growing extremism posed new threats to women's rights.

The Ahmadi religious community was a particularly frequent target of religious discrimination in 2007. Numerous blasphemy cases were registered against its members and scores were arrested.

Key International Actors

The US, UK, and EU all issued statements urging Musharraf to end the state of emergency, release those arrested, and hold free and fair elections. However, their actions did not match their words. At this writing, all three were continuing to prop up Musharraf with substantial military and economic assistance.

The Bush administration continues to provide significant political support to Musharraf. The United States has notably failed to press strongly for human rights improvements in the country or for the release and restoration to office of ousted Supreme Court Chief Justice Iftikhar Muhammad Chaudhry and other judges. As in previous years, the US muted its criticism in exchange for Pakistan's support in counterterrorism operations.

However, in a largely symbolic gesture, on November 20 Pakistan was suspended from the Commonwealth in response to Musharraf's actions. The suspension is expected to remain in force until the restoration of some form of constitutional rule.

Pakistan still has not signed the International Covenant on Civil and Political Rights or ratified the International Covenant on Economic, Social and Cultural Rights. Pakistan has played a negative role as a member of the UN Human Rights Council and has fought to prevent scrutiny and criticism of Organization of Islamic Conference (OIC) states.

PAPUA NEW GUINEA

Parliamentary elections in July 2007, although not without incident, concluded without the feared large-scale violence, resulting in Sir Michael Somare's return as prime minister and changes in key cabinet ministries. Again, only one woman, Dame Carol Kidu, was elected to parliament.

Police rape and torture, impunity for gender-based violence and discrimination, and abuses against people living with and affected by HIV/AIDS remain widespread.

Two men were sentenced to death in October for murder, although no executions have been carried out since the death penalty was reintroduced in 1991.

Police Violence, Juvenile Justice, and Detention of Children

Police continue to routinely use excessive force, torture, and sexual violence against individuals in custody. In the face of widespread violent crime, such tactics have proved ineffective as crime control, and have deeply eroded the public trust and cooperation crucial to policing. Impunity and corruption fuel abuse as police are rarely held accountable for violence, either through internal disciplinary mechanisms or by the criminal justice system.

Otherwise promising juvenile justice reforms have had little effect on widespread police violence against children and other vulnerable groups, as converting new standards into changed police practices remains elusive. However, progress in developing the juvenile justice system continues with additional training for police on new standards for dealing with children. A third juvenile policy monitoring unit opened in the highlands. The units are intended to divert children from the formal justice system into mediation or informal conflict resolution mechanisms, and to prevent detention with adults. However, in many areas, police continue to detain children with adults in police lockups, where they are denied medical care and placed at risk of rape and other forms of violence.

In prisons and other juvenile institutions, children awaiting trial are mixed with those already convicted. Many facilities lack blankets, beds, mosquito nets, clothes, or any education or rehabilitation programs. As children may face months or even years in detention awaiting trial, these are serious problems. Some prisons and rural lockups received additional funds in 2007, resulting in improvements to staff housing and conditions for some inmates.

A new juvenile justice act emphasizing rehabilitation and reintegration, with arrest and detention as measures of last resort, awaits parliamentary review at this writing.

Violence and Discrimination against Women and Girls

Violence against women and girls—including domestic violence, gang rape, and torture and murder for alleged sorcery—is pervasive and rarely punished. In October news reports of a man pulling the fetus from his pregnant wife's womb provoked widespread public outrage. Parliamentarian Kidu presented to parliament a petition on violence against women signed by more than 4,000 people. At this writing, parliament has declined to debate the issue. Police often ignore complaints or demand money or sex from victims. Nevertheless, in August the Supreme Court upheld the conviction of James Yali, a parliamentarian, for raping his 17-year-old sister-in-law; the ruling invalidated his reelection.

Girls' and women's low status also is reflected in disparities in education, health care, and employment; heavy household workloads; and polygyny.

Human Rights Monitoring Mechanisms

The Ombudsman Commission, which has taken useful steps to monitor government corruption, has a human rights unit, but the unit's capacity to pursue cases is weak. In June 2007 the police force signed an agreement with the Ombudsman's Commission to create a police ombudsman, but it remains to be seen whether the office will take up torture and cruel, inhuman, and degrading treatment, and, if it does, whether it will have the political backing and resources to hold officers accountable.

Prohibitive costs and procedural difficulties make it all but impossible for many citizens to pursue civil claims against police officers suspected of abuse.

Successful claims have limited deterrent effect because the costs are born by the state, not the police force or individual officers.

Nongovernmental organizations (NGOs) and women's rights activists play an essential role in obtaining services for victims of violence, but some face threats for their work.

HIV/AIDS

Papua New Guinea has the highest prevalence of HIV/AIDS in the Pacific: the government and UNAIDS estimate that almost 60,000 people were living with the disease at the end of 2007 (1.61 percent of persons ages 15-49).

Antiretroviral therapy remains inaccessible to most, and few have the tools to protect themselves from infection. People living with HIV/AIDS often face violence and discrimination in their communities. In August an activist's report that southern highlands villagers had buried alive at least three people living with HIV/AIDS received international condemnation. The government promised to investigate and, in the context of conflicting claims by some local groups, announced it had found no evidence of the practice.

Despite ongoing police training on HIV/AIDS, police undermine prevention efforts by targeting female sex workers, men and boys suspected of homosexual conduct, and street vendors for beatings and rape. Police also extort money from such individuals, using the threat of arresting them for illegal activities. Police are known to abuse people simply for carrying condoms; such actions deter condom use and undermine protection efforts. However, NGOs report some improvements on the part of individual officers as the result of training.

Education

Primary education is neither free nor universal. Gross primary enrollment is low—about 75 percent of school-age children in 2005—according to United Nations data, while secondary school enrollment rates are below 30 percent. School fees and related costs pose a significant barrier to children's education, despite partial government subsidies in some provinces. Fees, which are high compared with average annual income, are often linked to non-attendance, dropout, and the entry of children into child labor.

Key International Actors

The government has not at this writing responded to requests to visit Papua New Guinea from the UN special rapporteurs on torture, health, or education. Papua New Guinea is not a party to the Convention against Torture or to other major human rights treaties, apart from the Convention on the Rights of the Child, the Convention on the Elimination of All Forms of Discrimination Against Women, and the Convention on the Elimination of Racial Discrimination. The United Nations Children's Fund (UNICEF) continues to lead juvenile justice reform efforts.

Australia remains, by far, the most important external actor and largest foreign donor, playing a significant role in, among other areas, the law and justice sector and HIV/AIDS. However, Australia does not take a human rights approach to development, and relations between the two countries remain strained.

This summary does not address human rights developments in Bougainville.

THE PHILIPPINES

The Philippines is a multiparty democracy with an elected president and legislature, yet several key institutions, such as the judiciary and law enforcement agencies, remain weak. The legacy of the "people power" movement that helped end martial law in 1986 continues to bolster a thriving civil society sector and a vibrant media.

Members of the Armed Forces of the Philippines (AFP) are implicated in extrajudicial killings and enforced disappearances of people they suspect of being members or sympathizers of the insurgent communist New People's Army (NPA), the armed wing of the Communist Party of the Philippines (CPP). In its nearly four decades of armed rebellion, the NPA has killed its own members in internal purges, and has killed business or land owners, suspected government agents, and other perceived enemies. The AFP and Philippine National Police (PNP) dismiss killings of leftists attributed to them as being part of those NPA purges, despite considerable evidence to the contrary.

Extrajudicial Killings and Enforced Disappearances

Since President Gloria Macapagal Arroyo took office in 2001, hundreds of members of left-wing political parties, human rights activists, politically active journalists, and outspoken clergy have been killed or abducted. Although the government has adopted numerous measures it claims will stop extrajudicial killings and bring perpetrators to justice, at this writing no member of the military has been convicted for involvement in any case that occurred since 2001. Victims' families often complain that the PNP is reluctant to investigate cases involving the AFP, or puts the onus on them to produce evidence and witnesses themselves, while some witnesses have been reluctant to come forward due to inadequate witness protection. Even when police investigations have proceeded to court prosecution they have often been dismissed by prosecutors as lacking basic information, witnesses, or evidence. The PNP places the majority of blame for failed prosecutions on witnesses' unwillingness to cooperate.

Extrajudicial killings increased sharply in 2006. This coincided with President Arroyo's June declaration of "all-out war" against the NPA; she gave the AFP a

Scared Silent

Impunity for Extrajudicial Killings in the Philippines

**HUMAN
RIGHTS
WATCH**

two-year deadline to eradicate the insurgency. Two months later, however, in reaction to domestic and international criticism over extrajudicial killings, Arroyo established an investigating commission under former Supreme Court Justice Jose Melo. In January 2007 the Melo Commission concluded that members of the armed forces were involved in or tolerated the killings. The following month, the United Nations special rapporteur on extrajudicial, summary or arbitrary executions, Philip Alston, visited the Philippines at the government's invitation and concluded that "the AFP remains in a state of almost total denial … of its need to respond effectively and authentically to the significant number of killings which have been convincingly attributed to them."

In July the Supreme Court hosted a summit on extrajudicial killings and enforced disappearances, and in late September passed a resolution promulgating rules on the writ of amparo, which is designed to stop the AFP from stalling a case by denying it has the person in question in custody. Under the writ, an agency that has taken a person into custody will be ordered by the Supreme Court to produce evidence proving that the person is no longer in its custody. The new writ, which is retroactive in application, went into effect on October 24. Its effect on securing convictions in or preventing extrajudicial killings and enforced disappearances remains to be seen.

In a much publicized case, Jonas Burgos, who taught farmers organic growing techniques, was abducted in April 2007 in Quezon City. In early October the Court of Appeals repeatedly ordered the AFP to release a report by the provost marshal general who had conducted an investigation into the case, but the AFP invoked a lack of clearance to release the report. Almost simultaneously, President Arroyo issued an administrative order directing the Department of National Defense to draft a bill to prevent "disclosure of military secrets" and "interference in military operations inimical to national security." Local human rights activists expressed concern that this order could be used to block their inquiry into determining the fate of Burgos and other victims of enforced disappearance.

Attacks against Civilians by Armed Groups

In April, on Jolo, members of the Abu Sayyaf Group (ASG) kidnapped seven workers. ASG leader Albader Parad made a public ransom demand for the workers' return. On April 20 the ASG decapitated the seven. The ASG and Rajah Solaiman Movement (RSM), both violent Islamist groups, claimed responsibility in numerous attacks against civilians, and are implicated in many others. Although numerous suspects in such attacks have been arrested, very few have been successfully brought to trial. In some cases, prosecutions have been delayed for years.

In Davao and other areas, vigilante groups continue to kill individuals suspected of involvement in criminal activities.

The Human Security Act

The Human Security Act of 2007, a counterterrorism law passed by the Philippine Congress and signed by President Arroyo in March, took effect on July 15. The government said the law will be used to arrest and prosecute members of terrorist groups such as the ASG, but many civil society leaders, activists, and the UN special rapporteur on human rights and counterterrorism criticized the law. Human Rights Watch assesses it as having an overly broad definition of terrorism, overly harsh mandatory penalties applicable to even minor violations of the law, and it provides for the indefinite detention of terrorism suspects and rendition of persons to countries that routinely commit torture. Several domestic nongovernmental organizations (NGOs) have filed petitions to the Supreme Court asking it to nullify the law, on the grounds that it violates constitutional rights to freedom of speech, association, and assembly.

Government Blacklisting of Critics

The government is known to have put peaceful overseas critics on a blacklist used to ban them from entering the country. A copy of one such blacklist accused 504 individuals of links to al Qaeda or the Taliban, but many of those listed were affiliated with progressive NGOs and/or had previously been to the Philippines on human rights fact-finding visits. According to a Philippines Foreign Ministry official, that particular list was put in place at the time of the Association of Southeast Asian Nations ministerial meeting held in Manila from July 21 to August 2, 2007. It is not clear whether this or any other blacklist is currently in effect.

Key International Actors

The United States remains the Philippines' closest ally and a large donor. Their annual joint military exercises resumed in 2007 after having been cancelled in 2006 when the United States protested the detaining of a US marine convicted of raping a Filipino woman; the dispute was settled when President Arroyo had the marine transferred to the US Embassy compound in Manila. In fiscal year 2007 (October 2006–September 2007), the US government provided the Philippines almost US$30 million under Foreign Military Financing for procurement of military equipment and $2.9 million in the International Military Exchange Training program for training AFP officers in the United States.

In June 2007 a team of European Union experts conducted a fact-finding trip to the Philippines to assess possible assistance to help resolve extrajudicial killings. At this writing the mission results were not published.

The Philippines is a member of the United Nations Human Rights Council, and the country will be up for Universal Periodic Review in 2008.

Singapore

Singapore remains an authoritarian state with strict curbs on freedom of expression, assembly, and association. All political activities are tightly controlled.

Singapore also retains and continues to apply criminal and internal security laws that allow for prolonged detention of suspects without trial. Each year, several thousands of people, including illegal immigrants and other people convicted of crimes, are beaten—caned—as part of their punishment. Despite recent reforms, authorities also fail to guarantee basic rights for the roughly 160,000 migrant domestic workers in the country.

Freedom of Expression and Assembly

The People's Action Party (PAP) has been Singapore's governing party since 1959 and holds 82 of 84 seats in the legislature. Its political dominance is built on laws strictly limiting opportunities for opposition political activity and a draconian defamation law wielded as a political weapon. Opposition figures too often face a choice between speaking out and bankruptcy—and sometimes prison.

Opposition rallies and protests are largely prohibited by laws requiring that public assemblies of five or more persons have police permission, and by the Public Entertainment and Meetings Act, which requires a permit for almost all forms of public address and entertainment.

Both restrictions have been used repeatedly to prevent the opposition Singapore Democratic Party (SDP), headed by Dr. Chee Soon Juan, and other opposition parties from informing citizens of their political message and criticizing government policies. On October 8, 2007, for example, four members of the SDP protesting Singapore's links with Burma were arrested for "illegal assembly" under the Miscellaneous Offences (Public Order and Nuisance Act). In August 2007 the opposition Worker's Party was refused permission to celebrate its 50th anniversary in November with a bicycle party in a public park. Political parties are banned from sponsoring outdoor events to avoid any possibility of a public disturbance.

The government ruthlessly pursues politically motivated defamation cases to deprive political opponents of basic rights to liberty and freedom of movement. On September 7, 2007, Chee was sentenced to a three-week jail term for refusing to pay a fine of US$2,621, levied for his attempt to leave the country without permission in April 2006. He had needed clearance to leave as he had been declared bankrupt in February 2006 after he defaulted on $316,455 due in defamation damages to Lee Kuan Yew and ex-prime minister Goh Chok Tong. Other charges against Chee have included speaking in public without a permit. Between November and December 2006, he served a five-week sentence in lieu of a $3,268 fine.

On October 17, 2007 the *Financial Times* apologized publicly to Lee Kuan Yew; his son, Prime Minister Lee Hsien Loong; and the latter's wife, Ho Ching, for suggesting in an article entitled, "Sovereign funds try to put on an acceptable face," that "nepotistic motives" were involved in the appointments of Lee Hsien Loong and Ho Ching. The paper admitted that the allegations were "false and without foundation," and that damages and costs would be paid "by way of compensation." It is unclear whether the *Financial Times* settled because they believed the article was in error or because they did not want to be banned from distribution in Singapore, as has happened with the *Far Eastern Economic Review* (FEER).

The Singapore government restricted FEER's circulation in 1987 under a 1986 law that gave the government the right to limit sales if it deemed a publication had interfered in local politics. The full ban came in September 2006 along with a defamation suit instituted by Lee and his son over an article critiquing the way the government responded to a scandal at a charitable organization. The article went on to suggest that Singapore's government was less than "squeaky clean" and used defamation charges to hide "real misdeeds."

Free expression is further compromised by government monitoring of the internet and censorship of all media outlets. Movies, music, and video games are also censored. Political websites must register with the Media Development Authority. Singapore's Films Act prohibits the showing of films on issues of public controversy or that in any other way are "directed towards a political end in Singapore." In April 2007, the government banned the film "Zahari's 17 years," the story of an imprisoned journalist.

Due Process

Singapore's Internal Security Act (ISA), Criminal Law (Temporary Provisions Act) (CLA), Misuse of Drugs Act, and Undesirable Publications Act permit detention and arrest of suspects without a warrant or judicial review. Both the ISA and the CLA also authorize preventive detention. The drug act permits the Central Narcotics Bureau chief to send suspected drug users for rehabilitation without recourse to trial. The ISA, used in the past to detain political opponents and critics, is now used against suspected Islamist militants, many of whom have been detained for long periods without trial. In September 2006 the government said that 34 suspected Muslim militants were being held on national security grounds.

Caning

Singapore's penal code mandates caning, combined with imprisonment, for some 30 offenses, both violent and nonviolent, and permits caning for a variety of others. In 2006, 5,984 people reportedly were sentenced to caning and in some 95 percent of the cases the sentence was carried out.

Death Penalty

Although death penalty statistics are secret, available information indicates that Singapore's per capita execution rate is one of the world's highest. Not only are death sentences mandatory for drug traffickers, but Singaporean law shifts the burden of proof to suspects to prove that they did not knowingly carry drugs or had no intention to traffic in drugs. On January 26, 2007, a Nigerian and a South African were hanged for smuggling, even though the judge concluded that in the case of the Nigerian there was "no direct evidence that he knew the capsules contained diamorphine." Singapore's Home Affairs Minister, referring to the law's deterrent effects, commented that "there is no room to go soft."

Migrant Domestic Workers

Approximately 160,000 migrant domestic workers—primarily from Indonesia, the Philippines, and Sri Lanka—are employed in Singapore. Many domestic workers report excessive work hours without regular rest breaks, restrictions on freedom of movement, unpaid wages, and in some cases, physical abuse.

The government has prosecuted some employers who physically abuse domestic workers and imposed penalties on labor recruitment agencies for unethical practices. Singapore's labor laws, however, still exclude domestic workers from key protections guaranteed to other workers, such as a weekly day off, limits on working hours, and caps on salary deductions. The government also has failed to regulate exploitative recruitment charges. Many domestic workers must work for months just to pay off recruitment debts, making it difficult for them to leave abusive employers.

Lesbian, Gay, Bisexual, and Transgender Rights

In October 2007 Singapore's parliament rejected a proposal to repeal law 377A, which bans private and consensual sexual relations between men. Although prosecutions have been rare, those found in violation of law 377A can be jailed for up to two years on charges of "gross indecency."

Human Rights Defenders

State laws and political repression effectively prevent the establishment of human rights organizations and deter individuals from speaking out publicly against government policies.

The need for police permits prevents civil society groups from organizing outdoor events with ties to public issues. In October 2007, for example, police refused to grant permission for an outdoor "Peace Concert for Burma," forcing the concert indoors on grounds that an outdoor event had higher potential to "stir emotions and controversy."

Unless they are registered as political parties, associations may not engage in any activities the government deems political. Trade unions are under the same restrictions and are banned from contributing to political parties or using their funds for political purposes. Most unions are affiliated with the umbrella National

Trade Union Congress which does not allow union members supportive of opposition parties to hold office.

Burma

On September 27, 2007, Singapore's Minister for Foreign Affairs, George Yeo, the chair of the Association of Southeast Asian Nations (ASEAN), issued a statement expressing ASEAN's "revulsion" over the use of "violent force" to put down anti-government demonstrations in Burma. The statement called for a halt to the crackdown and the release of all political prisoners. ASEAN has since rejected interference in Burma's internal affairs and its members even refused to allow Ibrahim Gambari, UN special envoy to Burma, to address their meeting. At this writing, Singapore has yet to indicate its willingness to reexamine the human rights implications of its own economic ties to Burma, including in sectors that directly benefit the Burmese military. Singapore-registered companies are active in Burma's oil and natural gas industry, and the Burmese junta and its allies are believed to use Singapore for banking and other financial transactions.

Key International Actors

Singapore is a key member of the Southeast Asia Regional Centre for Counter-Terrorism, along with the US, Malaysia, and others, and is an active participant in regional and sub-regional security issues. Singapore and the US maintain an active partnership as outlined in the 2005 "Strategic Framework Agreement Between the United States of America and the Republic of Singapore for a Closer Cooperation Partnership in Defense and Security." Singapore is also an important financial and banking center for southeast Asia.

Singapore has not ratified important international human rights instruments, including the International Covenant on Civil and Political Rights, the International Convention on Economic, Social and Cultural Rights, and the Convention Against Torture.

SRI LANKA

In the continuing conflict between the Sri Lankan government and the Liberation Tigers of Tamil Eelam (LTTE), both sides show little regard for the safety and well-being of civilians—and violate international humanitarian law—by indiscriminately firing on civilian areas and unnecessarily preventing the delivery of humanitarian aid. Since the breakdown of the ceasefire and the resumption of major military operations in mid-2006, hundreds of civilians have been killed and over 208,000 persons remain displaced as of October 31.

Government security forces are implicated in extrajudicial killings, enforced disappearances, forcibly returning internally displaced persons (IDPs) to unsafe areas, restricting media freedoms, apparent complicity with the abusive Karuna group, and widespread impunity for serious human rights violations. Hundreds of people have been detained under newly strengthened Emergency Regulations that give the government broad powers of arrest and detention without charge. The regulations have been used to conduct mass arbitrary arrests of ethnic Tamils in the capital Colombo, as well as to detain political opponents, journalists, and civil society activists.

In areas under its control, the LTTE continues to forcibly conscript children and adults, control the media, and suppress freedoms of expression, association and assembly. In contested areas, the LTTE continues to conduct targeted killings of perceived political opponents. On November 28, two bombings attributed to the LTTE killed 18 civilians in Colombo.

The Karuna group, which has been aligned with government forces since breaking away from the LTTE in 2004, openly engaged in child recruitment, extortion, abductions for ransom, and political killings. Its expelled leader Colonel Karuna was arrested by UK immigration authorities in London in October.

Internal Displacement

Nearly 315,000 people, mostly Tamil and Muslim, have fled their homes in the north and east because of renewed hostilities. Currently over 200,000 remain displaced in the east; many have been displaced multiple times. Returning IDPs face

regular threats and occasional violence, including abductions, by both the LTTE and pro-government armed groups. In several instances during 2007, government authorities forced IDPs to return to insecure areas. Others are unlikely ever to be able to return to their homes following the government's announcement in May of the creation of "High Security Zones" that include "special economic areas" on land where thousands of families once lived.

Abductions and Enforced Disappearances

More than 1,100 new "disappearances" or abductions were reported between January 2006 and June 2007, the vast majority Tamils. While the LTTE has long been responsible for abductions, most recent reported "disappearances" implicate government forces or armed groups acting with government complicity, who target young Tamil men deemed to be part of the LTTE's civilian support network. On the northern Jaffna peninsula alone, in areas under strict military control, more than 800 persons were reported missing from December 2005 to April 2007. The national Human Rights Commission (HRC) does not publicize its data on "disappearances," yet credible sources maintain that about 1,000 cases were reported to the HRC in 2006 and over 300 cases in the first four months of 2007. A prominent Sri Lankan NGO, the Law and Society Trust, says that, on average, five persons are either killed or "disappeared" each day in Sri Lanka. The group recorded 540 cases of "disappearances" between January 1 and August 31, 2007.

In the lawlessness that has grown since the return to conflict, Tamil armed groups and criminal elements have committed numerous abductions for ransom. The victims were mostly businessmen from the Tamil community in Colombo.

Emergency Regulations

In December 2006 the government expanded the Emergency Regulations that were reintroduced in August 2005, labeling a range of peaceful activities as "terrorist offenses." Using sweeping language, the regulations criminalize any action threatening public order that aims to bring about "political or governmental change" or compels the government "to do or abstain from doing any act." The government has used the regulations to detain political opponents, journalists,

Complicit in Crime

State Collusion in Abductions and Child Recruitment by
the Karuna Group

HUMAN
RIGHTS
WATCH

and civil society activists, and at this writing has provided no information about the number of people held and their whereabouts.

On November 22, 2006, agents of the Terrorist Investigation Division arrested Munusamy Parameswary, a reporter for the weekly newspaper *Mawbima*, under the Emergency Regulations, accusing her of "helping the LTTE" and of being "a suspected suicide bomber." On March 22, 2007, the Supreme Court found no reasonable grounds for her detention and ordered her release.

Before Parameswary's release, on February 27, the Terrorist Investigation Division arrested Dushantha Basnayake, spokesman and financial director of Standard Newspapers Ltd., the company that publishes *Mawbima* and the English-language weekly *Sunday Standard*. They detained Basnayake for over two months also under the Emergency Regulations, eventually releasing him on bail. On March 13 the government froze the assets of Standard Newspapers, citing suspected links to the LTTE, and neither *Mawbima* nor the *Sunday Standard* have been published since March 29.

Impunity

The Sri Lankan government fails to hold members of the security forces and non-state armed groups accountable for abuses. Key parts of the criminal justice system, such as the police and the Attorney General's Office, have not effectively investigated human rights violations or brought perpetrators to justice. Victims of abuses by security forces and non-state armed groups are apprehensive about complaining to the authorities for fear of retaliation, especially in the absence of functioning victim and witness protection mechanisms. A draft witness protection bill is still pending.

Sri Lanka's Human Rights Commission is of limited capacity and political weight, and unable to investigate specific incidents and make recommendations for redress, primarily for lack of cooperation from the government. Independence of the Human Rights Commission and other constitutional bodies has been undermined since 2006, when Sri Lankan President Mahinda Rajapaksa directly appointed commission members, contrary to the constitution.

Given their limited resources and mandate, and lack of support from government agencies and the security forces, the Presidential Commission of Inquiry and the International Independent Group of Eminent Persons (IIGEP) have been ineffectual in investigating the 15 incidents of grave human rights abuses selected for inquiry. In its first statement in August 2007, the IIGEP noted that the Commission of Inquiry and the IIGEP are not a substitute for robust, effective national and international human rights monitoring to address the country's broader human rights problems. In early November the president extended the term of the Commission of Inquiry by an additional year, but determined that the body cannot examine practices of the Attorney General's Office.

The Nordic-led Sri Lanka Monitoring Mission (SLMM), created to monitor violations of the 2002 ceasefire, has had a significantly reduced role since the effective end of the ceasefire in mid-2006 and due to restrictions on its access.

Child Soldiers

The United Nations Children's Fund (UNICEF) documented 210 cases of recruitment and re-recruitment of children by the Karuna group from December 2006 to September 2007, and an almost identical number of cases of recruitment or re-recruitment by the LTTE in the same period. Fear often prevented parents from reporting cases, however.

Evictions of Tamils from Colombo

On June 7, 2007, 376 Tamils resident in Colombo were forcibly evicted and expelled from the city by security forces. While the government cited security reasons, those evicted included infants, the elderly, the sick; some evictees had been resident in Colombo for over a decade. Following an interim order halting the process arising from a fundamental rights petition filed by the Centre for Policy Alternatives, an NGO, the government reportedly brought back 140 of those expelled. The prime minister apologized on behalf of the government, although the defense secretary defended the decision. President Rajapaksa ordered a commission to investigate the evictions but it is unclear how the commission will be constituted or what action, if any, it will take.

Media Freedom

The environment for media freedom continues to worsen. Tamil journalists in particular work under severe threat from both the government and LTTE, but the government also pressures Sinhala-language outlets that present critical news and views.

The Karuna group impedes and at times has blocked circulation of some Tamil-language newspapers in the north and east, including by issuing death threats to newspaper distributors in Trincomalee. There was no apparent effort by the government to address these actions or arrest those responsible.

Sri Lankan Migrant Workers

More than 660,000 Sri Lankan women work abroad as domestic workers, nearly 90 percent in Saudi Arabia, Kuwait, Lebanon, and the United Arab Emirates. Poor monitoring of labor recruiters has allowed unscrupulous labor agents and their unlicensed sub-agents to demand illegal, exorbitant fees from prospective migrant domestic workers, leaving them highly indebted. Labor agents often deceive women about their conditions of employment, including the country where they will work and their salary. In mid-2007 the government instituted measures to provide migrant workers greater information about their employment contracts; the impact of these efforts is not yet clear. Once abroad domestic workers face a wide range of abuses, including long hours, no rest days, forced confinement, extremely low wages, physical and sexual abuse, and conditions that amount to forced labor (see Saudi Arabia and UAE chapters). Sri Lankan consular officials often provide little or no assistance to domestic workers who approach them with cases of unpaid wages and abuse.

Human Rights Defenders and Humanitarian Workers

Human rights defenders, community leaders, and humanitarian workers in Sri Lanka have particularly come under attack. The government tries to silence those questioning or criticizing its approach to the armed conflict or its human rights record. It has dismissed peaceful critics as "traitors," "terrorist sympathizers," and "supporters of the LTTE." The Law and Society Trust reported that from

SRI LANKA/MIDDLE EAST

Exported and Exposed

Abuses against Sri Lankan Domestic Workers in Saudi Arabia,
Kuwait, Lebanon, and the United Arab Emirates

HUMAN RIGHTS WATCH

January 2006 to August 2007, 40 humanitarian workers and religious leaders had been killed and 20 "disappeared." During an August 2007 visit, UN Under-Secretary for Humanitarian Affairs and Emergency Relief John Holmes described Sri Lanka as "one of the most dangerous places for aid workers in the world." The chief government whip and cabinet minister Jeyaraj Fernandupulle dismissed Holmes as a "terrorist."

In areas under its control the LTTE prevents development of any independent and effective human rights institutions. Domestic human rights organizations critical of the LTTE have justifiable concerns for their safety.

Key International Actors

Expressions of concern about the situation in Sri Lanka grew in 2007 but international action on human rights was slow and lacked cohesion.

In early May the UK suspended around US$3 million of debt relief aid to the Sri Lankan government, citing concerns over human rights and defense spending. In June the European Parliament Committee on Development conducted a hearing on the humanitarian and human rights situation in Sri Lanka since the December 2004 tsunami. There was little support within the Parliament to pass a resolution on Sri Lanka, however.

The US increasingly criticized the Sri Lankan government and the LTTE for failing to stem human rights abuses. Notably, at the end of a three-day visit in May, US Assistant Secretary of State for South and Central Asian Affairs Richard Boucher expressed strong concern about the spate of abductions, killings, and attacks on the media in Sri Lanka. In October the US for the first time called on the Sri Lankan government to cooperate with the United Nations in establishing an international human rights monitoring mission to investigate and report on human rights abuses by all sides to the conflict. The US government's Millennium Challenge Corporation suspended more than US$110 million in aid due to concerns about the country's human rights situation.

European Union members on the UN Human Rights Council sought unsuccessfully to adopt a resolution on human rights in Sri Lanka. The Sri Lankan government sought to thwart such efforts by inviting United Nations High Commissioner for

Human Rights Louise Arbour and Special Rapporteur on Torture Manfred Nowak. Both UN officials visited Sri Lanka in October 2007. At the end of the high commissioner's five-day visit, Human Rights Minister Mahinda Samarasinghe told Arbour that Sri Lanka would not agree to her call for UN monitoring of human rights in the country. Authorities tried to dismiss allegations of human rights violations as propaganda by separatist Tamil Tiger rebels, but Arbour stated she believed there were "credible allegations that deserved to be investigated." She also expressed concern about the culture of impunity and a disturbing lack of investigations that undermines confidence in institutions set up to protect human rights.

THAILAND

The military-installed government of General Surayud Chulanont has taken few steps to promote human rights. Martial law is still enforced in many parts of the country, and the government actively censors the internet, cracking down on dissidents. A proposed new internal security law would, if enacted, extend broad and unchecked powers to the prime minister to suppress fundamental rights and legalize government impunity, a major setback to efforts to restore democratic freedoms.

A military-sponsored referendum for a new constitution passed in August 2007, and general elections are at this writing scheduled for December 23, but prospects for a return to democracy remain uncertain.

The armed conflict in southern border provinces escalated in 2007 with brutal violence—much of it targeting civilians—by separatists and continuing counterinsurgency abuses by government forces. Since taking office in October 2006, the government repeatedly has announced an end to state-sponsored abuses and impunity, but with little visible success.

Refugee protection in Thailand is in crisis after the government pressured the office of the United Nations High Commissioner for Refugees (UNHCR) to stop conducting refugee status determinations in May 2007.

Media and Internet Censorship

Soldiers still patrol the T-iTV station, a station owned until 2006 by the family of the ousted Prime Minister Thaksin Shinawatra. Scripts of T-iTV's famous political talk programs often require pre-broadcast approval by the Public Relations Department of the Prime Minister's Office. Many community radio stations—initially blocked after the coup—have since returned to the airwaves but with considerable pressure to be less critical of the military.

Political websites established in opposition to the coup have faced harassment and blocking. The authorities also monitor critical opinions and debates on popular opinion boards of Prachatai (www.prachatai.com) and Pantip.com (www.pan-

THAILAND

"It Was Like Suddenly My Son No Longer Existed"

Enforced Disappearances in Thailand's Southern Border Provinces

HUMAN RIGHTS WATCH

tip.com) and have threatened both websites with closure if they fail to remove opinions critical of the military authorities. The Computer-Related Offences Act seriously threatens freedom of expression by giving authorities expanded powers to police online content. Two famous cyber dissidents, known as *Praya Pichai* and *Thon Chan,* were arrested in August 2007.

Martial Law

During the lead-up to the constitutional referendum in August, authorities used martial law to justify the stifling of Thaksin's political allies and those opposed to the coup. Authorities raided their houses, confiscated political campaign materials, and detained some of them in military facilities. The crackdown continued in the run-up to general elections. The Council for National Security announced on September 17 that martial law would remain in effect in 27 provinces. Most of those areas are Thaksin strongholds in the north and northeast, where people voted against the military-sponsored constitution. Under martial law, the military can ban political gatherings, censor the media, and detain people without charge.

Internal Security Law

On October 31 the government submitted the Draft Act on the Maintenance of National Security in the Kingdom to the National Legislative Assembly for debate. The draft passed its first parliamentary reading on November 11, and at this writing was being reviewed for the second and third readings. If enacted, this law would give the Internal Security Operations Command—under the control of the Prime Minister—emergency-style powers to restrict fundamental rights, override the civilian administration, and suspend basic due process rights at any time. No declaration of a state of emergency, or accountability to the parliament and the courts, would be required. This law would also shield from prosecution those who violate human rights under its provisions.

Violence in the Southern Border Provinces

Village-based militants called the Patani Freedom Fighters (Pejuang Kemerdekaan Patani) in the loose network of the National Revolution Front-Coordinate (BRN-

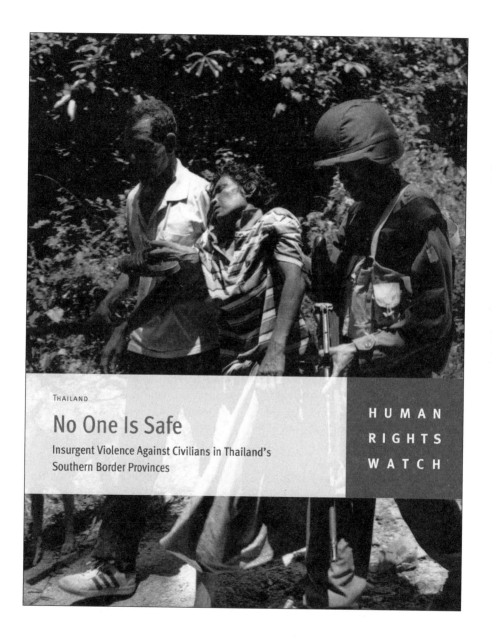

THAILAND

No One Is Safe

Insurgent Violence Against Civilians in Thailand's
Southern Border Provinces

**HUMAN
RIGHTS
WATCH**

Coordinate) have been responsible for more than 2,000 civilian deaths—both Buddhists and ethnic Malay Muslims—from January 2004 to November 2007. They have also carried out summary executions of civilians based on ethnicity. For example, on March 14, militants ambushed a passenger van in Yaha district of Yala province and shot all Buddhist passengers one by one. Some attackers aim to spread terror among the civilian population, most notably by beheading victims or setting their bodies on fire.

Militants have targeted the Thai education system. The Education Ministry reported in October that militants have killed more than 80 teachers and injured 70 more since January 2004. Militants have burned down some 200 schools during the same period. At least 1,600 teachers have requested transfers from the region due to security concerns. General Surayud acknowledged on June 18 that the government could not guarantee school safety everywhere and that some schools might have to be closed indefinitely.

Some parts of the southern border provinces lack access to public health services after separatist militants burned down community hospitals and murdered medical personnel.

In October 2006 the government announced a new counterinsurgency strategy, seeking to balance military operations with political reconciliation, justice, and human rights principles. At this writing, however, Thai security forces—both regular and volunteer units—continue to face little or no consequences for extrajudicial killings, torture, arbitrary arrests, and use of excessive violence against suspected militants.

There is no functioning mechanism for systematically and effectively monitoring the conditions of suspects locked up without charge in military camps across the southern border provinces. This is of major concern, especially since the June 2007 launch of security force sweep operations under the code name, "Battle Plan for the Protection of the Southern land." These sweeps resulted in nearly 2,000 arrests of ethnic Malay Muslim men, women, and children during the first two months alone. Among them, 384 men were further transferred to four-month vocational trainings in army-run camps until a court ruled on October 18 that the army has no legal power to keep anyone in such trainings against their will.

Security forces responsible for the large-scale killings of ethnic Malay Muslims in 2004 at Krue Se and Tak Bai had yet to be brought to justice at this writing.

Ongoing Impunity from Thaksin's War on Drugs

In August 2007 the government appointed a special committee chaired by former Attorney General Khanit na Nakhon, to investigate approximately 2,500 extrajudicial killings that took place in 2003 as part of Thaksin's "war on drugs." Nevertheless, it remains unclear whether the new investigations will lead to effective criminal prosecution of the perpetrators, who are believed to include senior police officers and members of the former Thaksin administration.

Refugee Protection

General Surayud's government pressured the UNHCR office in Thailand to stop the refugee status determination process in May 2007. Thousands of asylum seekers— particularly Rohingyas from Burma and Hmong from Laos—have been left with limited access to international protection. Without a determination of their status, asylum seekers can be summarily classified as "illegal migrants" and arrested, detained, and deported.

In June Thai authorities deported a group 163 Lao Hmong to Laos and since have held more than 7,000 Lao Hmong at a barbed-wire-enclosed camp in Petchabun province without access to UNHCR screening and protection mechanisms. The Thai-Lao Border Security Committee decided at a joint meeting in October to complete the repatriation of this group of in 2008.

The ongoing mistreatment of 149 UNHCR-recognized Lao Hmong refugees, including 77 children and nine infants, has sparked an international outcry. After a failed attempt to forcibly return them to Laos on January 30, Thai authorities refused international offers to resettle them in third countries. At this writing, refugees continued to be locked up in the Immigration Detention Center in Nong Khai province and faced harsh conditions, apparently to discourage other Lao Hmongs from trying to enter into Thailand illegally.

HIV/AIDS

About 180,000 people living with HIV/AIDS (more than 80 percent of those in need) received antiretroviral therapy (ART) by late 2007, making Thailand one of three developing countries worldwide—and the only one in Asia—to achieve this level of coverage. Yet many people in Thailand, particularly drug users, prisoners, and migrant workers, still face significant barriers in obtaining ART and other essential services, marring Thailand's reputation as a "success story" in the global fight against AIDS.

Human Rights Defenders

The government continues to have a poor record in protecting human rights defenders. On October 10 unidentified gunmen shot dead Ma-usoh Malong in Narathiwat province's Tak Bai district. It was the second deadly attack on individuals known to be closely involved in the campaign for justice for the Tak Bai victims. Ma-usoh's colleague, Muhammad Dunai Tanyino, was murdered in a nearby area on October 20, 2006.

There was little progress in official investigations into the cases of 20 human rights defenders killed during the Thaksin administration. This includes the disappearance and presumed murder of famous Muslim lawyer Somchai Neelapaijit.

Key International Actors

The United States has used its strong bilateral relationship with Thailand to raise human rights concerns and, on occasion, has intervened to protect refugees. In 2007, however, a joint effort with Australia, Canada, and the Netherlands failed to secure the release and resettlement of the 149 Lao Hmong refugees detained in Nong Khai province (see above).

The Election Commission of Thailand has refused to sign a memorandum of understanding with the European Union on election monitoring, saying that the request was an interference in its domestic affairs.

Despite unprecedented and strong condemnation of the violent crackdowns on protesters and Buddhist monks by Burmese authorities in September, Thailand remains the biggest trading partner of Burma.

Former Foreign Minister Surin Pitsuwan will begin a five-year term as secretary-general of the Association of Southeast Asian Nations (ASEAN) on January 1, 2008.

TIMOR-LESTE

Sporadic violence in Dili, Timor-Leste's capital, continued in 2007 with the worst outbreaks taking place in the run-up to June 30 elections and after the announcement of results in July and August. At times violence spilled over into some eastern districts.

While 2007 saw some prosecutions of officials and commanders responsible for deadly clashes between soldiers and police in 2006, many perpetrators were shielded from prosecution by a 2007 amnesty law.

Presidential and parliamentary elections brought in new leadership in 2007, but squabbling over the final result has left the country vulnerable to more insecurity and violence.

The government continues to ignore the recommendations of the Commission on Reception, Truth and Reconciliation for past crimes committed during Indonesia's occupation.

Police

In a marked step backwards in December 2006, the Timorese government handed back to the United Nations prime responsibility for police operations throughout the country. This followed the collapse of the National Police of East Timor (PNTL) in May 2006, after fighting between security force factions triggered wider violence in which at least 37 people were killed. The agreement with the UN, known as the Police Supplemental Arrangement, provides a legal framework allowing UN police to take responsibility as an interim law enforcement body. The arrangement also provides for the reform, restructuring, and rebuilding of the East Timorese national police force, including a registration and screening process for all Timorese police officers.

International forces failed in several attempts to arrest Alfredo Reinado, a fugitive rebel leader involved in the 2006 uprising. One attempt resulted in the death of five members of his armed group and provoked rioting by some of his supporters. Another failed attempt in May led the government to declare a state of emergency to quell pre-election violence. This gave peacekeepers and police the right to carry out arrests and searches without warrants and to break up public gatherings.

On June 19 President Jose Ramos-Horta halted police and military operations to arrest Reinado, and the two met in August to discuss terms of Reinado's surrender.

Accountability for 2006 Crimes

Despite a few high profile prosecutions, there has been little accountability for crimes committed during April and May 2006. Many violations identified by the Independent Special Commission of Inquiry are yet to be prosecuted. Delays have been due to a backlog of cases, weaknesses in the judiciary, and deliberations over a problematic Law on Truth and Clemency for Diverse Offenses, which was approved by the legislature in June but not yet promulgated by the president at this writing.

The Law on Truth and Clemency includes an amnesty provision for perpetrators of crimes committed between April 2006 and April 2007. Before signing the law, President Ramos-Horta referred it to the Court of Appeals for review. In August the court ruled that provisions relating to the time period covered by the law were unconstitutional but allowed other amnesty provisions to stand. There has been concern that, once promulgated, the law would not only prevent new prosecutions but might lead to the release of those already convicted.

In May Timor-Leste's Court of Appeals upheld the conviction and sentencing of former Interior Minister Rogerio Lobato for distributing arms to Vicente da Conceição, known as "Rai Los," a militia leader widely believed to have been responsible for instigating much of the 2006 violence. Lobato was sentenced to seven years and six months in prison for manslaughter and illegal distribution of weapons. Two co-defendants also had their convictions upheld. Rai Los was arrested on murder-related charges for his role in the events of May 25 and 26, 2006.

On August 8 the former deputy police commander of Dili District was sentenced to four years in prison for illegal possession of weapons in relation to an attack on the house of the military commander on May 24-25, 2006. Three co-defendants were also convicted.

The trial of 11 army officers and one police officer indicted for manslaughter in relation to the May 25, 2006, killing of eight unarmed police officers was still in progress at this writing.

In February 2007 the prosecutor-general closed the investigation into allegations of weapons distribution against former Prime Minister Mari Alkatiri, citing lack of evidence.

Elections and Dili Violence

Timor-Leste held three rounds of relatively free and fair elections in 2007 with a high voter turnout in all three.

Former Prime Minister Ramos-Horta was elected president in May after two rounds of presidential elections. Ramos-Horta polled almost 70 percent of the votes against Francisco Guterres, the candidate of the Revolutionary Front for an Independent East Timor (FRETELIN), the former ruling party.

No political party in Timor Leste's June 30 parliamentary elections managed to secure an outright majority. FRETELIN won 21 seats while the party of former president Xanana Gusmao, the new National Congress for the Reconstruction of East Timor (CNRT), won 18. FRETELIN argued that it should form the government as the party with the most votes, but CNRT countered this by forming an alliance with smaller parties, giving it 37 seats in the 65-member legislature.

After two months of bickering, President Ramos-Horta was forced to intervene in August to break the political stalemate. He appointed Gusmao as prime minister, heading a new ruling coalition called the Alliance for a Parliamentary Majority (AMP). Gusmao was sworn into office on August 8, 2007.

The announcement prompted violence and unrest from disaffected FRETELIN supporters in Dili and the eastern districts of Baucau and Viqueque. Rioters burned scores of houses and government buildings, displacing at least 7,000 people.

FRETELIN officials branded the new government illegal and said it would appeal the decision through Timor-Leste's courts.

Human Rights Defenders

There were no attacks on human rights defenders in Timor-Leste in 2007.

The Office of the Provedor, which has the power to investigate and report on complaints by government officials and institutions, is able to work without interference. In 2007 the office submitted 12 cases of alleged abuse of authority to the police.

Key International Actors

Marking decreasing international attention to Timor-Leste, the British government closed its embassy in Dili in October 2006, deciding that future consular issues should be dealt with from its embassy in Jakarta.

Relations between Timor-Leste and Indonesia remained cordial. President Ramos-Horta met Indonesian President Susilo Bambang Yudhoyono in Jakarta in June 2007 to discuss border demarcation, student exchanges, and business cooperation. The two presidents agreed to extend the mandate of the bilateral Commission for Truth and Friendship by a further six months. The commission held its final public hearing in Dili at the end of September. The hearings were poorly attended and accompanied by demonstrations, protesting it as a mechanism to perpetuate impunity. In July UN Secretary-General Ban Ki-moon effectively enforced a UN boycott by stating that UN staff would not testify before the commission, unless its amnesty provision was changed to make perpetrators of serious crimes ineligible.

On February 22 the United Nations Security Council extended UNMIT's mandate for 12 months and increased its police size by 140.

Commercial relations with Australia strengthened as a result of two bilateral treaties ratified in February to regulate exploration and exploitation of petroleum resources in the Timor Sea: the International Unitization Agreement (IUA) and the Certain Maritime Arrangements in the Timor Sea (CMATS) Treaty. Equal sharing of the upstream revenues from the Greater Sunrise gas and oil field under CMATS could result in Australia and Timor-Leste each receiving up to US$10 billion over the life of the project.

These new maritime arrangements are on top of the existing 2002 Timor Sea Treaty with Australia, where Timor-Leste receives 90 percent of revenue from production of petroleum resources, which may be worth as much as US$15 billion. Timor-Leste's Petroleum Fund, set up to receive and administer revenues from oil and gas sales, now has a balance of over US$1 billion from exploitation of resources in the Joint Petroleum Development Area.

In March 2007 the Australian New South Wales coroner issued an arrest warrant for retired Indonesian Lieutenant General Yunus Yosfiah after he failed to appear at an inquest in relation to the death of Brian Peters, one of five Australia-based journalists killed in Balibo, East Timor, in 1975. The warrant strained relations between Indonesia and Australia, but Timor-Leste officials refused to comment.

Timor-Leste remains dependent on international aid and assistance. It continues to receive its largest financial contributions from Japan, Portugal, the United Kingdom, the European Union, the United States, and Australia.

Vietnam

2007 was characterized by the harshest crackdown on peaceful dissent in 20 years. The government, emboldened by international recognition after joining the World Trade Organization in late 2006, moved to suppress all challenges to the Vietnamese Communist Party (VCP) by arresting dozens of democracy and human rights activists, independent trade union leaders, underground publishers, and members of unsanctioned religious groups. This reversed a temporary easing of restrictions in 2006, prior to Vietnam's hosting the Asia-Pacific Economic Cooperation summit, when independent activism and opposition political parties had surfaced.

Of nearly 40 dissidents arrested since the crackdown began, more than 20 were sentenced to prison in 2007, most under Penal Code article 88, conducting anti-government propaganda. In March Roman Catholic priest Nguyen Van Ly, a founder of the Bloc 8406 democracy group, was sentenced to eight years in prison. Others sentenced included human rights lawyer Nguyen Van Dai, labor activist Tran Quoc Hien, and at least five opposition party members. Members of independent churches were also imprisoned. Le Tri Tue of the Independent Workers' Union "disappeared" in May after claiming political asylum in Cambodia with the United Nations High Commissioner for Refugees (UNHCR). He was presumed to have been abducted and sent to prison in Vietnam.

Prior to the visit of Vietnamese President Nguyen Minh Triet to the United States in June, Vietnam released political prisoners Nguyen Vu Binh, who had served five years, and lawyer Le Quoc Quan, arrested in March 2007 and charged with attempting to overthrow the government after participating in a fellowship at the National Endowment for Democracy in the United States. Eleven people imprisoned on national security charges were reportedly released in a prisoner amnesty in October 2007, but the Vietnamese government did not publicize their names.

Despite flouting its international human rights commitments, in October Vietnam was elected to a two-year term on the UN Security Council.

Detention without Trial

Vietnamese law continues to authorize arbitrary detention without trial. Administrative detention decree 31/CP was repealed in 2007, but a more repressive law, Ordinance 44, authorizes placing people suspected of threatening national security under house arrest or in detention without trial in Social Protection Centers, rehabilitation camps, or mental hospitals. Lawyer Bui Thi Kim Thanh, who assisted farmers with land rights complaints, was arrested in November 2006 and involuntarily committed to a mental hospital. She was released in July 2007.

Prisons and Torture

Hundreds of religious and political prisoners remain behind bars in harsh conditions throughout Vietnam. Prisoners are placed in solitary confinement in dark, unsanitary cells, and there is compelling evidence of torture and ill-treatment of political prisoners, including beatings and electric shock. A disturbing number of Montagnard prisoners—even those in their thirties—have died shortly after release because of illness attributed to harsh conditions and mistreatment in prison.

Freedom of Expression, Information, and Assembly

All media in Vietnam is controlled by the government or the VCP. Criminal penalties apply to publications, websites, and internet users that disseminate information that opposes the government, threatens national security, or reveals state secrets.

Foreign internet service providers (ISPs) are prohibited from operating. Internet cafe owners are required to obtain customers' photo identification, which is supplied to Vietnamese ISPs. The ISPs are required to install monitoring software that identifies internet users and their online activities, and store the information for a year. The government monitors online activity and blocks websites covering human rights, religious freedom, democracy groups, and independent media. Website owners must obtain government approval for website content.

Internet users such as Truong Quoc Huy, whose trial is expected by the end of the year, have been imprisoned for alleged national security crimes after participating in pro-democracy discussion forums or using the internet to disseminate views disfavored by the government.

In February police detained and questioned Roman Catholic priests Chan Tin and Phan Van Loi, editors of Freedom of Speech. In April police arrested Tran Khai Thanh Thuy, an editor of the dissident bulletin Fatherland. In September the government ordered the closure of Intellasia, an Australian-owned website in Hanoi, charging that it disseminated "reactionary" material.

Decree 38 bans public gatherings in front of places where government, Party, and international conferences are held, and requires organizers to obtain advance government permission. In July Ho Chi Minh City police dispersed a month-long peaceful protest by hundreds of farmers—many of them elderly women—against government land seizures.

Religion

Vietnamese law requires that all religious groups register with the government and bans religious activities deemed to cause public disorder, harm national security, or "sow divisions."

During 2007 the Minh Ly Sect in southern Vietnam and the more pro-government part of the Mennonite church in Vietnam were granted legal registration. Other Mennonites in Vietnam, such as those affiliated with Rev. Nguyen Hong Quang in Ho Chi Minh City, a former prisoner of conscience, continued to be harassed.

While most Roman Catholics are able to practice their religion, those who advocate for political and civil rights have been harassed, imprisoned, or threatened with arrest.

Monks from the banned Unified Buddhist Church of Vietnam (UBCV), including top leaders Thich Huyen Quang and Thich Quang Do, have been largely confined to their pagodas, and after Thich Quang Do spoke at the farmers' demonstration in Ho Chi Minh City in July the government increased its harassment and surveillance of the UBCV. In March UBCV monk Thich Thien Mien, who formed an association of former political and religious prisoners following his release in 2005 after 26 years in prison, was interrogated by police for alleged anti-government activities.

Four Hoa Hao Buddhists in Dong Thap were sentenced to prison terms of four to six years in 2007 for "causing public disorder" after protesting the imprisonment of Hoa Hao members in 2006.

In February 2007 several hundred ethnic Khmer (known as Kampuchea Krom) Buddhist monks in Soc Trang peacefully demonstrated for religious freedom. Police dispersed the demonstration and arrested protest leaders, with five later sentenced to two to four years' imprisonment for "causing public disorder." Tim Sakhorn, a Kampuchea Krom monk from Cambodia who had been defrocked and deported to Vietnam in June by Cambodian authorities was sentenced to a year's imprisonment at a trial in Vietnam in November on charges of undermining national unity (see Cambodia chapter).

Ethnic minority Christians belonging to independent house churches continue to be harassed, pressured to join government-authorized churches, and arrested. Most congregations that tried to legally register were rejected or received no response. In Phu Yen province the government recognized-Evangelical Church of Vietnam reported that an Ede Christian died in April 2007 after being detained and beaten by police for not renouncing his religion. In July police and soldiers forcibly evicted ethnic minority Stieng Christians from their farms in Binh Phuoc, beating some of the villagers and bulldozing their crops and homes.

An independent report facilitated by UNHCR in 2007 found "severe forms of religion-based punitive action" against Montagnard Christians in the Central Highlands. During 2007 at least 13 Montagnards were sentenced to prison, joining more than 350 Montagnards imprisoned on national security charges since 2001 for peaceful political or religious activities, or trying to seek asylum in Cambodia. A steady trickle of Montagnard asylum seekers fled to Cambodia, with many forcibly turned back by Cambodian border police. Problems remained in monitoring conditions in the Central Highlands without hindrance: after a UNHCR visit to Dak Lak in June, police detained and beat a Montagnard who had helped translate for the delegation.

Labor

Members of independent trade unions are arrested and harassed, with at least six members of the United Worker-Farmers Organization arrested since 2006.

In 2007 the government announced it would raise the minimum monthly salary for workers in foreign companies for the first time in six years. Despite this, unprecedented numbers of workers—mostly at South Korean, Japanese, Taiwanese, and Singaporean enterprises—continued to strike for better pay and working conditions.

A new draft law would fine workers who participate in "illegal" strikes not approved by the VCP-controlled union confederation. Decrees issued in 2007 enable local officials to force striking workers back to work, and ban strikes in strategic sectors including power stations, railways, airports, post offices, and oil, gas, and forestry enterprises.

Women

While Vietnam's National Assembly has among the highest proportion of women representatives of any Asian country and laws prohibiting gender discrimination and trafficking, poor legal enforcement leaves many women disenfranchised and subject to domestic violence, trafficking, landlessness, growing rates of HIV/AIDS, and low school enrollment rates.

Vietnam continues to be a source of and transit point for women and children trafficked for forced prostitution, fraudulent marriages, and forced domestic servitude to China, Cambodia, Taiwan, Malaysia, and South Korea. Sex workers, trafficking victims, and street peddlers—officially classified by the government as "social evils"—are routinely rounded up and detained without warrants in compulsory "rehabilitation" centers, where they are subject to beatings and sexual abuse.

Key International Actors

Vietnam's donors, including the World Bank, Asian Development Bank, and Japan, pledged US$4.4 billion for 2007, which represents 15 percent of its annual budget. Vietnam's largest trading partners are China, Japan, the US, and Singapore.

In March 2007 33 countries made demarches to the Vietnamese government condemning the arrest of dissidents. In May the European Union called for the release of all nonviolent political activists, followed in July by a European Parliament resolution condemning the crackdown.

Relations with the United States continued to warm as the US granted Vietnam Permanent Normal Trade Relations at the end of 2006 and removed it from the US list of religious freedom violators. However, President Bush raised concerns about human rights with President Triet during their June 2007 White House meeting.

RUSSIA

The Stamp of Guantanamo

The Story of Seven Men Betrayed by Russia's Diplomatic
Assurances to the United States

HUMAN
RIGHTS
WATCH

WORLD REPORT
2008

EUROPE
AND CENTRAL ASIA

ARMENIA

The ruling Republican Party of Armenia (RPA) won almost 33 percent of the vote in the May 2007 parliamentary elections and controls nearly half of the seats in the National Assembly. Two other parties loyal to President Robert Kocharian won enough seats to guarantee a pro-presidential majority. Although the elections showed improvements over previous years, observers have documented irregularities and the opposition contested results in some locations. Harassment of opposition supporters and limits on media freedom marred the run-up to the February 2008 presidential election. Torture and ill-treatment remain a problem. Limits on media freedom and freedom of religion persist.

Elections

International observers have determined that the May 12 parliamentary elections largely met international standards, although they have noted pre-election irregularities, including pressure on employees to vote for the RPA, distribution of goods and services in exchange for votes, and abuse of administrative resources. Opposition parties held rallies without police harassment and had access to public television, although pro-government parties received disproportionate coverage. On election day there were reports of fraud and double voting as well as problems in transparency, counting, tabulation, and publication of results.

On April 27 President Kocharian publicly accused Orinats Yerkir Party leader Artur Bagdasarian of treason based on secret recordings of a February meeting between Bagdasarian and a British diplomat, during which reportedly Bagdasarian claimed that government officials were taking steps to rig the parliamentary elections and asked whether the European Union could respond. No charges have been brought against Bagdasarian.

On October 23 police in the capital Yerevan detained seven opposition activists who were informing passers-by about an October 26 rally for former Armenian president and prospective 2008 presidential candidate Levon Ter-Petrosian. The group was released, but five were later charged with assaulting police.

Narek Galstian, an activist with the youth group of the opposition Social Democratic Hnchakyan Party, was beaten on November 15 by a group of unknown assailants. Two days prior, police briefly detained Galstian and another opposition youth activist as they posted leaflets critical of Prime Minister (and prospective 2008 presidential candidate) Serzh Sargsian and warned them to stop antigovernment propaganda.

In mid-October, leading Armenian media figures expressed concern that the country's television outlets were curtailing political news, including coverage of news conferences by opposition politicians, and accused the authorities of restricting press freedom ahead of the presidential election. On November 12, the state tax service accused the Giumri-based independent Gala television channel of tax evasion. The station's leadership believes the tax inspection and other pressures from the authorities come in response to its broadcast of a September speech by Ter-Petrosian in which he called the government "corrupt and mafiosi."

On November 22 the Yerevan Press Club and the "TEAM" Research Center presented the initial results of a project analyzing eight broadcasters' evening news coverage of prospective presidential candidates and political party leaders ahead of the 2008 presidential elections. The research revealed that Prime Minister Sargsian has received disproportionately more positive coverage compared to opposition candidates.

Arrest with Possible Political Motivation

On May 7 police arrested former minister of foreign affairs Alexander Arzoumanian, now the head of the Civil Disobedience Movement, on charges of money laundering. Authorities claim that Arzoumanian, obtained funds for political activities from a fugitive Armenian-Russian businessman. Arzoumanian maintains that the money was given to him legally by friends and not for political purposes. Arzoumanian was released on September 6 pending investigation.

Torture and Ill-Treatment

The death in custody of Levan Gulyan highlights concerns about continuing torture and ill-treatment of suspects and witnesses. On May 9, 2007, Gulyan, a restaurant owner, witnessed a fight between several individuals, which resulted in one person being shot dead. Gulyan was called to the local police station repeatedly for several days for questioning. On May 12, after questioning Gulyan at the Ministry of Internal Affairs, officials informed Gulyan's family that he had died after supposedly jumping from a second-storey window. At the request of the family, Armenian authorities allowed international forensic experts to conduct an autopsy. Although the experts could not determine the circumstances in which Gulyan fell, they concluded that the severe injuries causing his death were consistent with a fall from a second-storey window and that "a few of the smaller bruises and abrasions could have been caused by another force, e.g. a punch or a blow, prior to the fall."

On August 25 Lori province prosecutor Albert Ghazarian was killed by an unknown assailant. According to local human rights groups and media reports, during the investigation into his death authorities subjected some witnesses to beatings and other ill-treatment in order to extract testimony. Officials deny the claims.

On December 22, 2006, the Court of Cassation overturned the murder conviction of three conscript soldiers, Razmik Sargsian, Musa Serobian, and Arayik Zalian, releasing them and returning the case to prosecutors for additional investigation. Sargsian testified that military investigators had beaten him and threatened him with rape, coercing him into signing a confession in which he named as accomplices Serobian and Zalian, who also claim to have been ill-treated by investigators.

Human rights groups reported that ill-treatment of military conscripts remains widespread as a result of impunity for perpetrators. In an exceptional case, military authorities arrested and charged with murder an officer who had in April 2007 shot and killed Gegham Sergoian reportedly because he believed Sergoian and another conscript were laughing at him.

Media Freedom and Freedom of Speech

In mid-July 2007 Armenian Public Radio ceased broadcasts of Radio Free Europe/Radio Liberty (RFE/RL), a United States government-funded program widely listened to in Armenia, notwithstanding that on July 3 parliament had narrowly voted against amendments to media laws that effectively would have banned RFE/RL and other foreign broadcasters from being rebroadcast through Armenian public television and radio. RFE/RL is currently being rebroadcast through private networks.

Journalists continue to face threats, harassment, and criminal charges. On September 15 unknown assailants beat Hovannes Galajian, editor of the opposition newspaper *Iskakan Iravunk* and a frequent government critic, outside his office moments after a man claiming to be from another Armenian newspaper telephoned Galajian requesting a meeting. Vandals burned the car of Suren Baghdasarian, the founder of *Football Plus* newspaper, on January 30 (his car had been similarly vandalized a year earlier), and on February 8 vandals set fire to the car of Ara Saghatelian, chair of the editorial board of *Im Iravunk* newspaper and Panorama.am news portal, both of which often criticize government institutions and prominent business people.

On June 6 a Yerevan court handed freelance journalist Gagik Shamshian a two-and-a-half-year suspended sentence, two years' probation, and a fine, for fraud, embezzlement, and "waste." In July 2006 Shamshian had published an article about a bank robbery for which relatives of the Nubarashen district administration head faced charges. Shamshian reported being harassed and assaulted in retaliation for the article, and pressed charges against his attackers, but then prosecutors instead charged him initially with insult, cheating, and extortion.

On January 12, 2007, an appeals court lessened the sentence of Arman Babajanian, editor of the opposition newspaper *Zhamanak Yerevan,* who had been convicted of forging documents in order to evade compulsory military service. The court cut six months from the original four-year sentence, which had been considered unnecessarily harsh.

Freedom of Religion

At least 80 Jehovah's Witnesses are in prison for refusing to perform military or civilian service. In accordance with its Council of Europe obligations, in 2004 Armenia established alternative service, but the allegedly civilian service remains under military control and regulations.

Human Rights Defenders

Armenia's Ombudsman Armen Harutyunyan received 1,353 complaints in the first six months of 2007, mainly against city administrations and police. His 2006 report described human rights protection in Armenia as "unsatisfactory." He noted the excessive use of pretrial detention, violence against journalists, and limits on freedom of speech, and the need for a more independent judiciary.

Key International Actors

Following the annual Partnership and Cooperation Council meeting between the European Union and Armenia in October 2007, the two parties underlined the "importance of the respect of the rule of law, democratic principles, protection of human rights and fundamental freedoms as essential elements in the bilateral dialogue." The conclusions further stressed the importance the EU attached to the government's ensuring that the 2008 presidential election is held in full compliance with international standards.

The United States presidential budget request for 2008 proposes reducing funding for civil society programs in Armenia, including human rights programs, by 66 percent, from US$8.3 million to US$2.9 million.

The Parliamentary Assembly of the Council of Europe adopted a resolution on Armenia in January acknowledging that Armenia's revised constitution is consistent with European standards but encouraging Armenia to fully implement electoral, media, and justice system reforms. It expressed disappointment over Armenia's failure to introduce a genuine civilian alternative to military service.

AZERBAIJAN

The government continues to use defamation and other criminal charges to intimidate independent and opposition journalists, some of whom have also been assaulted by unknown men. Media freedoms rapidly deteriorated in 2007, with at least ten journalists imprisoned. High-profile government officials, businessmen, and opposition politicians remain in custody, and politically-motivated arrests and trials, torture in police custody, and conditions of detention remain unresolved problems. Less than a year ahead of major presidential elections in Azerbaijan, the ground is set for an unfair presidential campaign.

Media Freedom

Independent and opposition media is subject to state intimidation. In April 2007 Eynulla Fatullayev, the outspoken founder and the editor-in-chief of two newspapers—*Realny Azerbaijan* and *Gundelik Azerbaijan*—was sentenced to two-and-a-half years in prison on charges of libel and insult for an internet posting blaming Azerbaijanis for a 1992 massacre in Nagorno-Karabakh. Fatullayev denied writing the posting. In July Azerbaijan's Ministry of National Security pressed additional charges against him for terrorism and inciting religious and ethnic hatred for articles printed in *Realny Azerbaijan*. Further tax evasion charges were filed against him in September. Both newspapers, which had the largest circulations among print outlets in the country, were effectively shut down in May after Emergency Ministry and National Security Ministry personnel evicted staff from the papers' premises, confiscated computer hard drives, and sealed the office shut.

In January, Faramaz Allahverdiev, correspondent for the *Nota Bene* newspaper, was sentenced to two years of imprisonment for libel and insult charges brought by the minister of interior and another official. In May, Samir Sadetoglu and Rafik Tagi, editor and correspondent for the weekly *Senet* were sentenced to five and three years of imprisonment, respectively, for inciting religious hatred because of an article in *Senet* unfavorably comparing Christianity to Islam. In the same month, Rovshan Kebirli and Yashar Agazadeh, editor and correspondent for the newspaper *Mukhalifet*, were sentenced to two-and-a-half years on libel and defamation charges brought by a member of parliament for an article exposing government corruption. In July, Mushfig Husseinov, who wrote a series of articles on government corruption for the newspaper *Bizim Yol*, was arrested on spurious charges, which NGOs believe were the result of entrapment. In November, Nazim Guliev, editor of *Ideal* newspaper, was sentenced to two-and-a-half years for defamation charges filed by a ministry of interior official. In the same month, a judge ordered Ganimet Zahid, editor-in-chief of opposition *Azadlig* daily, to be held for two months to await trial on spurious hooliganism charges. Mirza Sakit Zakhidov, a reporter and satirist for the daily *Azadlyg*, remains in prison after his 2006 conviction on spurious drug charges.

The government failed conclusively to investigate numerous reports of violence and threats of violence against opposition and independent journalists. In December 2006, Nijat Husseinov, an *Azadlyg* journalist, was attacked by four unknown assailants and required three weeks of hospitalization to recover from his injuries. The attack was precipitated by anonymous, threatening phone calls referring to his journalism. In April 2007 unknown assailants attacked *Realny Azerbaijan's* Uzeyir Jafarov, who sustained serious injuries. At least two other journalists, Hakimeldostu Mehdiev and Suhayla Gamberova, were hospitalized with injuries they sustained following assaults in 2007 related to their work.

The president appoints all nine members of Azerbaijan's National Television and Radio Broadcast Council, which grants broadcasting licenses. The independent television station ANS faced problems renewing its broadcast license for three years after it expired in 2003, and was taken off the air for a short time in November 2006. In April 2007 its license was extended for six years, but as a result of the licensing ordeal, ANS's content now appears to be prone to self-censorship.

Torture and Inhuman Treatment

Torture remains a widespread and largely unacknowledged problem in Azerbaijan. Emblematic of this is the June 2007 murder conviction of three boys, who were between the ages of 15 and 17 when they were arrested, based on confessions and incriminating statements that they stated repeatedly, including at trial, had been coerced under severe beatings and other forms of torture. The government has failed to conduct meaningful investigations into these and other allegations of abuse.

The Azerbaijani government says that it has invested in training for law enforcement officials, but this effort is not matched with rigorous prosecutions of abusive officers. Of 11 cases the government has investigated, 10 dealt with suspicious deaths in custody. Six cases were dismissed for lack of evidence, two are still pending, and three officers were convicted for such minor offenses as negligence and abuse of office, receiving prison sentences from one to three years.

Politically-Motivated Arrests and Convictions

In 2004 and 2005 Azerbaijan released more than 100 political prisoners, but the government has made no more progress in this area. The government officials, businessmen, and opposition politicians arrested in advance of the November 2005 parliamentary elections on allegations of attempting to overthrow the government remain in custody; some have been convicted, and many remain in detention pending trial. In almost all cases the government replaced accusations of coup plotting with charges of economic crimes or abuse of office. For example, in October 2007, former Economic Development Minister Farhad Aliyev was sentenced to 10 years of imprisonment for corruption, tax evasion, and other economic crimes. Similarly, in April, former Minister of Health, Ali Insanov, was convicted of abuse of office and other economic charges. Parts of Insanov's and Aliyev's trials were completely closed, and lawyers complain of numerous procedural violations. The March 2007 presidential pardon provided for the release of only one person out of what human rights activists estimate to be dozens of prisoners sentenced on politically motivated charges.

Human Rights Defenders

Human rights defenders are the targets of public smear campaigns on television and in print media, physical and verbal attacks, and other forms of pressure and harassment. For example, in July 2007 the pro-government Modern Musavat party held a protest outside of the Institute for Peace and Democracy (IPD), a human rights NGO, throwing eggs and tomatoes and shouting offensive remarks. The organization's head, Leyla Yunus, believes that the protest was prompted by the

IPD's May appeal to the Council of Europe calling for sanctions against Azerbaijan because of its deteriorating human rights record. Throughout 2007, staff of the Institute for Reporter Freedom and Safety (IRFS), an outspoken media monitoring organization, were subjected to police beatings, arbitrary detention, and surveillance by the security services. In July, an elderly man was brutally beaten just outside the IRFS's office. The IRFS believes the attackers assumed the victim was an employee of the organization. The police failed to respond promptly or open an investigation citing the victim's unwillingness to file a complaint. On August 29, the IRFS director and a staff member were detained while reporting on a protest, they were released after several hours of police questioning about IRFS's work.

Key International Actors

Key actors made public statements of concern about Azerbaijan's human rights record. These concerns appear to have little impact on these actors' relationships with Azerbaijan, likely due to the country's geostrategic importance and hydrocarbon resources. As part of the European Neighborhood Policy (ENP) Action Plan signed by the EU and Azerbaijan in 2006, the two parties adopted a European Neighborhood Policy Instrument (ENPI) for financial assistance totaling €92 million for 2007-2013. Funding priorities include strengthening democratic structures, good governance, and poverty reduction efforts.

The annual EU-Azerbaijan Partnership and Cooperation Council meeting in October underscored the "importance of the protection of human rights and fundamental freedoms" as "essential elements in the bilateral dialogue."

A March statement by the German Presidency of the EU on media freedom in Azerbaijan expressed concern that "criminal defamation suits initiated by public officials are being used in order to limit media freedom," and called the authorities to "create an environment where the media can work freely, effectively and without fear."

A strongly critical resolution adopted in April by the Council of Europe Parliamentary Assembly highlighted many shortcomings in Azerbaijan's record of honoring its membership obligations.

In its second report on Azerbaijan, the Council of Europe's Commission against Racism and Intolerance (ECRI) noted some positive steps, such as improved access to public school for children of non-citizens, but noted that "there are still cases of racist and inflammatory speech or promotion of religious intolerance by some media, members of general public and politicians."

In January, the European Court of Human Rights issued its Chamber judgment in the case of Mammadov (Sardar Jalaloglu) v. Azerbaijan, unanimously finding violations of Article 3 (prohibition of torture) and of Article 13 (right to effective remedy) of the European Convention on Human Rights. Police had arrested Jalaloglu, secretary general of the Democratic Party of Azerbaijan, following the October 2003 presidential elections for "organizing public disorder" and "use of violence against a state official."

In March 2007, the United States and Azerbaijan signed an agreement aimed at improving security and cooperation in the Caspian Sea region energy sector. In August, the US and Azerbaijan conducted the third round of their bilateral dialogue on democracy and human rights, initiated by the US in December 2006. Key issues were discussed, and some US concerns about Azerbaijan's human rights record were made public.

The Organization for Security and Cooperation in Europe (OSCE) Representative on Media Freedom, Miklos Haraszti, harshly criticized the Azerbaijani authorities in his report to the Permanent Council on June 21, 2007, expressing particular concerns "about the continuous harassment of independent media and journalists," and urging the government to decriminalize defamation. The OSCE in Baku issued numerous statements echoing the problems of media freedoms.

BELARUS

The Belarusian authorities' repressive grip on political and media freedom intensified after the March 2006 presidential election, which was considered by the
Office for Democratic Institutions and Human Rights of the Organization for
Security and Cooperation in Europe, United Nations Human Rights Council (HRC),
the US, and the EU to have failed to meet international standards for free and fair
elections. Opposition leaders and activists remain behind bars, and the authorities continue to beat, detain, and intimidate civil society groups, making it difficult for them to function.

Political Freedoms

Political opposition groups are not illegal in Belarus, but authorities make it
almost impossible for them to operate. Registration is obligatory but frequently
denied for arbitrary and unfounded reasons. In 2007 dozens of opposition
activists were beaten and arrested for a variety of trumped-up misdemeanors and
criminal offenses. For example, Alexander Kazulin, a former presidential hopeful
in the March 2006 election who was arrested during a peaceful post-election
opposition march, is serving a five-and-a-half-year prison term for hooliganism
and disturbing public order. When opposition leader Alexander Milinkevich organized a European March in October to show Belarus' commitment to become closer to Europe, more than 50 opposition activists were detained in advance. Among
them was the leader of the United Civic Party in the Homiel region, who was sentenced to seven days in jail allegedly for using obscene language in public.

In spring and summer 2007, more than 60 activists were beaten, fined, and jailed
for participating in and preparing for Freedom Day, the anniversary of the declaration of Belarus' sovereignty, an annual Chernobyl rally, and the European March.
A few members of the youth opposition group Young Front were charged with acting on behalf of an unregistered group, and several more were detained for showing their support for their fellow activists. Punishments ranged from large fines to
two years in jail; at the time of writing Young Front leaders Zmicier Dashkievich
and Artur Finkievich are still serving jail sentences. Young Front's registration
application has been denied several times; in May 2007, registration was refused

for supposed contradictions in the organization's charter. At least five activists were detained across Belarus in July for alleged petty hooliganism. Riot police beat the leader of the youth wing of the United Civil Party Young Democrats, breaking his arm.

The government of President Lukashenka shut down Belarus' only private university. Recently, students have been sometimes expelled from universities in retaliation for involvement in groups associated with the opposition. For example, three students were expelled from Belarusian State Pedagogical University in late 2006 for their political activities.

Yuri Aleynik, of the Movement for Liberty and member of the Belarusian Association of Journalists, a civil society group affiliated with Reporters Without Borders, was expelled from the Presidential Management Academy in July 2007, for allegedly missing too many classes despite his excellent grades; more likely, he was expelled for his association with civil society groups.

Human Rights Defenders and Civil Society

Only five human rights organizations remain registered in Belarus: the Belarusian Association of Journalists, Society for the Belarusian Language, Belarusian PEN Center, Belarusian Helsinki Committee, and Pravavaia Initsiativa (Legal Initiative). The authorities continually seek to intimidate and control these groups, including by penalizing them for association with unregistered organizations. Other human rights groups continue to operate without registration; their attempts to register legally are repeatedly denied.

For example, on September 21, 2007 the human rights group Viasna filed suit with the Belarusian Supreme Court, challenging the Ministry of Justice's refusal to register the organization. The ministry claimed that Viasna did not meet registration requirements of the Nongovernmental Organizations Law and had used in its application incorrect information on birthdates and the spelling of names. It also noted that 20 of the organization's 69 founders have been convicted for various misdemeanor offences. In July 2007, the United Nations Human Rights Committee found that the closure of the organization's predecessor (of the same name) was a violation of Article 22 of the International Covenant on Civil and Political Rights (ICCPR).

The Supreme Court upheld a ruling by the Economic Court of Minsk ordering the Belarusian Helsinki Committee (BHC) to pay 160m rubles (about US$6.4m) and confiscating property valued at 255,000 rubles (about US$10,000) in fees and back taxes for tax-exempt grants received from the EU's TACIS program (Technical Assistance to the Commonwealth of Independent States).

Religious Freedom

The Belarusian constitution provides for freedom of religion, but the government makes it difficult for religious institutions other than those affiliated with the Belarusian Orthodox Church to practice. The authorities often refuse to register spaces where religious organizations convene, choosing a strict interpretation of the housing code, therefore making such gatherings illegal, and have fined, threatened, and detained several religious leaders for holding religious services in "unauthorized" spaces. More than 25 foreign Catholic and Protestant clergy were expelled from Belarus between the summers of 2006 and 2007 for allegedly "posing a threat to national security."

Media Freedom

The government continues to tightly control the media. There are no independent television or radio stations. The authorities monitor the Internet, and politically sensitive sites are often temporarily shut down. Several privately-owned newspapers are printed in Russia because local, state-run printing companies are not permitted to print material that "discredits Belarus" by "fraudulent representation" of developments in the country. Before the 2006 presidential election the state postal service Belpochta stopped distributing several opposition newspapers.

In September 2007, 14,000 copies of the opposition newspaper *Tovarishch* were confiscated for being printed in Belarus.

All Internet access passes through the state-owned operator Beltelcom, and a subdivision of the special security services (KGB) is responsible for protecting state secrets and for running the country's top domain (.by). Following President Lukashenka's assertion that there is "anarchy on the Internet," Deputy Information Minister Alexander Slabadchuk announced that the government would create an inter-agency working group to create policies for controlling the Internet. The parliament is working on a law that will make registration of all Internet news sites obligatory.

The September 2007 conviction of opposition politician Andrei Klimov on charges of calling to overturn the constitutional order of Belarus with the use of mass media sent an unambiguous signal that the Internet was not a safe alternative to the print media for expressing criticism of the government. Klimov was sentenced to two years in jail following a closed trial.

Journalists from Reuters and Agence France Presse were detained in September 2007 without explanation. They were covering the trial of a member of the youth opposition movement; later an official of the Brest Interior Department explained that they participated in an "unauthorized street act." Leading up to the October 14 European March, Igor Bancar, a journalist from Magazyn Polski Na Uchodztwie (Polish Magazine on Emigration), was arrested and held for 10 days for "hooliganism."

Key International Actors

Multilateral organizations as well as the EU and the US remained deeply critical of Belarus' human rights record, while Belarusian authorities persisted in their refusal to heed key actors' recommendations to improve the situation or respond to penalties for failing to do so.

In June 2007, the EU suspended Belarus' trade benefits under the Generalized System of Preferences (GSP) after Belarus failed to implement recommendations made by the International Labor Organization to improve the treatment of independent unions. The United States had already suspended GSP in 2000 for failure to take steps to allow the right of association and collective bargaining.

United States Deputy Assistant Secretary of State, David Kramer, made an official visit to Belarus in April 2007. Kramer told the press that if Belarus wishes to improve relations with US, it must release all political prisoners and stop persecution of political activists.

In August 2007, the United States expanded the list of Belarusian governmental officials banned from the United States. The original visa ban list was created in May 2006, and included almost 40 names cited for violating human rights and committing fraud during presidential elections.

In March 2007 the United Nations General Assembly adopted Resolution 61/175 sharply criticizing Belarus for the failure to "hold free and fair elections, arbitrary use of State power against opposition candidates, routine harassment and detention of political and civil society activists," harassment and detention of journalists, implication of government officials in the enforced disappearance or summary execution of opposition politicians and a journalist, forced closure of the University of Belarus, harassment and closure of civil society organizations, and harassment and prosecution of human rights defenders. It also cited Belarus for failing to cooperate with the Human Rights Council.

In May the United Nations General Assembly rejected Belarus' bid for a seat on the HRC. A broad coalition of international and national nongovernmental organizations, including Human Rights Watch, raised strong objections about Belarus' candidacy, pointing to its poor human rights record and lack of cooperation with the HRC.

BOSNIA AND HERZEGOVINA

There was progress on accountability for war crimes from the armed conflict of the first half of the 1990s, including through domestic prosecutions. However, the number of refugees and displaced persons returning to their areas of origin continues to decline.

War Crimes Accountability

Improved Bosnian official cooperation with the International Criminal Tribunal for the former Yugoslavia (ICTY), including by Republika Srpska, delivered concrete results in 2007. Bosnia's War Crimes Chamber continued successfully to pursue its mandate of prosecuting those responsible for war atrocities. Nonetheless, there are concerns regarding the chamber prosecution's prioritization of cases, excessive use of closed sessions (justified on witness protection grounds), and inadequate public outreach.

Bosnian collaboration with Serbian authorities and the European Union peacekeeping force in Bosnia (EUFOR) resulted in the arrest of indicted Bosnian Serb army general Zdravko Tolimir in May and his transfer to the ICTY. The two most wanted ICTY indictees, Ratko Mladic and Radovan Karadzic, remain at large, however. Dragan Zelenovic pled guilty and was sentenced to 15 years' imprisonment by the ICTY in April for the rape and torture of Bosniak (Bosnian Muslim) women and girls in the Foca area. The ICTY Appeals Chamber reduced the sentences of Radoslav Brdjanin (convicted of failing to prevent war crimes against Bosniak and Croat civilians) and Vidoje Blagojevic (convicted for crimes against humanity at Srebrenica) in April and May, respectively.

In Bosnia's War Crimes Chamber defendants included former Yugoslav Army commander Marko Samardzija; Gojko Jankovic, the former commander of Republika Srpska military units operating in Foca; and 11 members of the Serbian special police and military charged with genocide over the Srebrenica massacre. Gojko Klickovic, former prime minister of Republika Srpska, was extradited to Bosnia from Serbia in June 2007. Klickovic is charged with crimes against humanity.

In May Radovan Stankovic, the first indictee to be transferred from the ICTY to Bosnia, escaped while being transferred to hospital. Stankovic was serving a 20 year sentence for crimes against Bosniak civilians in the Foca area, following his November 2006 conviction by the Bosnian chamber. At this writing he remains at large.

The ICTY transferred five cases to the chamber for trial during 2007, including that of Milorad Trbic, charged with involvement in the Srebrenica genocide. But the ICTY Appeals Chamber ruled in July 2007 against the transfer of the case of Milan and Sredoje Lukic for their alleged role in the killings of civilians in the Visegrad area, reversing an earlier decision. The court cited the enormity of crimes committed and possible distress to victims if the case was transferred.

War crimes prosecutions also continue in the Federation cantonal courts (26 cases at this writing), Republika Srpska district courts (nine cases), and Brcko special area court (one case). Local prosecutors and judges are increasingly proactive in investigating and prosecuting war crimes, but remain hampered by weak witness protection, a lack of funding, and limited political and public support. The unwillingness of the Banja Luka court (Republika Srpska) to classify wartime sexual crimes as war crimes drew criticism domestically.

The number of lawsuits filed in the Republika Srpska and Federation courts against both entities for compensation for wartime death and injury continue to grow. Neither entity has a strategy to systematically address the thousands of claims.

On February 26 the International Court of Justice ruled that the Serbian government was not directly responsible for genocide during the Bosnian war (see chapter on Serbia). Bosnian victims' associations were dismayed at the verdict and staged a number of peaceful protests.

The whereabouts of approximately 13,000 missing persons from the war remain unknown. The majority are Bosniak. Mass graves containing 200 victims of the Srebrenica massacre, including children, were discovered in September.

Return of Refugees and Displaced Persons

As of June more than 134,000 Bosnians remain internally displaced. The United Nations High Commissioner for Refugees (UNHCR) registered around 1,250 IDP and 300 refugee returns during the first half of 2007, around half the number from the same period in 2006. The majority of returning refugees in 2007 were Bosniak, while most returning IDPs were Bosniaks or Bosnian Serbs.

Not all of those registered as returning remained permanently, especially in areas where the returnees' ethnic group is now in a minority. Limited economic opportunity and perceptions of insecurity provide part of the explanation. Anti-minority violence remained sporadic, but in some instances—such as the violent assault in July on Bosnian Serb Bishop Hrizostom in Bosanski Petrovac, for which no one has yet been charged—it undermines confidence in return. Property repossessions by pre-war owners under a national restitution scheme increased, but most minority returnees then sell their property, particularly in urban areas.

Many of those who remain displaced lacked property before the war. Despite government housing schemes in 30 municipalities aimed at displaced persons, lack of housing remains an obstacle to return. Approximately 7,000 IDPs still live in collective centers, some of which are sub-standard.

Roma refugees in Bosnia, the majority of whom come from Kosovo, remain vulnerable and dependent on periodic extensions of their temporary protection status.

Citizenship and National Security

The Bosnian commission established to review wartime decisions on the naturalization of foreign citizens continues its work. At this writing around 1,300 cases have been reviewed, with around 500 individuals stripped of Bosnian citizenship, including some 350 of North African origin who came during the war. While the process is said to be motivated solely by concerns over irregularities in naturalization decisions, it is clearly linked to concerns about the presence in Bosnia of Islamist radicals with links to terrorism.

Many appealed against loss of their citizenship and were allowed to remain in Bosnia pending the outcome. At this writing none has been deported. National and international human rights organizations expressed concern that Bosnia lacks adequate safeguards against risk of return to serious human rights abuse, including torture or ill-treatment, for those subject to deportation.

The six Algerian national security suspects illegally transferred to Guantanamo Bay in 2002 with the complicity of the Bosnian authorities remain there at this writing. In May 2007 the men (four of whom are Bosnian citizens) filed a claim against Bosnia in the European Court of Human Rights for failing to intervene on their behalf with the United States government, resulting in ongoing human rights violations.

Police Decertification

In April 2007 the United Nations Security Council agreed to terms under which 598 Bosnian police officers disqualified from service on the grounds of alleged involvement in human rights abuses could reapply for police jobs. The decision followed concerns expressed by the Council of Europe's Venice Commission and commissioner for human rights that the decertification process lacked transparency and a meaningful appeals system. Decertified former police seeking reappointment must admit to the previous decertification when applying for a new position.

In July the international high representative dismissed Republika Srpska senior police officer Dragomir Adnan for using his position to protect fugitives, and 35 other police officers for their alleged role in the Srebrenica massacre.

Human Rights Defenders

The killing in February of Dusko Kondor, co-founder of the Helsinki Committee for Human Rights in Republika Srpska, in a machine gun attack carried out by local gangsters, in which his daughter was also severely injured, was viewed with alarm among Bosnian human rights defenders. Although the attack appeared unrelated to Kondor's human rights work, colleagues claimed that the police failed to give him adequate protection, despite requests for assistance following earlier threats. The trial of persons accused of involvement in Kondor's death is ongoing at this writing.

In March the Ministry of Justice simplified the requirements for nongovernmental organization registration at state level.

Key International Actors

The mandate of the international high representative was extended to June 2008, reversing a plan by the Peace Implementation Council to end it in June 2007 and retain only an EU special representative with limited powers. In July Slovak diplomat Miroslav Lajcak was appointed to both positions.

Bosnia's negotiations with the EU for a Stabilization and Association Agreement (SAA) remained stalled due to unresolved issues concerning police, public broadcasting, and public administration reform. The EU peacekeeping force in Bosnia was reduced from 6,000 to 2,500 in December 2006 in light of an improved security situation. The mandate of the EU Monitoring Mission (EUMM) expires in December 2007.

In May Bosnia was elected to the UN Human Rights Council. Members are required to "uphold the highest standards in the promotion and protection of human rights."

To its credit, the government of Bosnia and Herzegovina agreed in June to publish the report of the Council of Europe's Committee for the Prevention of Torture (CPT) following their March visit. The report published in July noted the failure to segregate dangerous prisoners and some incidents of mistreatment of prisoners by prison guards, and inadequate provisions and safeguards for juvenile and mentally ill offenders.

CROATIA

Croatia's human rights record saw modest improvement in 2007, linked in part to its candidacy for European Union membership. Key continuing problems relate to the legacy of Croatia's 1991-95 war. There was insufficient progress in removing the remaining obstacles to the return and reintegration of refugee Serbs. There was some movement toward genuine accountability for wartime abuses, but the impartiality and effectiveness of domestic prosecutions remains in question.

Return and Reintegration of Serbs

There was limited progress toward resolving the ongoing obstacles to the return and reintegration of displaced and refugee Serbs. As of July 2007 around 125,000 of the 300,000 to 350,000 Serb refugees who fled the conflict were registered as having returned to Croatia. Around 60 percent of those who return stay permanently in Croatia. Figures from the United Nations High Commissioner for Refugees (UNHCR) indicate that 1,745 Serbs returned between January and September 2007. More than 80,000 refugees in neighboring countries have yet to decide about their future.

Serbs, particularly returnees, continue to suffer violence and intimidation, although at a lower rate in 2007 than in previous years. Police showed improved efficiency in the apprehension of perpetrators of inter-ethnic criminal incidents. However, prosecutions frequently drag, with resolution long separated from incidents and attacks rarely qualified as "hate crimes."

In the most serious incident of the year, in July 2007 a Serb father and his son who were returning to Gornji Vrhovci village were beaten in their home following an alleged land dispute. Their assailants then locked them in a room and set fire to the house, but the victims escaped. At this writing, three suspects await trial on charges of attempted murder. In February the Serb Orthodox Church in Sibenik reported a series of attacks on church property and Serb returnees in the Kistanje area, and in October six Serb-owned reconstructed houses in the Zadar area were damaged. At this writing, three juveniles have been charged with criminal damage. In April seven members of Serbia's national hockey team were assaulted by a group of about 20 young men in Zagreb.

Serbs continued to face practical difficulties repossessing occupied homes, despite court judgments in their favor. Some cases were delayed in lengthy court proceedings. Access to reconstruction assistance for wartime damage is available to Serbs, but applications are frequently refused on procedural grounds and at least 9,000 appeals are pending. There remains no effective remedy for those seeking the return of occupied agricultural land.

There was little progress toward a viable solution for Serbs stripped during the war of the right to occupy socially-owned property (tenancy rights), an issue linked to the return of Serbs. Delays and flawed procedures mean that the number of Serb former tenancy-right holders allocated social housing remains small. As a result, a June 2007 decision allowing people allocated social housing in previously war-affected areas to buy their homes at below market prices is unlikely to benefit many Serbs. No comparable right to buy exists in urban areas, where limited housing stock further complicates access for Serb former tenancy-right holders.

There was no progress toward recognizing working time between 1991 and 1995 in Serb-occupied areas for the purposes of Croatian state pensions, compromising the financial security of returnee and other elderly Serbs.

There was movement toward the implementation of minority rights legislation at the national level in 2007, notably with the publication of the Central State Administration Office's annual employment plan that included for the first time statistics on minority employment and hiring targets at central and county level. No such plan exists for hiring in the judiciary, however, and the Council for National Minorities assessed that legal guarantees for minority representation in state administration are not fully respected.

War Crimes Accountability

The conviction in June 2007 of Milan Martic by the International Criminal Tribunal for the former Yugoslavia (ICTY) for war crimes against Croats, for which he received a 35-year sentence, was welcomed by Serbs and Croats alike. But the October ruling by the court in the so-called Vukovar Three trial was criticized by the Croatian parliament for lenience after Miroslav Radic was acquitted and

Veselin Sljivancanin given five years' imprisonment in a case dealing with the 1991 mass killing of Croats in Vukovar; the third defendant, Mile Mrksic, received a 20-year sentence. The ICTY prosecutor appealed against the sentence and verdict on Mrksic and Sljivancanin.

There were several high-profile trials of Croats in domestic courts in 2007, including that of Branimir Glavas and six others for the wartime murder of Serb civilians in Osijek, which began in October. The stripping of Glavas's immunity as a member of parliament in May 2006 had opened the way for proceedings against him. The first case transferred to Croatia from the ICTY (in September 2005), that of Rahim Ademi and Mirko Norac for the murder of Serb civilians in the Medak pocket, went to trial in June 2007. Both of these trials are ongoing at this writing.

Serbs continue to make up the vast majority of defendants and convicted war criminals in Croatia, a disproportion so large it suggests bias as a factor. According to statistics released by the state prosecutor's office in May, of 3,666 people charged with war crimes since 1991, 3,604 were prosecuted for involvement in aggression against Croatia, while 62 were members of the Croatian armed forces. The absence of an agreed threshold for determining when acts should be prosecuted as war crimes may also provide part of the explanation for the disparity. Prosecutors received evidence from the ICTY to facilitate the prosecution of Tomislav Mercep for crimes in 1991 against Serbs, but at this writing the trial has yet to begin. Serb victims of other wartime abuses, including the disappearance of over 100 civilians in Sisak, continue to wait for justice. The Sisak abuses were finally categorized as war crimes, allaying fears that they would be subject to the 15-year statute of limitation applied to ordinary murders.

Many prosecutions and trials against Serbs remain of questionable standard, with concerns relating to fairness—particularly for those tried in absentia or prosecuted in areas where the crimes occurred—and about the effectiveness of the court-appointed defense lawyers. In absentia trials are opposed by the prosecutor's office in Zagreb, but continue to take place for war crimes, defendants mostly being Serbs: at the end of October 2007, 19 of the 23 defendants on trial in absentia were Serbs.

Trials against Croats for wartime abuses were far more likely to result in acquittals. In March the Karlovac County Court acquitted for the third time Mihajlo Hrastov over the 1991 killing in the Karlovac area of 13 Yugoslav Army reservists who had surrendered, the Supreme Court having overturned two previous acquittals. The case highlighted the continued predominance of trials in local courts where the crimes occurred, rather than the four courts designated to try war crimes.

Efforts to improve Croatia's cooperation with neighboring states as a way to overcome barriers to prosecution posed by extradition rules bore fruit in May 2007, when Croatia's transfer of evidence to Serbia led to the latter's arrest of 12 people for crimes against Croats in Lovas, near Vukovar. However, as noted by the Human Rights and Legal Affairs Committee of the Council of Europe in May, further progress was required to lower barriers to inter-state judicial cooperation, particularly in relation to the participation of refugee and other witnesses living elsewhere. Securing the participation of Serb witnesses residing outside Croatia proved difficult in the Ademi-Norac case.

Human Rights Defenders

Findings and requests for information to the government by the Human Rights Ombudsman were routinely ignored by the authorities, in the absence of powers to sanction for non-compliance. The institution was also compromised by a continuing proliferation of specialized ombudsmen, including on children and gender, rather than the development of a single institution with specialized departments or deputies.

In January 2007 the head of the Office for Associations arranged for secret service vetting of members of the state Civil Society Development Council. The government rejected her claims that it had authorized the vetting, and she was subsequently relieved of her post.

Key International Actors

The future of the Organization for Security and Co-operation in Europe (OSCE) Mission to Croatia was called into doubt following signals from the OSCE chairman- in-office, the head of mission, and the United States government that it should close at the end of 2007. At this writing the OSCE Permanent Council has yet to take a decision. The uncertainty undermined the mission's effectiveness, particularly its engagement on Serb returns issues with recalcitrant local authorities.

As a candidate for membership of the European Union, Croatia is expected to move toward meeting the EU's human rights criteria, although the willingness of the EU to prioritize war legacy issues remains in question. The European Commission annual report on Croatia published in November made reference to the rights of Serbs and other minorities, including obstacles to the reintegration the returning refugees and displaced persons, and domestic war crime prosecutions.

European Union

Attacks and foiled plots in the United Kingdom, Germany, Denmark, and Spain underscored the ongoing threat of terrorism, some of it homegrown. The state response continues to weaken rights and the rule of law.

National security removals of persons remain an important tactic, but with inadequate safeguards against return to abuse, including the use of unreliable "diplomatic assurances" against torture. EU states show an increasing willingness to categorize as terrorism actions only remotely connected to the planning and commission of violent attacks, with damaging consequences for expression, privacy, and in some cases liberty.

Migration and asylum policy remain largely driven by border control rather than protection concerns. Removals without proper safeguards continue, including under agreements with countries that lack the capacity to protect migrants. Interdiction at sea, including through the EU border agency, largely focuses on keeping asylum seekers and migrants outside EU territory rather than protecting them.

Counterterrorism Measures and Human Rights

In February the European Parliament adopted the final report of a special committee tasked with investigating EU member states' complicity with the US Central Intelligence Agency (CIA) in the illegal detention and transfer of terrorism suspects to risk of torture and ill-treatment. The report criticized many EU countries including Germany, Italy, Sweden, and the UK for allowing their airspace to be used by the US agency for the practice, known as "extraordinary rendition." The report called on EU states to launch independent national investigations, seek the return of citizens and residents held illegally by US authorities, and compensate victims.

A joint declaration issued after the October 2007 G6 meeting of interior ministers from France, Germany, Italy, Poland, Spain, and the UK identified diplomatic assurances against torture and ill-treatment as an "effective way forward" for the forced removal of national security suspects. Austria, Germany, Italy, the

Netherlands, Sweden, and the UK have all sought to rely on such assurances, despite evidence that they fail to protect persons against abuse on return, and criticism from United Nations and European human rights bodies.

A committee of the Parliamentary Assembly of the Council of Europe (PACE) confirmed in a June report that the CIA operated illegal prisons for terrorism suspects in Poland and Romania in 2003-2005 in which prisoners were subjected to "interrogation techniques tantamount to torture." The Polish and Romanian governments continue to deny that such centers existed. The PACE report also deplored obstruction to its investigation by EU governments including Germany, Italy, Poland, and Romania.

Common EU Asylum and Migration Policy

The EU continues to pursue the externalization of its migration and asylum policy, notably through readmission agreements with third countries and coordinated naval patrols in the Mediterranean Sea, to the detriment of access to asylum and protection against return to risk of abuse.

The EU External Borders Agency FRONTEX conducted joint naval operations with Senegal and Mauritania in their territorial waters to intercept and turn back boats heading for the Canary Islands before they reached international waters. The EU pursued the participation of Tunisia, Algeria, Morocco, and Libya in similar joint patrols. The operations lacked clear guidelines to ensure access to asylum, and there was disagreement among states over responsibility when boats are intercepted in international waters, and among EU and other Mediterranean states over who should bear responsibility for rescuing shipwrecked migrants.

The EU signed readmission agreements with five western Balkan countries in September, and continued to negotiate agreements with other countries, including Morocco, Algeria, and Turkey. Agreements have already been reached with Ukraine, Sri Lanka, Albania, Hong Kong, and Macao. Under the agreements, states outside the EU accept the return of migrants from third countries who have transited their territory en route to the EU. Readmission agreements raise concerns that persons in need of protection will be removed to countries that lack effective asylum systems or protection against return to risk of human rights abuse.

In June the European Commission launched a consultation process on the common European asylum system with the publication of a green paper examining ways to increase and harmonize protection. The European Court of Justice concluded hearings on the European Parliament's petition to annul widely criticized provisions in the Asylum Procedures Directive establishing common lists of "safe countries of origin" and "safe third countries." In the first step to a decision, the Court's advocate general issued an opinion in September recommending the provisions be annulled.

Iraqis now represent the largest number of asylum applicants in the EU, with 19,375 asylum applicants in 2006 and 18,205 in the first half of 2007. Over half of the latter were in Sweden. Germany, the recipient of the third largest number of Iraqi asylum seekers in the first half of 2007 (820), continued to revoke the status of Saddam Hussein-era Iraqi refugees, citing changed circumstances. About 18,000 Iraqi refugees have had their status revoked since 2003.

There are continuing concerns over a draft directive proposed by the Commission establishing common EU standards and procedures for returning irregular migrants. As drafted, it would allow member states to detain migrants pending deportation for up to 18 months. At this writing the European Parliament has yet to debate the directive.

Human Rights Concerns in EU Member States

France

The new government of President Nicolas Sarkozy proposed new immigration legislation in September. Adopted by Parliament at the end of October, the law tightens the rules on family reunification and creates an in-country appeal for failed asylum seekers detained at the border; the latter is in response to a critical April ruling by the European Court of Human Rights (ECtHR) that the French asylum system lacks effective safeguards. Parliament failed to improve procedural safeguards for others at risk of return to human rights abuse, including asylum seekers under accelerated procedures and terrorism suspects subject to expulsion.

Inadequate safeguards were also highlighted in a May decision by the UN Committee Against Torture (CAT) that France had violated the torture convention when it expelled Adel Tebourski. The French-Tunisian dual national had been stripped of his French citizenship prior to his release from prison on terrorism charges and expelled to Tunisia in August 2006, before French courts and the CAT had fully examined his appeal alleging risk of torture on return.

Also in May 2007 the appellate court in Paris increased prison sentences for nine of the thirteen defendants in the so-called Chechen Network trial. A lower court had convicted 24 people, 16 of them foreign nationals, of the broad offense of "criminal association in relation to a terrorist undertaking" in June 2006. The court ordered 11 of the 16 foreigners to be deported upon completion of their sentences. A 12th man was expelled in February 2007 on order of the Interior Minister.

The forced removal of irregular migrants topped the agenda for the newly created Ministry of Immigration, Integration, National Identity and Development, which imposed a quota of 25,000 expulsions by year's end.

Germany

In June a Munich court ordered the arrest of 13 CIA operatives for their involvement in the 2003 kidnapping of Khaled el-Masri, a German citizen of Lebanese descent apprehended in Macedonia and flown to Afghanistan, where he was imprisoned for five months and tortured. The chief prosecutor for Bavaria formally requested that the German federal government seek to have the 13 extradited to Germany for trial, but in September the Ministry of Justice dropped the extradition effort because of non-cooperation from the US government.

A July report by the Council of Europe human rights commissioner accused the German government of assisting in el-Masri's abduction and noted that a German intelligence officer visited el-Masri in Kabul in May 2004. Foreign Minister Frank-Walter Steinmeier denied Germany had played a role in el-Masri's kidnapping.

In August prosecutors reopened an investigation into allegations that two German soldiers interrogated and mistreated Murat Kurnaz, a German-born Turkish citizen, at a detention camp in Afghanistan in 2002. Kurnaz later spent almost five

FRANCE

In the Name of Prevention

Insufficient Safeguards in National Security Removals

HUMAN
RIGHTS
WATCH

years at Guantanamo Bay. He was released without charge in 2006 and repatriated to Germany. Prosecutors dropped the charges against the soldiers in May 2007
due to lack of evidence, but reopened the case against them in August with plans
to question two new witnesses detained with Kurnaz in Afghanistan.

A German parliamentary panel continued its investigation into possible human
rights violations during counterterrorism operations by the German intelligence
services, including in the el-Masri and Kurnaz cases.

The arrest of two academics in July raised questions about academic freedom and
free speech in the context of counterterrorism. The federal police arrested Andrej
Holm, a professor from the University of Humboldt, and another academic identified only as "Mattias B.," citing their academic writings and accusing them of
being intellectual supporters of a militant left-wing faction allegedly responsible
for a series of arson attacks since 2001. Neither of the men is a suspect in the
arson investigation, but Holm is accused of meeting with one of the suspected
arsonists earlier in 2007. Holm was detained and placed in solitary confinement
until bail was granted in August. Charges of membership in a terrorist organization are pending against both men.

The German government tabled a draft law in September criminalizing "acts of
preparation" of violent terrorist attacks, following the arrests earlier that month of
three alleged Islamic militants. The offense would cover training in a terrorist
camp or flight training, but would apply only where there is intent to carry out a
terrorist attack. Another proposed offense, "instructions for an act of violence,"
would apply to anyone distributing instructions over the internet on building
bombs for use in an attack, or to anyone downloading such instructions.
Opponents argue that criminalizing internet use infringes privacy rights.

Italy

The trial of 26 US citizens (25 alleged CIA agents and a US air force officer) and
six Italians accused of abducting Muslim cleric Hassan Mustafa Osama Nasr
(known as Abu Omar) was suspended in June so the Constitutional Court could
consider a complaint by the government of Romani Prodi that Milan prosecutors
violated state secrecy during their investigations. At this writing the Constitutional

Court has not ruled on the complaint. The Italian government failed to forward the prosecutors' request for extradition of the US citizens, who will instead be tried in absentia, represented by court-appointed attorneys. Abu Omar, kidnapped in Milan in February 2003 and rendered to Egypt, remains there following his release from custody in February 2007.

Italy continued to expel terrorism suspects under an expedited procedure that explicitly denies the right to an in-country appeal. The UN CAT expressed concern in May that the procedure lacked effective protection against return to risk of torture and ill-treatment. In January Fouad Cherif Ben Fitouri was expelled to Tunisia where he was held incommunicado for 12 days and allegedly tortured. He was later charged with terrorism offences and at this writing awaited trial in prison. Interior Minister Giuliano Amato said in March that 30 expulsion orders had been made under the expedited procedure since its introduction in August 2005.

The ECtHR Grand Chamber was due to rule by the end of the year in the case of Nassim Saadi, a Tunisian man the Italian government sought to expel on the basis of unreliable diplomatic assurances of humane treatment upon return. Italy argued before the Grand Chamber in July (with support from the UK government, which intervened in the case) that the absolute prohibition on returns to ill-treatment under the European Convention on Human Rights should be reconsidered to allow a national security exception.

In October the Italian government adopted an emergency decree for the immediate expulsion of EU citizens considered threats to public security. By mid-November authorities had moved to expel more than 150 Romanians, and at this writing Parliament is considering improved safeguards for such cases. The emergency decree followed a brutal crime in October allegedly committed by a Roma man from Romania.

According to the Interior Ministry, 12,419 irregular migrants reached Italy by sea in the first eight months of 2007, a slight decrease from 2006. Migrants continue to die attempting the crossing in unseaworthy boats: according to one estimate, 491 people had died in the Strait of Sicily by September. In a development that risked discouraging rescues at sea, seven Tunisian fishermen were prosecuted for abetting illegal immigration after they rescued 44 migrants and brought them to

Lampedusa, an island off Sicily, in August. No verdict has been handed down at this writing.

Malta

Malta continued to be criticized for its failure to rescue migrants in distress at sea and unwillingness to allow ships carrying migrants rescued at sea to enter its ports. In May a Maltese fishing vessel refused to rescue a group of 27 shipwrecked African migrants, leaving them clinging to fishing nets for three days. The Maltese government declined to rescue the group on the grounds that they were outside its search and rescue area, and that it was Libya's responsibility to do so; the migrants were eventually rescued by an Italian military vessel. Days later the government refused to allow a Spanish fishing vessel carrying 26 migrants rescued at sea to enter Malta, again pointing to Libya. The migrants were subsequently admitted by Spain.

Irregular migrants who enter Malta are subject to mandatory detention in closed centers for up to 18 months (one year in the case of asylum seekers), unless they are pregnant women or minors in which case the maximum detention is six weeks. Detention conditions remain poor, with overcrowding, malnutrition, insufficient access to health care, poor sanitary conditions, and inadequate exercise. In September the government established an independent board of visitors to monitor detention centers.

The Netherlands

A new government took power in February. In June parliament approved the government's plan to grant amnesty to up to 30,000 failed asylum seekers who had applied for asylum prior to 2001. The move was seen as a clear break from the policies of the former government.

The asylum system remained problematic. The UN CAT expressed concern in May 2007 that the accelerated asylum procedure under the Aliens Act of 2000 could result in people being returned to risk of torture. The committee criticized the procedure's 48-hour timeframe for not providing an asylum seeker enough time to adequately access counsel; allowing only "marginal scrutiny" of appeals against rejected claims; and restricting the opportunity to submit additional documentation and information.

A new law expanding state powers to investigate and prosecute terrorist acts came into effect in February. The law lowers the standard upon which special surveillance powers, including wire-tapping, can be invoked from a "reasonable suspicion" to "indications" that a terrorist act is being planned; permits a public prosecutor to designate preventive cordons within which persons can be searched; and increases the maximum period of pretrial detention in terrorism cases from 90 days to two years. Human rights groups expressed concern that the new measures could violate the rights to privacy, liberty and security of person, and fair trial.

A bill aimed at preventing acts of terrorism passed the House of Representatives in March and is pending before the Senate at this writing. It contains provisions limiting the freedom of movement and the right to privacy of persons suspected of being "connected" to or supporting terrorist activities, including bans on residence in a defined part of the Netherlands and association with specific persons, and periodic reporting to the police. The bill has been criticized by rights groups for failing to define specifically what constitutes a terrorist activity or "support" for such activity. There is no requirement that a judge authorize the measures, and judicial supervision would only be triggered if an appeal is lodged.

Poland

The opposition Civic Platform party won early parliamentary elections in late October 2007 and formed a coalition with the Polish Peasants' Party a month later. The outgoing government blocked the EU's adoption of October 10 as the European Day against the Death Penalty. The day was subsequently proclaimed by the Council of Europe.

In April the European Parliament adopted a resolution that referred to the climate of state-sponsored homophobia in Poland. In May the ECtHR ruled that the Warsaw mayor's decision to ban the 2005 Equality Parade contravened free assembly and association under the European Convention. In June the Council of Europe human rights commissioner criticized Poland's policies towards lesbian, gay, bisexual, and transgender communities in a report on Poland's compliance with the European Convention.

Spain

In June 2007 the violent Basque separatist group ETA officially declared an end to the unilateral ceasefire it had announced in March 2006. ETA claimed responsibility for a car bomb explosion at Madrid's Barajas airport in December 2006 that killed two men. Spanish and French authorities arrested numerous suspected ETA members during 2007, including its alleged top explosives expert and its logistics chief. In October authorities arrested 21 alleged members of Batasuna, the banned Basque separatist political party, on charges of belonging to a terrorist organization.

In January the Supreme Court designated as a terrorist organization a Basque youth group involved in street violence in the Basque autonomous region, overturning a lower court's ruling. In May the National Court said the terrorism prosecution of seven former staff at the Basque-language newspaper *Egunkaria* could go to trial despite the prosecutor's December 2006 recommendation that all charges be dismissed. The decision reflects the involvement of two victims' rights organizations as civil parties in the case. The 16-month mass trial of over 50 members of organizations accused of providing support to ETA ended in March 2007. No verdict has been announced at this writing.

In October 2007 the National Court convicted 21 men of involvement in the Madrid train bombings in March 2004. Three men were sentenced to between 34,000 and 42,000 years in prison for hundreds of counts of murder, while 18 others were sentenced to between three and 23 years on other charges, including collaboration with a terrorist organization. Seven others were acquitted.

The regime that allows terrorism suspects to be held in incommunicado detention for up to 13 days remains in effect despite ongoing international criticism. In a July report on Spain, the European Committee for the Prevention of Torture (CPT) recommended improving safeguards, including access to a lawyer from the outset of detention, increased judicial oversight, and prompt and effective investiga-

Unwelcome Responsibilities

Spain's Failure to Protect the Rights of Unaccompanied
Migrant Children in the Canary Islands

**HUMAN
RIGHTS
WATCH**

MENOR
DE EDAD

CRUZ ROJA ESPAÑOLA

tions into allegations of mistreatment. The government responded that existing safeguards are sufficient.

There was a marked drop in arrivals by sea of irregular migrants—9,400 people in the first eight months of 2007 compared to 24,300 in the same period the previous year. Interception at sea, including by FRONTEX, and increased forced removals by Spain provide part of the explanation. By the end of August over 8,000 migrants had been removed. In July the Interior Ministry adopted new guidelines allowing for the use of straightjackets and helmets to restrain migrants resisting removal, after a Nigerian man died on a commercial flight while handcuffed and gagged.

A March agreement with Morocco on readmission of unaccompanied migrant children failed to include safeguards to protect children from potential harm and to ensure their best interests. Hundreds of unaccompanied migrant children continued to be housed in crowded emergency centers in the Canary Islands, where they were subjected to undue restrictions on freedom of movement, lack of access to public education, obstacles in applying for asylum, and instances of abuse and neglect by staff. The CPT included one of these centers in a September visit to Spain.

United Kingdom

Prime Minister Gordon Brown, who assumed office in June, was immediately tested by failed terrorist attacks in England and Scotland. Two men drove a burning car loaded with gas cylinders into the main terminal at Glasgow international airport on June 30. A day earlier, police discovered two car bombs in central London that had failed to explode. Of the seven people arrested in the UK in connection with the attacks, three were charged, three were released without charge, and one suspect died of burns sustained during the Glasgow attack. An eighth suspect was arrested in Australia but later released when Australian prosecutors dropped all charges.

In July the Brown government detailed new counterterrorism proposals, renewing the attempt to extend pre-charge detention beyond 28 days, already the longest in the EU. Other proposals included relaxing the prohibition on using intercept evidence in court, widening the already broad definition of terrorism, and enhancing sentences for ordinary criminal offenses when committed for a terrorist purpose. At this writing a bill has yet to be presented to Parliament.

Britain's highest court, the House of Lords Judicial Committee (Law Lords), ruled in October on four appeals relating to the system of control orders for terrorism suspects. The court held that orders based solely on secret evidence not properly disclosed to defendants violate the right to a fair hearing. It affirmed that orders confining suspects to their homes for 18 hours a day breached the right to liberty, but upheld the overall lawfulness of the control order regime, ruling that shorter periods are acceptable, and rejected arguments that the orders are criminal punishments.

Government figures showed that as of March more than half of all terrorism suspects arrested since September 2001 were released without charge. Nonetheless, several high-profile terrorism prosecutions ended in convictions in 2007. In July four men were sentenced to life imprisonment for conspiracy to murder in the failed attacks on London's transport system on July 21, 2005, while a fifth plotter was sentenced to 33 years in November. Five others were convicted in April and also sentenced to life for plotting to use fertilizer bombs against different targets. In June seven members of an alleged terrorist cell pled guilty to conspiracy to murder in 2006 and were sentenced to terms ranging from 15 to 26 years in prison.

Some prosecutions raised concerns about improper restrictions on free expression. In trials concluding in July, two men each tried separately and a group of five students tried together were sentenced to prison terms ranging from two to nine years for possession of terrorism-related documents. At this writing, two 17-year-olds face similar charges in ongoing cases. In the first trial of its kind in the UK, three men were given sentences, also in July, ranging from six-and-a-half to ten years after pleading guilty to inciting terrorism over the internet. Two men received eight and six-year jail terms, in October and November respectively, for distributing terrorist material and other terrorism offenses. In November the first woman to be convicted under the Terrorism Act was found guilty of possessing articles likely to be useful for terrorism, including the "Al Qaeda Manual."

Three men convicted in separate trials between November 2006 and July 2007 of soliciting to murder and incitement to racial hatred during a protest outside the Danish Embassy in London in February 2006, over the publication of offensive cartoons depicting the Prophet Muhammad, were each sentenced in July to six years in prison. A fourth man, convicted in February of incitement to racial hatred, was sentenced to four years.

UK efforts to deport foreign terrorism suspects on the basis of diplomatic assurances of humane treatment were delayed by challenges in the courts, with mixed results. In February the Special Immigration Appeals Commission (SIAC) ruled that Omar Othman (known as Abu Qatada) could be returned safely to Jordan under the terms of a memorandum of understanding negotiated with the UK in 2005. SIAC approved the deportation of another Jordanian in November on the same grounds, despite fresh evidence of torture in Jordan. The same court ruled in April, however, that two Libyan terrorism suspects risked torture and a "complete" denial of due process if deported, notwithstanding a similar 2005 memorandum agreed between London and Tripoli.

In July the Court of Appeal ordered the SIAC to reconsider its prior decisions to allow the deportation of three Algerians. The men were not permitted in court and the reasons for granting their appeals are secret, but the Court of Appeal accepted the SIACs conclusion that diplomatic assurances from Algeria would be effective. The SIAC ruled again in November that the men could be safely returned.

In a welcome reversal of policy, in August the UK officially requested the release from detention at Guantanamo Bay and return to the UK of Jamil al-Banna, a Jordanian with refugee status in the UK, and four other former UK residents. Another former UK resident, Bisher al-Rawi, was released and returned to the UK in April, after four years in Guantanamo.

GEORGIA

After several days of large-scale peaceful opposition demonstrations in November, the Georgian government initiated a violent crackdown on protesters, causing a serious human rights crisis. This crisis occurred in the context of an emerging but dominant view among the governing political elite and its supporters that short-term, supposedly minor sacrifices in human rights are justifiable to build a stronger state, which can better protect human rights in the long term. This approach, however, is leading Georgia away from international standards and represents a gamble with freedom. Prison conditions remain poor, and fair trial and property rights are restricted. Against international recommendations, in 2007 Georgia lowered the minimum age of criminal responsibility.

Freedom of Expression and Assembly

After several days of large-scale peaceful opposition protests in Tbilisi, the Georgian government initiated a violent crackdown on opposition protesters and instituted a nine-day state of emergency, saying that this was in response to a coup attempt. Riot police used excessive force to attack demonstrators, dispersing them with water cannons, large amounts of tear gas, and rubber bullets. Many policemen also beat individual protestors. According to official statistics over 550 protestors and 34 police were hospitalized with injuries. President Saakashvili announced snap presidential elections for January 2008, which helped diffuse the immediate political crisis.

According to the general prosecutor's office, 75 people were arrested for petty hooliganism and resisting police orders with regard to the November 7 events; of these, 21 were held in misdemeanor detention and 54 fined and released. In the lead-up and aftermath to the November 7 demonstration, unidentified attackers assaulted numerous opposition activists, and police detained several people on questionable charges such as hooliganism. For example, three activists from the Equality Institute, a human rights organization, and one from the youth wing of the opposition Republican Party were arrested during a peaceful protest in Tbilisi on October 16. On October 28 unidentified men, believed to be security officials, attacked protestors, injuring at least two severely, as they were leaving a demonstration in Zugdidi, a town in western Georgia. On November 8 police used excessive force to disperse students gathering in the Black Sea town of Batumi to protest the previous day's violence in Tbilisi.

On the evening of November 7 riot police raided the private Imedi television station, held the staff at gunpoint, destroyed archives, and smashed equipment. Both Imedi and another private station, Kavkasia, were taken off the air. The government then declared a state of emergency that lasted nine days, limiting freedom of assembly and banning all broadcast news programs except by the state-funded Georgian Public Broadcasting. The government lifted the state of emergency on November 16, but suspended Imedi's broadcasting license for three months.

The truncated pre-election period, the restrictions on assembly and media imposed during the state of emergency, and the absence of one of Georgia's key alternative media outlets all marred the pre-election campaign.

Prison Conditions

Despite a presidential pardon of 772 inmates in November 2007, overcrowding persists in almost all of Georgia's penitentiary facilities, leading to many human rights violations, including inadequate nutrition, medical care, and exercise. Although the courts began to use bail more frequently as a pretrial restraining measure, the number of prisoners rose monthly by an average of 400 in 2007. As of October 1, the prison population was 19,441, a 50 percent increase in one year, a result of the government's important crime-fighting campaign. The government's response to overcrowding has for the most part been to build new prisons, rather than explore more alternatives to pretrial custody. More inmates are expected to be released pursuant to an amnesty planned for the end of 2007. Its impact on overcrowding is unclear.

As of this writing, the government has not concluded an investigation into possible excessive use of force during the March 2006 disturbances in Tbilisi Prison No. 5, which resulted in the deaths of at least seven inmates and injuries to another 17.

Juvenile Justice

In May 2007 the government lowered the minimum age of criminal responsibility from 14 to 12 for certain crimes, further weakening the protection of children in conflict with the law. Although the decrease will come into effect in June 2008, Georgia has yet to build a juvenile justice system capable of rehabilitating young offenders.

A disturbance in the juvenile prison in August, which officials described as "a scuffle between several inmates," left at least 12 inmates and one guard injured. One hundred and seven children were transferred to a prison for adults where 64 remained for three months as punishment for the disturbance. They were deprived of the right to education and subjected to restrictions on meeting with their families.

Restrictions on Fair Trial

Thirteen persons from small opposition political organizations affiliated with fugitive ex-security chief Igor Giorgiadze were sentenced in August 2007 to prison terms of up to eight years and six months for plotting a coup. Citing witness protection needs the authorities closed the entire trial, thereby limiting public scrutiny of the evidence.

Irakli Batiashvili, leader of the very small opposition Forward Georgia movement, was sentenced to seven years' imprisonment in May 2007 for failing to report a crime and assisting a coup attempt by providing "intellectual support" to the leader of an illegal militia. Georgia's ombudsman, Sozar Subari, criticized the trial on the basis that the defense had inadequate access to the prosecution's evidence. For example, the defense was only given a transcript of tape recordings that were key to Batiashvili's conviction.

Restrictions on Property Rights

The government failed to adequately compensate owners for property confiscated for urban renewal or private development. Many cases related to property issues are pending in the courts.

In January and February 2007 the Tbilisi mayor's office confiscated and demolished small shops, booths, and stalls around metro stations and at other locations, saying they tarnished the city's image. In most cases the owners received verbal warnings, but their property was destroyed before they could challenge the demolition in court.

Another wave of property confiscations forced restaurant owners in Tbilisi and a nearby town to "voluntarily" hand over their property to the state or face criminal charges for obtaining their property through corrupt deals with officials during the era of former president Shevardnadze. In April 2007, several owners held a protest rally in Tbilisi, claiming that authorities pressured them into "gifting" their property to the state.

Residents of an apartment building in downtown Tbilisi were forcibly evicted by police in July 2007 after the city determined the building to have been built with construction violations. The building was demolished before residents could mount a court challenge. Residents believed that the reason for the eviction was the sale of the land to a foreign investor. They ultimately received a settlement from the investor which they believe is inadequate, and which they felt they were pressured into accepting.

In November 2007 the Georgian parliament passed a resolution instructing state agencies to cease probes into disputed properties, except in cases of "special interest" to the state. The effects of this resolution on property rights remain to be seen.

Key International Actors

Key actors made public statements condemning the November 7 violent dispersal of peaceful protestors. The US State Department and the Council of Europe called for the state of emergency to be lifted and media freedoms be restored; the European Union called for constructive dialogue between the government and the political opposition, NATO for restraint and respect for the rule of law, and UNHCHR expressed concern over the disproportionate use of force against the demonstrators.

But prior to the events, most international actors resisted robustly challenging Georgia's compromises on human rights. While calling for reform, they mostly gave the benefit of the doubt to a government that had come to power on the reform promise of the Rose Revolution, and that had a strong stated commitment to human rights and the rule of law. As part of the European Neighborhood Policy (ENP) Action Plan signed by the EU and Georgia in 2006, the two parties adopted a European Neighborhood Policy Instrument (ENPI) for financial assistance. The EU-Georgia Cooperation Council met in October 2007 to discuss the country's progress in the ENP implementation process, following which the EU "underlined the importance of ... protection of human rights and fundamental freedoms as essential elements in the EU-Georgia bilateral dialogue."

Matyas Eorsi and Kastriot Islami, co-rapporteurs of the Parliamentary Assembly of the Council of Europe's Monitoring Committee, called on the government to "fully restore the normal democratic practices and functioning of the institutions." They had also visited Georgia in September 2007, and commended the government for ratifying a number of Council of Europe instruments, but also called for reforms of the election code, judiciary, and penitentiary system. The co-rapporteurs made an urgent visit to Georgia in November following the government's November 7 crackdown on demonstrators.

An important, unambiguous statement about human rights in Georgia was the October report by the European Committee for the Prevention of Torture and Inhuman or Degrading Treatment (CPT), which noted progress in preventing ill-treatment of people in police custody, but stated that overcrowding is undermining any "efforts made to create a humane penitentiary system."

In its concluding observations on Georgia, in October 2007, the United Nations Human Rights Committee praised the government on legislative and institutional reform, while calling for improvements on a wide range of issues including improvement of prison conditions and promotion of freedom of speech.

The United States is one of Georgia's strongest allies and has openly supported Georgia's NATO aspirations. Prior to the November events, the US resisted publicly criticizing Georgia on its human rights record, though it did publicly call on the government to implement reforms on property rights, an independent judiciary, and the criminal procedural code.

Kazakhstan

Even though the Kazakhstan government launched a campaign to improve its image and establish itself as a prominent player in international politics, likely motivated by its bid for chairmanship of the Organization for Security and Cooperation in Europe (OSCE) in 2009, the human rights situation in the country remains poor. Despite considerable attention from the international community, in 2007 respect for human rights failed to improve, and according to Transparency International corruption in Kazakhstan significantly worsened.

While there were some minor improvements in legislation, there was little meaningful progress in civil and political rights protection. The lower chamber (*Majilis*) parliamentary elections were neither free nor fair, according to international observers. The government continued to stifle the political opposition and independent media.

Political Opposition

In May 2007 the Kazakh government passed an amendment to article 42 of the constitution, which prohibits more than two successive terms as president, paving the way for President Nursultan Nazarbaev to run for an unlimited number of terms. The constitutional amendment was condemned by the opposition, which was prevented by the police from demonstrating against it in Almaty. Sergei Duvanov, a journalist and the leader of the protest, was detained on May 24, held in police custody, and released later that day.

Other changes made to the constitution include an amendment to article 50, which increases the number of representatives in the *Majilis* from 77 to 107. This was ostensibly intended to give the parliament increased power and strengthen the role of opposition political parties, but has instead consolidated presidential power.

The government routinely misuses the criminal justice system against its political opponents. During 2007 a former member of the president's own family was the target of what appear to be politically-motivated charges. Rakhat Aliev, formerly the president's son-in-law until his recent divorce, who was considered at one time a possible successor to Nazarbaev, was dismissed as Kazakhstan's ambassador to Austria in May. He is now wanted in Kazakhstan on suspicion of having kidnapped and assaulted two employees of Nurbank, a commercial bank he partially owned. Austrian authorities refused to extradite Aliev because of fair trial concerns. His trial started in absentia on November 8.

The day after Aliev was charged, on May 28, the television station Kommerchesky Televizionny Kanal (KTK) and the weekly newspaper *Karavan,* both owned by Aliev, were ordered by an Almaty court to suspend operations. Aliev is currently seeking asylum in Austria.

Courts upheld a five-year sentence for Alibek Zhumabaev of the For a Just Kazakhstan Party for insulting the president in May 2006. Activists promoting free speech in Kazakhstan have called for Zhumabaev's release.

Elections

In *Majilis* elections held on August 18, Kazakhstan's ruling party, Nur Otan, won 88 percent of the vote. No opposition parties cleared the 7 percent threshold to win seats. Opposition leaders denounced the elections as fraudulent and called for new elections in an August 28 letter to the president. The OSCE said the elections reflected some democratic progress but still fell short of international standards.

President Nursultan Nazarbaev brushed off all criticism and claimed that the one-party parliament was a "wonderful opportunity to adopt all the laws needed to speed up our country's economic and political modernization."

Two opposition parties, Nagyz Ak Zhol and the National Social Democratic party, merged in June ahead of the August elections, but still failed to gain any seats in *Majilis*. The Social Democratic Party was registered in January, three months after it had applied. The Alga! (Forward!) Party and the Atameken (Homeland) Party were not able to register.

Freedom of Press

Although Kazakhstan's laws guarantee the media the right to report on political events, the independent media continues to be threatened and harassed for criticizing the president or government, and journalists run serious risks.

For example, Oralgaisha Omarshanova, an independent journalist working on corruption for the weekly publication *Zakon i Pravosudiye* (Law and Justice), was reported missing March 30. At this writing her whereabouts remain unknown.

Saken Tauzhanov, a journalist for several opposition websites was killed in a traffic accident on August 2. While the authorities concluded that Tauzhanov's death was a routine accident, some observers called for an investigation, pointing to the fact that at least six journalists have died in similar circumstances since 2002 and raising concern that they may have been targeted because of their political reporting.

Criminal libel laws are routinely used against opposition media. For example, in January 2007 Kaziz Toguzbayev, a reporter for the independent newspaper *Azat*, was given a two-year suspended sentence for "insulting the honor and dignity" of President Nazarbaev in two articles he published on the website *Kub* in April and May 2006.

Also in January, government officials in the city of Uralsk began to harass the newspaper *Uralskaya Nedelya* after the paper published a series of articles on local government corruption. Government officials repeatedly threatened local printing houses that they would be shut down if they printed or distributed the paper. Ultimately, the paper had to be printed outside the region.

The government continues to censor the internet and in 2007 "deregistered" or suspended several websites. The government also blocked several opposition websites that reported on Nazarbaev's feud with Rakhat Aliev.

HIV/AIDS

The HIV/AIDS epidemic in Kazakhstan, one of the fastest-growing in the world, continues to accelerate, despite a US$53 million government program for 2006-

2010 to fight the epidemic. There were 1,165 new cases of HIV/AIDS in the first half of 2007, compared to 958 cases for the same period in 2006.

The government has failed to take steps to end the human rights abuses that fuel the epidemic. Most infections are among injecting drug users and commercial sex workers, who face widespread stigmatization, police harassment and brutality, and false criminal charges. These abuses decrease the likelihood that such groups will access preventive and post-infection services; they are often denied humane medical treatment.

Uzbek Refugees

The Kazakh government admitted in August 2007 that in November 2005 security forces had forcibly returned nine Uzbeks who had fled persecution to Uzbekistan. Of the group, also known as the "Shymkent 9," four had been registered with the Kazakh office of United Nations High Commissioner for Refugees (UNHCR). While the government's admission is welcome, the authorities have still taken no steps to hold those responsible to account.

Key International Actors

Kazakhstan's bid for the OSCE chairmanship for 2009 has been the dominant recent theme in its international relations. After failing to come to a consensus on the issue in 2006, the OSCE in late November 2007 awarded Kazakhstan the chairmanship for 2010, despite the country's failure to improve its human rights situation. Opinions differed among Kazakhstan's international partners—the UK and the Czech Republic pointed to deteriorating political and social freedoms in the country to say that Kazakhstan was not appropriate for the role—while Germany took the lead in supporting Kazakhstan's bid, along with Russia and the Commonwealth of Independent States. The US, which initially opposed the bid, wavered on the issue and ultimately supported the chairmanship in exchange for commitments by Kazakhstan not to undermine the autonomy of the OSCE's Office for Democratic Institutions and Human Rights (ODIHR), as well as to reform its election law and to ease restrictions on political parties and the media.

In February ODIHR made public statements urging Kazakhstan to make progress on fair trial standards, including allowing the public to attend court hearings, equality between the parties, and the presumption of innocence. In March it called on the government to stop a draft amendment that would require all printing presses to be licensed.

Meeting in late April with Kazakh Prime Minister Karim Massimov and other officials in Astana, United Nations High Commissioner for Human Rights Louise Arbour pushed for Kazakhstan to adopt the optional protocol to the Convention Against Torture and the Convention for the Protection of Migrant Workers. Both Arbour and the OSCE called for increased media freedoms and for the decriminalization of libel.

The EU adopted a Central Asia Strategy in June, setting out its ambition to deepen cooperation with the region. While, in contrast to earlier drafts, the final strategy acknowledged the centrality of human rights in the EU's relations with the region, it fell short of formulating specific benchmarks for improvement the EU would seek as part of its engagement.

The UN high commissioner on refugees, Antonio Guterres, met with President Nazarbaev in mid-November 2007, calling for a national mechanism to give refugees protection and for the country to cooperate more fully with international practices.

The UN Committee on the Rights of the Child conducted a review of Kazakhstan in May, and was critical of the government for failing to address the economic exploitation, sexual exploitation, and trafficking of children, among other issues.

KYRGYZSTAN

The government of President Kurmanbek Bakiev, who came to power after the March 2005 "tulip revolution," largely abandoned a democratic reform agenda in 2007. Constitutional reform has been impeded by a power struggle between parliament and the president, which Bakiev sought to resolve by calling parliamentary elections for December. The year was characterized by a dramatic increase in politically motivated prosecutions of civil society and opposition activists, as well as the murder of an independent journalist.

Constitutional Reform and Referendum

On September 14 the Constitutional Court nullified constitutional amendments adopted in November–December 2006. The decision prompted parliament to adopt a vote of no confidence in the court. The next day President Bakiev put forward a new version of the constitution and electoral code, which were adopted in a referendum on October 21. Bakiev then dissolved parliament, in a clear attempt to consolidate presidential power. New parliamentary elections are scheduled for December 16.

According to official data, over 81 percent of voters took part in the October referendum, and approximately 76 percent voted in favor of the proposed constitutional changes. Independent domestic monitors, however, concluded that voter participation had not reached the 50 percent required by law. There were significant violations during the voting, including massive ballot stuffing by members of the precinct election commissions and voting with fraudulent identification documents. Referendum observers in several cities reported being threatened by representatives of local government and precinct commissions.

Prosecution of Civil Society Activists

Valentina Gritzenko, chairperson of the board of the nongovernmental organization (NGO) Justice, and her two colleagues Abdumalik Sharipov and Mamadjan Abdujaparov, continue to stand trial for libel, in a case initiated in 2006 by a senior investigator of Jalalabat's Department of Interior. The charges against them are based on Justice's report alleging the investigator's involvement in the ill-treatment of a pregnant woman.

On April 19, 2007, opposition demonstrations in the capital Bishkek calling for constitutional reform and for Bakiev's resignation were dispersed by police. The State Committee of National Security detained and interrogated dozens of protesters. Several leaders of the opposition movement United Front were charged with organizing mass disturbances, but the charges were ultimately dropped; however, four members of the movement were convicted on what appear to be politically motivated charges. Adilet Aitikeev of the youth movement Kanzhar, who had initially been arrested in April and then released on condition that he not leave the country, was re-arrested on October 25, allegedly for having violated the terms of his release. He is currently in detention awaiting trial.

In May charges were brought against 11 individuals, including eight environmental activists, opposing the development of gold mines in Talas province. The charges, which include "assault against a government official," were initiated as a result of protests that occurred during a visit of then-Prime Minister Almazbek Atambaev on May 26 to Talas. The activists face up to 10 years' imprisonment if found guilty. Six of the activists fled Kyrgyzstan and are seeking asylum abroad.

On several occasions authorities prevented protestors from reaching the site of a demonstration, confiscated posters, temporarily seized equipment, and sentenced organizers for administrative misdemeanors on what appear to be politically motivated grounds. The leader of the Green party, journalist Erkin Bulekbaev, was arrested on August 10 while filming a police operation at the Issyk-Kul Investbank in Bishkek and sentenced to 10 days' imprisonment for "petty hooliganism." The appellate court reduced his sentence to six days' imprisonment. On October 18 police searched the office of the Green party and confiscated leaflets printed for a planned demonstration. On November 30 Bishkek City Council adopted new rules for holding demonstrations in the city: only three sites were approved for demonstrations; notification must be submitted 10 days in advance; and fees are imposed on the organizers to ensure order during the demonstration.

Media Freedom

The authorities' interference with independent media intensified during 2007 and reached a peak during the April protests. Between March 1 and April 20 the NGO "Journalists" counted more than 20 threats and assaults against independent media, including physical attacks on journalists and the seizure of entire editions of the opposition newspapers *Agym* and *Kyrgyz Rukhu*. Aziz Egemberdiev, a journalist with the 24.kg news agency, was severely beaten during the April protests in Bishkek and hospitalized with concussion; the assailant's identity remains unknown.

On October 24 Alisher Saipov, an independent journalist who criticized human rights abuses in Kyrgyzstan and neighboring Uzbekistan, was shot dead in the southern city of Osh. President Bakiev announced that he had taken the investigation into Saipov's murder under his personal control, but at this writing no arrests have been made.

Parliament failed to adopt legislation to decriminalize libel, maintaining provisions in Kyrgyz law that provide for up to three years' imprisonment for libel and slander. On a positive note, a law was adopted in April to transform the National Television and Radio Corporation (NTRC) into a public broadcasting entity, and the new advisory board to the NTRC was created.

Persecution of Independent Muslims

The government intensified its persecution of independent Muslims. Law enforcement bodies repeatedly brought criminal charges against individuals for "fostering religious hatred," often simply because they possessed leaflets of Hizb ut-Tahrir, an Islamic organization banned in Kyrgyzstan. On August 1 and August 2 police raided the homes of Muslim families in Jalalabat province. The Air NGO documented at least four cases in which police used excessive force and beat individuals suspected of involvement in Hizb ut-Tahrir during the raids.

On June 1 Kyrgyzstan secretly returned Otabek Muminov, a suspected Hizb ut-Tahrir member, to Uzbekistan, despite his facing a high risk of torture or other ill-treatment there. On the same day another Uzbek citizen allegedly related to Hizb ut-Tahrir, Mukimzhan Makhmudov, was arrested by security forces in Kyrgyzstan; he was released on August 9 by order of an appellate court.

Judicial Reform

The death penalty was formally abolished in June. A new law introducing life imprisonment only provides for possibility of parole after the person has served at least 30 years. The fate of more than 170 persons on death row remains unresolved.

Other legislative amendments in June included introducing judicial review of detention; improving lawyers' access to their clients in detention; and creating a framework for jury trials. An amendment that requires an acquitted person to remain in detention for an additional 10 days until the verdict enters into force was troubling.

Deaths in Custody

At least two cases of death in custody were reported during 2007, both in the town of Naryn. Bektemir Akunov, a participant in the April protests in Bishkek, was arrested after returning from the capital and was found dead in his cell the next morning. Police claimed the death was a suicide. However, two policemen stand accused of "negligence"; the case has been sent back for additional investigation. No criminal investigation has been launched into the August death of Kurmanbek Kalmatov.

Violence against Women

Violence against women, including domestic violence and kidnapping of women and girls for forced marriage, is on the rise. The authorities have not yet developed a systematic approach to stop this negative trend and deal with the problem more effectively. There were some indications of growing willingness to enforce the laws against forced marriage: countrywide in the first nine months of 2007, 15 cases involving forced marriage were brought to court, and in all cases the defendant was found guilty. The courts dealt with only three cases addressing domestic violence, however; the defendants in each case received a fine.

Key International Actors

Kyrgyzstan continues to develop and balance relations with the European Union, the United States, Russia, China, and its neighbors in Central Asia.

A key international event in 2007 was the Summit of the Shanghai Cooperation Organization (SCO) in Bishkek on August 16. The participants pledged to intensify the fight against terrorism, separatism, and extremism, including the search for, and detention and return of suspects. In July SCO representatives compiled a list of religious organizations deemed "extremist" and that are banned in the SCO states. The SCO did not make the full list public, nor did it specify the criteria by which organizations were characterized as "extremist."

Strong debates on the future of the US military presence in Kyrgyzstan were prompted by the December 2006 killing of a Kyrgyz citizen, Alexandr Ivanov, by an American serviceman. The US Millennium Challenge Corporation on August 9, 2007, approved Kyrgyzstan's participation in its Threshold Program, under which the US will provide some US$16 million in assistance to help the government to "address judicial, criminal justice and law enforcement reforms." In September a US-Kyrgyz Comprehensive Policy Dialogue was inaugurated, intended to "bring bilateral relations to a new level."

The EU's first-ever Central Asia Strategy adopted in June acknowledges human rights as one of its priorities but falls short of formulating country-specific benchmarks. The focus on vaguely worded "human rights dialogues" raises doubts about the effectiveness of the EU's approach in addressing human rights concerns. The European Bank for Reconstruction and Development adopted a new country strategy for Kyrgyzstan in June, hailing the country's political pluralism but acknowledging a range of problems such as poverty, deep-seated corruption, nepotism, child labor, trafficking, and discrimination.

The UN Committee on the Elimination of Racial Discrimination, which reviewed Kyrgyzstan in August, highlighted numerous shortcomings in the government's record, including in relation to its asylum procedures, and urged the government to ensure its asylum procedures are not applied in a discriminatory manner and to respect the principle of *nonrefoulement*.

RUSSIA

As parliamentary and presidential elections in late 2007 and early 2008 approached, the administration headed by President Vladimir Putin cracked down on civil society and freedom of assembly. Reconstruction in Chechnya did not mask grave human rights abuses including torture, abductions, and unlawful detentions.

International criticism of Russia's human rights record remains muted, with the European Union failing to challenge Russia on its human rights record in a consistent and sustained manner.

Elections and Political Participation

In 2007 Russian authorities beat, detained, and harassed activists participating in and planning peaceful political protests. Authorities banned or severely restricted a series of opposition demonstrations known as "Dissenters' Marches," which were nonetheless held across Russia. In April riot police and special forces used excessive force to break up a Moscow Dissenters' March, beating numerous demonstrators and detaining hundreds. Authorities prevented activists and observers from traveling to Samara to participate in a May Dissenters' March, which coincided with the EU-Russia summit held there.

In November the Office for Democratic Institutions and Human Rights of the Organization for Security and Co-operation in Europe cancelled its mission to observe Russia's December 2 parliamentary elections, citing operational concerns. The Russian government had imposed unprecedented restrictions on the size of the mission and did not issue visas to observers in a timely manner.

Also in November, riot police used excessive force to disperse Dissenters' Marches in Moscow and St. Petersburg, and made arrests. Among those detained were several march organizers and prominent opposition candidates including Garry Kasparov, leader of the Other Russia coalition, who subsequently received a five-day prison sentence.

In late November Farid Babaev, a human rights activist and opposition parliamentary candidate from Dagestan, was shot dead by unidentified assailants.

Civil Society

The government is tightening controls over civil society through new legislation, interference with peaceful assembly, and harassment of nongovernmental organizations (NGOs) and government critics.

The 2006 NGO law increased government oversight and restrictions on NGOs. It requires NGOs to submit regular activity reports or face liquidation, and allows intrusive and punitive inspections that often result in warnings for minor, technical violations. Two warnings lead to liquidation even if the organization corrects the violation.

The Registration Service demanded the liquidation of several NGOs for failure to provide timely activity reports. For example, in June 2007 a court in Nizhni Novgorod ordered the liquidation of the Youth Human Rights Movement (YHRM) for this failure, even though the organization submitted the reports as prescribed by law. The YHRM is appealing the liquidation.

During a two-month inspection of the St. Petersburg rights organization Citizens' Watch, the Registration Service demanded all of the organization's outgoing correspondence, including that containing confidential information. In April police conducted an 11-hour search of the Educated Media Foundation (EMF) in Moscow, a prominent media training organization, seizing all financial documents and computers. Police linked the search to criminal proceedings against EMF's director for failing to declare excess cash on returning to Russia, a violation ordinarily treated as an administrative offense. In July, after a court refused to return the confiscated items, the organization could no longer function and was forced to liquidate. Similarly, in August Federal Security Service agents searched the Nizhni Novgorod Center for Assistance to Migrants in connection with criminal charges of document forgery against the center's head. Agents confiscated financial documents, computer equipment, and archives, paralyzing the center's work.

In August new amendments to the Law on Extremism entered into force, prohibiting the media from mentioning any group found by a court to be extremist with-

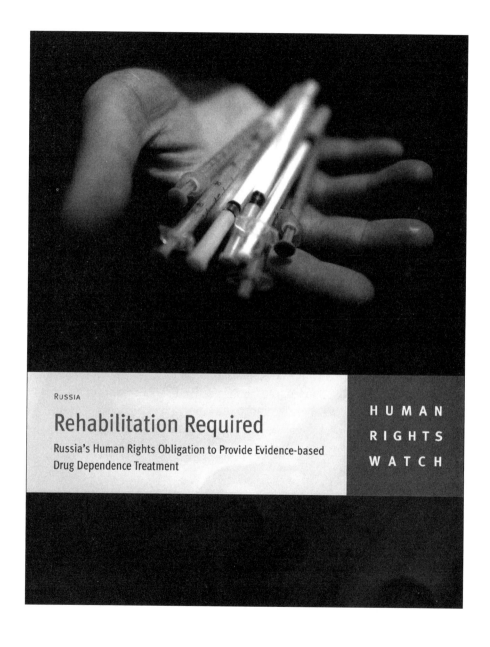

RUSSIA

Rehabilitation Required

Russia's Human Rights Obligation to Provide Evidence-based
Drug Dependence Treatment

H U M A N
R I G H T S
W A T C H

out referencing the court's designation. The amendments also allow any political-ly or ideologically-motivated crime to be designated extremist, raising concerns that the law will be used to silence critics of the government.

The Prosecutor General's Office arrested three suspects for the 2006 murder of investigative journalist Anna Politkovskaia, but serious questions remain about the case, which officials claim was organized by "opponents abroad." The defen-dants' lawyers do not have access to the case materials.

On May 27 several dozen Russian lesbian, gay, bisexual, and transgender people, and their supporters, tried to hold a peaceful demonstration outside Moscow's City Hall. Police arrested 21 demonstrators and observers as the event's organiz-ers attempted to deliver a petition to the mayor's office protesting its ban on a gay pride parade, which Moscow Mayor Yury Luzhkov had declared "satanic." Dozens of anti-gay protesters, including skinheads, nationalists, and Russian Orthodox adherents, beat and kicked peaceful participants as riot police stood by.

Moscow city police announced that it would recruit volunteers from the pro-Kremlin youth group Nashi (Ours) to patrol Moscow streets, including at demon-strations and opposition events. Members of Nashi have stated that they will mobilize Nashi patrols to prevent "destabilization" of the country from opposition groups. Federal Migration Service (FMS) officials also used members of a nation-alist youth group called Mestnye (Locals) to find and detain migrants allegedly working illegally at a Moscow market. The head of the FMS announced that it would continue collaboration with Mestnye.

The North Caucasus

Ramzan Kadyrov, a former security chief, became president of Chechnya and is presiding over significant reconstruction of civilian infrastructure, changing the face of Grozny, the capital. Russian federal and Chechen officials have claimed that the conflict in Chechnya is "solved," though sporadic armed clashes and counterinsurgency operations continue. These are carried out chiefly by forces under Kadyrov's command, known as "kadyrovtsy," who torture those suspected

Singled Out

Russia's Detention and Expulsion of Georgians

HUMAN
RIGHTS
WATCH

of ties to rebels and hold them in unlawful detention, including in secret detention centers.

Local human rights groups continued to report a decline in the number of enforced disappearances, documenting 25 abductions leading to five disappearances by August 2007. However, few efforts have been made to address the cases of as many as 5,000 people "disappeared" since 1999.

In November uniformed and masked men in Nazran, Ingushetia, robbed, kidnapped, and brutally beat Oleg Orlov, leader of prominent human rights organization Memorial, and three television journalists, before leaving them at the border with Chechnya.

Violence continued elsewhere in the North Caucasus, with armed clashes between rebels and police in Ingushetia and Dagestan. In October the trial of 59 alleged participants of the 2005 Nalchik uprising, in Kabardino-Balkaria, began. Many of the defendants have alleged torture and other abuses while in custody.

Entrenched Problems

Denial of food and other abuses against conscripts continue in the armed forces, with several horrific cases in 2007 underscoring the government's failure to sufficiently acknowledge or address the problem. After one conscript was severely beaten and not given timely medical care, later requiring multiple transplants, the minister of defense denied that the violence exemplified a broader problem. The rare prosecutions in such cases are not proportional to the scope of violent hazing, which results in the death of dozens of young soldiers every year and serious injuries to thousands more. Many conscripts commit or attempt suicide and thousands defect from their units to escape harm. In October the term of conscription was reduced from two years to 18 months.

While Russia continues to make progress in making antiretroviral treatment (ART) available to people living with HIV, a disproportionately low number of HIV-positive injection drug users receives such treatment. The ban on the use of substitution therapy in treating injection drug users and, more generally, the poor quality of drug dependence treatment at state clinics are key barriers to improving injection drug users' access to ART.

Key International Actors

While many global leaders expressed concern over developments in Russia, such as restrictions on civil society, human rights issues remain on the margins of Russia's bilateral and multilateral relations, with many key interlocutors failing to press Russia to reform or to challenge it on continuing problems, especially Chechnya.

The EU held two rounds of human rights consultations with Russia, meetings ultimately undermined by the lack of high-level Russian participation and adequate follow-up mechanisms. Human rights did not figure prominently in the broader EU-Russia agenda. Although the German EU presidency raised human rights issues at the May EU-Russia summit, particularly around freedom of assembly, this stance was compromised by subsequent statements made by the Portuguese presidency equating the raising of human rights issues with inappropriate "lecturing." Due to a standstill over concerns unrelated to human rights, the EU made no progress on strengthening the human rights component of its Partnership and Cooperation Agreement with Russia, set to expire in December 2007.

The United States government issued several strong statements on human rights but lacked the leverage to challenge Russia meaningfully on its worsening human rights record.

Russia has served on the new United Nations Human Rights Council since its inception in May 2006. However, the government has not fulfilled its obligation to cooperate fully with UN human rights mechanisms, including the UN special rapporteur on torture, who has remained unable to visit the country due to the government's continued failure to allow a visit in accordance with the mandate's terms of reference.

In March 2007 the European Committee for the Prevention of Torture (CPT) took the rare step of issuing a public statement on its 2006 visits to the North Caucasus, expressing concern about torture, unlawful detention, and a failure to investigate allegations of abuses, as well as lack of cooperation and improvements by Russia. Russia remains the only Council of Europe member state that regularly fails to voluntarily allow the publication of the CPT's reports. The

Parliamentary Assembly of the Council of Europe failed to reverse its misguided 2006 decision to discontinue the assembly's monitoring mandate on Chechnya.

2007 proved a landmark year for international justice on Chechnya. Unable to secure justice domestically, hundreds of victims of abuse have filed applications with the European Court of Human Rights (ECtHR). In 11 rulings to date, the ECtHR found Russia responsible for serious human rights abuses in Chechnya, including torture, extrajudicial executions, and enforced disappearances. In every ruling the court has found a failure by the Russian government to launch a meaningful investigation. Russia has taken insufficient steps to implement the general measures recommended by the ECtHR to remedy systemic problems and prevent the reoccurrence of abuses. Russia remains the only Council of Europe member not to have ratified Protocol 14 of the court's charter, which would streamline the court's procedures and reduce backlog.

SERBIA

The government formed in May 2007 signaled a greater willingness to address accountability for war crimes, although it failed to deliver to justice the most wanted suspect, Ratko Mladic. There was less progress on other human rights issues: the situation of ethnic and religious minorities remains of concern, and independent journalists face threats and violence.

War Crimes Accountability

Serbia improved its cooperation with the International Criminal Tribunal for the former Yugoslavia (ICTY). The apprehension in May of Bosnian Serb army general Zdravko Tolimir near Bosnia's border with Serbia followed Serbian collaboration with Bosnian authorities and EU peacekeepers in Bosnia. Similar collaboration between Serbia and Montenegrin authorities contributed to the apprehension of former Yugoslav Army general Vlastimir Djordjevic in Budva, Montenegro in June. ICTY Chief Prosecutor Carla Del Ponte positively assessed the two arrests and the government's handover of long-requested files related to ongoing cases, during her visit to Belgrade in June. After reporting a subsequent dip in cooperation, she gave an upbeat assessment in November.

Indicted war crimes suspect and Bosnian Serb general Ratko Mladic remained at large in Serbia, despite repeated commitments from Belgrade that he would be brought to justice.

Prosecutions continued at the ICTY in a number of high-profile cases involving former Yugoslav and Serbian army and government officials, including Dragoljub Ojdanic, Sreten Lukic, Milan Milutinovic, Nikola Sainovic, Nebojsa Pavkovic, and Vladimir Lazarevic. The Serbian public's largely negative perceptions of the institution and its work remain.

The Belgrade War Crimes Chamber continued efforts to create accountability for wartime abuses, despite limited funding, political support, and public awareness of its work. In April the chamber convicted four former members of the "Scorpions" paramilitary unit filmed participating in the 1995 killing of six Bosniaks (Bosnian Muslims), sentencing two to 20 years' imprisonment and the others to 15 and five years; a fifth defendant was acquitted. The court's finding that the crimes were an isolated incident, the relatively short sentences, and the acquittal, provoked anger from the relatives of the victims and some nongovernmental organizations. The war crimes prosecutor has appealed against the acquittal and the five-year sentence.

Notable ongoing prosecutions included the "Suva Reka" trial—related to the killing of Kosovo Albanian civilians in 1999—and the "Zvornik" trial, in which former Serbian paramilitaries are charged with the killing of Bosniak civilians in 1992. At this writing around 35 further cases remain in the pretrial or investigative stage, most relating to killings of non-Serbs by Serbs in Bosnia, Croatia, and Kosovo. Significant improvements were made in the field of cooperation with other countries (the joint investigation with Bosnia in the "Zvornik" case being a notable example). There were improvements to witness protection, allowing witnesses to give evidence remotely or with their identities concealed, and to outreach efforts.

In December 2006 the Supreme Court controversially overturned the chamber's ruling in the "Ovcara" case (in which 14 people were convicted for the 1991 murder of 200 non-Serbs in Vukovar, Croatia), ordering a retrial. In April it affirmed the conviction of Kosovo Albanian Anton Lekaj for the 1999 murder and torture of Roma in Kosovo.

In February 2007 the International Court of Justice rendered judgment in the case of *Bosnia and Herzegovina v. Serbia and Montenegro*, the first-ever ruling on the application of the 1948 Genocide Convention. While finding that Serbia was not directly responsible for genocide during the Bosnian war, the court determined that Serbia was in continuing breach of its obligations under the Genocide Convention to prevent and punish genocide, including by its failure to arrest Ratko Mladic and cooperate fully with the ICTY.

Administration of Justice

There were ongoing reports of political interference in the work of prosecutors. Nevertheless, the verdict in the former Prime Minister Zoran Djindjic assassination trial, delivered on May 23, demonstrated the courage of prosecutors and judges, who managed to bring 12 individuals to justice despite political pressure and threats. Milorad "Legija" Lukovic-Ulemek, the most prominent figure among the accused, was sentenced to 40 years' imprisonment.

Treatment of Minorities

There was limited progress toward improving the status of the Albanian minority in southern Serbia and Bosniaks in Sandzak, despite Serbia's welcome ratification of the European Charter of Self-Government in September. Negotiations continued over increasing budgetary control for minority-run municipalities, improving minority input into school curricula, and greater official use of minority languages. In a positive development, textbooks in five minority languages were approved for use in state schools.

Roma continued to face substandard economic and social conditions as well as instances of verbal abuse and physical assault. In August around 100 Serbian Roma were caught crossing illegally into Romania. The group claimed asylum, saying they had fled harassment and ill-treatment in Serbia. In April the Belgrade Municipal Court handed down a six-month suspended sentence to a nightclub doorman for racial discrimination after he denied three Roma access to a club.

More than 30 attacks on religious minorities were recorded during the year. Churches, cemeteries, and religious community centers were damaged or desecrated across Serbia, with Catholic, Jewish, Protestant, and Muslim communities targeted, as well as Jehovah's Witnesses and Hare Krishna devotees. The Serbian government usually condemned these attacks, and the police opened investigations in most cases, but few led to perpetrators being punished.

Internally Displaced Persons and Refugees

With large numbers of internally displaced persons (around 208,000) and refugees (around 106,000), Serbia has one of the highest proportions of displaced people among its population in Europe. Around 6,000 displaced persons from Bosnia, Croatia, and Kosovo remain in collective centers, often in substandard conditions. IDPs and refugees continue to experience severe problems with obtaining documentation, and accessing housing and employment. Elderly and unaccompanied child IDPs and refugees are particularly vulnerable.

Forced removals of Roma from Western Europe continued, including Kosovo Roma sent to other parts of Serbia, placing a burden on the already limited resources within Roma communities in the absence of any programs to assist forced returnees.

Media Freedom

Independent journalists faced threats and violence. In April a hand grenade exploded outside an apartment of Dejan Anastasijevic from the *Vreme* daily newspaper. The same month Dinko Gruhonjic from the Beta news agency received death threats from nationalist organization Nacjonalni Stroj. In August Stefan Cvetkovic from the radio-TV station TNT received an anonymous death threat. The police opened investigations into these incidents, but at this writing no one has been charged. All three journalists are renowned for their high-quality journalism and willingness to tackle difficult topics, including organized crime. There was no progress in solving earlier murders of journalists, including Slavko Curuvija in 1999 and Milan Pantic in 2001.

Human Rights Defenders

In July neo-Nazis repeatedly attacked young human rights activists from Serbia, Bosnia, and Croatia during a "Caravan of Differences" peace and tolerance festival in Novi Sad. According to the organizers, Youth Initiative for Human Rights, the police failed to provide security despite several requests. In September 2007 President Boris Tadic pardoned a member of the same group, Maja Stojanovic, following her 2005 conviction for unauthorized public display of posters urging Ratko Mladic's arrest.

Key International Actors

After the ICTY prosecutor's November assessment, European Union Enlargement Commissioner Olli Rehn initialed a Stabilization and Association Agreement (SAA) with Serbia the same month. The EU had resumed negotiations with the SAA in

June after suspending them for over a year because of Belgrade's failure to hand over Ratko Mladic and otherwise to cooperate with the ICTY. The resumption drew criticism from the human rights community as unjustified and premature, given Serbian authorities' continued failure to transfer Mladic to The Hague. The EU indicated that signing of the SAA would still depend on full cooperation with the ICTY, despite some member states arguing for a more lenient approach.

Serbia's admission to the NATO Partnership for Peace program in December 2006 drew criticism for rewarding Serbia while Mladic remained at large. Proponents claimed it would stimulate long-awaited reforms in the army, aimed at introducing more democratic oversight and transparency into the institution.

Russia's veto threat in the United Nations Security Council derailed the UN-backed settlement for Kosovo (see also below). Russia's unqualified support for Serbia's position in the status process, and the scale of its investment helped to cement its renewed influence in Serbia.

Kosovo

Kosovo's final status negotiations overshadowed its bleak human rights situation. Minorities continued to face violence, intimidation, discrimination, and difficulties accessing public services. There was limited progress on the return of displaced persons and refugees to their homes. Weaknesses in the criminal justice system frustrated efforts to create accountability. Elections to the Kosovo Assembly (parliament) took place on November 17. Many Serbs heeded Belgrade's call to boycott.

Protection of Minorities

Roma, Ashkali, and Egyptian (RAE) communities remain the most vulnerable and marginalized in Kosovo. Their political, economic, and social demands were largely ignored during the final status negotiations. RAE face persistent discrimination, particularly in employment and access to public services, and have the highest unemployment, school drop-out, and mortality rates in the province. Measures to improve their access to education were inadequate.

Violence against minorities continued, although the number of registered cases continued to fall. The decline reflected the geographic separation of communities and the practice of classifying offenses as "regular crimes" before ethnic motivation is determined. In April a bus carrying Kosovo Serbs was stoned in Rudnik, and the same happened to a train in Lipjan carrying Serbs in August. In March a mortar-grenade was detonated in the vicinity of the Visoki Decani Serbian Orthodox monastery. Six Serbian Orthodox churches and monasteries experienced lesser incidents. Overall, almost 200 inter-ethnic incidents have been registered in 2007 at this writing, most in ethnically mixed locations, with robbery, threats, and assault being most common. The victims were mainly Kosovo Serbs, but Bosniaks, Roma, Croats, and Montenegrins were also affected.

Return of Refugees and Displaced Persons

The number of voluntary returns to Kosovo, including from Serbia, remains small. In the first half of 2007, 308 persons were registered as voluntary returnees.

Internally displaced RAE inside Kosovo are a target group for organized return. Plementina, one of the largest RAE camps in Kosovo, was largely dismantled during 2007, with the majority of its inhabitants moved to newly constructed housing located close to the camp in Obilic municipality. Fifty-seven families returned in September and October from the lead-contaminated area near the Trepca mine to South Mitrovica's "Roma Mahalla," the first returns to the area since 1999. While there were no reports of violence against returnees during 2007, those who returned were subject to verbal harassment. Around 800 RAE remain displaced in Kosovo, with thousands more in Serbia.

Forced returns to Kosovo continued. Some 1,900 individuals, around 10 percent of them from RAE communities, have been forcibly returned to Kosovo in 2007 from Western European countries at this writing. They include more than 550 people, the majority ethnic Albanian, returned from Germany under a 2004 readmission agreement between the UN Interim Administration in Kosovo (UNMIK) and the German government.

UNHCR guidelines indicate that Serbs, Roma, and Albanians risk persecution if returned to areas where they would be in a minority. While the guidelines assess that Ashkali and Egyptians are generally not at risk on return, those subject to forced return are ineligible for international or local assistance, imposing a significant burden on the already limited resources of existing RAE communities. In November the provisional government and UNMIK agreed a draft readmission and reintegration policy covering forced returns to Kosovo. At this writing it awaits parliamentary approval.

Impunity and Access to Justice

Kosovo's criminal justice system remains its weakest governmental institution, despite ongoing reform efforts. Coordination between international and local judges and prosecutors is insufficient, despite attempts to provide mentoring and foster collaboration. Implementation of an electronic case management system remains poor, with court staff reluctant to use it. Oversight by the newly created Kosovo Judicial Council of local judges and prosecutors has improved accountability, but international judges and prosecutors remain answerable only to the special representative of the UN secretary-general (SRSG). The absence of designated judicial police hampers the ability of the Kosovo Police Service to meaningfully assist prosecutors.

Inadequate witness protection has created mistrust and a reluctance to cooperate with prosecutors. Arrangements for protection continue to be made on an ad hoc basis while comprehensive legislation is drafted. Reluctance on the part of Western governments to host witnesses and their families hampers witness relocation. Progress has, however, been made in supplying all regional courts with booths, video links, and other means to disguise the voices and identities of witnesses.

There was belated progress in bringing to justice persons involved in the March 2004 riots. During the first eight months of 2007, 29 defendants were convicted on charges of arson, looting, inciting racial, religious and ethnic hatred, and assault, in cases managed mainly by international prosecutors. Twelve of the convicted received prison terms ranging from six months to 18 years. One suspect was acquitted. At this writing, seven additional defendants awaited trial.

There was movement on several notorious crimes against minorities. In October the trial of Florim Ejupi, the main suspect in the February 2001 "Nis Express" bus bombing, began in the Pristina District Court. Ejupi is accused of blowing up a bus full of Serbs in Kosovo, killing 10 people and injuring 40. Also in October UNMIK police arrested an ethnic Albanian man suspected of the 1999 killing of 14 Serb farmers in the village of Staro Gracko.

UNMIK's lack of accountability was highlighted in February when a Romanian police unit, acting under the command of UNMIK police, responded to a violent protest with rubber bullets and teargas, killing two protesters and injuring many others. The UNMIK police commissioner subsequently resigned, but an international investigation led by the UNMIK chief prosecutor was unable to assign criminal responsibility for the deaths. After initially good cooperation, the Romanian police contingent left Kosovo in March while the investigation was ongoing, leading to accusations from the media and local campaigners that their departure had impeded the investigation.

There were concerns around UNMIK's prosecution of Albin Kurti, leader of the Vetevendosje Self-Determination Movement, for directing the violence at the February protest. Several international and local nongovernmental organizations and the Kosovo Ombudsperson criticized the duration and scope of Albin Kurti's house arrest, and expressed concerns about possible bias on the part of international judges. In November 2007 the house arrest conditions were significantly relaxed.

In May 2007, After a six-year wait, the Grand Chamber of the European Court of Human Rights ruled inadmissible two cases filed by Kosovo Albanian families against contingents of the NATO-led Kosovo peacekeeping force (KFOR) from France, Norway, and Germany. The Behrami family had sought redress for the death of a child killed by an unexploded cluster bomb in 2000, while Ruzhdi Saramati challenged his extrajudicial detention by KFOR during 2001-2002. The court reasoned that it lacked jurisdiction because the KFOR troops were operating under a UN mandate and outside the territories of the respondent countries.

The trial of former Kosovo Prime Minister Ramush Haradinaj at the ICTY began in March. Haradinaj had returned to The Hague the previous month for the start of the trial, after spending more than a year on provisional release with the unprecedented ability to engage in political activities. Haradinaj was permitted by UNMIK to top the list of his Alliance for the Future of Kosovo party in the November 2007 elections.

The total number of domestic war crimes prosecutions remained low. In August the war crimes trial of Miroslav Vuckovic resumed in the Mitrovica District Court. Vuckovic is accused of manslaughter, assault, and other crimes against Kosovo Albanians in the town of Suvi Do in 1999. In June Idriz Gashi was sentenced to 15 years' imprisonment in the Pristina District Court for involvement in killing a Kosovo Albanian alleged collaborator with Serbian forces, and in imprisoning and torturing others.

There was little progress in determining the fate of missing persons. As of August 2007, 2,047 persons, the majority Kosovo Albanian, remained missing. All known remains exhumed in Serbia have been transferred to Kosovo.

Human Rights Defenders

Human rights defenders are largely free to operate without hindrance from UNMIK or the provisional government. An arson attack in September on the home of independent journalist Milaim Zeka, known for investigating organized crime, highlighted the potential for violence against those who document abuse, however.

The important work of the Ombudsperson Institution was overshadowed by the continued failure of the Kosovo Assembly to appoint an ombudsperson and uncertainty over its mandate. UNMIK indicated that the institution's old mandate to oversee UNMIK (ostensibly removed in 2006) applies while the institution has an acting ombudsperson. In practice, however, UNMIK's cooperation was limited. The appointment process was also marred by criticism that the shortlisted candidates lacked human rights experience necessary for the position.

The Human Rights Advisory Panel held its inaugural session in Pristina in November, more than a year-and-a-half after it was first mandated by UNMIK. The body was created to oversee UNMIK following the change in the Ombudsperson's mandate.

Key International Actors

The UN-sponsored status proposal for Kosovo, presented in February, recommended internationally supervised independence with broad guarantees for the rights of the Serb minority. The proposal was removed from Security Council consideration after a Russian veto threat. A "troika" consisting of the EU, the United States, and Russia was created in July to oversee fresh talks between Pristina and Belgrade, with a December 10, 2007 deadline.

Planning continued for an EU-led international mission, including an EU police and justice component, but deployment remained contingent on settlement of Kosovo's status. In the interim, UNMIK continued to act as Kosovo's international administrator under UN Security Council resolution 1244.

In April UNMIK and KFOR facilitated a visit by the Council of Europe Committee for the Prevention of Torture (CPT), permitting access to all detention facilities in Kosovo, including the US KFOR Bondsteel camp.

TAJIKISTAN

Tajikistan's human rights situation continues to be characterized by lack of access to justice, due process violations, incommunicado detention, and ill-treatment in custody. The government interferes with opposition political parties. Government harassment of non-traditional religious groups and Muslim groups that are independent of state-controlled religious bodies has intensified.

The government announced an amnesty in June to mark the 10th anniversary of the end of the civil war, but it remains unclear how many people were released from prison. The amnesty excluded persons convicted of "extremism," which is the most common charge in religious and politically-motivated cases.

Nongovernmental Organizations

On May 12 the Tajik parliament adopted a new law "on public associations." The law grants the government excessive powers to monitor the activities of public associations, including nongovernmental organizations (NGOs). Only groups that have representative offices or branches in all provinces are registered as national associations and allowed to carry out activities countrywide; local associations are restricted to activities in the district where they are registered. The law also requires all NGOs in Tajikistan to re-register no later than January 1, 2008. All prior registrations will be automatically nullified.

On April 30, 2007, President Emomali Rahmon (he publicly dropped the Russified name by which he was previously known—Emomali Rahmonov—in March) announced an initiative to establish an Ombudsman's institution. Seventeen local human rights organizations in November issued an open letter calling for NGO participation in drafting the law on the Ombudsman and for more transparency in the process.

Freedom of Expression

The government continues to tighten control over independent media activities. Critical journalists are routinely threatened with prosecution or are called before state bodies to "explain" their publications. The pressure sometimes results in self-censorship. Under the new law on public associations, media outlets will also be required to re-register by January 1, 2008.

On July 30, 2007, President Rahmon signed into law widely criticized amendments to articles 144, 307, and 396 of the criminal code (publishing false information, slander, and libel in the mass media) and an additional provision for information published on the internet. These offenses are punishable by up to two years' imprisonment, and by up to five years for criminal defamation of the president.

Two judges filed a lawsuit against Firuza Vohidova for insult to their "honor, dignity and business reputation" after she named them in a letter to the president about what she considered to be the judges' unfair decision. On October 1 the Dushanbe City Court fined Vohidova 4,000 somoni (approximately US$1,500) in a flawed proceeding. She is appealing against the ruling. Human rights organizations and journalists are concerned that Vohidova's case may prevent others from complaining about unfair treatment or procedural violations.

An ongoing licensing dispute means that the BBC has been unable to restart FM radio broadcasts in Tajikistan, which were initially suspended by Tajik government order in early 2006.

Torture and Ill-Treatment

Human rights organizations and lawyers continue to receive reports of arbitrary arrests, violations of detention procedures and fair trial standards, and credible, serious allegations of ill-treatment and torture in detention. Defense lawyers themselves are subject to threats and harassment if they insist on effective assistance of counsel.

Tajikistan has not amended its law on torture to comply fully with the UN Committee Against Torture's recommendations to the country in December 2006. Law enforcement officials can be charged with "abuse of professional competency" (criminal code article 314), but not with torture. National legislation does not prohibit torture evidence from being admitted at trial.

Impunity for ill-treatment in detention continues to be widespread. There were, however, at least two cases in 2007 in which law enforcement officers were prosecuted for ill-treatment. In April police lieutenant Nurullo Abdulloev was sentenced to seven years' imprisonment by a court in Kulyab for the unlawful detention and ill-treatment of two detainees. In another case in April, two police officers were each sentenced to two years' imprisonment for beating and torturing with electrical shock a 15-year-old boy in the capital, Dushanbe. All three men were convicted under article 314.

Tajikistan continues to return individuals to Uzbekistan in violation of its *nonrefoulement* obligations. In January the Prosecutor General's Office announced that two "Andijan suspects" (see Uzbekistan chapter) had been returned.

Actions in the Name of Countering Terrorism and Extremism

In 2007 law enforcement bodies continued to arrest individuals simply because they were accused of possessing leaflets of Hizb ut-Tahrir, a banned Islamic organization, and at least three alleged Hizb ut-Tahrir members were sentenced to more than 10 years' imprisonment each for "incitement of ethnic and religious hatred" and "membership in extremist organizations." In the first case of a child being imprisoned for membership in Hizb ut-Tahrir, Muminbek Mamedov, a 17-year-old boy, was sentenced to eight years' imprisonment.

In January the Supreme Court banned another 10 organizations, including the Islamic Movement of Turkestan, as "extremist." In August a small Islamist group, Mavlavi, was banned on the grounds that it holds "unsanctioned gatherings."

Uzbek and Tajik citizens continue to be arrested for alleged membership in the Islamic Movement of Uzbekistan. In these highly political cases involving terrorism charges, the suspects are frequently denied procedural protection and the right to a fair trial, and routinely suffer from inhumane treatment in detention.

Freedom of Religion

In early 2007 the Prosecutor General's Office and officials of the Committee on Religious Affairs conducted an investigation into the membership and finances of all religious groups in Tajikistan. Religious leaders were asked to present lists of all members who regularly attend their services, and to provide tax and land-use documentation. A draft religion law is currently under consideration. If adopted, it would require all religious groups to re-register, subject to conditions that are draconian, such as requiring that each of the group's followers has had legal residence in the country for at least 10 years, with documentary proof to that effect. At least three unregistered mosques were demolished in Dushanbe in 2007, and more were reportedly forced to close.

In October Jehovah's Witnesses were banned from conducting any religious activities in Tajikistan. According to Forum 18, an independent, international religious freedom group, the ban was because of the sect's position of conscientious objection to military service, and because Jehovah's Witnesses "propagate faith in public places."

Housing Rights and Forced Evictions

Violations of housing rights, including deprivation of property and mass eviction, gained momentum in Dushanbe in late 2006 and 2007, when the government began forcibly resettling residents of some areas of central Dushanbe to the city outskirts without just compensation and sometimes to unsafe buildings. The government justified the evictions as part of a longstanding reconstruction plan and claimed public and governmental need for the sites, but local human rights organizations allege that the land has not always been used for public purposes but sold for commercial use. The project was ultimately postponed until 2009 after it triggered protests.

Political Parties

In April the Ministry of Justice tried to suspend the opposition Social Democratic Party (SDP) for six months for allegedly failing to report on its activities and funding sources. The SDP rejected the charges as groundless. The ministry later withdrew its lawsuit, stating that the SDP had "rectified the violations."

Mahmadruzi Iskandarov, the leader of the opposition Democratic Party of Tajikistan (DPT), did not benefit from the June amnesty and at this writing remains in prison on terror-related charges. The DPT accused the government of interfering with the party's efforts to identify new leadership. The Ministry of Justice officially recognized one faction, led by Masud Sobirov, after the party split into three groups.

Key International Actors

Visiting Tajikistan in April, United Nations High Commissioner for Human Rights Louise Arbour called on the government to ensure better access to justice and to allow local and international monitors, including the International Committee of the Red Cross, to visit detention places. Asma Jahangir, the UN special rapporteur on freedom of religion or belief, visited Tajikistan in February, concluding that religious communities and individuals faced "challenges," and underscoring the importance of the government's ensuring that "especially vulnerable individuals" be protected "from harassment by non-State actors in the name of religion."

In March the UN Human Rights Committee issued two decisions on applications alleging abuses by Tajik authorities. It found that in both *Ashurov v. Tajikistan*, and *Karimov and Nursatov v. Tajikistan* the victims had been subjected to torture and unfair trial. The decisions urge Tajik authorities to ensure effective remedy to the applicants, including compensation, and in the *Ashurov* case to immediately release the victim. At this writing the government has not implemented the decisions.

The European Union's first-ever Central Asia Strategy adopted in June acknowledged human rights as one of its priorities but fell short of formulating country-specific benchmarks. The focus on vaguely worded "human rights dialogues" raises doubts about their effectiveness.

Russia remains a key partner for Tajikistan, although relations are tense. The plight of approximately 50,000 Tajik citizens who were deported from Russia in recent years because of irregularities in their migration documents is a particularly sensitive issue between the two countries.

The United States' relationship with Tajikistan focused primarily on border control, security, and law enforcement. The 2007 US Department of State's Country Reports on Human Rights expressed concern about a number of issues in

Tajikistan, including torture, restrictions on freedom of speech and press, harassment of international NGOs, and access to prisons.

TURKEY

Recent trends in human rights protection in Turkey have been retrograde. 2007 saw an intensification of speech-related prosecutions and convictions, controversial rulings by the judiciary in defiance of international human rights law, harassment of pro-Kurdish Democratic Society Party (DTP) officials and deputies, and a rise in reports of police brutality. The state authorities' intolerance of difference or dissenting opinion has created an environment in which there have been instances of violence against minority groups. In January 2007 Turkish-Armenian journalist and human rights defender Hrant Dink was murdered. Armed clashes between the military and the Kurdistan Workers' Party (PKK) rose in the lead-up to elections in July and intensified yet further in the second half of the year, with heavy loss of life; some attacks—such as a suspected PKK bombing in Ankara in May—have targeted civilians.

Prior to the general election, the Turkish military intervened directly in the political arena by voicing opposition to the ruling Justice and Development Party (AKP) government and by decisively influencing a constitutional court decision to block the presidential candidacy of the AKP's Abdullah Gül. The AKP nevertheless won 47 percent of the vote in the early general election precipitated by the presidential crisis, and subsequently secured the election of Abdullah Gül as president. The AKP government embarked on plans for a new constitution to replace that put in place under the military regime in 1982.

Human Rights Defenders

The criminalization of speech remains a key obstacle to the protection of human rights in Turkey, contributing to an atmosphere of intolerance that assumed violent proportions in 2007. On January 19 the journalist and human rights defender Hrant Dink was shot dead outside his office. Dink came to public notoriety because he was repeatedly prosecuted for speech-related crimes and, in 2006, convicted for "publicly insulting Turkishness" under article 301 of the penal code. The trial of 12 suspects indicted for Dink's murder, among them the 17-year-old gunman, began on July 2, but the authorities have to date failed to act on significant evidence of negligence or possible collusion by the security forces.

Other public figures associated with human rights advocacy also received death threats. Burdensome registration procedures and legal restrictions on associations continued. The LGBT organization Lambdaistanbul, for example, was prosecuted for having aims that were against "law and morality" and faced possible closure.

Freedom of Expression and Assembly

After its electoral victory in July, the new AKP government failed to take immediate steps to restart the stalled reform process by lifting restrictions on freedom of expression such as article 301, and elements of the legal establishment opposed to reform continued to prosecute and convict individuals for speech-related offences, as well as for staging unauthorized demonstrations. Over 2007 hundreds of individuals, among them journalists, writers, publishers, academics, human rights defenders, and, above all, officials of Kurdish political parties and associations, were prosecuted. Some were convicted.

In October 2007 Arat Dink, son of Hrant Dink and editor of the bilingual Turkish-Armenian newspaper Agos (Furrow), and the newspaper's owner Serkis Sarkopyan were given one-year suspended sentences for "insulting Turkishness" under article 301. They had reported a July 2006 Reuters interview with Hrant Dink in which he had referred to the "Armenian genocide." No other newspaper that reported Hrant Dink's words to Reuters has been prosecuted.

Officials of the pro-Kurdish Democratic Society Party (DTP)—which stood independent in the election and gained 22 seats—were repeatedly convicted for speech-related offences during the year. Some were detained for several months pending trial. The number of prosecutions was significantly higher than in previous years, lending credence to suggestions that concerted efforts were being made to block their political activity and restrict their freedom of assembly in an election year. In November the closure of the DTP was pending before the Constitutional Court. Officials of the Kurdish party HAK-PAR were also sentenced for using the Kurdish language in their political party activities; a Constitutional Court closure case is still pending against the party.

Torture, Ill-Treatment, and Killings by Security Forces

Ill-treatment appeared to be on the rise in 2007 and was regularly reported as occurring during arrest, outside places of official detention, and in the context of demonstrations, as well as in detention centers. This trend was further exacerbated by the passing in June of a new police law granting wide-ranging powers of stop and search. After the new law came into force, cases of police brutality were also reported in the context of the routine identity checks permitted in the new law. There were continuing reports of ill-treatment in prisons and, in January, conscientious objector Halil Savda was ill-treated at the Tekirdağ military barracks.

Fatal shootings of civilians by members of the security forces remain a serious concern. Although police typically state that the killing occurred because the individual has failed to obey a warning to stop, in some cases these may amount to extrajudicial executions. The fatal shooting of Bülent Karataş near Hozat, Tunceli, in September 2007, bore the hallmarks of a summary execution. His companion, Rıza Çiçek, who survived serious gunshot wounds, explained how he was shot by military personnel while on a beekeeping trip. Another suspected summary execution was that of the villager Ejder Demir, shot dead near Özalp, Van, in September. Nigerian asylum seeker Festus Okey died of gunshot wounds incurred while in police custody in Istanbul in August.

Attacks on Civilians

Suspected PKK bomb attacks targeting civilians have continued at intervals in 2007, including a suicide bombing in May in the shopping district of Ulus, Ankara, which resulted in eight deaths, and two bombings in Izmir in October, killing one man. In September a minibus was fired upon near a village in Beytüşşebap, Şırnak province, killing five civilians and seven village guards. As of this writing, the perpetrators had not been identified.

Impunity

Turkish courts are notoriously lenient towards members of the security forces who are charged with abuse or misconduct, contributing to impunity and the persistence of torture and the resort to lethal force. Many allegations of torture or killings in disputed circumstances never reach the courts and are not investigated. Some controversial court rulings in the first half of 2007 stand out. In May the Court of Cassation quashed the 39-year sentences of two gendarmerie intelligence officers for the November 2005 bombing of a bookshop in the southeastern town of emdinli that resulted in one death. This bombing was widely condemned by human rights groups in Turkey as evidence of a resort to lawlessness in the name of counterterrorism. Controversially the court ruled that the crime had been committed in the course of a counterterrorism operation and that the defendants should be retried in a military court. The decision is on appeal.

In April a court in Eskişehir acquitted four police officers for the killing of Ahmet and Uğur Kaymaz, in November 2004 in the southeast town of Kızıltepe. The court ignored substantial forensic evidence demonstrating that the father and son may have been the victims of a summary execution. The case is on appeal.

There was no progress in the investigation into the widespread allegations of police torture following arrests during violent protests in March 2006 in Diyarbakır, or into the deaths of 10 demonstrators (eight shot dead) during the protests.

Key International Actors

The European Union (EU) remained the most important international actor in fostering respect for human rights in Turkey. However, the December 2006 EU summit decision to partially freeze membership negotiations because of Turkey's relations with Cyprus contributed to the perception in Turkey that EU member states were reneging on their commitment to Turkey's candidacy. After the election in France of President Nicolas Sarkozy in 2007, who has repeatedly stated his opposition to Turkey joining the EU, in June France used its veto power to block two minor chapters of the accession negotiations. In its annual progress report, published in November, the European Commission commented on the failure to advance reforms in 2007, continuing restrictions on free speech, the interference of the military in political affairs, the need to strengthen the independence of the judiciary, and the failure to further minority rights.

As of this writing, the European Court of Human Rights has issued 242 judgments against Turkey in 2007 for torture, unfair trial, extrajudicial execution, and other violations. In an October judgment that may have implications for the draft constitution, the court found that the failure to grant an Alevi schoolgirl exemption from constitutionally enshrined compulsory religious education classes focused on Sunni Islam constituted a violation of the right to education (Hasan and Eylem Zengin v. Turkey). In a controversial decision in January the court ruled that the existence of the 10 percent electoral threshold, which has been argued to deprive in particular pro-Kurdish parties of political representation in parliament, did not violate the right of the people to freely express their opinion of the choice of the legislature (article 3 of protocol 1 of the convention). Two judges dissented, pointing to the fact that the Parliamentary Assembly of the Council of Europe had in 2004 urged Turkey to lower the threshold, and that the threshold was twice as high as the European average (see Yumuk and Sadak v. Turkey). In November the case was heard by the Grand Chamber of the European Court and judgment is awaited.

TURKMENISTAN

Turkmenistan remains one of the most repressive countries in the world, despite a change in leadership brought about by the death of president-for-life Saparmurat Niazov in December 2006. The new president, Gurbanguly Berdymukhamedov, has taken steps to reverse some of the most ruinous social policies of Niazov's rule and to end the country's international isolation. But the human rights situation in Turkmenistan remains disastrous, and the government has yet to commit to a reform agenda that guarantees fundamental rights.

New President

Berdymukhamedov, formerly a deputy prime minister and health minister, was named acting president upon Niazov's death, and on February 11, 2007, he was elected president. The election was neither free nor fair: five low-ranking "alternative" candidates ran against Berdymukhamedov, but no opposition leaders were able to return from exile abroad to stand as candidates, and all candidates represented the country's sole political party.

To his credit, after his election Berdymukhamedov announced a number of reforms, including reinstating pensions and social allowances and restoring the tenth year of secondary education and the five-year course of university-level education.

Persecution of Civil Society Activists

On December 17, 2006, environmental activist Andrei Zatoka was arrested in Dashaguz. He was charged with possession of firearms and poison, but the arrest appears to have been motivated by his contacts with environmental groups abroad. As a result of intense international pressure, Zatoka was ultimately given a three-year suspended sentence in January 2007.

The new government has continued to harass and persecute civil society actors and independent media. The unofficial ban on registering independent non-governmental organizations remains in effect, and these groups face ongoing harassment.

During the year, government agents prevented activists from meeting with visiting international delegations. In February six persons were warned not to leave their homes during a visit to Turkmenistan by a delegation of the Organization for Security and Co-operation in Europe's (OSCE) Parliamentary Assembly. Three activists reported that their telephone lines did not work and that Ministry of National Security agents waited in cars parked close to the activists' homes the day of the visit. This intimidation was repeated several days later, during a visit by EU Special Representative for Central Asia Pierre Morel. Similarly, one activist was held at the Ministry of National Security (MNB) for an entire day during the visit of the United Nations high commissioner for human rights in May.

Freedom of Expression and Access to Information

The new government continues to severely limit free expression and to harass those who express their peaceful opinions or seek independent sources of information, as well as to use a variety of means to intimidate and impede the work of independent journalists. The government continues to restrict much foreign media access to the country.

Radio Free Europe/Radio Liberty (RFE/RL) reported the ongoing harassment and surveillance of its correspondents by security officials. At least seven RFE/RL correspondents had their land-line and mobile telephones blocked during the spring. On April 26 the son of an RFE/RL correspondent and his girlfriend were detained and questioned for eight hours in Ashgabat; the woman was threatened with unspecified consequences should she marry the correspondent.

In April an independent journalist, Sona Chuli-Kuli, was barred from leaving Turkmenistan to attend the Eurasian Media Forum in Almaty, Kazakhstan. She was taken to the MNB, where she was held for three days and questioned about the contents of her computer's hard drive. The hard drive was confiscated for examination and returned to her only after she signed a statement promising not to cooperate with international media. Human Rights Watch is aware of two other cases in which journalists were subjected to similar intimidation.

Despite Berdymukhamedov's pledge early in his presidency to increase access to the internet, the state does not permit independent service providers. Most websites that contain information perceived to be critical of the government are blocked. Security services reportedly visit internet cafes and intimidate customers.

Freedom of Religion

Forum 18, an independent, international religious freedom group, has reported a rise in arrests, deportations, raids, and threats against religious minorities since Niazov's death.

Some individuals have been arrested and harassed simply for their peaceful religious expression, according to Forum 18. On May 14, 2007, Vyacheslav Kalataevsky, a Turkmenistan-born Baptist with Ukrainian citizenship, was sentenced to three years in a labor camp. Although charged with illegal border crossing, his family reports that most of the questions asked of him during pretrial interrogations related to his religious activities. Russian citizen Yevgeny Potolov, a Baptist pastor arrested with Kalataevsky, was expelled from Turkmenistan in early July after having been detained for seven weeks. Although the grounds for his deportation remain unclear, Potolov reported that while he was detained, officials of the MNB reported to the Migration Service that he was a "dangerous person," an accusation he rejects. On August 12 local officials in the city of Turkmenbashi also threatened to deport Potolov's wife and children.

Members of a Protestant church near the northeastern town of Turkmenabat reportedly had their houses raided by local officials and secret police on May 20. On the following two days, public meetings were held at which church members were humiliated and warned to stop attending Protestant services. Local government representatives accused the believers of "conducting criminal activity and political action against the government."

Freedom of Movement

The government under President Berdymukhamedov has softened some restrictions on freedom of movement. In July 2007 it formally abolished the requirement that residents wishing to travel to closed areas along the border obtain prior government permission. At least seven individuals are known to have been removed from the list of people forbidden from travel abroad. Nonetheless, numerous people, including journalists, religious minorities, and perceived dissidents and their relatives, remain on a blacklist banning them from leaving the country. While it is difficult to estimate the exact number of people forbidden from foreign travel, knowledgeable sources believe the number to be in the thousands.

Political Prisoners

Large numbers of prisoners who were convicted in closed, unfair trials during the Niazov era are still believed to be imprisoned. During 2007 Berdymukhamedov granted two presidential pardons that affected approximately 9,000 prisoners. Among those released were 15 persons believed to have been sentenced on politically motivated charges, as well as more than 10 relatives of dissidents and former high-ranking officials. They included Nasrullah Ibn Ibadullah, the former chief mufti of Turkmenistan, who had been serving a 22-year sentence on politically motivated charges of involvement in a 2002 plot to assassinate Niazov. However, well-known Niazov-era political prisoners including Mukhametkuli Aymuradov, Annakurban Amanklychev, and Sapardurdy Khajiev, remain deprived of their liberty. Dozens of prisoners are held incommunicado. The fate of imprisoned former foreign minister Boris Shikhmuradov and former ambassador to the OSCE Batyr Berdiev remains unknown, although Berdymukhamedov told an audience at New York's Colombia University in September he was "positive that they are alive."

Politically motivated arrests continue to be a concern under Berdymukhamedov. Ovezgeldy Ataev, the constitutionally designated successor to Niazov as interim president, was removed from succession in December 2006 and imprisoned on charges of driving a relative to attempt suicide.

The government has taken no steps to investigate credible allegations of torture or to outline a process for reviewing the convictions that are the basis for ongoing imprisonment for thousands. No independent investigation has been conducted into the 2006 death in custody of human rights defender Olgusapar Muradova.

Key International Actors

In contrast to previous years of self-imposed isolation, the new president demonstrated a willingness to engage with the international community. This greater openness presented a significant opportunity to press specific reform, such as the release of all political prisoners—an opportunity the many foreign diplomatic visitors to Turkmenistan during 2007 have largely squandered.

The government continues to refuse access to places of detention for any independent national or international observers, including the International Committee of the Red Cross. With the exception of the special rapporteur for religious freedom, it has failed to extend invitations to the special procedures of the United Nations Human Rights Council that have requested to visit Turkmenistan, including those on torture, education, health, human rights defenders, independence of judges and lawyers, the right to freedom of opinion and expression, and on arbitrary detention.

The European Union held a first round of its newly established human rights dialogue with Turkmenistan in September, in the framework of the EU's new Central Asia strategy, but it failed publicly to articulate any specific human rights reforms it intended to advance through this dialogue. Rights issues were raised during Berdymukhamedov's November visit to Brussels, though no benchmarks for progress were set.

The United States government increased its engagement with the government of Turkmenistan after the death of Niazov, including on issues of human rights concern. The US Department of State's Country Reports on Human Rights Practices continued to cite serious human rights violations in Turkmenistan. In August the Turkmen government received a delegation from the US Commission for International Religious Freedom, which considers Turkmenistan a "country of particular concern" and which sought to assess the government's commitments to improve human rights, in particular the right to freedom of religion. At this writing the report of the visit has not been made public.

UKRAINE

Political deadlock, continuing for much of 2007, again hindered Ukraine's implementation of necessary reforms. New laws limiting presidential powers sparked a conflict between parliament and President Victor Yushchenko over cabinet appointments. On April 2 Yushchenko dissolved parliament and called for new elections after dozens of politicians from pro-presidential parties defected to a coalition headed by Yushchenko's political rival, Viktor Yanukovich. The political crisis abated when Yushchenko and Yanukovich agreed to parliamentary elections on September 30. Yanukovich's Party of Regions won the elections, with the Yulia Timoshenko Bloc coming second and Yushchenko's Our Ukraine—People's Self Defense party third.

Torture and ill-treatment remain serious problems. Media generally operate without government interference, but harassment of media outlets and journalists persists. Concerns remain about inadequate protection of the rights of migrants and asylum seekers. The government is not taking adequate steps to address human rights abuses fueling the HIV/AIDS epidemic.

Elections

An observer mission led by the Organization for Security and Co-operation in Europe (OSCE) determined that the parliamentary elections mostly met standards for democratic elections and that freedoms of expression and assembly were respected. However, observers noted shortcomings including incomplete voter lists, the elimination of absentee voting for snap elections, the Central Election Commission's lack of independence, and the failure of the Constitutional Court to rule on election-related complaints in a timely manner. In the months prior to the elections there were credible reports of misconduct, including the distribution of unsigned brochures containing false information about political parties.

Torture and Ill-Treatment

Ukrainian and international organizations reported incidents of torture and ill-treatment in 2007. Ukraine appeared before the UN Committee Against Torture

(CAT) in May, and in its concluding observations the CAT expressed concern about torture and ill-treatment in detention, as well as other violations of detainees' rights, and noted the government's failure to effectively investigate torture complaints. The CAT also noted that Ukraine had returned persons to countries where there are substantial grounds for believing that they would be subjected to torture.

At the request of the Ukrainian authorities, the European Committee for the Prevention of Torture (CPT) in June published the report on its visit to Ukraine in 2005. The report concluded that persons detained by the police face a risk of ill-treatment, in particular during initial questioning. The CPT deplored the continuing practice of holding people for weeks or months in police station lockups, which often are overcrowded and may lack basic material conditions such as drinking water, natural light, mattresses, heat, and toilets. The CPT cited significant improvements in conditions in some temporary holding facilities and prisons, but found that work requirements in the women's prison amounted to inhuman treatment.

Media Freedom

Journalists and media outlets continue to work free of direct government interference, but threats and physical attacks against journalists critical of government officials or other prominent figures remain a problem.

For example, on August 14 two unidentified assailants attacked Artem Skoropadsky, a journalist for the *Kommersant-Ukraina* newspaper, who linked the attack to a story he had written citing controversial remarks by Kyiv Mayor Leonid Chernovetsky. Skoropadsky said the mayor's press department had threatened a libel suit over the story. On February 18 two men beat Anatoly Shinkarenko, news director at the local 9 Kanal television station in Dnipropetrovsk. The attackers threatened the journalist, promising to destroy him if he continued to report on an internal conflict at 51 Kanal, a rival television station.

The trial of three former police officers suspected of kidnapping and murdering investigative journalist Georgy Gongadze in 2000 continues, after being opened in January 2006 and repeatedly delayed. Media freedom activists lament that still no charges have been brought against former senior government officials implicated in organizing Gongadze's killing.

Migrants

Multiple reforms in recent years still have not led to a clear migration policy or a unified, efficient migration service. Detention conditions for migrants remain poor in most facilities, and fundamental rights to a lawyer, to inform a third party of detention, and to be informed of one's rights are routinely denied. Many asylum seekers in need of protection are denied refugee status on procedural grounds or because migration officials fail to evaluate country-of-origin situations. Many migrants, especially Chechens, remain at risk of being returned to countries where they may face torture or ill-treatment.

On June 18, 2007, the European Union and Ukraine finalized agreements on visa facilitation for Ukrainian nationals and on readmission of irregular migrants who transit Ukraine and are apprehended in the EU. The readmission provisions will become applicable after a transitional period of two years, and a special accelerated procedure will apply to persons apprehended in common border regions. Nongovernmental organizations (NGOs) believe that the readmission agreement fails to provide sufficient human rights safeguards.

Human Rights Abuses Fueling the HIV/AIDS Epidemic

The government is not addressing the human rights problems fueling the HIV/AIDS epidemic. The Ukrainian National AIDS Center reported over 6,000 newly registered cases of HIV infection in the first three months of 2007, primarily among injection drug users. NGOs report that police interference with the delivery of HIV prevention information and services continues. Those at highest risk of HIV/AIDS, including drug users and sex workers, are particularly vulnerable to police harassment and are frequently driven away from lifesaving services.

Despite its promises to increase access for drug users to medication-assisted treatment (MAT) with methadone or buprenorphine, which is widely recognized as among the most effective means to treat opiate dependence, the government has failed to expand successful MAT pilot programs to more regions. The Ministry of Interior has publicly opposed medication-assisted treatment.

The Ministry of Health has taken measures to expand provision of antiretroviral therapy for people living with HIV, although not on a scale sufficient to address the need for it. When selecting candidates for antiretroviral therapy, medical institutions frequently discriminate against drug users on the unfounded assumption that they will not adhere to a rigorous course of treatment.

Key International Actors

The EU continues to deepen its engagement with Ukraine, seeking to bolster the country's democratic reforms and secure its own economic and energy policies. In the December 2006 progress report on European Neighborhood Policy implementation in Ukraine, the EU noted that political dialogue had intensified, and that Ukraine had made progress toward consolidating respect for human rights and the rule of law, including by removing pressure on the media and civil society. The report also stated that reforms are hindered by endemic corruption, lack of an independent judiciary, and long periods of political instability. During a September 2007 summit in Kyiv, the EU and Ukraine "reaffirmed strong and sustained ties," stressing that Ukraine's strengthening of the rule of law and respect for human rights will lead to closer relations with the EU.

In November Giovanni Fava, an Italian member of the European Parliament, claimed to have information suggesting that in 2005 a Ukrainian airstrip was used by Central Intelligence Agency (CIA)-operated planes involved in the United States government's extraordinary rendition program. Ukrainian authorities deny the allegations.

At its spring session, the Parliamentary Assembly of the Council of Europe held an urgent debate on the functioning of democratic institutions in Ukraine and issued a resolution noting that the April political crisis was a result of "systematic failure by the successive Ukrainian governments to establish coherent policies backed by substantial legal, administrative and economic reforms."

In October 2007 the Council of Europe's human rights commissioner presented the report on his December 2006 visit to Ukraine. The report noted the problem of torture and ill-treatment, the lack of access to a lawyer for detainees, and over-crowding and poor health conditions in pretrial detention facilities. The commis-sioner called on the Ukrainian authorities to improve access to treatment and social reintegration for people living with HIV. The report also noted as problems violence against women, human trafficking, and abuse of children's rights.

The European Court of Human Rights found Ukraine responsible for subjecting Vladimir Kucheruk to inhuman treatment in a pretrial detention facility in 2002. Officials used rubber truncheons allegedly to subdue Kucheruk, kept him hand-cuffed for seven days in a disciplinary cell, and denied him proper medical care. Authorities also illegally detained Kucheruk for nearly two weeks in violation of a court order committing him to compulsory psychiatric treatment.

In its June 2007 concluding observations on Ukraine's initial report on the Optional Protocol to the Convention on the Rights of the Child on the Sale of Children, Child Prostitution, and Child Pornography, the UN Committee on the Rights of the Child encouraged Ukraine to adopt an action plan to prevent crimes against children and to establish a juvenile justice system in conformity with international standards.

UZBEKISTAN

The government of Uzbekistan has taken no meaningful action to improve its atrocious human rights record. In 2007 the authorities continued to suppress independent civil society activism and independent religious worship, and to resist investigation of and accountability for the 2005 Andijan massacre. Yet international pressure on the Uzbek government to improve its human rights record saw a steady decline.

Uzbekistan is to hold presidential elections on December 23, 2007. The Central Election Commission has approved four candidates, including President Islam Karimov, amid doubts about the legality of his seeking another term: Karimov has already served the maximum two consecutive terms allowed by the constitution and extended his second term by a referendum in 2002 from five to seven years. His current term expired in January 2007.

Persecution of Human Rights Defenders and Independent Journalists

Uzbekistan continues to hold at least 13 human rights defenders in prison on politically-motivated charges. These activists languish in prison following sham trials, serving lengthy sentences solely because of their legitimate human rights activities. Authorities continue to detain independent journalist Jamshid Karimov in a closed psychiatric ward, where he has been confined since September 2006.

Two human rights activists detained in January 2007 on politically-motivated grounds were eventually conditionally released, but only after they "confessed" to their "crimes," renounced human rights work, and denounced their colleagues. Gulbahor Turaeva, a doctor from Andijan, was arrested on January 14. On April 27 she was convicted for anti-constitutional activities and sentenced to six years' imprisonment. In a second trial on May 7 she was convicted for slander and fined. On June 12 an appeals court commuted Turaeva's prison term to a suspended sentence. Umida Niazova, an independent journalist from Tashkent and a former translator for Human Rights Watch's Tashkent office, was initially detained for a day in December 2006, and her passport and laptop were confiscated. Shortly after Niazova left Uzbekistan for neighboring Kyrgyzstan in early January

UZBEKISTAN

Nowhere to Turn

Torture and Ill-treatment in Uzbekistan

HUMAN
RIGHTS
WATCH

2007, her lawyer was informed that she would not face criminal charges and that she could collect her passport and computer. However, while traveling back to Tashkent on January 22 she was arrested by the Uzbek authorities, held incommunicado for four days, and charged with smuggling and illegal border crossing. On May 1 Niazova was sentenced to seven years' imprisonment, commuted to a suspended sentence on May 8.

Two other activists who had previously served prison sentences fled Uzbekistan in fear for their personal security after being subjected to ongoing surveillance, harassment, and threats of re-arrest. Ulugbek Khaidarov, a journalist from Jizzakh, had been sentenced to six years' imprisonment on extortion charges in October 2006. One month later his sentence was changed to three years' non-custodial corrective labor, and after release Khaidarov publicly alleged that he had been tortured in pretrial detention and at Navoi prison. He fled Uzbekistan in late 2006. Yagdar Turlibekov, a human rights defender from Kashkadaria province, had been sentenced in October 2006 to three-and-a-half-years' imprisonment but was released under a general amnesty in December 2006. After release Turlibekov reported on prison conditions and ill-treatment of prisoners, but after suffering constant surveillance and threats he too fled Uzbekistan in September 2007.

In March Komil Ashurov, an activist from Samarkand, was attacked by two people in his neighborhood. Witnesses who tried to help Ashurov were also attacked. Several men believed to be police or security officers watched the incident without intervening. Hate rallies against human rights defenders remain common. For example, in February Vasila Inoiatova, chair of the human rights organization Ezgulik, was attacked by a crowd of women in Samarkand throwing eggs and clay. Because of the attack the local branch of Ezgulik had to cancel its annual meeting.

The authorities continue their practice of denying exit visas to activists to prevent their participation in international conferences or similar events. For example, in January 2007 the police department in Margilan city seized the passport of Ahmadjon Madumarov, a recipient of the Front Line Award for Human Rights Defenders at Risk 2006. As a result he was not able to participate in a human rights seminar in Istanbul. If activists manage to travel abroad, they face interrogations and harassment upon their return to Uzbekistan. In April human rights defender Elena Urlaeva, returning from a workshop in Kyrgyzstan, was held for eight hours at a border police station while officials recorded every piece of paper she had with her.

Authorities have also persisted in their obstruction of Human Rights Watch's work in Tashkent, denying work accreditation to our sole staff person without any explanation and refusing to extend her visa, thereby forcing her to leave the country. As a result, Human Rights Watch has not been able to have a presence in Tashkent since late July 2007.

The Andijan Massacre and Situation of Refugees

The Uzbek government has adamantly rejected numerous and repeated calls for an independent international inquiry into the May 2005 Andijan massacre when hundreds of unarmed protestors were killed by government forces. The circumstances surrounding the massacre have not been clarified, and those responsible for the killings have not been held accountable.

The government continues to persecute anyone whom it deems to have any connection to or information about the Andijan events. Refugees who fled Uzbekistan in the immediate aftermath of the massacre but later returned to Uzbekistan, as well as their families, have been a particular target of government pressure. They have been subjected to interrogations, constant surveillance, ostracism, and in some cases overt threats to life, which has triggered a new wave of refugees.

Refugees must fear for their security even in neighboring countries, because Uzbek security services are operating in areas geographically close to the Uzbek border, such as in Osh, Kyrgyzstan. For example, in February 2007 a court in Andijan sentenced Isroil Kholdarov, activist with the banned Erk party, to six years' imprisonment for illegal border crossing, anti-constitutional activities, and distributing threatening and extremist materials. There is evidence that Kholdarov, who fled Uzbekistan after the Andijan events, was kidnapped by Uzbek security services in Kyrgyzstan and returned to Uzbekistan. The Uzbek and Kyrgyz Ministries of Interior agreed in August to extend their cooperation and to create "branches" reciprocally in Osh and Andijan.

Religious Persecution

Uzbek authorities continue their unrelenting, multi-year campaign of unlawful arrest, torture, and imprisonment of Muslims who practice their faith outside state controls or who belong to unregistered religious organizations. Peaceful religious believers are often branded as "religious extremists." Dozens were arrested or convicted in 2007 on charges related to religious "extremism." Human Rights Watch documented allegations of ill-treatment in several of these cases.

Torture

In a long-awaited move in July 2007, the Uzbek parliament adopted significant legislative reforms introducing habeas corpus and abolishing the death penalty as of January 1, 2008. Yet the government has not ended the culture of impunity for torture and continues to refuse to acknowledge the main conclusion of the UN special rapporteur on torture, that "torture or similar ill-treatment is systematic." In 2007 Human Rights Watch continued to receive credible, serious allegations of torture, the documented cases showing that torture in Uzbekistan is not a marginal problem caused by only a handful of errant police or security agents but rather a widespread practice that has become endemic to the criminal justice system. The United Nations Committee Against Torture (CAT), reviewing Uzbekistan in November, gave a similar assessment, finding that torture and ill-treatment remain "routine." The CAT called on the government to "apply a zero-tolerance approach to the continuing problem of torture and to the practice of impunity," and detailed numerous urgent measures the Uzbek authorities should take to address the concerns identified.

Key International Actors

The UN Human Rights Council in March 2007 voted to end scrutiny of Uzbekistan under the confidential monitoring procedure known as "1503" (after the resolution that created it), despite the government's persistent refusal to cooperate with the independent expert appointed under the procedure. Uzbekistan also continued to refuse access to other UN monitors, and failed to take meaningful measures to address longstanding recommendations made by a range of UN bodies.

The European Union continued to use every opportunity to chip away at its already modest sanctions policy toward Uzbekistan, first introduced post-Andijan. It dropped four names off the visa ban list in May 2007 and, although it renewed the arms embargo and the visa ban for an additional 12 months in October 2007, immediately suspended the visa ban for six months to encourage the Uzbek government "to take positive steps to improve the human rights situation." Given the EU's failure to vigorously enforce the conditions it had previously articulated for lifting the sanctions, it was unclear whether it could muster the required political will to obtain concrete concessions from the Uzbek government in the upcoming six-month period.

As part of its Central Asia strategy, adopted in June 2007, the EU also entered into a "structured human rights dialogue" with the Uzbek government. The first round was held in Tashkent in May, as the strategy was being finalized. Apart from general statements emphasizing the importance of the dialogue "achieving concrete and sustained results," it was unclear what specific objectives the EU was seeking to advance through this dialogue, and what its strategy was for achieving the desired outcomes. At this writing there have been no further rounds of the dialogue, after the Uzbek government made clear that it was not prepared to engage in such talks again until early 2008.

457

LEBANON

Rot Here or Die There

Bleak Choices for Iraqi Refugees in Lebanon

HUMAN
RIGHTS
WATCH

WORLD REPORT
2008

MIDDLE EAST
AND NORTH AFRICA

BAHRAIN

Human rights conditions in Bahrain worsened in 2007. Although the king, Shaikh Hamad bin `Isa al-Khalifa, undertook important reforms in 2001-2002, the government still has done little to institutionalize human rights protections in law. The government continued to subject freedom of expression, assembly, and association and to arbitrary restrictions.

Bahrain's counterterrorism law as well as a new Drugs and Psychotropic Substances Law, enacted in August 2007, prescribe the death penalty for certain offences. In December 2006, the government executed a Bangladeshi man and woman and a Pakistani man convicted in separate murder cases. Except for a single execution in 1996, a time of great political turmoil, Bahrain had not executed anyone since 1977.

Bahrain held National Assembly and municipal elections in November and December 2006. Opposition political societies that boycotted the first elections, in 2002, participated in 2006, but some groups continue to boycott the Assembly, protesting what they regarded as the absence of real legislative authority for the elected representatives.

Freedom of Expression

Authorities continue to use the press law (Law 47/2002) to restrict coverage of controversial matters, particularly issues such as official corruption. In the first nine months of 2007, authorities referred the cases of 15 journalists to the public prosecutor, in most instances for alleged defamation of a government official or department. In May 2007, the government-appointed Shura Council, the upper chamber of the parliament, approved draft legislation that would remove criminal penalties for journalistic offenses, but as of November the government had not forwarded the draft to the elected National Assembly for approval.

In mid-November 2006 authorities arrested a 35-year-old dentist and a 32-year-old insurance salesman for attempting to distribute leaflets calling on Bahrainis to boycott the upcoming parliamentary elections. On January 30 a court sentenced them to prison terms of six months and one year, respectively, for dissemination and possession of materials that could "damage the public interest." The government released them several weeks later, apparently following a pardon from the king.

In early February authorities arrested `Abd al-Hadi Khawaja, president of the Bahrain Center for Human Rights (BCHR), and Hassan Mushaima, head of Al Haq, a political opposition group, on charges of circulating false information, insulting the king, and inciting hatred against the government. In May, following demonstrations protesting their prosecution, the king declared the court proceedings against them "frozen."

The country's sole residential internet service provider, Batelco, is government-owned; the BCHR said in November that the authorities were blocking 23 discussion forums and other websites, including its own.

Freedom of Assembly

Law 32 of 2006 requires the organizers of any public meeting to notify the head of Public Security at least three days in advance and authorizes that official to determine whether a meeting warrants police presence on the basis of "its subject ... or any other circumstance." The law stipulates that meeting organizers are responsible for "forbidding any speech or discussion infringing on public order or morals," but leaves "public order or morals" undefined.

During 2007 Bahraini authorities, citing Law 32/2006, banned meetings and on several occasions forcibly prevented or dispersed unauthorized gatherings. In several instances the police used what appeared to be excessive force and inflicted severe beatings on persons they seized, sometimes amounting to torture. On May 20 police reportedly fired rubber bullets at a gathering at which opposition political figures, including members of parliament, were speaking, injuring Ibrahim Sharif, a leader of the opposition National Democratic Action Society. The next evening, when riot police confronted a street demonstration protesting the May 20 incident, security forces seized and beat 22-year-old Ali Sa`id al-Khabaz and 46-year-old Hamid Yusif Ahmad, inflicting serious injuries on both men.

Freedom of Association

The government continues to deny legal status to the BCHR, which it ordered dissolved in 2004 after the BCHR's president publicly criticized the prime minister. Several other groups, including the National Committee for the Unemployed and the Bahrain Youth Human Rights Society, attempted in 2005 to register with the Ministry of Social Development, as required by law, but at this writing had received no response to their application.

In 2007 the Ministry of Social Development drafted new legislation on civil society organizations, but at this writing the ministry had not submitted the draft to the Shura Council or the Chamber of Deputies. The draft law contains some improvements over the existing Law 21/1989, but includes numerous provisions incompatible with international standards and best practices regarding freedom of association. For example, the draft law maintains the authority of the minister of social development to close any organization for up to 60 days without having to provide any justification or court order, and includes criminal penalties for "any" violation of the law.

Bahrain has ratified some conventions of the International Labor Organization, but neither of the two core conventions governing freedom of association. Law 33/2002 permits workers to form and join unions, but the General Federation of Bahrain Trade Unions (GFBTU) filed a complaint with the ILO in June 2005 protesting what it said was the government's repeated refusal to register six trade unions in the public sector. In 2007 the GFBTU filed another complaint protesting a November 2006 edict by the prime minister prohibiting strikes in numerous sectors of the economy.

Counterterrorism Measures

In August 2006 the king signed into law the "Protecting Society from Terrorist Acts" bill, despite concerns expressed by the UN special rapporteur on human rights and counterterrorism that it contained excessively broad definitions of terrorism and terrorist acts. Article 1 prohibits any act that would "damage national unity" or "obstruct public authorities from performing their duties." Article 6 prescribes the death penalty for acts that "disrupt the provisions of the Constitution or laws, or prevent state enterprises or public authorities from exercising their duties." The law also allows for extended periods of detention without charge or judicial review. The first trial of suspects, four Bahrainis and a Qatari, charged under the new law with funding and preparing terrorist attacks abroad, was scheduled to begin in late November 2007.

Women's Rights

Bahrain has no written personal status law. Instead, separate Sharia-based family courts for Sunni and Shia Muslims hear marriage, divorce, custody, and inheritance cases. Family court judges, who are generally conservative religious scholars with limited formal legal training, render judgments according to their individual reading of Islamic jurisprudence. They have consistently favored men in their rulings and are unapologetically adverse to women's equality. In June, a Sharia court denied the former wife of a Bahraini policeman custody of their three children and any rights to the marital home. Prior to the ruling, the 29-year-old woman appeared on television criticizing these judges for their handling of the case and the Ministry of Interior for failing to take any action against her ex-husband despite numerous allegations of physical abuse and harassment. The government has intensified its harassment of women's rights activist Ghada Jamsheer following an April letter she addressed to Shaikh Hamad calling for the dissolution of the Supreme Council for Women (chaired by the king's wife) for failing to do more to advance women's status in the kingdom. Women's rights organizations continued to call for a written unified personal status law.

Human Rights Defenders

As already noted, the Bahrain Center for Human Rights (BCHR) was ordered dissolved in 2004 and remains closed. Authorities arrested BCHR president `Abd al-Hadi Khawaja in early February 2007 on charges that included circulating false information, but in May the king "froze" judicial proceedings against him. In March the public prosecutor summoned BCHR Vice President Nabeel Rajab for questioning on the violation of a gag order prohibiting public discussion of alleged government efforts to manipulate National Assembly elections November 2006. The Bahrain Human Rights Society (BHRS), another independent rights organization, visited Jaw prison, a major detention facility, in December 2005, but despite requests, the government did not grant further access to detention centers in 2007.

Decree 56/2002, which confers immunity from investigation or prosecution on government officials alleged to be responsible for torture and other serious human rights abuses committed prior to 2001, remains on the books. The BCHR and BHRS together led a coalition of rights groups and opposition political societies in sponsoring workshops in June and September 2007 on setting up a truth and reconciliation mechanism to address such violations. The government continues to insist that it considers such matters closed. In its November 2006 response to the review conducted by the UN Committee Against Torture, the government said that the king's reform project had "paved the way for the provision of humanitarian assistance and the realization of transitional justice, beginning with a general amnesty ... closing a chapter on the past." The authorities, however, did not prevent the transitional justice meetings from taking place and the minister of social development addressed the opening session of the June conference.

Key International Actors

Bahrain hosts the headquarters of the US Navy's Fifth Fleet as well as "important air assets." The US State Department's Fiscal Year 2007 budget justification submitted to Congress identified access to Bahrain-based military facilities and airspace as "critical" to US military operations in Iraq, Afghanistan, and the Horn of Africa as well as "any contingency operations and/or force projections in the Gulf and Southwest Asian areas."

In June 2007 the UN Human Rights Council initiated its Universal Periodic Review (UPR) process, in which the council will review the human rights record of every country once every four years. The United Nations announced in September that Bahrain would be among the first 16 countries reviewed at the first UPR session in February 2008.

EGYPT

Egypt stepped up attacks on political dissent in 2007. In March the government enshrined aspects of emergency rule via amendments to the constitution, providing a continued basis for arbitrary detention and trials of civilians before military and state security courts. The government arrested thousands of Muslim Brotherhood members and tried senior members in military courts. It brought charges against journalists and bloggers who criticized human rights abuses, and closed human rights and labor rights organizations.

Emergency Rule

The government renewed the Emergency Law (Law No. 162 of 1958) in April 2006 for an additional two years. Egyptian human rights organizations estimate that between 4,000 and 5,000 people remain in prolonged detention without charge under the law. On March 21, 2007, parliament approved changes to article 179 of the constitution that removed safeguards requiring judicial warrants before authorities search people's homes or communications in cases deemed "terrorist-related." The president may now send such cases to "exceptional" courts or military tribunals. On March 26, voters approved these amendments in a referendum that Egyptian rights monitors and independent media said was marked by vote-rigging.

Political Violence and Torture

On November 30, 2006, a State Security Emergency Court in Isma`iliyya sentenced three men to death after convicting them in connection with the October 7, 2004, bombings in and around the resort city Taba. This court, established under Egypt's Emergency Law, does not provide the right of appeal; the defendants said they had been tortured into signing false confessions while held incommunicado.

Human rights organizations received credible reports that security services and police tortured and mistreated detainees, particularly during interrogations. On November 7, 2007, Judge Samir Abu al-Mati sentenced two police officers to three years in prison on charges that they tortured `Imad al-Kabir, a microbus driver detained in January 2006 on charges of resisting arrest. Al-Kabir said that the officers beat him on the street and then, in a police station, bound and whipped him, and sexually assaulted him with a stick while another officer filmed the episode with a mobile phone. On January 9, 2007, Judge al-Mati sentenced Al-Kabir to three months in prison for "resisting authorities" and assaulting a civil servant.

On September 4, 2007, a Cairo court acquitted State Security Investigations (SSI) officer Ashraf Mustafa Hussain Safwat on charges that he tortured to death Muhammad `Abd al-Qadir, who died in SSI custody in 2003. An autopsy performed soon after `Abd al-Qadir's death showed bruises as well as burns on his mouth, nipples, and penis. A forensic doctor said he had sustained these injuries shortly before his death.

Egyptian border guards reportedly killed three Sudanese nationals trying to cross Egypt's border into Israel. The killings followed a reported informal agreement in June between President Mubarak and Israeli Prime Minister Ehud Olmert that Egypt would accept the return of third-country nationals who had crossed the border illegally into Israel. Egyptian border guards reportedly shot and killed a woman from Darfur on July 22 and Israeli soldiers reportedly saw Egyptian guards shoot and beat to death three Sudanese as they tried to cross the border on August 1. Egypt did not acknowledge killing anyone. In another incident, on November 10, Egyptian border guards shot and killed an Eritrean national who was attempting to cross into Israel.

On August 18 Israel returned to Egypt 44 Sudanese, three Ivorians, and one Somali. Egypt reportedly forcibly returned at least five of the 48 to Sudan on October 28 after holding the larger group at an unknown location. At this writing, Egypt continues to hold the remaining 43 in incommunicado detention, refusing to allow the United Nations or others access to them.

Freedom of Expression

The government jailed numerous peaceful critics over the course of 2007. On March 12, the Alexandria Court of Appeals upheld a four-year prison sentence against `Abd al-Karim Nabil Sulaiman, a blogger who had criticized Islam and President Hosni Mubarak.

On May 2, a Cairo criminal court sentenced Al-Jazeera journalist Huwaida Taha Mitwalli, an Egyptian national, to six months in prison for "possessing and giving false pictures about the internal situation in Egypt that could undermine the dignity of the country," in connection with an Al-Jazeera documentary about torture in Egypt. The court also fined her 20,000 Egyptian pounds (US$3,518). At this writing, Mitwalli is free on appeal.

On September 13, a Cairo misdemeanor court sentenced four editors of independent opposition newspapers, `Adil Hamuda (*Al-Fagr*), Wael al-Ibrashi (*Sawt al-Umma*), `Abd al-Halim Qandil (*Al-Karama*), and Ibrahim `Issa (*Al-Dustur*), to a maximum one year in prison and a US$3,500 fine on charges of publishing "with malicious intent, false news, statements or rumors likely to disturb public order."

Freedom of Association

Egypt's law governing associations, Law 84/2002, gives the government unwarranted control over the governance and operations of nongovernmental organizations (NGOs). The law provides criminal penalties for carrying out activities prior to an NGO's official authorization and for receiving foreign donations without prior approval from the Ministry of Social Affairs. It also provides criminal rather than civil sanctions for activities such as "engaging in political or union activities." The prohibitions are broadly framed to discourage legitimate NGO activity.

In April 2007 security officers closed the headquarters and two branches of the Center for Trade Union and Workers' Services (CTUWS), which offers legal aid to Egyptian factory workers and reports on labor-rights issues. Authorities blamed the CTUWS for inciting labor unrest around the country. On October 12, a court sentenced the group's general coordinator, Kamal Abbas, and his lawyer, Muhammad Hilmi, to a year in prison on criminal libel charges after the CTUWS magazine published a story about alleged corruption at a youth center whose board is chaired by a member of the ruling party.

On September 4 the government shut down the Association for Human Rights Legal Aid, which reports on human rights violations and provides legal assistance to victims, charging that it used funds from abroad prior to getting government permission.

The Political Parties Law (Law 40/1977), as amended in 2005, empowers the Political Parties Affairs Committee (PPC), headed by the chair of the ruling National Democratic Party, to suspend an existing party's activities if it judges this to be "in the national interest" and to refer alleged breaches of the law to the prosecutor general.

The government detained more than 1,000 members of the Muslim Brotherhood, the banned organization that is the country's largest opposition group. On June 3, 2007, authorities prevented Egyptian and international human rights organizations from attending the military trial of 40 leading members of the Muslim Brotherhood. In January, a Cairo criminal court had dismissed all charges against 16 of the defendants and ordered their immediate release. Security forces rearrested the men moments after their release, and President Hosni Mubarak ordered their cases, and those of 24 others, transferred to the military court. At this writing, the accused are in custody pending the conclusion of their trial.

Ill-Treatment of Street Children

The government periodically conducts arrest campaigns of homeless or truant street children who have committed no crime. In custody many face beatings, sexual abuse, and extortion by police and adult suspects, and police at times deny them access to food, bedding, and medical care. The authorities do not routinely monitor conditions of detention for children, investigate cases of arbitrary arrest or abuse in custody, or discipline those responsible. In many cases, the police detain children illegally for days before taking them to the public prosecutor on charges of being "vulnerable to delinquency."

Women's Rights

Despite reforms, particularly of nationality laws, Egypt's family and penal laws still discriminate against women and girls. The penal code does not effectively deter or punish gender-based violence and police are routinely unsympathetic to the concerns of victims. A series of well-publicized cases of sexual harassment

Prohibited Identities

State Interference with Religious Freedom

**H U M A N
R I G H T S
W A T C H**

EIPR

affecting large groups of women in October 2006 in Cairo's streets resulted in hardly any prosecutions, highlighting the government's tacit acceptance of abuses against women and girls.

The government took some positive measures in 2007 to advance the rights of women and girls. On March 14, the Supreme Judicial Council appointed Egypt's first group of female judges to the bench. In June, the Ministry of Health issued a decree that fully criminalizes female genital mutilation, eliminating a legal loophole allowing girls to undergo the procedure for ostensible health reasons. The ban followed the death of an 11-year old girl at a private clinic.

Religious Intolerance and Discrimination against Religious Minorities

Although Egypt's constitution provides for equal rights without regard to religion, discrimination against Egyptian Christians and official intolerance of Baha'is and some Muslim sects continue. Egyptians are able to convert to Islam generally without difficulty, but Muslims who convert to Christianity face difficulties amending their identity papers. Baha'i institutions and community activities are prohibited by law.

In August and October 2007 security agents detained two activists, Muhammed al-Dereini and Ahmad Sobh, who had promoted the rights of Egypt's Shia Muslim minority. At this writing they ere being held in solitary confinement in Tora prison outside Cairo on charges of "promoting extreme Shia beliefs with the intent of causing contempt of the Islamic religion" and "spreading false rumors" that could "undermine trust in security agencies by claiming that prisoners and detainees died as a result of torture."

Key International Actors

The US remains Egypt's largest provider of foreign military and economic assistance. In 2006 it provided approximately US$1.3 billion in military aid and US$490 million in economic assistance. In June 2007 the US House of Representatives' Appropriations Committee approved an amendment that would make $200 million of the aid package conditional on efforts to curb police abuse and increase the independence of the judiciary, as well as measures unrelated to human rights.

In April 2006 the European Parliament voted to make respect for human rights a priority in negotiations for Egypt on an EU-Egypt Action Plan under the European Neighborhood Policy, but EU officials have yet to indicate how they plan to do this. The January 2007 Action Plan agreement made human rights and the participation of civil society important components of the action plan, but lacked specific benchmarks.

IRAN

Respect for basic human rights in Iran, especially freedom of expression and assembly, continued to deteriorate in 2007. The government of President Mahmoud Ahmadinejad routinely detains people solely for peacefully exercising their rights to freedom of expression and association, and regularly tortures and mistreats those detained. The Judiciary, which is accountable to Supreme Leader Ali Khamenei, is responsible for many serious human rights violations. The government increasingly cites "national security" as a pretext for silencing expressions of dissent or calls for reform.

Freedom of Expression

Iranian authorities systematically suppress freedom of expression and opinion by imprisoning journalists and editors and strictly controlling publishing and academic freedom. The few independent dailies that remain heavily self-censor. The government has fired dissident university professors or forced them into early retirement. Many writers and intellectuals who have evaded imprisonment have left the country or have ceased to be critical. The Ministry of Culture and Guidance increasingly denies publication permits to publishing houses, including republication permits for books previously in circulation.

In 2007 the authorities also targeted student and internet journalists in an effort to prevent the independent dissemination of news and information. The government systematically blocks websites inside Iran and abroad that carry political news and analysis.

Freedom of Assembly

The Ahmadinejad government shows no tolerance for peaceful protests and gatherings. In March 2007 security forces arrested over 30 women peacefully demonstrating outside a courthouse in Tehran to protest the prosecution of three prominent women's rights activists. That same month security forces arrested hundreds of teachers peacefully protesting outside parliament in Tehran and in other cities for wage and benefits improvements. After releasing them the government prosecuted some of the protesters, leading mainly to suspended sentences. Some protesters were suspended from teaching or had their jobs transferred to other cities. In July security forces arrested six Amir Kabir University students who were staging a peaceful sit-in in commemoration of the anniversary of the 1999 student protests that the government had violently suppressed. The government released the six on bail and their cases remain open at this writing.

Torture and Ill-Treatment in Detention

Under Ahmadinejad the treatment of detainees has worsened in Tehran's Evin prison as well as in detention centers operated clandestinely by the Judiciary, the Ministry of Information, and the Islamic Revolutionary Guard Corps. The authorities subject those imprisoned for peaceful expression of political views to torture and ill-treatment, including beatings, sleep deprivation, and prolonged solitary confinement. Judges often accept coerced confessions. In July 2007 former student detainees and the families of three imprisoned student journalists, Majid Tavakoli, Ahmad Ghasaban, and Ehsan Mansouri, made public allegations that Ministry of Information agents had physically and psychologically tortured the three detained students and five others whom the government had held in relation to student publications.

Authorities broadcast statements obtained from detainees who were denied access to lawyers. In July the government aired the "confessions" of Haleh Esfandiari and Kian Tajbakhsh, two Iranian-American scholars detained since May on vague charges of "endangering national security." The government released Esfandiari and Tajbakhsh on bail in late August and September, respectively.

Impunity

There is no mechanism for monitoring and investigating human rights violations perpetrated by agents of the government. The closure of independent media in Iran has helped to perpetuate an atmosphere of impunity.

In recent years public testimonies by numerous former detainees have implicated Tehran's public prosecutor Saeed Mortazavi and his office in some of the worst cases of human rights violations. Despite extensive evidence, Mortazavi has not been held responsible for his role in illegal detentions, torture of detainees, and coercing false confessions. The case of Iranian-Canadian photojournalist Zahra Kazemi, who died in the custody of judiciary and security agents led by Mortazavi in June 2003, remains unresolved. Mustafa Pour-Mohammadi, the current interior minister, has been implicated in extrajudicial killings of thousands of political prisoners in 1988.

Human Rights Defenders

In 2007 the authorities intensified their harassment of independent human rights defenders and lawyers in an attempt to prevent them from publicizing and pursuing human rights violations. In July Branch Six of Iran's Revolutionary Court sentenced human rights activist Emad Baghi, as well as his wife and daughter, to suspended sentences of three years for their work in documenting and publicizing human rights violations. In October court authorities arrested Baghi after he responded to a summons to appear before an interrogator, and at this writing he remains in detention.

The government closed nongovernmental organizations that encourage civil society participation and raise awareness of human rights violations. In March authorities raided and closed the offices of the Civil Society Organizations Training and Research Center, and closed the offices of Rahi Institution, a nongovernmental organization providing legal and social aid to women victims of violence.

Juvenile Death Penalty

Iran leads the world in the number of death sentences handed down to defendants for crimes they committed under age 18. At least 70 juvenile offenders are presently on death row, and at this writing Iran has executed two juvenile offenders in 2007: Syed Mohammad Reza Mousavi Shirazi, 20, executed in Adel Abd prison in Shiraz city on April 22 for a murder he allegedly committed when he was 16, and Sa'id Qanbar Zahi, 17, executed in Zahedan on May 27. In 2003 the head of the Judiciary, Ayatollah Shahrudi, circulated an order among Iran's judges prohibiting death sentences for juvenile offenders, but courts continue to issue such sentences.

Minorities

Iran's ethnic and religious minorities are subject to discrimination and, in some cases, persecution.

After a February 2007 bombing of a bus carrying members of Iran's Revolutionary Guards Corps in the southeastern province of Sistan and Baluchistan, the government arrested dozens of members of the Baluchi minority. Less than a week after the bombings, the government publicly hanged Nasrollah Shanbezehi after televising his "confession" and following a rushed trial in which he had no access to a lawyer. In a March interview, Iranian parliament member Hossein Ali Shahryari stated that 700 people awaited execution in Sistan and Baluchistan. In May authorities hanged seven in connection with the bombings; one of them was Said Qanbar Zahi, mentioned above.

The government increased its surveillance of the ethnic Arab population of Khuzistan after bombings in 2005 in this southwestern province. In 2006 Revolutionary Courts, whose secret proceedings did not meet international fair trial standards, condemned at least 16 Iranians of Arab origin to death on charges of armed activity against the state. In 2007 at least seven Iranian Arabs were executed in connection with the bombings after secret trials during which they were denied due process rights.

In the northwestern provinces of Azarbaijan and Kurdistan the government restricts cultural and political activities that stress local languages and identities. The government harassed editors of Kurdish newspapers on the grounds that their coverage of events in Iraqi Kurdistan was aimed at instigating separatist ambitions among Iranian Kurds. The authorities similarly persecuted local newspapers in the provinces of East and West Azarbaijan that covered events in the neighboring country Azarbaijan.

The government continues to deny Iran's Baha'i community permission to publicly worship or pursue religious activities. In 2007 the government prevented at least 800 Baha'i students access to National Entrance Examination scores needed for admission to universities in Iran.

Forced Returns to Afghanistan

Iran announced in 2006 that it would "voluntarily repatriate" all of the more than one million Afghans remaining in Iran by March 2008, saying that none of those people are refugees. Between April and June 2007 the Iranian government forcibly deported back to Afghanistan nearly 100,000 registered and unregistered Afghans living and working in Iran.

HIV/AIDS

Iran is reporting increasing rates of HIV infection due to injecting drug use and unsafe sex. In February 2007 Health Minister Kamran Baqeri Lankarani announced that Iranian scientists had produced a new HIV/AIDS medication, made from seven native Iranian herbs. Iranian health officials claimed that scientists tested the drug on over 200 people over five years. However, Iranian AIDS and human rights activists raised concerns that scientists enrolled people living with HIV in these tests without consent and that the study was conducted with a control group of patients receiving an inert placebo in place of effective medicines.

Key International Actors

In 2007 Iran's nuclear program dominated discussions and policies in the international arena. Two key international actors, the European Union and the United Nations, addressed Iran's human rights situation, but the nuclear program remained their major preoccupation: the UN Security Council increased sanctions on Iran in March 2007, and the European Union's meetings with Iran have focused on the nuclear issue. The EU has pledged to tie progress in broader cooperation to Iranian respect for human rights, but the pledge has had little impact.

In June the UN Human Rights Council decided to end scrutiny of the situation in Iran under the confidential monitoring procedure known as "1503" (after the resolution that created it). In January the UN Human Rights Council's experts on extrajudicial executions urged Iran to refrain from executing the seven members of Iran's ethnic Arab community mentioned above, a request that Iran ignored. In September UN High Commissioner for Human Rights Louise Arbour visited Iran.

In 2007 the already poor relations between the United States and Iran further deteriorated. The US and Iran traded accusations about support for various armed groups in Iraq and Afghanistan. The US continues to hold five Iranian diplomats detained in northern Iraq, despite protests from the Iraqi and Iranian governments.

The US government frequently invokes Iran's human rights record as a matter of concern. Since February 2006 the State Department has budgeted US$75 million "to support democracy promotion activities in Iran," but many Iranian dissidents, human rights defenders, and civil society activists inside Iran have publicly dissociated themselves from the initiative, making clear they did not seek or accept any financial help from the US government. The Iranian government uses the US program to justify cracking down on dissidents.

IRAQ

Human rights conditions in Iraq deteriorated for much of 2007 with sectarian violence swelling the ranks of Iraq's displaced to some 4.4 million, half of them outside the country. Attacks on civilians by various insurgent and militia groups continued, including the single deadliest attack since the war began, targeting Iraq's Yazidi minority and resulting in the deaths of almost 500 civilians in August.

Iraq's government executed former President Saddam Hussein in late December 2006 and his one-time intelligence chief Barzan al-Tikriti two weeks later following deeply flawed trials. The manner of the executions further inflamed minority Sunni apprehensions about the Shia majority government.

The sectarian cleansing of Baghdad by both Sunni and Shia groups proceeded despite a major US troop deployment aimed in part at stopping it. US military operations continued against Shia and Sunni insurgents throughout the country, leading to an unknown number of civilian casualties.

The US and Iraqi security offensive was accompanied by alliances between the military and Sunni tribal and insurgent factions in Anbar province and Baghdad, some of which had begun fighting al Qaeda in Mesopotamia.

During the course of the year, Iraq's government grew more fragmented and dysfunctional. Legislation on oil revenue, one index of the chances of a cohesive national government, languished in a paralyzed parliament. Defections from the government left its political and sectarian base even narrower, and made the prospect of national political reconciliation seem distant.

The US and Iraqi security offensive in Baghdad led to a sharp increase in the numbers of detainees. Iraqi detention facilities strained to accommodate them, and the justice system often foundered in reviewing their cases, leading to a backlog in Iraqi detention centers where reports of physical abuse and torture were common. The US military said in October its detainee population had grown by about two-thirds from the year before, to about 25,000. Some detainees have spent years in US custody without charge or trial.

Government and the Political Process

In January 2007, Prime Minister Nouri al-Maliki outlined a drive to pacify Baghdad in which operations against Sunni insurgents would be coupled with disarming of Shia militias. The Bush administration pledged to send more than 20,000 troops to Baghdad and western Iraq to shore up the security plan, which began in mid-February amid devastating suicide bombings in Baghdad. The cabinet agreed to a draft oil law on February 27 but parliament had not ratified it at this writing. The main Sunni bloc, the Iraqi Accordance Front, quit the government in August, citing failure to release detainees not charged with crimes, disband militias, and grant Sunnis a say in security matters; it was followed by a secularist bloc which withdrew ministers from the government.

Shia cleric and militia leader Muqtada al-Sadr pulled his ministers from the cabinet in April over government reluctance to demand a timetable for US military withdrawal. In September, he pulled his parliamentary bloc out of the governing coalition. Sadr ordered his Jaysh al-Mahdi militia to stand down for six months after bloody August clashes in Karbala with government forces loyal to its main Shia rival, the Supreme Iraqi Islamic Council (SIIC). The Allawi and Sunni al-Tawafuq blocs also left the cabinet. At this writing, Maliki's government—reliant on Kurdish parties and a Shia group hostile to Sadr—clung to power with a slender majority in the 275-seat parliament.

Attacks on Civilians and Displacement

Civilians were once again the targets of attacks by Sunni and Shia armed groups across the country, though the number of such attacks decreased following the US and Iraqi security offensive. Many attacks appeared to be intended to cause the greatest possible civilian casualties and spread fear, notably those occurring in marketplaces, schools, and places of worship. Iraq's government and US military officials blamed Sunni insurgents for waves of car bombings in the capital in early 2007. Bombings in a Shia area of the northern town of Tel Afar in March that killed some 150 people were followed by revenge killings of dozens of Sunnis by Shia policemen. Suicide truck bombings targeting minority Yazidis near the northern town of Sinjar in August killed as many as 500 people, the worst single attack since 2003. Shia armed groups, including Jaysh al-Mahdi and SIIC's Badr militia, were reported to have carried out numerous abductions and killings in Baghdad and elsewhere.

Sectarian violence spurred large-scale flight: over a million Iraqis were displaced following the February 2006 shrine bombing, according to figures from the International Organization for Migration (IOM), most of them leaving mixed areas for more homogenous ones within the capital and outside Baghdad province. Eighty-nine percent of displaced Iraqis cited their sectarian identity as the source of threats to their safety, the IOM said in its mid-year review. There were signs at this writing, however, that some refugees and IDPs were starting to return.

The situation of Iraqis seeking refuge outside the country was little better: Jordan, which hosts more than 500,000 Iraqi refugees, began turning back most Iraqis arriving by land and air in January 2007. Syria, which hosts some 1.5 million Iraqis, began enforcing strict visa requirements in October that restricted entry to Iraqis entering for specific commercial or educational purposes. Many other countries—notably the United States—have taken very few refugees. In October, the US State Department said 1,608 Iraqi refugees had been admitted for resettlement in fiscal year 2007, with a target of 12,000 for the next fiscal year.

MNF Operations and Contractors

Stepped-up military operations by the US-led Multinational Forces (MNF) during the security offensive led to an increase in civilian casualties. UN officials reported that MNF airstrikes between March and May killed 88 civilians and called for investigations into the deaths.

The killing of at least 17 Iraqi civilians by employees of US-based security firm Blackwater in September focused attention on the impunity with which private contractors operate in Iraq. Iraq's government demanded over $100 million in compensation for victims' families and called for Blackwater's departure. Non-Iraqi contractors have been exempt from prosecution in Iraqi courts under a 2004 decree by the US occupation authority. A draft law approved by Iraq's government in late October 2007, still not approved at this writing, would end their immunity from prosecution.

Detention and Torture by Iraqi Forces

Reports of widespread torture and other abuse of detainees in detention facilities run by Iraq's defense and interior ministries and police continue to emerge. In October 2007, officials from the United Nations Assistance Mission for Iraq (UNAMI) reported that detainees had been hung by their limbs, subjected to electric shocks, forced to sit on sharp objects, and burned by their jailers. Officials in Iraq's Interior Ministry, which had previously vowed to investigate instances of detainee abuse, disputed the charges.

The number of detainees in Iraqi government custody grew by nearly 4,000 from April through June, according to UNAMI officials. Detainees often had limited access to counsel and faced lengthy delays in review of their cases.

Kurdish officials, responding to Human Rights Watch research documenting torture and denial of due-process rights to detainees in northern Iraq, released some detainees in 2007 and began reviewing cases of others. Conditions for remaining detainees were unchanged at this writing.

US Detention

As of October 2007, the US military was holding about 25,000 people in Iraq, an increase of some 10,000 from a year earlier, according to Major General Douglas Stone, head of detainee operations. Stone estimated the average detention period at 300 days, but noted detainees involved in criminal proceedings had remained in custody for several years. Many security detainees are also sometimes held for years without charge or trial and only limited review.

According to press accounts, US arrests of children allegedly involved in insurgent activities rose from an average of 25 per month to 100 per month in 2007, with over 800 children held at Camp Cropper by mid-September. In August the US opened Dar al-Hikmah, a non-residential facility intended to provide 600 detainees ages 11-17 with education services pending release or transfer to Iraqi custody. Officials have said children would be subject to the same detention review process as adults, which does not guarantee detainees access to lawyers when presenting their cases.

Accountability for Past Crimes

The Iraqi government executed Saddam Hussein on December 30, 2006, following his conviction by the Iraqi High Tribunal (IHT) for crimes against humanity in
Dujail in 1982. The government executed his half-brother and former security
chief Barzan al-Tikriti and former chief judge of the Revolutionary Court `Awwad
al-Bandar on January 15 after convictions in the same case. Their trials were
marred by the failure to disclose key evidence to the defense, government actions
that undermined the independence and impartiality of the court, and violations of
defendants' right to confront witnesses against them.

Taha Yassin Ramadan was executed in March after the IHT's Appeals Chamber
ordered the trial chamber to change his life sentence to death by hanging.

The IHT in June convicted five of Saddam's aides of genocide, war crimes, and
crimes against humanity for their actions during the 1988 Anfal campaign, in
which Iraqi forces used chemical weapons and killed as many as 100,000 Iraqi
Kurds. Three of them were sentenced to death.

Gender-Based Violence

Violence against women and girls in Iraq continues to be a serious problem, with
members of insurgent groups and militias, soldiers, and police among the perpetrators. Even in high-profile cases involving police or security forces, prosecutions
are rare.

Violence within the family also continues to be a serious issue. In 2007, UNAMI
officials recorded 40 alleged "honor" crimes in the Kurdish region alone within a
three-month period.

Key International Actors

In June 2007 the UN Security Council re-affirmed the mandate of the MNF for
2007. As of October, the United States had approximately 165,000 troops in Iraq;
the United Kingdom, the other principal contributor of foreign forces, planned to
halve its troop presence based in southern Iraq to about 2,500 in 2008.

In November 2007 the US and Iraqi governments announced they would negotiate an agreement on bilateral relations, including the status of US forces in the country in the years to come. Iraq's government said 2008 would be the last year of the United Nations mandate for multinational forces in the country, which had been expanded in 2007 to include political reconciliation, displacement, and human rights protection. The Human Rights Office of the UNAMI monitors, reports on, and follows up on human rights violations as part of a plan aimed at developing Iraqi mechanisms for addressing past and current abuses.

ISRAEL/OCCUPIED PALESTINIAN TERRITORIES (OPT)

The heavy toll of fighting among Palestinian groups, Hamas's armed takeover of Gaza, and the intensified humanitarian crisis in Gaza as a result of the Israel-led blockade dominated events in 2007.

In 2007, for the first time since Israel occupied the West Bank and Gaza in 1967, more Palestinians died as a result of internal Palestinian fighting than from Israeli attacks. The Israeli and Western economic embargo of Gaza, Israel's almost total closure of Gaza's border crossings, ongoing lawlessness in the OPT, and heightened Israeli restrictions on freedom of movement in the West Bank contributed to a serious human rights and humanitarian crisis.

This overview begins with an assessment of Israel's human rights practices followed by a separate section on the record of the Palestinian Authority and Hamas.

Israel

Gaza

In the aftermath of the Hamas armed takeover in June 2007, described below, Israel moved to isolate Gaza. It closed the crossings for people (Rafah and Erez) and for goods (Karni), and sharply limited the passage of imports to Gaza at the secondary crossings of Kerem Shalom and Sufa. The Israeli Customs Authority banned the export of Israeli goods bound for Gaza except for limited humanitarian supplies (basic foods, medicine, and medical equipment).

The general population has borne the brunt of Israel's measures. The border closure has led to the shut-down of 75 percent of Gazan factories, further crippling a local economy already weakened by past Israeli border closures. Shortages have led to a steep rise in food prices. According to the UN Office for the Coordination of Humanitarian Affairs (OCHA), as of June 2007 87 percent of Gazans lived below the poverty line and 85 percent were dependent on humanitarian aid.

While Israel has usually allowed urgent medical cases to leave Gaza through the Erez crossing, by mid-September it stopped allowing most patients out, reducing

Indiscriminate Fire

Palestinian Rocket Attacks on Israel
and Israeli Artillery Shelling in the Gaza Strip

**HUMAN
RIGHTS
WATCH**

the average number of patients leaving Gaza each month to five, down from 40 in the preceding months. Israel denied exit to many seriously ill patients on unspecified security grounds; at least five patients died in Gaza after being denied treatment in Israel.

At this writing, 670 Palestinian university students were also trapped in Gaza, unable to continue their higher education in the West Bank or abroad. On October 22 some of these university students from Gaza petitioned Israel's Supreme Court to grant them permission to travel. Israel has continued to ban Palestinian students from the West Bank and Gaza from studying at Israeli universities despite a 2006 Supreme Court decision requesting the military to change its policy.

Following Palestinian militants' continued firing of homemade rockets from Gaza, Israel's cabinet declared Gaza a "hostile entity," on September 19, paving the way for Israel to impose additional measures to deter Palestinian rocket attacks. On October 26 Defense Minister Ehud Barak approved cutting supplies of electricity and fuel, measures that constitute collective punishment of Gaza's civilian population in violation of international humanitarian law.

Palestinian Deaths and Israeli Impunity

Between January and October 2007, 245 Palestinians, about half of whom were not participating in hostilities, were killed by Israeli security forces. The Israeli army's continued failure to investigate civilian death and injury where there was evidence of a laws of war violation reinforces a culture of impunity in the army and robs victims of an effective remedy.

In a welcome development, Israel's State Prosecution agreed in September, following a decision of the High Court of Justice, to establish an independent commission of inquiry to investigate the circumstances around the Israeli air force's July 2002 targeted killing of Hamas military leader Salah Shehadeh in Gaza that also killed 14 civilians, nine of them children. Minister of Defense Barak announced that he will not cooperate with the commission and that he will forbid Israeli soldiers from appearing before it.

Freedom of Movement

Israeli authorities in 2007 expanded already extensive, often arbitrary restrictions on freedom of movement in the West Bank and East Jerusalem. In September 2007 UN OCHA reported that the army had set up 572 West Bank roadblocks, an increase of 52 percent in just two years. The restrictions make it impossible for many Palestinians, including UN doctors and teachers, to get to work, access education and health services, and visit family, friends, and religious and cultural institutions.

The Wall and Settlements

In 2006 then-Acting Prime Minister Ehud Olmert stated publicly for the first time that the route of the wall the government had said it was constructing to prevent Palestinian armed groups from carrying out attacks inside Israel also reflected official aspirations for a future border. Currently, 85 percent of the wall's route extends into the West Bank, carving out approximately 10 percent of the West Bank, including almost all major Israeli settlements there—which are illegal under international humanitarian law—as well as some of the most productive Palestinian farmlands and key water resources.

Israel continues to expand illegal settlements in the West Bank and the Israeli settler population has been growing by around 5.5 percent each year. In 2007 approximately 450,000 settlers were living in the West Bank, including East Jerusalem; more than 38 percent of the West Bank now consists of settlements, military bases, and other Israeli-controlled areas, most of which are off limits to Palestinians. Settler violence against Palestinians and their property continues with virtual impunity.

Discriminatory Legislation

Israel continues to apply laws and policies that discriminate on the basis of ethnic or national origin. Since 2002, Israel has prohibited Palestinians from the OPT who are spouses of Israeli citizens from joining their partners in Israel. In March 2007 the Knesset amended the Citizenship and Entry into Israel Law, expanding the scope of the existing ban on family reunification and extending it through

2008. The new law also bans residents or citizens of Iran, Iraq, Syria, and Lebanon married to Israelis from living with their spouses in Israel.

In July 2007 the Ministry of Justice issued draft legislation, in the form of a proposed amendment (Number 8) to the Civil Wrongs (Liability of the State) Act, which would reintroduce a sweeping ban on Palestinians from filing tort claims for injuries caused by Israeli security forces. Israel's Supreme Court had struck down a previous amendment to this effect in December 2006.

Expulsion of Asylum Seekers

On August 18, 2007, Israel expelled approximately 50 Sudanese nationals, mostly from Darfur, who were presumably entering Israel to seek asylum. The summary expulsion violated Israel's international obligations and marked a departure from prior Israeli policy, which had been to allow Sudanese asylum seekers to remain temporarily in Israel pending refugee status determination by the UN High Commissioner for Refugees.

Palestinian Authority and Hamas

Attacks on Israeli Civilians

Palestinian armed groups in Gaza continue to fire locally made rockets into civilian areas in Israel, disrupting life in the border town of Sderot. At this writing, two Israelis had been killed and several more wounded in such attacks in 2007. These attacks, whether targeted at civilian areas or indiscriminate in their impact, are serious violations of international humanitarian law.

In January 2007, Islamic Jihad and the Fatah-affiliated al-Aqsa Martyrs' Brigade carried out a suicide bombing in Eilat, killing three Israeli civilians. The Palestinian Authority failed to take action to apprehend those who had ordered or organized the attack.

At this writing, Palestinian armed groups still held hostage Israeli Corporal Gilad Shalit, captured in June 2006.

ISRAEL AND THE OCCUPIED PALESTINIAN TERRITORIES

Civilians under Assault

Hezbollah's Rocket Attacks on Israel in the 2006 War

HUMAN RIGHTS WATCH

Intra-Palestinian Fighting and Lawlessness in the OPT

Palestinian armed groups, rival security forces, and powerful clans continue armed attacks on one another. At this writing, 318 Palestinians, including many civilians, had died in such fighting in 2007, most of them in Gaza.

By far the worst round of fighting broke out in June 2007 and left 161 Palestinians dead, including 41 civilians. By the end of the eight-day battle, Hamas had taken full control of the Gaza Strip. Both sides engaged in serious violations of international humanitarian law, such as torturing and summarily executing captured and incapacitated fighters, including inside hospitals; unnecessarily endangering civilians by deploying in populated areas during the fighting; and blocking the access of medical teams to injured persons.

Despite the gravity of the violations committed by both sides, the Ramallah-based Palestinian Authority and the de facto Hamas government in Gaza made no efforts to investigate these crimes or hold anyone to account, further entrenching impunity.

Since June 2007, the Qassam Brigades, the armed wing of Hamas, has been policing the Gaza Strip, carrying out arrests and running detention centers, although it is not a law enforcement agency nor is it empowered by law to exercise these functions. Both the Qassam Brigades and the Hamas-affiliated Executive Force have reportedly engaged in torture and inhumane and degrading treatment of detainees during interrogation. In the West Bank, the PA's Military Intelligence and Preventive Security forces, which are dominated by Fatah members, have been responsible for arbitrary arrests and detention as well as ill-treatment and torture of Hamas activists in the West Bank.

A Palestinian armed clan, the Army of Islam, kidnapped BBC correspondent Alan Johnston on March 12, 2007, and held him for 114 days before Hamas forces freed him following that group's takeover of Gaza.

Violence against Palestinian Women and Girls

Violence against women and girls inside the family is a serious problem in the OPT. Law enforcement and health officials lack adequate training, guidelines, and commitment to report and investigate the problem. Even in the rare instances where the authorities pursue cases, perpetrators benefit from laws that reduce penalties for men who attack female relatives suspected of dishonoring the family, relieve from criminal prosecution rapists who agree to marry their victims, and allow only male relatives to file incest charges on behalf of minors. The Palestinian Centre for Human Rights reported that as of late August, 11 women had been murdered by relatives in so-called "honor killings" in Gaza in 2007.

Key International Actors

The United States and key European countries have continued their steadfast support of President Abbas and the PA, but have not used their economic and political support to leverage improvements in the PA's human rights record. Nor have these countries pushed the PA to investigate human rights violations committed by Fatah-linked security forces and militias. In June 2007 the US, EU, and Israel announced the end of their economic embargo of the Palestinian Authority after Abbas dismissed the Hamas-led government and created a new emergency government based in Ramallah in the West Bank.

The Quartet (the EU, US, Russia, and UN) continues to funnel limited humanitarian aid to Gaza, even as the US, EU, and Israel continue their economic blockade of the de facto Hamas government in Gaza. This blockade is one of the primary factors behind the dire humanitarian situation in Gaza at present.

Israel remains by far the largest recipient of US aid, receiving US$2.28 billion in military aid and $280 million in financial aid in 2007. This amount is set to increase to $3 billion for each of the next 10 years. Despite its leverage, the US has not made the funding conditional on Israel improving its human rights record.

JORDAN

In 2007 Jordan regressed in protecting the exercise of basic rights. A proposed NGO law would severely restrict freedom of association, and new laws on the press and on the right to information fell short of expectations. A new political parties bill threatened the existence of small parties by raising the required minimum number of founding members to 500, representing at least five governorates.

Municipal elections in July were marred by serious fraud, as documented by local civil society groups, including multiple voting and voter list manipulation. Parliamentary elections were held in November under the old electoral law, the government having not fulfilled a 2006 promise to reform it. The existing law favored pro-regime rural tribal regions against opposition strongholds in urban population centers.

Arbitrary Detention, Administrative Detention, and Torture

The General Intelligence Department (GID) arrests suspects mostly in the name of counterterrorism, sometimes without charge and frequently on spurious charges. Three security detainees—'Adnan Abu Nujila, Samir al-Barq, and 'Isam al-'Utaibi (better known as Abu Muhammad al-Maqdisi)—have been held for years without trial. The GID routinely obstructs detainees' access to legal representation and delays family visits. Security detainees as recently as 2006 have alleged torture and ill-treatment to extract confessions in the form of beatings and psychological abuse such as mock executions, sleep deprivation, and prolonged solitary confinement. Human Rights Watch inspected the GID facility from August 19 to 30, 2007.

In 2006 provincial governors administratively detained 11,597 persons without proof of criminal action or to circumvent the obligation to present suspects to the prosecutor within 24 hours. Administrative detainees must meet a financial bail guarantee to gain release, but indigent detainees frequently resort to hunger strikes instead.

JORDAN

Shutting Out the Critics

Restrictive Laws Used to Repress Civil Society in Jordan

H U M A N
R I G H T S
W A T C H

In April, and from June through August 2007, prison strikes and riots occurred. Reasons included withdrawal of visiting and book privileges, prolonged solitary confinement, delayed trials, and beatings. In visits to six regular prisons in August and October, Human Rights Watch found rampant beatings of inmates for perceived infractions of prison rules. Mass beatings took place in Swaqa prison on August 22, and in Swaqa, Qafqafa, and Juwaida prisons in June after a guard facilitated an escape. Any officers charged with abusing prisoners face an appointed police court instead of an independent regular court. Police officials prosecuting Aqaba prison guards for beating an inmate to death in May only upgraded charges from neglect of duty to murder following the intervention of King Abdullah II.

The GID offered the governmental National Center for Human Rights the same conditions of unannounced visits at any time and private interviews with detainees agreed with Human Rights Watch; at this writing this offer has not been taken up. The Public Security Directorate at times allowed the Jordanian Engineers' Association's Freedom Committee to visit imprisoned engineers.

Protective Custody of Women

Governors detain women—in one case for over 20 years—to protect them against family violence, instead of providing voluntary shelters. Between 400 and 800 women at risk are detained every year. The purpose of the first governmental women's shelter for victims of violence, which opened in 2007, is to reconcile the women with their family rather than offer protection. Judicial accountability for perpetrators of violence, or threats thereof, remains weak, although improved prosecutorial performance has secured convictions in 2007.

Freedom of Expression, Association, and Assembly

Criticisms of the king, government officials, and the intelligence forces are strictly taboo and carry serious penalties. Prosecutors also rely on the penal code to criminalize speech diminishing the prestige of the state, and harming relations with other states.

The State Security Court in October found ex-parliamentarian and current head of the unlicensed Jordan National Movement Ahmad al-`Abbadi guilty of diminishing the prestige of the state for a web article alleging corruption by the interior minister and sentenced him to two years in prison; the court did not investigate the truth of the allegations. A royal court official said the government filed charges to avoid violence within the large 'Abbadi tribe. Also in October the State Security Court sentenced Muhammad al-Zuhairi to 18 months in prison for *lese majeste* over online postings he had made.

Parliament reversed its initial position and agreed in March to a new press and publications law that dropped imprisonment as a sanction for breaching its requirement for "precision, neutrality and objectivity in presenting national material, human rights or the values of the Arab and Islamic nation," among other provisions. The new law retains fines as high as 20,000 dinars (US$28,000). In September the government announced that the law extended to material published on websites. Other laws retain imprisonment for prohibited speech, especially the penal code. Jordan also passed in April the Arab region's first law on access to information, that experts criticized for allowing broad exclusions under the rubric of national security and for maintaining government control over any decision to release information

Foreign Minister Abd al-Ilah al-Khatib in January initiated a criminal defamation suit against weekly newspaper *al-Hilal's* editor-in-chief Nasir Qamash and journalist Ahmad Salama. He objected to the content of a January article, and said his tribe had threatened to beat up Salama if he failed to take action. The case remains in the courts at this writing.

Since December 2006 parliamentarians or policemen have assaulted journalists on four occasions, and intelligence forces twice pre-censored media content, confiscating an Al Jazeera interview with Jordan's Prince Hasan in April and in May stopping the weekly *al-Majd's* publication of a plan to aid Palestine's President Mahmoud Abbas.

In April the government passed a regulation bringing non-profit companies (primarily nongovernmental organizations (NGO) registered under the more permissive companies law) more in line with the stricter measures of the NGO law, giving the government the right to monitor their work and to dissolve them for minor breaches of their articles of association. In October the Cabinet proposed without broader consultation a new NGO law that is more restrictive than the current law. Foreign funding of NGOs or non-profit companies requires government approval under the new regulation and the proposed new law.

In July 2006 the Ministry of Social Development installed temporary government management of the Islamic Center Society, and led a massive recruitment of new members in 2007 to oust the Center's Muslim Brotherhood leadership in members' elections for a new management. By law these elections should have happened within two months of the appointment of a temporary management board. Similarly, the ministry in September 2006 installed temporary management at the General Union of Voluntary Services (GUVS), an NGO umbrella group, and in June 2007 at the Amman branch of GUVS. The new management postponed elections.

Jordan's restrictive law on public gatherings gives local governors the right to ban any meeting or demonstration, without having to provide a reason. In July, for example, Amman's deputy governor refused the `Afaf Society, run by a former three-time president of parliament, permission to hold a conference entitled "The Family is the Nursery of Values and Identity." In other examples, Amman's governor in May withheld permission for a rally that 28 opposition parties had planned to protest the new law on political parties and on several occasions he denied the student organization Dhabahtuna permission to demonstrate.

Iraqi Refugees

Jordan hosts at least 500,000 Iraqi refugees, the majority of whom arrived after 2003 (only Syria hosts a comparable number of Iraqis). After Iraqis killed 57 people in the Amman hotel bombings of November 2005, Jordan's traditional tolerance toward Iraqis eroded. Jordan's government, which does not have an established mechanism to determine refugee status, has practically shut its land borders and airport to fleeing Iraqis, and continued in 2007 to deport visa overstayers despite official promises to recognize their right to stay. The office of the United Nations High Commissioner for Refugees in Jordan greatly expanded its still inadequate provision of asylum seeker cards to Iraqis, but, in deference to the government, only exceptionally provides them with refugee documents.

Ending its ban of prior years, Jordan admitted Iraqi children to public schools for the 2007-2008 school year.

Migrant Worker Rights

Reports documenting abuses of mostly Southeast Asian migrants working in Jordan's Qualified Industrial Zones led the government to shut down some factories, help transfer abused workers to other employers, and waive fines for visa overstayers. Nevertheless, there are few criminal prosecutions of abusive employers, and abusive conditions continue including beatings, long working hours, withholding of passports and paychecks, pay discrimination based on sex or nationality, preventing workers from leaving the work site at any time, and denying medical care. The provisions of Jordan's labor code, including the right to unionize, exclude non-Jordanians as well as agricultural and domestic workers. In early October the governor of Zarqa had Bangladeshi workers detained for striking.

Key International Actors

The United States gave Jordan US$532 million in economic and security-related assistance in 2007 (compared to the European Union's €265 million for 2007-2010), praising Jordan's cooperation in the so-called global war on terrorism. US Ambassador David Hale was quick to praise Jordan's municipal elections, and a US congressional bill further praised these elections, causing disbelief among Jordanians who witnessed the electoral fraud.

The United Kingdom continues to try to return at least two Jordanians to Jordan, saying that it relies on a 2005 memorandum of understanding with Jordan to prevent torture, under which the government permits Adaleh, a Jordanian NGO with limited experience and little track record of criticizing the government, to monitor the treatment of a returned detainee.

LEBANON

Lebanon endured another year of instability in 2007, with political and security crises weakening state institutions and undermining human rights. The three-month military confrontation between the Lebanese armed forces and the armed Islamist group Fatah al-Islam destroyed most of the Nahr al-Bared Palestinian refugee camp. More than 40 civilians died in the fighting.

As the security situation deteriorated, torture and ill-treatment of security suspects increased. Palestinian refugees continue to face widespread discrimination, and their situation worsened following the Nahr al-Bared fighting. Iraqis fleeing their war-torn country to Lebanon find themselves facing a real risk of coerced return. Lebanese law continues to discriminate against women by, among other things, denying them the right to pass their nationality to their children or spouses. Migrant domestic workers face exploitation and abuse from their employers with little possibility for legal remedy.

In May 2007 the UN Security Council passed a resolution to establish an international tribunal to try those responsible for the murder of former Prime Minister Rafiq Hariri in 2005. Access to redress remains elusive for the approximately 900 civilians who died in last year's war between Israel and Hezbollah and for the families of the estimated 17,000 who "disappeared" during and after Lebanon's deadly civil war (1975-1990).

The Nahr al-Bared Battle and Palestinian Refugees

The battle between the Lebanese army and the armed Islamist Fatah al-Islam from May to September 2007 in the Nahr al-Bared Palestinian refugee camp was the worst internal fighting since the end of the civil war in 1990. Over 30,000 camp residents left the camp, which lay in ruins. According to military and government sources, the battle resulted in the deaths of 166 Lebanese army soldiers, 220 Fatah al-Islam militants, and at least 40 civilians, most of whom were Palestinians. The Lebanese government appealed to international donors for almost US$400 million to rebuild the camp and its surrounding areas and to care for those forced out of their homes.

The Lebanese army and internal security forces arbitrarily detained and physically abused some Palestinian men fleeing the fighting. On June 29, 2007, the Lebanese army killed two Palestinian civilians when it opened fire on demonstrators demanding to return to their homes in Nahr al-Bared. The government failed to investigate the cases of arbitrary detention and abuse or the shooting incident, reinforcing a climate of impunity.

The fighting exacerbated existing tensions between Lebanese and an estimated 300,000 Palestinians living in Lebanon. Harassment and abuse of Palestinian civilians at checkpoints on account of their identity discouraged some Palestinians from moving around the country. Palestinians remain subject to wide-ranging restrictions on housing and work despite some efforts by the authorities to relax some of these restrictions in 2005.

Torture and Ill-Treatment

As the security situation deteriorated in 2007, reports of torture and ill-treatment of security detainees increased. While the exact scope of torture remains unknown, credible reports indicate that the Military Intelligence unit of the Ministry of Defense, the Information Branch of the Internal Security Forces, and the police—notably in their anti-drug trafficking operations—engage in torture of certain detainees.

Lebanese law prohibits torture, but accountability for ill-treatment and torture in detention remains elusive. In a rare exception, in March 2007, a Lebanese court sentenced a policeman for torturing an Egyptian man, but the 15-day sentence and the monetary fine were insignificant penalties.

Conditions in prison and detention facilities remain poor, with overcrowding a perennial problem. At least five people died in custody in 2007 without independent investigations to credibly determine their exact cause of death.

Legacy of War between Hezbollah and Israel

More than a year after the end of the war between Israel and Hezbollah, neither the Israeli nor the Lebanese governments have investigated the serious violations of the laws of war committed by the warring parties. The war resulted in approximately 900 civilian deaths in Lebanon and 39 civilian deaths in Israel.

The estimated one million cluster submunition "duds" left behind by Israel's bombing campaign continue to kill and injure civilians, resulting, at this writing, in at least 34 deaths and 216 injuries. Israel continues its refusal to turn over detailed information on the location of its cluster munition attacks, hampering demining efforts, which the United Nations estimates will last until the end of 2008.

The reconstruction of the infrastructure and of the tens of thousands of homes damaged by Israeli attacks has stalled amidst allegations of corruption and rising tensions between the government and Hezbollah.

In October 2007 Israel and Hezbollah agreed to exchange the remains of an Israeli civilian who had drowned and whose body had washed ashore in Lebanon for a captive Hezbollah member and the bodies of two of the group's fighters. The two Israeli soldiers abducted by Hezbollah at the beginning of the July 2006 war remained in captivity at this writing.

Political Assassinations, Hariri Tribunal, and Lack of Accountability

The targeting of politicians continued in 2007, with two separate explosions killing pro-government parliamentarians Walid Eido and Antoine Ghanem in June and September respectively. The UN-appointed International Independent Investigation Commission continues its investigations into the killing of former Prime Minister Hariri in 2005 and other politically motivated assassinations, but it has not named any official suspects.

In June 2007 Security Council Resolution 1757 established a tribunal to try those responsible for the Hariri killing, and the UN began the process of setting up the tribunal. Four former heads of Lebanese intelligence and security services—General `Ali al-Hajj, General Raymond Azar, Brigadier General Jamil al-Sayyed, and Mustafa Hamdan—remain in detention without charge following their arrest in August 2005 on suspicion of their involvement in Hariri's assassination.

"Disappearances"

No progress was made in 2007 to uncover the fate of the Lebanese, Palestinians, and other nationals who "disappeared" during and after the 1975-1990 Lebanese civil war. The Lebanese government estimates that there were a total of 17,415 such cases, but no criminal investigations or prosecutions have ever been initiated. Relatives and friends of the "disappeared" have been holding a sit-in in front of the UN offices in Beirut since April 2005 to demand information on the fate of people still unaccounted for.

According to Lebanese human rights groups, Syria has committed at least 640 enforced disappearances, detaining Lebanese incommunicado in Syrian prisons. An official joint Syrian-Lebanese committee established in May 2005 to investigate the cases had not published any findings at this writing.

Iraqi Refugees

An estimated 50,000 Iraqis are now living in Lebanon. Since January 2007, the UN High Commissioner for Refugees (UNHCR) has recognized all Iraqis from central and southern Iraq seeking asylum in Lebanon as refugees on a prima facie basis. However, Lebanon has refused to give legal effect to UNHCR's recognition of Iraqi refugees, and it treats the vast majority of them as illegal immigrants, subjecting a number of them to arrest, fines, indefinite detention, and coerced return. Lebanon provides almost no services to the Iraqis and no effective process for regularizing their status.

Human Rights Defenders

Human rights groups operate freely in Lebanon, but the tense political and security situation creates a challenging environment for activists. In September 2007 judicial police formally questioned a Human Rights Watch researcher with respect to a legal complaint accusing him of "weakening national sentiment" and other such crimes in connection with the release of a report by Human Rights Watch documenting Hezbollah violations in their rocket attacks on Israel. The prosecutor did not proceed with the case for lack of evidence to prove the elements of the crime.

Samira Trad, whose organization Frontiers Center promotes the rights of refugees, continues to face ill-defined defamation charges dating from 2003, apparently related to her work on behalf of refugees. Her court session is scheduled for January 2008.

Discrimination against Women

Despite women's active participation in all aspects of Lebanese society, discriminatory provisions continue to exist in personal status laws, nationality laws, and criminal laws relating to violence in the family. Current Lebanese law does not allow Lebanese women to confer nationality on either their spouses or children.

Women migrants employed as domestic workers, most of whom come from Sri Lanka, face exploitation and abuse by employers, including excessive hours of work, nonpayment of wages, and restrictions on their liberty. Many women migrants suffer physical and sexual abuse at the hands of employers, in a climate of complete impunity for employers. According to media reports, over 200 migrant domestic workers in Lebanon reportedly committed suicide over the last four years with no real investigation of their deaths.

Key International Actors

Multiple international actors compete for influence in Lebanon, but none contribute effectively to improving Lebanon's human rights record.

Since the ceasefire between Israel and Hezbollah in 2006, 13,000 UN peacekeepers monitor Lebanon's southern border and its territorial waters. The UN Security Council passed Resolution 1757 in May 2007 to establish an international tribunal to try those responsible for the Hariri killing. Meanwhile, the Security Council continues to follow-up on the implementation of Resolution 1559, which calls among other things for the Lebanese government to extend its control over all Lebanese territory and the "disarmament of all Lebanese militias."

France and the United States retain a strong role in Lebanon. In 2007, the US sharply increased its military assistance to Lebanon to US$270 million, more than five times the amount it provided a year earlier.

Regionally, Syria, Iran, and Saudi Arabia maintain a strong influence on Lebanese politics through their local allies. Despite the withdrawal of Syrian troops from Lebanon in April 2005, Lebanese-Syrian relations remain tense, and members of the parliamentary majority accuse Syria of killing some of its members. As Hezbollah's main foreign ally, Iran is seen by many as key to any long-term solution to the conflict between Hezbollah and Israel.

Libya

Libya's international reintegration accelerated in 2007 despite the government's ongoing human rights violations. In July the government released six foreign medical workers who had been tortured, unfairly tried, and imprisoned for eight years for allegedly infecting children with HIV. In October Libya won a seat on the UN Security Council. Driven by business interests and Libya's cooperation on counterterrorism, the United States and some European governments strengthened ties with Libya throughout the year. Yet the Libyan government continues to imprison individuals for criticizing the country's political system or its leader, Mu`ammar al-Qadhafi, and maintains near-total restrictions on freedom of expression and assembly. It forbids opposition political parties and independent organizations. Torture remains a concern.

Political Prisoners

Libya continues to detain scores of individuals for engaging in peaceful political activity. According to the Geneva-based group Libyan Human Rights Solidarity, Libya has forcibly disappeared 258 political prisoners, some for decades. Many were imprisoned for violating Law 71, which bans any group activity opposed to the principles of the 1969 revolution that brought al-Qadhafi to power. Violators of Law 71 can be put to death.

In February 2007 Libyan security agents arrested 14 organizers of a planned peaceful demonstration intended to commemorate the anniversary of a violent crackdown on demonstrators in Benghazi in 2006. At least 12 of the detainees are on trial and could face the death penalty on charges of planning to overthrow the government, arms possession, and meeting with a foreign official. Dr. Idris Boufayed, the demonstration's main organizer, is an outspoken critic whom the government previously detained in November 2006. Jamal al-Haji, also detained, is a Danish citizen to whom Libya has refused consular access. Two other detainees, Ahmad Yusif al-`Ubaidi and Al-Sadiq Salih Humaid, are reportedly not being treated for medical ailments. The government has "disappeared" `Abd al-Rahman al-Qotaiwi, a fourth-year medical student involved in planning the demonstration, and Jum`a Boufayed, who had given media interviews following the arrest of his brother Idris Boufayed. To Human Rights Watch's knowledge, none of the men has advocated violence.

Fathi al-Jahmi remains Libya's most prominent political prisoner. Libya has imprisoned al-Jahmi since March 2004 for calling for democratization and criticizing al-Qadhafi. Authorities have prevented al-Jahmi's family from visiting him since August 2006.

Freedom of Association and Freedom of Expression

Libya has no independent nongovernmental organizations. Law 19, "On Associations," requires a political body to approve all such organizations and does not allow appeals of negative decisions. The government has refused to allow an independent journalists' organization and has reportedly imposed unwanted leaders on the lawyers' union.

Freedom of expression is severely curtailed. Negative comments about al-Qadhafi are strictly punished, and self-censorship is rife. Uncensored news is available via satellite television and Libyan websites based abroad, which the government occasionally blocks. In April Libya's legislative body, the General People's Congress, passed Decree 146, creating a committee to examine the state-controlled media. In a bold statement, journalists and writers inside Libya described "press content" as "dependent solely on propaganda and positive government messages," and called on the committee to promote a free press. The government has announced no further information about the committee's work.

The exception to these rules are organizations run by one of Mu`ammar al-Qadhafi's sons, Seif al-Islam al-Qadhafi, who has criticized the lack of representative government and called for a free press. His quasi-official Qadhafi Development Foundation helped negotiate the release of the six healthcare workers. In August his al-Ghad company launched Libya's first private newspapers and television station. One of these papers criticized the secretary-general of the General People's Congress for poorly planned building demolitions in Tripoli, and another urged the authorities to allow exiled opposition members to return.

Benghazi HIV Case

In July Libya released five Bulgarian nurses and a Palestinian doctor who had been jailed since 1999 and convicted of deliberately infecting 426 children with HIV, based on dubious evidence. The Libyan High Judicial Council commuted the healthcare workers' death sentences, following a deal with the European Union to compensate the victims' families with a reported US$1 million per child. In an interview in August, Seif al-Qadhafi said the release was also tied to arms deals worth over $400 million.

The case raised serious concerns about due process and torture. Four of the healthcare workers told Human Rights Watch that they had confessed under torture by Libyan authorities, but a Libyan court had acquitted 10 security officials charged with their torture in 2005. The healthcare workers reportedly waived their right to seek redress from Libya shortly before their release.

Violence against Women and Girls

Although the extent of violence against women in Libya is unknown, the government's position in 2007 continued to be one of denial, leaving victims unprotected and without remedies. There is no domestic violence law in Libya, and laws punishing sexual violence are inadequate. The government prosecutes only the most violent rape cases, and judges have the authority to propose marriage between the rapist and the victim as a "social remedy" to the crime. Rape victims themselves risk prosecution for adultery or fornication if they attempt to press charges. Many victims' families coerce them into marriage in order to avoid public scandal.

Government services for victims of violence against women remain inadequate. Police officers are not trained to handle cases of violence against women, and there are no women's or girls' shelters. Instead, the government detains dozens of victims, particularly rape victims, in "social rehabilitation" facilities. Many are denied legal representation and the opportunity to challenge the legality of their detention. The authorities subject them to forced virginity examinations and punitive treatment, including solitary confinement. The only way out of these facilities is if a male relative takes custody of the woman or girl, or if she consents to marriage.

Abu Salim Prison

The government still has not released any findings on the large-scale killings in Tripoli's Abu Salim prison in June 1996. According to an ex-prisoner interviewed by Human Rights Watch, Internal Security Agency forces killed as many as 1,200 inmates who had revolted over prison conditions. In 2005 the government said it had established an investigatory committee, but it has released no information since. In October 2006 guards fired on another group of prisoners after a reported revolt, killing at least one and reportedly injuring nine.

Treatment of Foreigners

The government continues to forcibly deport foreigners who lack proper documentation, sometimes to countries where they could face persecution. Foreigners reported arbitrary arrests, beatings, and other abuse during their detention and deportation. On July 8, 2007, Libya reportedly rounded up approximately 70 Eritrean men, some of whom may have fled conscription into the Eritrean military. (Eritrea has no conscientious objector status, and military offenders are frequently subjected to torture.) Reportedly at Eritrea's request, Libyan security agents photographed the 70 men, who said guards had threatened them with deportation. The men remain in detention at this writing.

Libya has no asylum law, has not signed the 1951 Refugee Convention, and has no formal working agreement with the United Nations High Commissioner for Refugees (UNHCR). However, the government is drafting a law on asylum and reportedly grants UNHCR representatives regular access to detention facilities.

Promises of Reform

In 2007 the government continued to review proposals for a new penal code and code of criminal procedure, a process that began at least three years before. In 2005 the secretary of justice stated that, under the new penal code, the death penalty would remain only for the "most dangerous crimes" and for "terrorism."

However, a 2004 draft of the new code suggests the government might accept a very broad definition of terrorism, which could be used to criminalize people expressing peaceful political views. The government has yet to present either draft code to the General People's Congress.

Key International Actors

In 2007 the US and European governments upgraded relations with Libya despite its human rights abuses. In March the US State Department's annual human rights report found that Libya's "human rights record remained poor." Subsequently, President Bush nominated an ambassador to Libya and the US secretary of state met with Libyan officials in New York. EU representatives signed a memorandum of understanding in July on trade and other issues. In October the Council of the EU proposed negotiating a framework agreement on "areas of mutual interest, such as human rights [and] migration among others." Since 2004 the US, European, and other governments have approved billions of dollars in business deals with Libya, notably in the oil and gas sectors.

Libya continues to share intelligence on militant Islamists with Western governments. On April 27, 2007, a British court ruled that the United Kingdom could not return two terrorism suspects to Libya due to the risk of torture and unfair trials. In September the US government sent a Libyan citizen, Sofian Hamoodah, back to Libya after over five years of detention at Guantanamo Bay; the whereabouts of Hamoodah, who consented to return, are currently unknown. Another Guantanamo detainee returned in 2006, Mohamed al-Rimi, also remains missing.

Cooperation continued in controlling illegal migration from Libya to southern Europe, often without adequate regard for the rights of migrants or the need to protect refugees and others at risk of abuse on return to their home countries.

MOROCCO/WESTERN SAHARA

Morocco continues to present a mixed picture on human rights. It has made great strides in addressing past abuses, allowed considerable space for public dissent and protest, and reduced gender inequality in the family code. But authorities, aided by complaisant courts, continue to use repressive legislation to punish peaceful opponents, especially those who violate the taboos against criticizing the king or the monarchy, questioning the "Moroccanness" of the Western Sahara, or "denigrating" Islam. The police continue to use excessive force to break up demonstrations, especially in outlying areas.

Controls are particularly tight in the restive and disputed Western Sahara region, which Morocco administers as if it were part of its national territory. A pro-independence movement known as the Polisario Front (Popular Front for the Liberation of the Saguia al-Hamra and Rio de Oro) contests Moroccan sovereignty and demands a referendum on self-determination for the Sahrawi people. The Polisario rejected a Moroccan proposal, presented in April 2007, for enhanced autonomy for the region, mainly because that proposal nowhere mentions a referendum in which independence would be an option.

International observers pronounced Morocco's multiparty legislative elections in September 2007 to be generally clean, but many attributed the 63 percent abstention rate to a prevailing sense that parliament wields little power relative to the king and the executive branch.

Terrorism and Counterterrorism

Hundreds of suspected Islamist extremists arrested since the Casablanca bombings of May 2003 continue to serve prison terms, despite a series of royal pardons that freed a few hundred of them. The remaining prisoners staged hunger strikes during 2007 to demand their freedom or a review of their convictions, and improvements in prison conditions. At least 20 of the suspected militants were among the more than 100 prisoners facing death sentences. Many of those rounded up in 2003 were held that year in secret detention for days or weeks, subjected to mistreatment and sometimes torture while under interrogation, and convicted in unfair trials.

Since August 2006, police have arrested at least 500 additional suspected Islamist militants. The intelligence agencies continue to use an unacknowledged detention center at Temara to interrogate some of those suspected of serious offenses, according to numerous reports from detainees and their lawyers. Suspects continue to allege that they have been tortured while under interrogation, although there were fewer complaints of torture and excessive incommunicado pre-arraignment detention in 2007 than in the immediate aftermath of the 2003 Casablanca bombings.

Morocco was on edge after three incidents in March and April 2007 in which would-be suicide bombers in Casablanca narrowly missed inflicting heavy casualties.

The Justice System and Legal Reforms

Police are rarely held accountable for human rights violations. However, in June 2007 a court in al-Ayoun sentenced two policemen to ten years in prison for their role in the beating death of Hamdi Lembarki, a Sahrawi, during political unrest in al-Ayoun in October 2005.

In cases with political overtones, courts routinely deny defendants fair trials, ignoring requests for medical examinations lodged by defendants who claim to have been tortured, refusing to summon exculpatory witnesses, and convicting defendants solely on the basis of apparently coerced confessions. Courts in the cities of Agadir and Ksar al-Kbir convicted and imprisoned seven members of the Moroccan Human Rights Association (Association Marocaine des Droits de l'Homme, AMDH) for "attacking sacred values" by allegedly chanting slogans against the king during May Day marches. Agadir defendants Abderrahim Kerrad and Mehdi Berbouchi attempted unsuccessfully to challenge their own incriminating statements, claiming the police had beaten and threatened them into signing. The court also denied them the opportunity to confront the policeman whose testimony helped to convict them. The appeals court confirmed their sentence of two years in prison. The court in Ksar al-Kbir sentenced five other AMDH members to three years in prison on the same charges, increased to four years on appeal.

511

Freedom of Association, Assembly, and Movement

Authorities generally tolerate the work of the many human rights organizations active in Rabat and Casablanca. They also do not hamper foreign human rights organizations visiting Morocco, and often respond to their letters of concern. However, in the Western Sahara, surveillance is tighter, and harassment of rights defenders more common.

Most types of public assemblies require authorization from the Interior Ministry, which can refuse permission if it deems them liable to "disturb the public order." This discretion is exercised more often when the demonstrators' agenda is critical of government policies. Although many of the frequent public protests in Rabat run their course undisturbed, baton-wielding police have broken up others with brutality. For example, they forcibly dispersed a small demonstration on June 15, 2007, in front of parliament in Rabat called to demand the release of the imprisoned AMDH members (see above). Police violently dispersed demonstrations in various cities in May by pro-independence Sahrawi students, and courts later sentenced some of them to prison terms on trumped-up charges of engaging in violence.

Repression of public protests was fiercer in the Western Sahara than elsewhere. Police regularly used force to disperse peaceful sit-ins in favor of self-determination, and often used excessive force in responding to incidents when demonstrators lay stones across streets or threw rocks or, very occasionally, threw Molotov cocktails.

Authorities continue to restrict foreign travel for some Sahrawi activists, although such measures have decreased in recent years. Authorities have refused to grant legal recognition to any Sahrawi human rights organization dedicated to exposing Moroccan abuses, and prevented one such group, the Coalition of Sahrawi Human Rights Defenders, from holding its constitutive assembly in al-Ayoun on October 7.

Press Freedom

Media criticism of the authorities is often quite blunt, but is nevertheless circumscribed by a press law that provides prison terms for libel and for expression deemed critical of "Islam, the institution of the monarchy, or [Morocco's] territorial integrity."

Since mid-2005, a series of prosecutions of independent weeklies, the most outspokenly critical sector of the Moroccan news media, showed the continuing limits on press freedom. During 2007, authorities tightened those strictures. In January, a court convicted Driss Ksikes and Sanaa al-Aji, publisher and reporter, respectively, at the popular Arabic weekly *Nichane*, for a December 2006 article on how popular jokes reflected Moroccan attitudes about sex, politics, and religion. The court gave them three-year suspended sentences for "denigrating Islam." The prime minister temporarily suspended the weekly after that issue appeared, invoking his authority under the 2002 press code. In August, prosecutors charged Ahmed Benchemsi, editor of *Nichane* and its sister French-language weekly *TelQuel*, with disrespect for the king, apparently because of a pre-election editorial questioning the king's commitment to democracy. The interior minister ordered the police to confiscate copies of both publications from printers and newsstands. Benchemsi was still on trial at this writing.

On July 17 police arrested journalist Moustapha Hormatallah of *al-Watan al-Aan* shortly after that weekly published an article about classified government documents regarding terrorism threats in Morocco, reproducing one of the purportedly secret documents. A Casablanca court on August 15 handed Hormatallah an eight-month sentence and magazine publisher Abderrahim Ariri a six-month suspended sentence for "concealing items derived from a crime."

Family Law

Reforms to the family law enacted in 2004 have raised the minimum age of marriage for women from fifteen to eighteen, made the family the joint responsibility of both spouses, rescinded the wife's duty of obedience to her husband, expanded access to divorce for women, and placed the practice of polygamy under strict judicial control. In January 2007, Morocco reformed its nationality code to give women the right to pass their nationality to their children. Concerns remain that these reforms are being implemented at a slow pace.

Children

Child labor is widespread, despite the Labor Code's ban on children under 15 working. Young girls working as live-in servants in private homes are especially vulnerable to abuse, including sexual abuse, and frequently must work up to 100 hours a week without access to education or adequate food and medical care. Authorities rarely punish employers who abuse child domestics, and labor inspectors are not authorized to enter private homes. At this writing draft legislation to regulate employment conditions for domestic workers was still pending.

Large numbers of unaccompanied Moroccan children continue to attempt dangerous and illegal journeys to Europe. On March 6, 2007, Morocco and Spain concluded a readmission agreement that would allow Spain to repatriate an estimated 3000 unaccompanied Moroccan children (see Spain chapter). The agreement lacks explicit safeguards against abuse and provides no independent monitoring of its implementation, despite a pattern of earlier forced returns that exposed children to police abuse and often failed to reunite them with their parents or guardians.

Acknowledging Past Abuses

In 2005, Morocco's Equity and Reconciliation Commission (ERC) issued its report into grave human rights of the past, stimulating taboo-breaking discussions. The ERC provided an official acknowledgement of past repression, gave a long-overdue voice to victims, and elucidated many individual cases. However, non-cooperation by public officials prevented it from resolving other cases. Despite ERC recommendations, authorities took no steps to bring to trial those implicated in past abuse, including some who continue to hold high government posts. Nor has the government implemented the ERC's recommendation that it ratify the International Criminal Court statute and abolish the death penalty. But during 2007 the state did pay compensation to victims of past abuse, pursuant to guidelines established by the ERC.

Key International Actors

In June 2004, the United States designated Morocco "a major non-NATO ally," easing restrictions on arms sales. The US government-backed Millennium Challenge Corporation (MCC) approved on August 31, 2007, a five-year US$697.5 million economic aid package to Morocco—the largest grant made by the MCC since its creation in January 2004—to fight poverty and promote economic growth.

In public comments, US officials in 2007 praised Morocco's commitment to political and economic reform and counterterrorism cooperation. President George W. Bush saluted Morocco along with six other countries that "have recently taken strides toward liberty" in his address before the U.N. General Assembly on September 25. US officials rarely spoke out about human rights problems in Morocco, but the US embassy engaged in some public advocacy in favor of press freedom and reforming laws that criminalize libel.

Morocco has sought a privileged relation with the EU, which is in turn eager for Morocco's cooperation in combating terrorism and illegal immigration, among other issues. The EU considers Morocco's process of democratization and consolidation of the rule of law "as the most advanced in the region," according to its Morocco "Strategy Paper" for 2007-2013. Public criticism by EU officials of Morocco's human rights practices was rare. In July, the EU and Morocco signed an agreement for €654 million in EU financial aid for the period 2007-2010. The agreement designates "human rights and governance" as one of its priority areas.

France is Morocco's leading trade partner and the leading source of public development aid and private investments. President Nicolas Sarkozy made a three-day visit to Morocco in October 2007. Addressing parliament on October 23, he evoked "this democratic Morocco" and the "pluralism and openness that Morocco is experiencing today." He endorsed Morocco's autonomy plan for the Western Sahara, but said nothing during his visit publicly about continuing human rights problems in Morocco or the disputed Western Sahara region.

SAUDI ARABIA

Human rights conditions remain poor in Saudi Arabia. International and domestic pressure to implement human rights reforms have considerably weakened and the government undertook no major reforms in 2007. Curbs on freedom of association and expression, unfair trials, arbitrary detention, mistreatment and torture of detainees, restrictions on freedom of movement, and lack of official accountability remain serious concerns. Saudi law and policies discriminate against women, foreign workers, and religious minorities, especially Shia and Ismaili Saudis.

In May in its first public report the government-approved National Society for Human Rights (NSHR) highlighted major areas of rights abuses. The governmental Human Rights Commission's 24-member board began its work in January 2007 after a two-year delay. The government allowed Human Rights Watch to conduct research in the country in December 2006, but did not honor its promise to allow a return visit in May 2007, or similar promises made to Amnesty International.

Arbitrary Detention and Unfair Trial

Detainees are commonly the victims of systematic and multiple violations of due process and fair trial rights, including arbitrary arrest and torture and ill-treatment during interrogation. The authorities rarely inform them of the crime of which they are accused, or the evidence supporting the accusation. Detainees do not have access to a lawyer, face excessive pretrial delays, and at trial they often cannot examine witnesses or evidence or present a defense. Saudi Arabia in October 2007 adopted a new Judiciary Law setting up specialized courts, but has yet to write a penal code or ensure its criminal procedure code is consistently adhered to.

Saudi Arabia's secret police (*mabahith*) detains without trial or access to lawyers, in many cases for several years, around 3,000 security detainees suspected of sympathies with or involvement in terrorism.

In February the *mabahith* arrested seven reformist academics and lawyers, allegedly for funding terrorism. The authorities did not formally charge them or bring them to trial within the six months of pretrial detention allowed under Saudi law, and kept them in solitary confinement without family visits for five months. At this writing they remain detained without charge, and have had no access to lawyers.

Torture, Ill-Treatment, and the Death Penalty

In 2007 the government undertook the first prosecutions against religious police for abuse of power and for beating two detainees to death. However, not all alleged perpetrators of such abuses have faced trial, officials arrested innocent witnesses, and the religious police failed to appear in court. Minister of Interior Prince Nayef in July decreed that religious policemen must not detain persons they arrest, but instead promptly deliver them to the police.

Human Rights Watch found numerous allegations of ill-treatment and torture in al-Ha'ir prison in a December 2006 visit. In May 2007 a video showing torture there appeared on the internet. Prisoners in Najran, Buraiman, Ruwais, Dammam, al-Hasa, and Buraida prisons also alleged abuse.

Saudi judges routinely sentence defendants to thousands of lashes, often carried out in public. *Okaz* newspaper reported in October that a court sentenced two men in southern Baha to 7,000 lashes for "sodomy," the most severe sentence with lashes known to Human Rights Watch.

The kingdom carried out some 147 executions by decapitation with a sword as of November 2007, over four times the figure for 2006. There is no obvious explanation for this rise, as the most recent Ministry of Justice statistics for 2006 showed a downward trend in court cases for two years. Judges sentence persons as young as 13 to death. On July 21, 2007, Saudi Arabia executed Dhahiyan al-Thawri al-Sibai`i for a murder he committed when he was 15 or 16.

Freedom of Expression and Freedom of Religion

Freedom to voice criticism or openly discuss controversial ideas in the media and internet is limited. In early 2007 the government closed Ra'if al-Badawi's website www.saliberal.com, which spotlights the practices of the religious police, and in

517

October it closed the human rights and current affairs website www.menbar-alhe-war.com, run by former political prisoner Ali al-Dumaini. In late 2006 the government banished journalist Qinan al-Ghamdi for an article lamenting the slow implementation of reforms.

The Ministry of Interior routinely orders Saudis hosting private intellectual salons to desist or not invite certain individuals. In November 2006 King Abdullah prohibited any official from "opposing the policies or programs of the state ... by participating in any discussion through media channels or through domestic or foreign communications."

The governor of al-Ahsa province has detained without charge over 150 Shia prayer leaders for short periods, including during 2007. The Ministry of Education in June expelled a Shia girl from school for insulting the Prophet Muhammad's companions.

Freedom of Assembly and Association

The *mabahith* in July 2007 arrested five women peacefully demonstrating for the release or trial of their relatives detained for over two years without trial. Also arrested and later convicted for instigating a public demonstration were prominent reformers Abdullah al-Hamid, a lawyer for the detained husband of one of the demonstrators, and his brother 'Isa. Human rights activist Muhammad al-Bajadi remains detained following a second demonstration in September. In October Matrook al-Faleh, who publicized these rights violations, alleged that *mabahith* agents threatened his life by trying to run his vehicle off the road.

In December 2006 the appointed national Shura (Advisory) Council amended a first-ever draft law regulating nongovernmental organizations (NGOs) to reduce governmental control over them, but its recommendations are not binding. Currently, licensing NGOs is an arbitrary process. The government's National Dialogue platform promoting tolerance and dialogue has barred Ibrahim al-Mugaiteeb, president of the still unlicensed NGO Human Rights First in Saudi Arabia, from participating in its online forum because it was "a non-registered society."

Women's Rights

The Saudi system of male legal guardianship denies women their fundamental rights. Women must obtain permission from their father, husband, even sons, acting as male guardians to work, travel, study, marry, receive health care, and access government agencies, including when they seek protection or redress as victims of domestic violence. Strictly enforced gender segregation denies women full participation in public life.

In January 2007 a court finalized the forcible divorce of the consenting, adult couple Fatima `Azzaz and Mansour al-Timani after her half-brothers filed for the divorce citing his socially inferior tribal affiliation. Ministry of Interior officials have harassed the couple since, enforcing their complete separation by detaining Fatima with their two-year old son, while denying visits by Mansur, who has custody of their daughter.

In November 2007 a judge doubled on appeal—from 90 lashes to 200 lashes and six months' imprisonment—an October 2006 sentence handed down to a 20-year-old rape survivor for unlawful mixing with the opposite sex after she met a man who had blackmailed her. A gang kidnapped both of them at the meeting place and raped them. Up to the point of the judge's earlier verdict the woman had been unaware of facing any charges herself. The rapists also had their sentences doubled on appeal, to up to 10 years' imprisonment.

Saudi Arabia detains girls indefinitely without judicial review for "guidance."

Migrant Worker Rights

Restrictive immigration laws and inadequate labor protections place many of the estimated eight million foreign workers at risk of unpaid wages, excessively long working hours, confinement in the workplace or dormitories, confiscation of passports, and, in some cases, physical or sexual abuse. A visa sponsorship system ties migrant workers to their employers, whose agreement is needed for a host of bureaucratic procedures and who can terminate the worker's legal status at any time. Employers can also withhold permission to change employers, although a recent policy reform, if implemented, would strip that right from employers who do not pay their workers. Isolation in private homes and abuse of domestic workers often amount to conditions of forced labor, as evidenced by the thousands of complaints the Philippines, Indonesian, and Sri Lankan embassies receive. Saudi plans to codify protections for domestic workers, whom the labor law currently excludes, remain on hold since 2005.

Migrant workers suing their employers for abuse or labor violations risk imprisonment and deportation as a result of spurious countercharges in a justice system skewed against them. In August employers severely beat four Indonesian domestic workers, killing two of them, and police subsequently removed the survivors from hospital intensive care to investigate charges of witchcraft, and have denied the Indonesian embassy access to them. In June a Saudi court sentenced a Sri Lankan domestic worker, Rizana Nafeek, to death for murdering a baby in her care. Nafeek was 17 when the incident she described as an accident occurred, did not have access to legal or consular assistance during the trial, and alleged she was forced to confess. A lawyer, paid for by a foreign charity, has filed an appeal.

Key International Actors

Saudi Arabia is a key United States ally. US pressure for human rights improvements lessened: for example, the 2007 US State Department's international religious freedom report found "some improvements" in protecting the right to private worship for non-Muslims in Saudi Arabia, and the US chose not to impose sanctions. The US in July announced arms sales to the kingdom totaling US$7 billion.

The United Kingdom in December 2006 halted a governmental inquiry into illegal payments in connection with a UK-Saudi arms deal, claiming that the halt was in the national interest. During the Saudi king's first state visit in 20 years to the UK in October 2007, the government stressed shared Saudi-UK values, but did not publicly mention concern over Saudi Arabia's human rights record.

SYRIA

Syria's poor human rights situation deteriorated further in 2007, as the government imposed harsh sentences on a number of political and human rights activists. Emergency rule, imposed in 1963, remains in effect. President Bashar al-Assad was endorsed for a second term in May 2007 with 97 percent of the vote and parliamentary elections held in April 2007 delivered no reforms.

The Supreme State Security Court, an exceptional court with almost no procedural guarantees, sentenced over 100 people, mostly Islamists, to long prison terms. Syrian Kurds, the country's largest ethnic minority, continue to protest their treatment as second-class citizens. Iraqi refugees arrived in Syria at the rate of about 2,000 per day until October 2007, when Syria introduced strict entry and visa controls directed at stopping the refugee flow.

Political Activists on Trial

On May 10, 2007, a Damascus criminal court sentenced Dr. Kamal al-Labwani, a physician and founder of the Democratic Liberal Gathering, to 12 years in prison with hard labor for "communicating with a foreign country and inciting it to initiate aggression against Syria" after he called for peaceful democratic change in Syria during a visit to the United States and Europe in the fall of 2005.

Also in May a Damascus criminal court imposed harsh sentences on four activists arrested in 2006 for signing a petition calling for improved relations between Lebanon and Syria. The court sentenced prominent writer and political activist Michel Kilo and political activist Mahmud `Issa each to three years in prison. Khalil Hussain, a member of the Kurdish Future movement, and Sulaiman Shummar, a member of the unauthorized Worker's Revolutionary Party and a leader of the National Democratic Gathering, were tried in absentia and each sentenced to 10 years in prison.

At this writing, Fatih Jamus, a member of the Communist Action Party, was on trial for calling for peaceful reform in Syria during a trip to Europe in 2006. Faeq al-Mir, another communist activist who heads the Syrian People's Democratic Party, faces charges in connection with a visit he made to Lebanon following the 2005 assassination of Lebanese communist leader Georges Hawi.

Dr. `Arif Dalila, a prominent economics professor and a proponent of political liberalization, continues to serve a 10-year prison term imposed in July 2002 for his nonviolent criticism of government policies. He is suffering from heart problems and diabetes.

Arbitrary Detention, Torture, and "Disappearances"

Syria's multiple security services continue to detain people arbitrarily and frequently refuse to disclose their whereabouts for months—in effect forcibly disappearing them. For instance, Military Intelligence detained Ali al-Barazi, a Damascus-based translator, in July 2007, and refused to disclose his whereabouts for three months.

Torture remains a serious problem in Syria, especially during interrogation. Syrian human rights groups documented a number of cases in 2007 including the torture of 10 men detained in Hasake in April.

The Supreme State Security Court (SSSC), an exceptional court not constrained by the usual rules of criminal procedure, sentenced over 100 people in 2007, most of whom had Islamist leanings. The SSSC sentenced a group of seven young men in June 2007 to prison terms ranging between five and seven years because of their involvement in developing a pro-democracy youth discussion group online. Some of the group members said that the authorities had extracted "confessions" from them under torture.

As in previous years, the government in 2007 again failed to acknowledge security force involvement in the "disappearances" of an estimated 17,000 persons since the 1970s, the vast majority of whom remain unaccounted for and many of whom are believed to have been killed. The "disappeared" are mostly Muslim Brotherhood members and other Syrian activists detained by the government in the late 1970s and early 1980s, as well as hundreds of Lebanese and Palestinians detained in Syria or abducted from Lebanon by Syrian forces or Lebanese and Palestinian militias.

Hundreds and possibly thousands of political prisoners remain in detention in Syria. The authorities continue to refuse to divulge information regarding numbers or names of people in detention on political or security-related charges.

Human Rights Defenders

Human rights activists continue to be targets of government harassment and arrest. On April 24, 2007, a Damascus criminal court sentenced prominent human rights lawyer Anwar al-Bunni to five years in prison in connection with his statement that a man had died in a Syrian jail because of the inhumane conditions under which authorities had held him.

The government continues to prevent activists from traveling abroad and in 2007 expanded its list of those banned from leaving the country. While the exact number of activists banned from traveling is unknown, it is estimated to be in the hundreds. On August 12, 2007, State Security officials denied Riad Seif, a former opposition member of the Syrian parliament and a leader of the Damascus Declaration movement, permission to travel abroad to receive urgent medical care. Also among those banned from traveling in 2007 was Naser Al-Ghrazali, director of the Damascus Centre for Theoretical Study and Civil Rights and a media official in the Arab Committee for Human Rights.

All Syrian human rights group remain unlicensed, as Syrian officials consistently deny their requests for registration.

Discrimination and Repression against Kurds

Kurds, the largest non-Arab ethnic minority in Syria, comprise about 10 percent of the population of 18.5 million. They remain subject to systematic discrimination, including the arbitrary denial of citizenship to an estimated 300,000 Syria-born Kurds. Syrian authorities also suppress the use of the Kurdish language in schools and suppress other expressions of Kurdish identity.

Despite a general presidential pardon for those involved in the March 2004 clashes between Kurdish demonstrators and security forces in the northeastern city of Qamishli, an estimated 49 Kurds still face trials before the military court in

Damascus on charges of inciting disturbances and damaging public property. Kurdish political leaders are subject to frequent harassment and arrests. Syrian state security officials detained Ma`rouf Mulla Ahmed, a leading member of the Syrian Kurdish Yekiti Party, at the Syrian-Lebanese border in August 2007. At this writing, he remained in incommunicado detention.

Discrimination against Women

Syria's constitution guarantees gender equality, and many women are active in public life, but personal status laws as well as the penal code contain provisions that discriminate against women and girls. The penal code allows a judge to suspend punishment for a rapist if the rapist chooses to marry his victim, and provides leniency for so-called "honor" crimes. In January 2007, a Syrian human rights group reported that Zahra al-`Azu, age 16, was killed by her brother to protect the family's "honor" after a man had kidnapped her.

In May 2007, Syria submitted its initial report to the United Nations Committee on the Elimination of Discrimination against Women, and its delegation announced that Syria would take steps to amend laws that discriminate against women.

Situation of Refugees Fleeing Iraq

An estimated 1.4 million Iraqis are now living in Syria. While Syria continues to provide Iraqi refugees with access to public hospitals and schools, Syrian attitudes and policies towards these refugees hardened in 2007 with the implementation of increasingly restrictive visa and entry requirements. Iraqis are also banned from working, but many work illegally. Syrian authorities have forcibly returned a number of Iraqis to Iraq, but maintain that these Iraqis committed criminal acts.

Syria continues to refuse entry to Palestinians fleeing Iraq. In May 2006 Syria closed its border to Iraqi Palestinians and, at this writing, several hundred remained at makeshift camps in the no-man's-land between Iraqi and Syrian border checkpoints.

Key International Actors

Syria's relationship with the US and European countries remains strained over Syria's role in Iraq and Lebanon and its ties to Iran. While Syria remains isolated and under sanctions from the US, Damascus received high level visits by Javier Solana, the EU foreign policy chief, in March 2007, and US House Speaker Nancy Pelosi in April 2007.

The EU and the US have issued a number of public statements condemning the ongoing harassment and arrests of human rights activists. However, these condemnatory statements have had little impact on Syrian authorities.

The Association Agreement between Syria and the European Union, initialed in October 2004, remains suspended at the final approval stage as European countries remain divided over how to engage with Syria.

The UN Security Council continues to pressure Syria to cooperate with the ongoing international investigation into the assassination of former Lebanese Prime Minister Rafiq Hariri. On May 30, 2007, the UN Security Council adopted resolution 1757, which agreed to the establishment of a tribunal under Chapter VII. In his July 2007 interim report, Serge Brammertz, the head of the UN International Independent Investigation Committee, wrote that Syria's cooperation "remained generally satisfactory."

Iran continues to be Syria's main regional ally, and the two countries increased their cooperation in military and economic spheres. Iraqi Prime Minister Nouri al-Maliki visited Damascus in August 2007, following restoration of diplomatic ties in 2006, to discuss border security and Iraqi refugees. Saudi Arabia and Syria exchanged sharp criticism over regional roles, highlighting tensions between the two countries.

TUNISIA

President Zine al-Abidine Ben Ali and the ruling party, the Constitutional Democratic Assembly, dominate political life in Tunisia. The government uses the threat of terrorism and religious extremism as a pretext to crack down on peaceful dissent. There are continuous and credible reports of torture and ill-treatment being used to obtain statements from suspects in custody. Sentenced prisoners also face deliberate ill-treatment.

The government tolerates small opposition parties up to a point. On October 1, 2007, in a ruling that appeared politically motivated, a court in Tunis ordered the eviction of the Progressive Democratic Party's weekly organ al-Mawkef from its premises of 13 years on the grounds that the party had been using the office as a headquarters, in violation of the lease. The PDP is one of the rare outspoken legal parties. Authorities denied any role in what they said was a private dispute. However, the publication was spared eviction after President Ben Ali reportedly urged the landlord to resolve the dispute, following a month of domestic and international protests in support of al-Mawkef.

In July Ben Ali pardoned or conditionally released 21 political prisoners, and another 10 in November. Most were leaders of the banned Islamist party al-Nahdha who had been in prison since the early 1990s, when a military court convicted 265 party members and sympathizers on dubious charges of plotting to topple the state. Despite these releases the number of political prisoners continued to grow, as authorities arrested scores of young men in sweeps around the country and charged them under the 2003 anti-terror law. Authorities made life difficult for released political prisoners, monitoring them closely, denying them passports and most jobs, and threatening to rearrest some who spoke out on human rights or politics.

Human Rights Defenders

Authorities have refused to grant legal recognition to every truly independent human rights organization that has applied over the past decade. They then invoke the organization's "illegal" status to hamper its activities. For example, on June 6, 2007, police encircled the Tunis office of the non-recognized National

Council on Liberties in Tunisia and blocked entry to representatives of civil society who had come to show solidarity with the Council. Police also blocked meetings by the non-recognized International Association of Solidarity with Political Prisoners.

The independent Tunisian Human Rights League, a legally recognized group, continued to face lawsuits filed by dissident members. The broader context showed these supposedly private suits to be part of a pattern of repression: the courts ruled systematically in favor of the plaintiffs, providing a legal veneer for large-scale police operations to prevent most League meetings at its branches around the country.

Human rights defenders and dissidents are subject to heavy surveillance, arbitrary travel bans, dismissal from work, interruptions in phone service, physical assaults, harassment of relatives, suspicious acts of vandalism and theft, and slander campaigns in the press. On July 24 authorities freed on parole lawyer Mohamed Abbou, who had served two-thirds of a three-and-a-half year sentence that was imposed after he published harsh critiques of President Ben Ali in online forums. As of November, authorities were refusing to let Abbou travel abroad. In June authorities arbitrarily extended by two years a five-year-old order banishing released political prisoner Abdallah Zouari to a remote region 500 kilometers from his family's home in Tunis. Zouari is an outspoken government critic and human rights activist.

The Justice System

The judiciary lacks independence. Prosecutors and judges usually turn a blind eye to torture allegations, even when the subject of formal complaints submitted by lawyers. Trial judges convict defendants solely or predominantly on the basis of coerced confessions, or on the testimony of witnesses whom the defendant does not have the opportunity to confront in court.

The International Committee of the Red Cross continued its program of visiting Tunisian prisons. However, authorities refuse to allow access by independent human rights organizations. During 2007 prison authorities placed a small number of inmates in prolonged solitary confinement, an abusive practice that had reportedly stopped after the government pledged in 2005 to end it.

Detainees report a range of methods of torture and ill-treatment during police interrogation. Most common, according to human rights lawyers and organizations, are sleep deprivation; threats to rape the detainee or women family members; beatings, especially on the soles of the feet (*falaka*); and tying and suspending detainees from the ceiling or from a rod in the "roast chicken" (*poulet rôti*) position.

Tunisia has ratified the Convention against Torture and enacted strong legislation defining and criminalizing acts of torture. However, despite the submission of formal complaints by lawyers on behalf of defendants in hundreds of cases in recent years, no case has come to public attention of a state agent being held accountable for torturing persons held for politically motivated offenses.

Media Freedom

None of the domestic print and broadcast media offers critical coverage of government policies, apart from a few low-circulation magazines that are subject to occasional confiscation. Tunisia has privately-owned radio and television stations, but private ownership is not synonymous with editorial independence. The government blocks certain domestic and international political or human rights websites featuring critical coverage of Tunisia.

Authorities have refused to accredit the correspondent of the Arabic satellite television channel Al Jazeera, Lotfi Hajji. Plainclothes police prevented Hajji from attending several news events during the year. Hajji is also president of the independent Tunisian Journalists Syndicate, which authorities have refused to legalize.

Counterterrorism Measures

Since 1991 there has been one deadly terrorist attack in Tunisia: an April 2002 truck bomb that targeted a synagogue on the island of Djerba, for which al Qaeda claimed responsibility. Tunisian authorities claim that they have long been at the forefront of combating terrorism and extremism. The 2003 Law in Support of "International Efforts to Fight Terrorism and the Repression of Money-Laundering" contains a broad definition of terrorism. Like that found in the Penal Code, the definition encompasses "acts of incitement to racial or religious hatred or fanaticism regardless of the means employed," thereby leaving open the possibility of prosecuting political opinion or association as crimes of terrorism.

Since the law's enactment, authorities have rounded up hundreds of youths in towns around the country and charged them under its provisions. The government never accuses the majority of those whom it subsequently convicts of having planned or committed specific acts of violence; rather, it charges them with planning to join jihadist movements abroad or inciting others to join. Authorities routinely deprive suspects detained under this law of their rights. Many are held in pre-arraignment incommunicado police custody (*garde à vue*) beyond the six-day legal limit. The police subject many to torture and other mistreatment. Investigating judges question many defendants without informing them of their right to a lawyer at this stage, and routinely ignore their requests for a medical examination to check for evidence of mistreatment.

Between December 2006 and January 2007 security forces clashed with an armed insurgent group outside the capital, the first such incident in Tunisia in recent memory.

On June 18 the US sent to Tunisia two Tunisian nationals, Abdallah Hajji and Lotfi Lagha, who had been held for five years as suspected terrorists in the Guantanamo Bay detention facility. Tunisia immediately transferred them to detention—Lagha to face new charges of serving a terrorist organization while abroad, and Hajji to face a retrial after having been convicted in absentia on similar charges. Hajji accused the police of slapping and threatening him upon his arrival. Both spent their first six weeks in strict solitary confinement. A civilian court sentenced Lagha on October 24 to three years in prison and a military court on November 14 sentenced Hajji to seven years in prison.

Key International Actors

The United States enjoys good relations with Tunisia, while urging human rights progress there more vocally than in most other countries in the region. While the US gives minimal financial aid to Tunisia, the Department of Defense provides counterterrorism training and exchange programs for the military.

The US embassy frequently sends diplomats to observe political trials and to meet civil society activists. The State Department report "Supporting Human Rights and Democracy: The U.S. Record" notes, "U.S. officials … urged the government to respect freedoms of assembly and association after observing first-hand incidents where the government prevented human rights organizations from conducting meetings." Ambassador Richard C. Godec on September 28 visited PDP party members who were hunger-striking to protest *al-Mawkef's* threatened eviction.

With respect to the transfer of security detainees held at Guantanamo Bay, Ambassador Godec said, "We would not transfer individuals where it is more likely than not they would be tortured or mistreated." However, neither he nor other US officials commented on Tunisia's imprisonment and alleged mistreatment of Abdallah Hajji and Lotfi Lagha after their transfer from US custody.

The European Union-Tunisia Association Agreement continues to be in force, despite the government's human rights record and its blocking of EU grants to some nongovernmental organizations. EU officials occasionally criticize their partner's rights record, while taking pains to praise the state of bilateral relations overall.

France remains Tunisia's leading trade partner and foreign investor, and in 2007 provided Tunisia with more development aid per capita than it gave any other country. On July 10 newly elected French President Nicolas Sarkozy visited Tunisia, in the company of Foreign Minister Bernard Kouchner and Minister of State for Foreign Affairs and Human Rights Rama Yade. Sarkozy had nothing but praise for the Tunisian authorities in his public comments, but told journalists he had raised some human rights cases in private with President Ben Ali, including that of Mohamed Abbou. On this first visit, the French president did little to distance himself from the staunch support that his predecessor, Jacques Chirac, had shown for President Ben Ali in spite of the latter's human rights practices.

UNITED ARAB EMIRATES (UAE)

While the economy of the UAE continues its impressive growth, civil society continues to stagnate and human rights progress has been slow. Authorities have exerted censorial pressure on a wide range of activists, impeding the kind of vigorous monitoring and reporting that can draw attention to and help curb human rights abuses.

The UAE is a federation of seven emirates: Abu Dhabi, `Ajman, Al Fujayrah, Sharjah, Dubai, Ra's al-Khaymah, and Umm al-Qaywayn. The rulers of each emirate, sitting as the Federal Supreme Council, elect the president and vice president from among their number. In December 2006, the UAE held its first-ever elections for 20 seats in the 40-member Federal National Council (FNC), an advisory body to the president. Only members of the electoral colleges, a group of 6,595 UAE citizens chosen by the rulers of the emirates, were allowed to cast ballots and to stand as candidates. One woman was elected to the FNC, and the rulers of the emirates appointed seven other women as council members.

Freedom of Association and Expression

The government approved the formation of the first human rights organization in the country, the Emirates Human Rights Association, in February 2006, but the organization has remained largely inactive.

The government has actively discouraged the creation of other human rights organizations. In July 2004 a group led by Muhammad al-Roken, a former president of the independent Jurists Association, applied to the Ministry of Labor and Social Welfare for permission to establish the Emirates Human Rights Society. In April 2005 another group of 30 activists headed by Khalifa Bakhit al-Falasi applied to the ministry to set up another human rights association. As of November 2007, the ministry had not responded to either application.

The UAE has barred prominent UAE commentators and academics from disseminating their views and harassed and prosecuted human rights activists. The government has imprisoned and punished journalists for expressing views critical of the government.

In August, a court sentenced Mohammad Rashed al-Shehhi, the owner of a popular website Majan.net, to one year in prison for defamation of a public official, ordered him to pay $19,000 in damages, and closed down the website. In September, the court sentenced Khaled al-Asli to five months in prison for writing the website article in question. The court released Asli on bail pending his appeal. In September, a court sentenced two journalists working for the English-language daily Khaleej Times to two months in prison for libel, but released them on bail pending their appeal.

In September, UAE Prime Minister Sheikh Mohammad issued instructions "not to imprison journalists for reasons related to their work," but indicated that other measures should be taken to penalize journalists for "violations." On September 30, the prime minister ordered Shehhi's release on bail. It's unclear whether or not the charges will be dropped.

In June 2006, a Federal Supreme Court judge issued an arrest warrant for Muhammad al-Mansoori, president of the Jurists Association, for allegedly "insulting the public prosecutor." After spending most of 2007 outside of the country, Mansoori returned to the UAE in early September. The UAE government has reportedly warned him to cease his human rights advocacy.

Security agents detained Muhammad al-Roken twice in the summer of 2006, questioning him about his human rights activities. They also confiscated his passport and barred him from leaving the country. In January 2007, in what appears to be a politically-motivated case, a lower court sentenced Roken to three months in prison for sex out of wedlock. The sentence has been stayed and is currently on appeal. In May 2007, the government returned Roken's passport.

While it closed City of Hope, the country's only shelter for abused women, children, and domestic workers, the government has created a new quasi-governmental body called the Dubai Foundation for Women and Children, which will manage a facility providing the same services with capacity to house 260 people, a significant increase. City of Hope's former director Sharla Musabih is on the board of directors of the new organization, and the government has dropped what appears to have been a politically motivated criminal prosecution of her.

Migrant Labor

Roughly 85 percent of the UAE's population are foreigners, and foreigners account for nearly 99 percent of the workforce in the private sector, including domestic workers. As of August 2007, according to the Ministry of Labor, there were 4.5 million foreigners in the country, compared to 800,000 Emirati citizens. The UAE's economic growth has attracted large domestic and foreign investments and the current construction boom is one of the largest in the world. Exploitation of migrant construction workers by employers is particularly severe. Immigration sponsorship laws that grant employers extraordinary power over the lives of migrant workers exacerbate the problem.

Abuses against migrant workers include nonpayment of wages, extended working hours without overtime compensation, unsafe working environments, squalid living conditions in labor camps, and withholding of passports and travel documents.

Over the course of 2007, the UAE has made incremental progress toward improving the conditions of migrant workers. Most significantly, a substantial number of employers have made improvements to workers' living quarters, including improving sanitary conditions and easing overcrowding. The ministry of labor also claims to have shut down over one-hundred companies that have violated labor laws, but has not divulged the names.

On February 5, in a step toward greater transparency, the ministry of labor published a draft of a revised labor law on the internet and invited public comment. The draft law falls far short of international standards in several critical areas. It contains no provisions on workers' rights to organize and to bargain collectively, it explicitly allows authorities to punish striking workers, and it arbitrarily excludes from its purview all domestic workers employed in private households. The ministry had not indicated at this writing when the revised labor law would be enacted.

Women domestic workers are at particular risk of abuse, including food deprivation, forced confinement, and physical or sexual abuse. In April, the UAE introduced a standard contract for domestic workers which provides some protections, but contains no limit on working hours, no provisions for a rest day or overtime pay, no workers' compensation, and only provides for unspecified "adequate breaks" and one month of paid vacation every two years. The standard contract does not serve as an adequate substitute for extending equal protection to domestic workers under the labor law.

The government failed in 2007 to put in place a minimum wage as required by the UAE Labor Law of 1980.

In 2007, migrant workers continued to engage in public demonstrations to protest their treatment. In February 2007, 3000 construction workers went on strike for five days in Abu Dhabi. The strike ended when management agreed to raise daily wages, include pay for Fridays, and provide basic health insurance to workers. Following the strike, the ministry of labor ordered the expulsion from the country of 14 of the protest "instigators." Also, in February 2007, 300 to 400 construction workers blocked a busy highway in Dubai, protesting low wages, non-payment of wages, and substandard living conditions. The police ended the protest and escorted the workers back to their labor camps. In July 2007, the government sent in the armed forces to put an end to a four-day strike at a gas processing plant.

Following a surge in heat-related illnesses and injuries at construction sites in July 2005, the Labor Ministry directed construction companies to give their workers a break from 12:30 p.m. to 4:30 p.m. during July and August. In the summer months, temperatures often reach 110 degrees Fahrenheit. However, in July 2006, after intense lobbying by construction companies, the government reduced the afternoon break to the hours of 12:30 p.m. to 3 p.m., which remains in force.

Trafficking

According to the US State Department, human trafficking to the UAE for commercial sexual exploitation and involuntary servitude continues to be a serious problem. In its 2007 annual report on human trafficking, the US State Department placed the UAE on its Tier 2 Watch List for "failing to take meaningful steps to address the problem of foreign women trafficked for commercial sexual exploitation and of foreign male and female workers subjected to conditions of involuntary servitude."

Until recently, the trafficking of young boys to the UAE to be trained as camel jockeys was a widespread problem. Responding to international criticism, UAE President Sheikh Khalifa bin Zayed al-Nahyan decreed in July 2005 that all camel jockeys must be age 18 or older. In 2006 the government cooperated with UNICEF to identify and return 1,071 children to their home countries. In 2007, the UAE government continued to work with UNICEF to exclude all underage children in camel racing and to repatriate former underage camel jockeys.

Key International Actors

The UAE has emerged as a major business and trading hub in the Middle East, attracting substantial foreign investments. In April 2004 the UAE signed a Trade and Investment Framework Agreement (TIFA) with the US. The UAE is currently negotiating free trade agreements with the US, the European Union, and Australia.

In October 2004 the UAE acceded to the Convention on the Elimination of All Forms of Discrimination against Women. However, it is not a signatory to other major international human rights instruments such as the International Covenant on Civil and Political Rights, the International Covenant on Economic, Social and Cultural Rights, the Convention on the Protection of the Rights of All Migrant Workers and Members of Their Families, and the Convention against Torture.

UNITED STATES

Forced Apart

Families Separated and Immigrants Harmed
by United States Deportation Policy

H U M A N

R I G H T S

W A T C H

WORLD REPORT
2008

UNITED STATES

UNITED STATES

Bush administration resistance to scrutiny of its counterterrorism policies and past abuses continues to be a major obstacle to human rights improvement in the United States. Despite some efforts in Congress to change practices violating basic human rights, there was no evident progress concerning the treatment of so-called enemy combatants, including those held at Guantánamo Bay, or the use of secret detention facilities.

Domestically, undocumented migrant workers faced an increased risk of detention, and other non-citizens were blocked from vindicating their rights in court. Persons convicted of crimes faced harsh sentencing policies and in some cases abusive conditions in US prisons.

Racial discrimination again emerged as a prominent issue in 2007, when six African-American high school students in Jena, Louisiana, were charged as adults with a range of serious crimes for the 2006 beating of a white student. The case sparked protests and the charges were widely viewed as excessive and discriminatory, especially as compared with the treatment of white Jena youths involved in other incidents.

Guantanamo Bay, Indefinite Detention, and Military Commissions

The Department of Defense released over 100 detainees from Guantanamo Bay in 2007, but about 305 remained at this writing. Most of these men have been held without charge for six years. Over a dozen Chinese Uighurs, and likely several more individuals of other nationalities, were long ago cleared for release yet remain incarcerated at Guantanamo. The government acknowledges the Uighurs likely would be ill-treated if returned to China.

In other cases, the United States, in violation of its international obligations, has repatriated detainees without any meaningful or independent assessment of the risk of torture or abuse they faced upon return. In such cases the US has claimed that "diplomatic assurances"—or promises of humane treatment—from the receiving government were sufficient protection against abuse, despite compelling evidence to the contrary.

In December 2005 Congress passed the Detainee Treatment Act, preventing Guantanamo detainees from bringing future habeas corpus petitions to challenge the lawfulness of their detention or any mistreatment. In September 2006 the Military Commissions Act made these provisions retroactive and extended them to all detained non-citizen "unlawful enemy combatants." After the November 2006 congressional elections, legislation that would have lifted the habeas-stripping provisions passed the Senate, but fell short of the 60 votes needed to overcome a filibuster. The Supreme Court agreed to review the constitutionality of the habeas-stripping provisions, with a decision expected by mid-2008.

In June a federal appellate court ruled that these same habeas-stripping provisions could not be applied to Ali Saleh Kahlah al-Marri, a Qatari in the US on a student visa, whom the US administration had declared an "enemy combatant" just weeks before his trial for financial fraud and giving false statements. Having already spent four years in solitary confinement in a military brig in South Carolina, al-Marri's only outside contact has been with his lawyers, who had to sue in US court for access to him. The appeals court ruled that al-Marri could not be stripped of his right to bring a habeas challenge to his detention and ordered the government to either charge him in federal court or release him. At this writing, the order was stayed pending appeal.

Congress authorized a new system of military commissions in 2006 after the US Supreme Court in *Hamdan v. Rumsfeld* declared unlawful the military commissions set up in 2001 by the Bush administration to try non-citizens accused of terrorism. While these new commissions, which are entirely separate from the federal court system, address some of the concerns of the old commissions, they still fall far short of the due process standards provided by federal courts. For example, statements obtained through "cruel, inhuman, or degrading treatment" prior to December 30, 2005, are admissible so long as a judge finds that they are probative and "reliable." The ad hoc nature of the process raises further fair trial concerns.

Australian David Hicks, whose plea agreement in March 2007 makes him the only Guantanamo detainee to be convicted of a criminal offense, was scheduled to be released from custody in Australia in December, upon completion of his nine-month sentence.

To date only three other Guantanamo detainees had been charged under the commissions: Salim Hamdan, Omar Khadr, and Mohamed Jawad. Both Khadr and Jawad were juveniles—15 and 17, respectively—when they were first brought to Guantanamo close to six years ago. The Bush administration has said that it ultimately plans to try up to 80 Guantanamo detainees before the commissions.

Jose Padilla was convicted in federal court in 2007 of conspiracy to aid terrorism, but prosecutors did not pursue long-trumpeted allegations that he had been planning to detonate a radioactive "dirty" bomb in Chicago. The government agreed not to use any statements made by Padilla during his more than three years in incommunicado military detention, presumably because such statements were elicited during abusive interrogation.

Torture Policy

Over the past two years, Congress and the courts have repudiated the Bush administration's authorization of abusive interrogation techniques that amount to torture. In response the Pentagon announced new rules applicable to all interrogations carried out by the United States armed forces and disavowed many abusive techniques. The Central Intelligence Agency (CIA), however, contends that it is not bound by these rules, and the administration has gone to great lengths to justify the CIA's continued use of certain techniques banned for use by the military. According to an October 2007 *New York Times* article, the Department of Justice issued legal memoranda in 2005 that authorized the use of waterboarding (simulated drowning), head slapping, and exposure to frigid temperatures, and ruled that neither these techniques, nor any other techniques being employed by the CIA, violated the then-pending legislation prohibiting cruel, inhuman, and degrading treatment. In October 2007 the Bush administration's candidate for attorney general, Michael Mukasey, refused to repudiate waterboarding as a form of torture in his confirmation hearings.

In July 2007 the administration issued an executive order providing legal authorization for the so-called "CIA program" in which detainees are held incommunicado and subject to reportedly abusive interrogations. Michael McConnell, Director of National Intelligence, said on July 22, 2007 that he "would not want a US citizen to go through the process" of being subjected to some of the techniques approved for use by the CIA.

Secret Prisons

In April 2007 the Department of Defense announced the transfer to Guantanamo of another detainee who was previously held in CIA custody, suggesting that secret prisons (temporarily closed after President Bush's admission that they existed in 2006) were up and running again. Human Rights Watch has identified 39 other people we believe were held in secret prisons; administration officials have indicated the total number to be about 100. Under international law those persons remain unlawfully "disappeared" until the United States can account for them. In July President Bush issued an executive order providing authorization for this "CIA program," despite the patent illegality of incommunicado detention under international law.

Accountability for Detainee and Civilian Abuse

Despite a number of official investigations into abuse of detainees in US custody in Afghanistan, Iraq, and Guantanamo Bay, the United States has done little to hold those involved accountable. Prosecutions of military personnel have focused almost exclusively on low-ranking personnel, and no one has been charged under the doctrine of command responsibility. Over a dozen cases referred to the Department of Justice for prosecution by the military and others have been sitting idle for years. No CIA agents have been prosecuted for abuse, and only one civilian contractor has faced criminal charges.

On September 16, 2007, a convoy of contractors from the Blackwater security firm fired into a crowded street in Baghdad, killing at least 17 civilians. This incident has galvanized international attention to the effective immunity from prosecution under Iraqi and US law enjoyed by many of the almost 180,000 contractors supporting US operations in Iraq. At this writing, legislation expanding federal jurisdiction over felonies committed by contractors overseas was pending before Congress.

Khaled el-Masri, a German citizen arbitrarily arrested and transferred by the US to Afghanistan, where he was beaten and held incommunicado for several months, and Maher Arar, a dual Canadian-Syrian citizen secretly detained and sent by the US to Syria, where he was tortured and imprisoned for 10 months, brought lawsuits against the US challenging their mistreatment. US courts have dismissed both cases, accepting the administration's position that the courts should not review the government's actions. El-Masri asked the Supreme Court in 2007 to review the dismissal of his case, but the court declined to do so.

Denial of Refugee Protection

US law allows authorities to deny refugee protection to people believed to have associated with or provided "material support" to any armed group. The broad terms of the law have led authorities to deny rights to persons who fit the refugee definition under international law, including rape victims forced into domestic servitude by rebel groups. In 2007 the administration began to issue a small number of waivers to prevent innocent civilians from being barred as terrorists. Over 3,000 refugees—mostly from Burma—and a handful of asylum seekers have benefited, but implementation has been slow, the administration's waiver authority is limited, and families have been separated as a result. Legislation that would expand the waiver authority was pending before Congress at this writing.

Incarceration

There are more than 2.2 million persons in US prisons and jails, an increase of 500 percent from 30 years ago. A June 2007 report by the Justice Department's Bureau of Justice Statistics (BJS) found that the incarcerated population continued to grow in 2006, experiencing its largest one-year increase in six years. The United States now has both the largest incarcerated population and the highest per capita incarceration rate in the world, with a rate five times that of England and Wales, seven times that of Canada, and more than 10 times that of Japan.

The burden of incarceration falls disproportionately on members of racial and ethnic minorities. Black men are incarcerated at 6.5 times the rate of white men, and 11.7 percent of *all* black males age 25 to 29 are in prison or jail. The US government failed to explain or address these rates in its 2007 report to the United Nations Committee on the Elimination of Racial Discrimination, hearings on which are expected in February 2008.

As the prison population grows, so does the challenge of providing adequate medical and mental health care. A September 2006 BJS report found that more than half of all prisoners—and nearly three-quarters of all female prisoners—suffer from a mental health problem such as major depression or a psychotic disorder.

In California a federal judge found that medical care in the state's prisons violated the US Constitution's prohibition on cruel and unusual punishment. In 2006 the judge appointed a receiver to oversee prison medical care, stripping that function from the state government. In September 2007 the receiver issued a report finding that 15 percent of California prisoner deaths were either preventable or possibly preventable.

Enacted by the US Congress in 1996, the Prison Litigation Reform Act (PLRA) creates a variety of obstacles for prisoners seeking to challenge their conditions of confinement or otherwise vindicate their rights in court. In January 2007 the US Supreme Court issued a decision overturning some particularly restrictive interpretations of the PLRA by lower federal courts.

The Death Penalty and Juvenile Life without Parole

State governments executed 42 prisoners between January and October 2007, bringing the total number of men and women executed in the United States to 1099 since 1977. Almost all were killed by lethal injection; one was electrocuted.

With growing evidence that lethal injection may be a very painful way to die, executions in many states were halted in 2007. In September 2007 the US Supreme Court agreed to consider the constitutionality of lethal injection in the case of two Kentucky death row prisoners claiming that lethal injection amounts to cruel and unusual punishment. Lethal injections in the US are expected to decrease substantially until the court issues its decision sometime in 2008.

In 2007 Human Rights Watch revised upward, from 2,225 to at least 2,380, our estimate of the number of US prisoners serving sentences of life without parole for crimes committed when they were under 18. The number of such prisoners in the rest of world combined is eight. Efforts at reforming this excessively punitive sentence for young offenders continued in several states across the country, including in Michigan and California.

Women's Rights

Women's rights in the United States suffered major setbacks at the Supreme Court in 2007. One court decision severely restricted challenges to unequal pay (women earn only 77 cents for every dollar earned by men), another upheld the exclusion of in-home care workers from certain federal wage and overtime protections (89 percent of such workers are women), and a third upheld a ban on a medically approved late-term abortion method, adding to existing regulatory and financial obstacles to safe abortion.

The US continues to channel its international assistance toward programs that compromise sexual and reproductive health and rights. In 2007, a significant portion of US funding for HIV/AIDS prevention continued to be earmarked for programs that promote abstinence until marriage, regardless of whether such programs were likely to be effective and without sufficient regard for abuses that put women, even those who abstain until marriage, at high risk for HIV.

In a positive step, the Senate in 2007 approved a bill that would overturn the "global gag rule"—a series of restrictions on what recipients of US reproductive health aid can do and say on abortion. At this writing, it remained unclear whether the bill would become law.

Jena

In August 2006 an African-American high school student in Jena, Louisiana, challenged the de facto racial segregation of his school's grounds by asking permission to sit under the "white tree" on campus. The next day three nooses hung from the tree. School authorities responded inadequately, further stoking racial tensions. In December 2006 six African-American youth at the high school beat up a white youth, who suffered a concussion and other injuries. The six youth were charged as adults with a range of serious crimes including attempted murder, spurring a nationwide outcry over what were seen as excessive, racially discriminatory charges. In September 2007 an appeals court vacated the conviction for aggravated battery of the first of the six to be tried, Mychal Bell; the prosecutor said he would appeal the ruling.

Sex Offenders

In a 2007 report, *No Easy Answers,* Human Rights Watch found that, as currently conceived, many sex offender registry laws do little to prevent sexual violence and violate fundamental human rights. Offenders on publicly available registries find it difficult to obtain or keep employment and housing. Some have been murdered and many are harassed by strangers who find their information online. Residency restrictions lead to homelessness and transience for some convicted sex offenders, which interfere with their effective tracking, monitoring, and supervision by law enforcement officers; this in turn may make repeat offenses more likely.

Sex offender laws ignore the full reality of sexual violence in the US. Child safety advocates question the focus in current law on "stranger danger" and already convicted offenders because more than 90 percent of child sexual abuse is committed by someone the child knows and trusts. Authoritative studies show that three out of four sex offenders do not re-offend within 15 years of release from prison and 87 percent of sex crimes are committed by individuals without a previous conviction for a sex offense.

Rights of Non-Citizens

Immigration reform legislation continued to be stymied in 2007 by disagreements among lawmakers on whether or how to regularize the status of millions of undocumented migrant workers. According to the US Census, there were 37.5 million non-citizens living in the United States in 2006.

UNITED STATES

No Easy Answers

Sex Offender Laws in the US

HUMAN
RIGHTS
WATCH

State and local governments passed at least 182 laws in 2007 limiting access to public benefits and state-issued identification cards, or punishing landlords or employers for doing business with undocumented workers. Many of these laws were found unconstitutional or temporarily halted by courts. Federal immigration authorities stepped up workplace raids in California, Nevada, New Mexico, New York, and elsewhere, splitting many families and leading to mistaken arrests and transfers of migrants to detention centers in remote locations far from their legal counsel.

A 2007 Human Rights Watch report, *Forced Apart*, found that non-citizens who have lived in the country for decades, including lawful permanent residents, have been summarily deported after criminal convictions, even for minor crimes. In fact, 64 percent of the non-citizens deported in 2005 were deported for non-violent crimes such as drug possession or theft. The deportations occur after the non-citizen has finished serving his or her sentence.

According to US Citizenship and Immigration Services, 672,593 non-citizens were deported for crimes between 1997 and 2005. Human Rights Watch estimates that at least 1.6 million spouses and children, many of whom are US citizens, were separated from their family members as a result. US law gives immigration judges no opportunity to balance the individual's crime against his or her family relationships, other connections to the United States such as military service or economic ties, or likelihood of persecution in the country of origin.

Deportation and workplace raids are enforcement measures that US Immigration and Customs Enforcement (ICE) authorities combine with the daily detention of some 28,000 non-citizens. Endemic problems in detention facilities continued in 2007, including deaths in custody, inadequate medical care, inappropriate and punitive housing for non-citizen children, interference with access to counsel and to family members, and prolonged detention.

The death in July 2007 of Victoria Arellano, a 23-year-old transgender detainee, in US immigration custody is an extreme, but not surprising, example of the suffering experienced by immigration detainees with HIV/AIDS. The US fails to ensure that detainees with HIV/AIDS receive medical care that complies with recognized standards for correctional health care. Medical care in facilities operated or

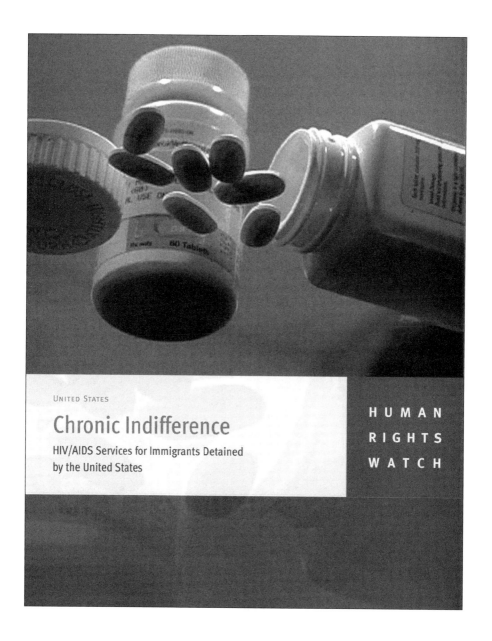

Chronic Indifference

HIV/AIDS Services for Immigrants Detained
by the United States

H U M A N
R I G H T S
W A T C H

supervised by ICE is delayed, interrupted, and inconsistent to an extent that endangers the health and lives of many detainees.

Lawsuits, congressional hearings, and proceedings before the Inter-American Commission on Human Rights have brought increased scrutiny to detention of non-citizen children, though generally not improved conditions. In one notable exception, lawyers in Texas won a settlement that improved conditions and ensured the release of dozens of children.

CHINA

"No One Has the Liberty to Refuse"

Tibetan Herders Forcibly Relocated in Gansu, Qinghai, Sichuan, and the Tibet Autonomous Region

HUMAN
RIGHTS
WATCH

2007
HUMAN RIGHTS WATCH
PUBLICATIONS

BY COUNTRY

Afghanistan

The Human Cost: The Consequences of Insurgent Attacks in Afghanistan, 04/07, 125pp.

Angola

"They Pushed Down the Houses": Forced Evictions and Insecure Land Tenure for Luanda's Urban Poor, 05/07, 101pp.

Bangladesh

Judge, Jury, and Executioner: Torture and Extrajudicial Killings by Bangladesh's Elite Security Force, 12/06, 81pp.

Bosnia and Herzegovina

Narrowing the Impunity Gap: Trials before Bosnia's War Crimes Chamber, 01/07, 62pp.

Burma

Crackdown: Repression of the 2007 Popular Protests in Burma, 12/07, 131pp.

Sold to be Soldiers: The Recruitment and Use of Child Soldiers in Burma, 10/07, 146pp.

Burundi

Paying the Price: Violations of the Rights of Children in Detention in Burundi, 03/07, 60pp.

Central African Republic

State of Anarchy: Rebellion and Abuses against Civilians, 09/07, 110pp.

笑

Chad

Early to War: Child Soldiers in the Chad Conflict, 07/07, 45pp.

The Trial of Hissène Habré: Time is Running Out for the Victims, 01/07, 23pp.

"They Came Here to Kill Us": Militia Attacks and Ethnic Targeting of Civilians in Eastern Chad, 01/07, 70pp.

China

"You Will Be Harassed and Detained": China Media Freedoms Under Assault Ahead of the 2008 Beijing Olympics Games, 08/07, 40pp.

"No One Has the Liberty to Refuse": Tibetan Herders Forcibly Relocated in Gansu, Qinghai, Sichuan, and the Tibet Autonomous Region, 06/07, 78pp.

A Great Danger for Lawyers: New Regulatory Curbs on Lawyers Representing Protesters, 12/06, 71pp.

Colombia

Maiming the People: Guerrilla Use of Antipersonnel Landmines and other Indiscriminate Weapons in Colombia, 07/07, 36pp.

Côte d'Ivoire

"My Heart is Cut": Sexual Violence by Rebels and Pro-Government Forces in Côte D'Ivoire, 08/07, 135pp.

Democratic Republic of Congo

Renewed Crisis in North Kivu, 10/07, 87pp.

Egypt

Prohibited Identities: State Interference with Religious Freedom, 11/07, 99pp.

From a Flood to a Trickle: Neighboring States Stop Iraqis Fleeing War and Persecution, 04/07, 19pp.

Monopolizing Power: Egypt's Political Parties Law, 01/07, 17pp.

France

In the Name of Prevention: Insufficient Safeguards in National Security Removals, 06/07, 94pp.

Guinea

Bottom of the Ladder: Exploitation and Abuse of Girl Domestic Workers in Guinea, 06/07, 110pp.

Dying for Change: Brutality and Repression by Guinean Security Forces in Response to a Nationwide Strike, 04/07, 66pp.

India

Protecting the Killers: A Policy of Impunity in Punjab, India, 10/07, 125pp.

Last Hope: The Need for Durable Solutions for Bhutanese Refugees in Nepal and India, 05/07, 88pp.

Hidden Apartheid: Caste Discrimination against India's "Untouchables," 02/07, 113pp.

Indonesia

Out of Sight: Endemic Abuse and Impunity in Papua's Central Highlands, 07/07, 81pp.

Protest and Punishment: Political Prisoners in Papua, 02/07, 40pp.

Iraq

Caught in the Whirlwind: Torture and Denial of Due Process by the Kurdistan Security Forces, 07/07, 57pp.

The Poisoned Chalice: The Decision of the Iraqi High Tribunal in the Dujail Case, 06/07, 34pp.

Israel/Occupied Palestinian Territories

Why They Died: Civilian Casualties in Lebanon during the 2006 War, 09/07, 249pp.

Civilians under Assault: Hezbollah's Rocket Attacks on Israel in the 2006 War, 08/07, 128pp.

Indiscriminate Fire: Palestinian Rocket Attacks on Israel and Israeli Artillery Shelling in the Gaza Strip, 07/07, 145pp.

Jordan

From a Flood to a Trickle: Neighboring States Stop Iraqis Fleeing War and Persecution, 04/07, 19pp.

Lebanon

Why They Died: Civilian Casualties in Lebanon during the 2006 War, 09/07, 249pp.

Civilians under Assault: Hezbollah's Rocket Attacks on Israel in the 2006 War, 08/07, 128pp.

Nepal

Last Hope: The Need for Durable Solutions for Bhutanese Refugees in Nepal and India, 05/07, 88pp.

Children in the Ranks: The Maoists' Use of Child Soldiers in Nepal, 02/07, 72pp.

Nicaragua

Over Their Dead Bodies: Denial of Access to Emergency Obstetric Care and Therapeutic Abortion in Nicaragua, 10/07, 19pp.

Nigeria

Criminal Politics: Violence, "Godfathers," and Corruption in Nigeria, 10/07, 123pp.

Election or "Selection"? Human Rights and Threats to Free and Fair Elections in Nigeria, 04/07, 42pp.

Chop Fine: The Human Rights Impact of Local Government Corruption and Mismanagement in Rivers State, Nigeria, 01/07, 107pp.

North Korea

North Korea: Harsher Policies against Border Crossers, 03/07, 14pp.

Pakistan

Ghost Prisoner: Two Years in Secret CIA Detention, 02/07, 50pp.

The Philippines

Scared Silent: Impunity for Extrajudicial Killings in the Philippines, 07/07, 86pp.

Lives Destroyed: Attacks on Civilians in the Philippines, 07/07, 32pp.

Russia

Rehabilitation Required: Russia's Human Rights Obligation to Provide Evidence-based Drug Dependence Treatment, 11/07, 112pp.

Singled Out: Russia's Detention and Expulsion of Georgians, 10/07, 78pp.

Justice for Chechnya: The European Court of Human Rights Rules against Russia, 07/07, 20pp.

"We Have the Upper Hand": Freedom of Assembly in Russia and the Human Rights of Lesbian, Gay, Bisexual, and Transgender People, 06/07, 22pp.

The Stamp of Guantanamo: The Story of Seven Men Betrayed by Russia's Diplomatic Assurances to the United States, 03/07, 48pp.

Rwanda

"There Will Be No Trial": Police Killings of Detainees and the Imposition of Collective Punishments, 07/07, 39pp.

Killings in Eastern Rwanda, 01/07, 20pp.

Serbia

Unfinished Business: Serbia's War Crimes Chamber, 06/07, 32pp.

Better Late Than Never: Enhancing the Accountability of International Institutions in Kosovo, 06/07, 44pp.

Spain

Unwelcome Responsibilities: Spain's Failure to Protect the Rights of Unaccompanied Migrant Children in the Canary Islands, 07/07, 117pp.

Sri Lanka

Abuses against Sri Lankan Domestic Workers in Saudi Arabia, Kuwait, Lebanon, and the United Arab Emirates, 11/07, 133 pp.

Return to War: Human Rights Under Siege, 08/07, 129pp.

Complicit in Crime: State Collusion in Abductions and Child Recruitment by the Karuna Group, 01/07, 100pp.

Somalia

Shell-Shocked: Civilians Under Siege in Mogadishu, 08/07, 115pp.

South Africa

"Keep Your Head Down": Unprotected Migrants in South Africa, 03/07, 111pp.

Sudan

Darfur 2007—Chaos by Design: Peacekeeping Challenges for AMIS and UNAMID, 09/07, 77pp.

Syria

No Room to Breathe: State Repression of Human Rights Activism in Syria, 10/07, 46pp.

Thailand

Deadly Denial: Barriers to HIV/AIDS Treatment for People Who Use Drugs in Thailand, 11/07, 59pp.

No One Is Safe: Insurgent Violence Against Civilians in Thailand's Southern Border Provinces, 08/07, 104pp.

"It Was Like Suddenly My Son Never Existed": Enforced Disappearances in Thailand's Southern Border Provinces, 03/07, 67pp.

Tunisia

Ill-Fated Homecomings: A Tunisian Case Study of Guantanamo Repatriations, 09/07, 43pp.

Turkey

Human Rights Concerns in the Lead-up to July Parliamentary Elections, 07/07, 21pp.

Unjust, Restrictive, and Inconsistent: The Impact of Turkey's Compensation Law with Respect to Internally Displaced People, 12/06, 40pp.

TUNISIA

Ill-Fated Homecomings

A Tunisian Case Study of Guantanamo Repatriations

HUMAN
RIGHTS
WATCH

Turkmenistan

Human Rights Reform in Turkmenistan: Rhetoric or Reality?, 11/07, 33pp.

Uganda

"Get the Gun!": Human Rights Violations by Uganda's National Army in Law Enforcement Operations in Karamoja Region, 09/07, 92pp.

Third Memorandum on Justice Issues and the Juba Talks: Particular Challenges for Uganda in Conducting National Trials for Serious Crimes, 09/07, 15pp.

United Kingdom

Counter the Threat or Counterproductive? Commentary on Proposed Counterterrorism Measures, 10/07, 26pp.

Hearts and Minds: Putting Human Rights at the Center of United Kingdom Counterterrorism Policy, 06/07, 24pp.

United States

No Easy Answers: Sex Offender Laws in the US, 09/07, 144pp.

Ill-Fated Homecomings: A Tunisian Case Study of Guantanamo Repatriations, 09/07, 43pp.

Forced Apart: Families Separated and Immigrants Harmed by United States Deportation Policy, 07/07, 88pp.

Off the Record: US Responsibility for Enforced Disappearances in the "War on Terror," 06/07, 29pp.

Discounting Rights: Wal-Mart's Violation of US Workers' Right to Freedom of Association, 05/07, 212pp.

The Stamp of Guantanamo: The Story of Seven Men Betrayed by Russia's Diplomatic Assurances to the United States, 03/07, 48pp.

Ghost Prisoner: Two Years in Secret CIA Detention, 02/07, 50pp.

Uzbekistan

Nowhere to Turn: Torture and Ill-Treatment in Uzbekistan, 11/07, 92pp.

Zimbabwe

Bashing Dissent: Escalating Violence and State Repression in Zimbabwe, 05/07, 39pp.

BY THEME

Arms issues

Landmine Monitor Report 2007: Towards a Mine-Free World, 11/07, 1,124pp.

Business and Human Rights Issues

Criminal Politics: Violence, "Godfathers," and Corruption in Nigeria, 10/07, 123 pp.

Discounting Rights: Wal-Mart's Violation of US Workers' Right to Freedom of Association, 05/07, 212pp.

Chop Fine: The Human Rights Impact of Local Government Corruption and Mismanagement in Rivers State, Nigeria, 01/07, 107pp.

Children's Rights Issues

Sold to be Soldiers: The Recruitment and Use of Child Soldiers in Burma, 10/07, 146pp.

Early to War: Child Soldiers in the Chad Conflict, 07/07, 45pp.

Unwelcome Responsibilities: Spain's Failure to Protect the

Rights of Unaccompanied Migrant Children in the Canary Islands, 07/07, 117pp.

Bottom of the Ladder: Exploitation and Abuse of Girl Domestic Workers in Guinea, 06/07, 110pp.

Paying the Price: Violations of the Rights of Children in Detention in Burundi, 03/07, 60pp.

Children in the Ranks: The Maoists' Use of Child Soldiers in Nepal, 02/07, 72pp.

Sri Lanka—Complicit in Crime: State Collusion in Abductions and Child Recruitment by the Karuna Group, 01/07, 100pp.

HIV/AIDS Issues

Deadly Denial: Barriers to HIV/AIDS Treatment for People Who Use Drugs in Thailand, 11/07, 59pp.

Rehabilitation Required: Russia's Human Rights Obligation to Provide Evidence-based Drug Dependence Treatment, 11/07, 112pp.

International Justice Issues

Third Memorandum on Justice Issues and the Juba Talks: Particular Challenges for Uganda in Conducting National Trials for Serious Crimes, 09/07, 15pp.

Unfinished Business: Serbia's War Crimes Chamber, 06/07, 32pp.

The Poisoned Chalice: The Decision of the Iraqi High Tribunal in the Dujail Case, 06/07, 34pp.

A Summary of the Case Law of the International Criminal Court, 03/07, 12pp.

The Trial of Hissène Habré: Time is Running Out for the Victims, 01/07, 23pp.

Narrowing the Impunity Gap: Trials before Bosnia's War Crime Chamber, 01/07, 62pp.

Weighing the Evidence: Lessons from the Slobodan Milosevic Trial, 12/06, 80pp.

Refugees/Displaced Persons Issues

Singled Out: Russia's Detention and Expulsion of Georgians, 10/07, 78pp.

Unwelcome Responsibilities: Spain's Failure to Protect the Rights of Unaccompanied Migrant Children in the Canary Islands, 07/07, 117pp.

"No One Has the Liberty to Refuse": Tibetan Herders Forcibly Relocated in Gansu, Qinghai, Sichuan, and the Tibet Autonomous Region, 06/07, 78pp.

Last Hope: The Need for Durable Solutions for Bhutanese Refugees in Nepal and India, 05/07, 88pp.

From a Flood to a Trickle: Neighboring States Stop Iraqis Fleeing War and Persecution, 04/07, 19pp.

"Keep Your Head Down": Unprotected Migrants in South Africa, 03/07, 111pp.

Unjust, Restrictive, and Inconsistent: The Impact of Turkey's Compensation Law with Respect to Internally Displaced People, 12/06, 40pp.

Terrorism and Counterterrorism Issues

Counter the Threat or Counterproductive? Commentary on Proposed Counterterrorism Measures, 10/07, 26pp.

Ill-Fated Homecomings: A Tunisian Case Study of Guantanamo Repatriations, 09/07, 43pp.

No One Is Safe: Insurgent Violence Against Civilians in Thailand's Southern Border Provinces, 08/07, 104pp.

Lives Destroyed: Attacks on Civilians in the Philippines, 07/07, 32pp.

Hearts and Minds: Putting Human Rights at the Center of United Kingdom Counterterrorism Policy, 06/07, 24pp.

Off the Record: US Responsibility for Enforced Disappearances in the "War on Terror," 06/07, 29pp.

France—In the Name of Prevention: Insufficient Safeguards in National Security Removals, 06/07, 94pp.

The Human Cost: The Consequences of Insurgent Attacks in Afghanistan, 04/07, 125pp.

The Stamp of Guantanamo: The Story of Seven Men Betrayed by Russia's Diplomatic Assurances to the United States, 03/07, 48pp.

Ghost Prisoner: Two Years in Secret CIA Detention, 02/07, 50pp.

Women's Rights Issues

Abuses against Sri Lankan Domestic Workers in Saudi Arabia, Kuwait, Lebanon, and the United Arab Emirates, 11/07, 133 pp.

Over Their Dead Bodies: Denial of Access to Emergency Obstetric Care and Therapeutic Abortion in Nicaragua, 10/07, 19 pp.

"My Heart is Cut": Sexual Violence by Rebels and Pro-Government Forces in Côte D'Ivoire, 08/07, 135pp.

6 45 2

ARCHBISHOP ALEMANY LIBRARY
DOMINICAN UNIVERSITY
SAN RAFAEL, CALIFORNIA 94901